Violence and Nihilism

Violence and Nihilism

Edited by
Luís Aguiar de Sousa and Paolo Stellino

DE GRUYTER

ISBN 978-3-11-152100-8
e-ISBN (PDF) 978-3-11-069921-0
e-ISBN (EPUB) 978-3-11-069936-4

Library of Congress Control Number: 2022934201

Bibliographic information published by the Deutsche Nationalbibliothek
The Deutsche Nationalbibliothek lists this publication in the Deutsche Nationalbibliografie; detailed bibliographic data are available on the internet at http://dnb.dnb.de.

© 2024 Walter de Gruyter GmbH, Berlin/Boston
This volume is text- and page-identical with the hardback published in 2022.
Cover image: Antonio Secci, "Squarcio", 2000, mixed technique, 70 x 60 cm, photo by Antonello Fancello

www.degruyter.com

Table of Contents

List of Abbreviations —— VII

Introduction —— 1

Part 1: Philosophy and Politics

Nolen Gertz
Nihilism and Violence from Plato to Arendt —— 7

George Pattison
Kierkegaard's Aesthetic Stage and the Ideology of Nihilism —— 25

Luca Lupo
"To smear his boots with the other's fat": Conscious and Unconscious Violence —— 45

Luís Aguiar de Sousa
Cruelty, Bad Conscience, and the Sovereign Individual in Nietzsche's *Genealogy of Morality* —— 65

Agata Mergler
Walter Benjamin's Media Theory in the Times of Platform Nihilism —— 89

Gianfranco Ferraro
'Like ants': The Mafia's Necropolitics as a Paradigm of Nihilistic Violence —— 111

Francescomaria Tedesco
Against the Kinship: State, Terror, Nihilism —— 139

Part 2: Literature and Film

Derek Offord
Nihilism in Nineteenth-Century Russian Literature and Thought —— 161

Marco Piazza
Violence, Evil and Nihilism: Nietzschean Traces in Guimarães Rosa's *Grande Sertão: Veredas* —— **189**

Joseph G. Kickasola
Signifying Nothing? Nihilism, Violence, and the Sound/Silence Dynamic in Cinema —— **203**

Paolo Stellino
Aestheticizing Murder: Hitchcock's *Rope*, **Nietzsche, and the Alleged Right to Crime of Superior Individuals** —— **231**

Kevin Stoehr
Nihilism, Violence, and the Films of Michael Haneke —— **255**

John Marmysz
"Supposing Truth is a Woman?": Nihilism and Violence in Nietzsche's *The Antichrist* **and Von Trier's** *Antichrist* —— **275**

Bülent Diken and Carsten Bagge Laustsen
"Is Something Funny, Asshole?": *Joker*'s **Nihilist Violence** —— **297**

Notes on the Contributors —— **315**

Names index —— **319**

List of Abbreviations

Per house style, references to Nietzsche's works, posthumous fragments, and letters are abbreviated. Nietzsche's works are identified by the standard abbreviations listed below, followed by chapter (when applicable) and section number. For the sake of brevity, the chapter is identified only by a key word (for instance, *Clever* instead of *Why I Am so Clever*). Nietzsche's posthumous fragments (NL) are cited by year, group, and fragment number, followed by a reference to the standard Colli and Montinari edition (*Sämtliche Werke, Kritische Studienausgabe* [KSA]). Nietzsche's letters are identified by the recipient, date, KGB (*Briefwechsel, Kritische Gesamtausgabe*) section/volume number, and letter (Bf.) number. The English translations are listed in the final bibliography of each chapter.

A *The Anti-Christ*
BGE *Beyond Good and Evil*
BT *The Birth of Tragedy*
D *Daybreak*
EH *Ecce Homo*
HH *Human, All Too Human*
GM *On the Genealogy of Morality*
GS *The Gay Science*
TI *Twilight of the Idols*
Z *Thus Spoke Zarathustra*

Introduction

Nihilism seems to be linked to violence by definition. The term 'nihilism' comes from the Latin *nihil*, which means "nothing." The nihilist is thus someone who "acknowledges nothing," as Nikolai Petrovich remarks in Turgenev's *Fathers and Sons*, that is, someone who acknowledges no moral or religious authority, or someone who believes in nothing, as the nihilists in the Coen brothers' *The Big Lebowski* claim. If this is so, then what is stopping the nihilist from committing even the worst of crimes? Dostoevsky repeatedly calls attention to this danger in his novels. The result of the nihilistic ideas defended by the main characters of his late works is nothing but violence and destruction, directed either towards oneself (as in the case of Kirillov) or towards others (as in the case of Raskolnikov and Ivan Karamazov). As von Lembke, one of the characters in Dostoevsky's *Demons*, puts it: "It's all arson! It's nihilism! If anything's ablaze, it's nihilism!" (Dostoevsky 1994, p. 515).

Dostoevsky saw in the denial of God's existence the *peccatum originale* of the Russian nihilists. The destruction of the idea of God in mankind inevitably opened the way to man's self-deification. Qua new God, man was allowed to act as he pleased, for, as the devil who appears to Ivan in *The Brothers Karamazov* puts it: "There is no law for God!" (Dostoevsky 1992, p. 649). Although from a very different perspective, Nietzsche, too, emphasized the potentially dangerous consequences of the death of God and the collapse of Judeo-Christian morality. As he wrote in a posthumous note dedicated to European nihilism: "morality was the great *antidote* to practical and theoretical *nihilism*" (NL 1886, 5[71], KSA 12, p. 211). Unlike Dostoevsky, however, Nietzsche saw in the death of God the possibility of a new beginning—or as he puts it in section 343 of *The Gay Science*, "a new dawn" (GS 343).

Given the historical events of the twentieth century, it is reasonable to say that Nietzsche's expectations have been disappointed. Beyond the question of whether the twentieth century was the most violent in history, as is often claimed, there is no doubt that the past century has been characterized by an extreme degree of violence, which has often gone hand in hand with a nihilistic reduction of the *other* to a nonperson, a mere thing (the term used by the Nazis to refer to those they considered inferior was *Untermensch*, that is, "underman" or "subhuman"). At the same time, the seemingly definitive crisis of any attempt at theodicy after the Shoah, the increasingly invasive role of technology and media (especially social media) in our lives, and the end of metanarratives (as Lyotard claims in his well-known *The Postmodern Condition*), among others, strongly suggest that the crisis announced by Dostoevsky and Nietzsche about a century and a half ago is far from over.

If, on the one hand, it may be a matter of debate whether we live in a nihilistic age, on the other hand, there is little doubt that nihilism has been and remains a recurrent topic not only in philosophy but also in other academic disciplines and the arts. Given the importance of this topic and the degree of exposure to violence that characterizes daily life, it is surprising that the existing literature on the relation between violence and nihilism is so scarce. The goal of this volume is precisely to remedy this lacuna by exploring modern and contemporary configurations of this connection, both in the real world and in fiction.

The first part of the volume contains contributions that approach the relation between violence and nihilism from the perspective of philosophy and politics, whereas the essays contained in the second part consider the same relation from the perspective of literature and film. As every contribution is prefaced by an abstract, there is no need to present a detailed summary of the content of the volume.

Of course, this volume does not purport to exhaustively capture the many ways in which the relation between violence and nihilism can be addressed. We are aware that many philosophers, writers, and directors who have dealt with this topic have been left out. Still, we strongly believe that the contributions presented in this volume address the abovementioned relation in such depth and variety that anyone interested in better understanding the phenomenon of nihilism and its connection to violence will find many important reflections here.

Some of the contributions to this volume were first presented at the International Conference *Gratuitous Violence and Free Will in a Nihilistic Age*, which was held in Lisbon on September 19 and 20, 2019. We would like to thank Ana Falcato, with whom we co-organized the conference, and those authors who, having presented their papers, accepted our invitation to take part in this volume. Our sincerest gratitude also goes to those authors who agreed to join the project at a later stage.

We are most grateful to the reviewers for providing very useful critical and constructive comments on the essays in this volume. We would also like to thank de Gruyter for publishing the volume, Christoph Schirmer, Senior Acquisitions Editor at de Gruyter, for supporting the initial proposal, and Aaron Sanborn-Overby, Acquisitions Editor, and Anne Hiller, Content Editor, for taking care of the different stages of the editorial process.

Lisbon, 19 October 2021
Luís Aguiar de Sousa
Paolo Stellino

Bibliography

Dostoevsky, Fyodor (1992): *The Brothers Karamazov*. New York: Vintage Books.
Dostoevsky, Fyodor (1994): *Demons*. New York: Vintage Books.
Nietzsche, Friedrich (2001): *The Gay Science*. Translated by Josephine Nauckhoff. Cambridge: Cambridge University Press.
Nietzsche, Friedrich (2003): *Writings from the Late Notebooks*. Edited by Rüdiger Bittner and translated by Kate Sturge. Cambridge: Cambridge University Press.

Part 1: **Philosophy and Politics**

Nolen Gertz
Nihilism and Violence from Plato to Arendt

Abstract: In this chapter, I will attempt to answer the question of whether nihilism is inherently violent insofar as it is destructive, or inherently nonviolent insofar as it is indifferent. I do this by, first, turning to Nietzsche to determine if there is a parallel between violent and nonviolent nihilism to be found in his distinction between active and passive nihilism. I then turn to Plato, as we can find an illustration of the violent potential of nihilism in his famous allegory of the cave. Next, I examine Heidegger's lecture on Plato's allegory of the cave, as Heidegger there provides an investigation into the various forms of violence that can be found in Plato's allegory, and an analysis of what those forms of violence can tell us about what it means to be human. Subsequently, I turn to Simone de Beauvoir, for we find an evolutionary account of how someone becomes a nihilist in her analysis of nihilism, an account that brings together various threads found in Nietzsche, Plato, and Heidegger on the relationship between violence and nihilism. Finally, this will lead us to Hannah Arendt, for through her work we can expand our understanding of the relationship between nihilism and violence to include violence that is not merely personal, but that is also political.

1 Introduction

What is the relationship between nihilism and violence? Depending on your definition of nihilism, it can seem that either violence and nihilism go hand-in-hand, or that violence and nihilism are opposed to each other. In a world that appears to be becoming increasingly nihilistic (see, for example, climate change denialism), it is imperative to determine precisely the nature of this relationship between nihilism and violence.

If you think that nihilism is destructive, that it is a rejection of traditions, values, and norms, then it would seem to be violent by its very nature (Turgenev 1991; Dostoevsky 1995). If, however, you think that nihilism is the embrace of meaninglessness, that to be nihilistic is to be uncaring, indifferent, and apathetic, then it would seem to be too passionless to ever be violent (Tartaglia 2016). So, should we think of one of these definitions of nihilism as correct and the other as mistaken? Or is it possible to reconcile these two visions of nihilism? Should we think of nihilism as somehow being both violent and nonviolent at the same time?

In this chapter, I will attempt to answer these questions by, first, turning to Nietzsche in order to determine if there is a parallel between violent and nonviolent nihilism to be found in his distinction between active and passive nihilism. I then turn to Plato, as we can find an illustration of the violent potential of nihilism in his famous allegory of the cave. Next, I examine Heidegger's lecture on Plato's allegory of the cave, as Heidegger there provides an investigation into the various forms of violence that can be found in Plato's allegory, and an analysis of what those forms of violence can tell us about what it means to be human. Subsequently, I turn to Simone de Beauvoir, for we find an evolutionary account of how someone becomes a nihilist in her analysis of nihilism, an account that brings together various threads found in Nietzsche, Plato, and Heidegger on the relationship between violence and nihilism. Finally, this will lead us to Hannah Arendt, for through her work we can expand our understanding of the relationship between nihilism and violence to include violence that is not merely personal, but that is also political. Through the analyses of nihilism we find in de Beauvoir and Arendt, we can see the vital importance of trying to understand the causes and goals of nihilistic violence, as such violence can consume not only individuals, but entire nations. This conclusion can then help us to understand both why authoritarian governments can rise to power while pursuing agendas that can seemingly only be described as nihilistic, and why even democratic governments that are viewed as pursuing agendas promoting individualism should be described as nihilistic.

2 Nietzsche and Active vs Passive Nihilism

If we follow the path set out by Nietzsche, we can distinguish two views of nihilism, one as essentially violent and the other as essentially nonviolent. Nietzsche calls these "active nihilism" and "passive nihilism," respectively:

> Nihilism. It is ambiguous:
> A. Nihilism as a sign of increased power of the spirit: as active nihilism.
> B. Nihilism as decline and recession of the power of the spirit: as passive nihilism...
> It reaches its maximum of relative strength as a violent force of destruction—as active nihilism.
> Its opposite: the weary nihilism that no longer attacks; its most famous form, Buddhism; a passive nihilism, a sign of weakness. (NL 1887, 9[35], KSA 12, pp. 350–351)

This distinction is important to Nietzsche as it allows him to simultaneously honor nihilism when it seeks to destroy the world in order to create a new one in its place, and to criticize nihilism when it seeks to hide from the world by erecting fantasy worlds in its place. Active nihilism can indeed be seen as our only hope of overcoming passive nihilism, as active nihilism seeks to explode the myths, illusions, and rituals that passive nihilism needs to survive (Gertz 2019). Whereas Nietzsche sees the desire to create a new world on the ashes of the old as noble, he views the desire to cling to fantasies in order to escape from reality as dangerously destructive. Active nihilism is willing to confront reality while trying to overcome it, but passive nihilism hides from reality and is desperate to avoid any encounter with it.

This evasion often results in the mere escapism that earns it the name of "passive." In our contemporary technological world, this escapism has become increasingly more prevalent and more normalized, as for example in the rise of "binge-watching" television as an accepted, if not celebrated, way to avoid facing reality (Gertz 2018, pp. 70–74). Given the rapid progress of technological means for pursuing passive nihilism—from video games to virtual reality—it would seem that passive nihilism will become ever more prevalent and ever more normalized.

Nevertheless, might passive nihilists be so desperate to shelter from the truth of the world that they, too, could turn violent? After all, Nietzsche does describe passive nihilism as "the weary nihilism that no longer attacks" (NL 1887, 9[35], KSA 12, p. 351), suggesting that it was once violent and so perhaps could become so again. We must therefore ask how passive nihilists would respond when reality can no longer be avoided. Would an attempt to force passive nihilists to face reality lead them to ever greater attempts at evasion? Or could it lead them to furiously fight against reality and anyone who forces them to again pay attention to reality? In other words, is it possible that both active nihilism and passive nihilism can be violent?

3 Plato and Liberation vs. Violence

The famous allegory of the cave in Plato's *Republic* offers an illustration of the potentially violent side of passive nihilism. According to Plato, we can understand what it is like to lack education by thinking of ourselves as being like prisoners who have been kept in a cave since birth, who know nothing more about the world than the shadows projected on the wall in front of them by the people who have imprisoned them. After one of the prisoners is freed and forced to travel out of the cave to discover the truth about the world, he returns to free the other prisoners. According to Plato, and contrary to the claims of Dick Cheney, the freed prisoner would not be "greeted as a liberator" (NBC News 2003, para. 3). As Plato writes, "And, as for anyone who tried to free them and lead them upward, if they could somehow get their hands on him, wouldn't they kill him?" In response to this question Plato has Socrates pose to Glaucon, Plato has Glaucon answer without hesitation, "They certainly would" (*Republic* 517a).

Plato establishes at the outset that the prisoners are meant to stand in for humans generally, since "they are like us" (*Republic* 515a). It is thus in our nature, according to Plato, to not only resist attempts to enlighten us against our will, but to put up violent and even murderous resistance if necessary. Of course, Plato wrote this after Socrates was put to death by his fellow Athenians for the crime of "corrupting the young" (*Apology* 24c) by having attempted to enlighten them against their wills. So, for Plato, this claim is not mere speculation but is rather based on empirical evidence. Arguably, such evidence has grown since Plato's time, as the deaths of such figures as Jesus Christ, Martin Luther King, Jr., and Mahatma Gandhi could be viewed similarly as having been executed by those they were attempting to enlighten.

However, one could argue that we should not see the prisoners in the cave as passive nihilists. Having grown up in a cave and having no knowledge that their cave is a prison, the prisoners would view the returning prisoner who attempts to liberate them as the one who is violent, as the one who wants to force them to abandon their *home*. Consequently, their violence toward him could be viewed, not as resistance to enlightenment, but as *self-defense*.

4 Heidegger and Liberation as Violence

In order to determine whether the prisoners in Plato's allegory are passive nihilists, we can turn to Heidegger. In his lecture on Plato's *Republic*, *The Essence of Truth*, Heidegger notes that violence actually occurs in the cave more than once. When the would-be liberator is freed, he does not immediately try to leave the cave, but, like his fellow prisoners after him, he initially resists liberation.

We are told by Plato that the freed prisoner prefers the shadows to the light and so must be forced to leave the cave against his will. Heidegger writes:

> Removal of the shackles is thus not genuine emancipation, for it remains external and fails to penetrate to man in his ownmost self. The circumstances of the prisoner change, but his inner condition, his willing [*Wollen*] does not. The released prisoner does indeed will, but he wills to return to his shackles. Thus willing, he wills not-willing: he does not want to be involved himself. He avoids and shrinks back from the demand to fully give up his previous situation. He is also a long way from understanding that man truly *is* only in so far as he demands this of himself. (Heidegger 2002, p. 28)

On Heidegger's reading, then, being released from one's shackles is not the same thing as being liberated, especially if the shackled individual does not want to have the shackles removed. However, Heidegger argues that the prisoner's response to the attempted emancipation is more than simple unwillingness. Rather, according to Heidegger, the prisoner "wills not-willing."

This way of describing the prisoner's reaction as willing to not will seems to be echoing one of the ways Nietzsche describes nihilism in his *Genealogy of Morals*. In the third essay of the *Genealogy*, Nietzsche writes: "*That* the ascetic ideal has meant so many things to man, however, is an expression of the basic fact of the human will, its *horror vacui: it needs a goal*—and it will rather will *nothingness* than *not* will" (GM III 1). Nietzsche then ends the essay by returning to this "basic fact of the human will" with which he opens the essay. Nietzsche writes:

> We can no longer conceal from ourselves what is expressed by all that willing which has taken its direction from the ascetic ideal: this hatred of the human, and even more of the animal, and more still of the material, this horror of the senses, of reason itself, this fear of happiness and beauty, this longing to get away from all appearance, change, becoming, death, wishing, from longing itself—all this means—let us dare to grasp it—*a will to nothingness*, an aversion to life, a rebellion against the most fundamental presuppositions of life; but it is and remains a *will!*. ... And, to repeat in conclusion what I said at the beginning: man would rather will *nothingness* than *not* will. (GM III 28)

According to Nietzsche, asceticism, the choice to make oneself suffer, was idealized by humanity, as, for example, when we see self-denial and selflessness as moral ideals. This idealization of suffering took place because it could give life meaning, and this was preferable to the alternative choice of having to face the meaninglessness of life.

Nihilism, according to Nietzsche, is therefore not found in seeing life as meaningless, as many often presume (Tartaglia 2016), for it is precisely the opposite that is the case (Gertz 2019). Nihilism is found in fleeing from the meaninglessness of life, in the unwillingness to accept the meaninglessness of life, and in the embrace of false meaningfulness. Even if that meaningfulness is destructive, as in the case of asceticism, in the case of finding meaning in denying one's own nature and one's own urges, nihilism clings to any false meaningfulness that can fill the void in life where meaning is expected to be found. In other words, nihilism is found in choosing to continue to be a prisoner in a cave, even after having been shown that one is a prisoner in a cave, because to do otherwise would mean having to accept the truth, the truth that one's life has been spent staring at shadows on a wall.

If we now return to the hypothetical counterargument that I raised at the end of the previous section, we can see that we should not think of passive nihilism and self-defense as rival interpretations of the reaction of the prisoners in Plato's cave. Rather, one could argue that the prisoners' passive nihilism is what provokes their self-defense. The first freed prisoner defends himself from the truth of the light by trying to return to the shadows. The other prisoners defend themselves from the truth of the freed prisoner by trying to kill the freed prisoner. The prisoners do not experience the truth *as truth*, they experience the truth *as violence*, a violence that they feel they must fight with violence in order to protect themselves.

As Heidegger argues in the passage quoted above, this experience of truth as violence provokes a counter-violence, which is not only violent against any would-be liberator, but also *violent against oneself*. Heidegger writes: "He is also a long way from understanding that man truly *is* only in so far as he demands this of himself" (Heidegger 2002, p. 28). We can understand this to mean that the prisoner, in wanting to remain a prisoner, is not only trying to avoid having to leave all that he has ever known but is also preventing himself from becoming truly human.

Just as the shadows are not as real as what exists outside the cave but only resemble that which is real, so the prisoners are not as human as they could be if they left the cave, and thus only resemble real humans. Consequently, the decision to remain living in a world that is not fully real is a decision to remain being not fully human. We can therefore view passive nihilism as not only violent in the sense of *self-defense*, but also violent in the sense of *self-destruction*. In wanting to protect themselves from having to face a truth that would be damaging to their sense of reality, and to their sense of who they are, the prisoners end up preventing themselves from becoming who they are supposed to be.

5 De Beauvoir and Adulthood vs. Annihilation

Another objection we might raise here, however, is that these prisoners are not acting *violently*, but rather they are acting *childishly*. Like children, the prisoners do not want to leave the only shelter they have ever known, the only caregivers they have ever known, the only world they have ever known, because they simply do not know any better. In other words, the prisoners do not want to grow up.

Wanting to remain in childhood, in innocence, in ignorance, in irresponsibility, in not being who one is, is how Simone de Beauvoir defines nihilism. In *The Ethics of Ambiguity*, de Beauvoir describes the evolution of a nihilist from being a child to being an adult who wants to return to being a child. Children, according to de Beauvoir, are like the prisoners in Plato's cave, finding themselves in a world not of their own making, a world in which they have no responsibility, a world where they can play carefree while blindly trusting and obeying the adults who take care of them. Upon reaching adolescence, however, children are faced with a choice, a choice like that experienced by the prisoners, to either become full human beings by leaving their childhood behind and by embracing their freedom and with it their responsibility, or to become what de Beauvoir calls "sub-men" (de Beauvoir 1948, p. 42).

According to de Beauvoir, sub-men are those who refuse to be human by refusing to accept their freedom, wanting to be a thing rather than a human being. However, since these sub-men are still human, they choose to become thing-like by replacing the meaning in their lives that would come from embracing freedom by instead embracing already-existing sources of meaning that they find in the world, and which allow them to subsume their freedom. As de Beauvoir writes:

> He would like to forget himself, to be ignorant of himself, but the nothingness which is at the heart of man is also the consciousness that he has of himself. His negativity is revealed positively as anguish, desire, appeal, laceration, but as for the genuine return to the positive, the sub-man eludes it. He is afraid of engaging himself in a project as he is afraid of being disengaged and thereby of being in a state of danger before the future, in the midst of its possibilities. He is thereby led to take refuge in the ready-made values of the serious world. He will proclaim certain opinions; he will take shelter behind a label; and to hide his indifference he will readily abandon himself to verbal outbursts or even physical violence. One day, a monarchist, the next day, an anarchist, he is more readily anti-semitic, anti-clerical, or anti-republican. Thus, although we have defined him as a denial and a flight, the sub-man is not a harmless creature. (de Beauvoir 1948, pp. 43–44)

The "serious world" that de Beauvoir refers to here as the place where the sub-man seeks to take refuge is how she describes the world as it is experienced as a child. The sub-man thus wishes to return to the life of a child, and like a child, will pretend to be someone who has serious concerns and serious opinions, and even violently uphold them, in order to avoid having to actually *be* concerned or actually *be* opinionated, like an adult.

Though the sub-man violently rejects the freedom that makes him a human being, he is nevertheless not yet fully a nihilist, according to de Beauvoir. To reach that stage, she argues that the sub-man first must become so engrossed in pretending to be serious that he actually turns himself into a "serious man" (de Beauvoir 1948, p. 45). A serious man is someone who escapes his freedom by identifying himself with a cause to such a degree that he becomes a fanatic absolutist about the cause. What the cause is does not matter. What matters is that, in blindly serving the cause, the cause is able to give the life of the serious man meaning and order, in much the same way that children are able to find meaning and order in life by blindly obeying their parents.

The serious man does not simply follow a cause but follows the cause absolutely and loses himself in it because the cause is and must be right. The serious man is like a child who believes his parents must be right. This is not because the child agrees with his parents, but because the idea of his parents being wrong is simply incomprehensible. So, too, the serious man believes the realization of his chosen cause is the only thing that matters and that can provide life with meaning because the alternative is incomprehensible. The serious man therefore views the success of the cause as inevitable, and it is the belief in this inevitability that allows the serious man to see any obstacles in the way of the cause, even if those obstacles are people, as meaningless. This willingness to reduce anything or anyone to nothing is what makes the serious man even more violent than the sub-man.

As de Beauvoir argues, the serious man not only rejects his own subjectivity and freedom but also "ignores the value of the subjectivity and the freedom of others, to such an extent that, sacrificing them to the thing, he persuades himself that what he sacrifices is nothing" (de Beauvoir 1948, p. 49). Like the prisoners in the cave when confronted by the freed prisoner, the serious man is not only willing to dismiss the objections of anyone who would question the meaningfulness of his chosen cause but would kill such people because he sees their lives as meaningless when compared to the cause. In other words, shadows can not only be found to be meaningful, but can also be found to be more meaningful than the lives of other human beings.

According to de Beauvoir, seeing everything in such stark all-or-nothing terms is what finally turns the serious man into a nihilist. As de Beauvoir writes, "Nihilism is disappointed seriousness which has turned back upon itself" (de Beauvoir 1948, p. 52). Having first lost the childlike belief in the serious world of adults, the serious man came to find a cause that he thought could give life meaning, and thus free him from the anxiety of freedom, the anxiety of having to himself give life meaning. Consequently, should the cause prove incapable of giving life meaning and freeing the serious man from his freedom, the serious man becomes a nihilist, according to de Beauvoir. The serious man does not seek out another cause, but rather comes to see all causes, all pursuits, all existence, as nothing. And so, his previous willingness to reduce anything to nothing in the pursuit of his cause becomes a willingness to reduce everything to nothing in the pursuit of turning himself into nothing.

When the cause that was supposed to free the serious man from his freedom proves unable to achieve this goal, the serious man moves from trying to annihilate his own freedom to nihilistically trying to annihilate freedom itself. And it is here, according to de Beauvoir, that we see how truly violent nihilism can be. As de Beauvoir writes:

> The attitude of the nihilist can perpetuate itself as such only if it reveals itself as a positivity at its very core. Rejecting his own existence, the nihilist must also reject the existences which confirm it. If he wills himself to be nothing, all mankind must also be annihilated; otherwise, by means of the presence of this world that the Other reveals he meets himself as a presence in the world. But this thirst for destruction immediately takes the form of a desire for power. The taste of nothingness joins the original taste of being whereby every man is first defined; he realizes himself as a being by making himself that by which nothingness comes into the world. Thus, Nazism was both a will for power and a will for suicide at the same time. (de Beauvoir 1948, pp. 55–56)

The nihilist is someone who wants to be nothing. But to be nothing is impossible since, first, to be nothing is to be not-being, which is a contradiction, just as being a nihilist still requires the nihilist to be something. Second, so long as other people are around, the nihilist cannot even pretend to be nothing since other people will always see the nihilist as something and force him to "meet himself" as something. Unable to be nothing, the nihilist instead becomes destructive, seeking to destroy himself by destroying everyone else, because it is everyone else who he feels forces him to continue to be a self.

By describing nihilism as being able to be "both a will for power and a will for suicide at the same time," de Beauvoir here reaffirms the idea that nihilism can be not only violent, but that this violence can take the form of either self-defense or of self-destruction. Or, to be more precise, the self-defensive violence of nihilism is self-destructive. It is the desire to protect oneself from one's freedom that leads to the desire to destroy the freedom of others in order to prevent being recognized by others as having freedom. So for de Beauvoir the resistance of the prisoners we see in Plato's cave should not be seen as being either violent or childish, as it is the childishness of the prisoners—in the sense of wanting to remain like children, to remain free from having to face their freedom—that provokes their violence.

6 Arendt and Violence vs. Power

In the analysis of nihilistic violence found in de Beauvoir's work we find an account that brings together the previously discussed analyses of nihilistic violence found in Plato, in Nietzsche, and in Heidegger. However, by linking nihilism to Nazism, de Beauvoir seemingly goes further than Plato, Nietzsche, and Heidegger. Whereas they describe the violence of nihilism as conducted by individuals against individuals, or prisoners against prisoners, de Beauvoir provides the provocative suggestion that this violence could grow and become violence by nations against nations. This raises the question then of whether we should think of the violent capabilities of nihilism not only on an interpersonal level, but also on an international level, in the form of political violence.

The connection that de Beauvoir makes between nihilism, violence, and power is a connection that we can find explored further in the work of Hannah Arendt. In her 1969 work *On Violence*, which was written primarily in response to the uprisings of 1968, Arendt argues that violence has been taken for granted by political theorists and thus left undefined and unappreciated. Against this, Arendt warns that we must be careful to avoid what she sees as the tendency among political theorists to treat violence as merely a manifestation of power. Arendt strives to show that we should not see violence and power as synonymous, as though violence is merely a way to gain power and power is merely the ability to exercise violence. Arendt attempts to provide a more nuanced account of the relationship between violence and power, an account that can help us better understand the relationship between violence and nihilism.

Seeing violence as insufficiently understood by both activists and academics, Arendt argues that we can begin to properly understand the nature of violence if we not only distinguish violence from power but recognize that they are actually opposed to each other. Whereas violence can be performed by one individual against countless others just by picking up a gun, power instead requires a group of people to act in concert with each other. As Arendt writes, "The extreme form of power is All against One, the extreme form of violence is One against All" (Arendt 1969, p. 42).

The idea that violence and power are opposed to each other is vital to Arendt's larger claim that if violence is successful, it is not because *violence is power* but rather because *power is absent*. In response to the idea that a small group of students can overpower a larger group through the use of violence, Arendt writes:

> What actually happens in such cases is something much more serious: the majority clearly refuses to use its power and overpower the disrupters; the academic processes break down because no one is willing to raise more than a voting finger for the *status quo*. What the universities are up against is the "immense negative unity" of which Stephen Spender speaks in another context. All of which proves only that a minority can have a much greater potential power than one would expect by counting noses in public-opinion polls. The merely onlooking majority, amused by the spectacle of a shouting match between student and professor, is in fact already the latent ally of the minority. (Arendt 1969, p. 42)

The success of a disruptive minority is due, according to Arendt, not to the power of their violence, but rather to the unwillingness of the majority to use their power to counter the violence. This unwillingness of the majority to use the power of their numbers, moreover, should not be presumed to be due to their *fear* of the violent minority. Instead, Arendt suggests it could be because the majority are *entertained* by the violence.

The majority, simply "amused by the spectacle" caused by the violent minority, becomes the "latent ally" of the violent minority and so, like the audience at a play, or at an execution, wait to see what happens next rather than use their power to intervene. Though Arendt does not develop this idea further, we can see an important connection between violence and nihilism here. The entertainment value of violence—a value that Nietzsche focuses on in his discussion of the "pleasure" of cruelty, a pleasure that could even become a "festival" (GM II 6) —provides us with an insight into why passive nihilism would be attracted to violence, and why violence would be attracted to passive nihilism.

As mentioned in section 2 above, passive nihilism seeks out distractions in order to avoid having to face reality. Though we often think of such distractions in terms of calm activities like drinking, sleeping, or meditating, the "spectacle" of violence, as Arendt points out, can also provide such a distraction. Like watching TV, in watching rather than performing violence, the passive nihilist is able to be absorbed by the actions of others and so can experience life through their actions while being allowed to just sit and do nothing. Even if threatened by the violence unfolding, the passive nihilist can nonetheless still be afforded the perceived freedom from responsibility that comes from being able to feel that there is nothing to do but *just follow orders*. Consequently, we can think of what Arendt describes as the "latency" of the audience, witnessing violence unfold without using the power of their numbers to intervene to stop it, as another way of describing passive nihilism.

Arendt's focus in this essay, however, is less on the latency of the witnesses to violence than on the *impotency* of the perpetrators of violence. Power, according to Arendt, does not need violence in order to achieve its aims. Even if power is only thought of in terms of ruling and of domination, a group can rule over others and can dominate others without violence because commanding and oppressing can be achieved instead through the use of authority. If Arendt defines power as the ability of people to come together to operate together in unison (Arendt 1969, p. 44), and authority as the "unquestioning recognition by those who are asked to obey" such that "neither coercion nor persuasion is needed," then the unity that defines power can be achieved solely through the obedience that defines authority (Arendt 1969, p. 45). It is thus when a group loses its authority, and its cohesiveness begins to break down, that, in its impotence, the group turns to violence to fill the void.

The resort to violence, in other words, is not a sign of power, of the ability to act with impunity, but a sign of weakness, of the inability to command obedience by respect rather than by fear. Arendt is careful to point out that though violence can indeed produce obedience and therefore the semblance of authority, violence cannot produce power but only destroy it. The attempt by the powerful to use violence to remain in power is "self-defeating" precisely because the fear it inspires leads people, not to unite, but to turn against each other (Arendt 1969, p. 54). Violence used for political purposes creates an atmosphere of terror, the result of which, according to Arendt, is "social atomization" (Arendt 1969, p. 55).

Due to the threat of other groups similarly attempting to take power through the use of violence, those who rule through fear come to fear those they rule. Historically, governments that rule by terror—such as the Nazis and the Soviets—try to root out the possibility of such threats by creating police states, societies of suspicion where everyone is incentivized to see each other as a potential informer rather than as a potential ally. As Arendt writes:

> The decisive difference between totalitarian domination, based on terror, and tyrannies and dictatorships, established by violence, is that the former turns not only against its enemies but against its friends and supporters as well, being afraid of all power, even the power of its friends. The climax of terror is reached when the police state begins to devour its own children, when yesterday's executioner becomes today's victim. And this is also the moment when power disappears entirely.... To sum up: politically speaking, it is insufficient to say that power and violence are not the same. Power and violence are opposites; where the one rules absolutely, the other is absent. Violence appears where power is in jeopardy, but left to its own course it ends in power's disappearance. (Arendt 1969, pp. 55–56)

Arendt here argues that a state that would resort to violence when their "power is in jeopardy" would end up "being afraid of all power, even the power of its friends." Violence can force people to act together, but it cannot force people to *willingly* act together, and so it cannot create power for the state but only be used continuously to prevent anyone else from having power. Since any group willing to work together as one to achieve a common goal—even if that goal was to be a "friend" of the state—would have the power that the state no longer had, it would present itself as a threat to the violent state and so it would have to be destroyed by the state's violence.

When those in power resort to violence to stay in power, this results in the self-defeating destruction of power. This conclusion of Arendt's analysis of the antagonistic relationship between power and violence shows why we should think of political violence by the state as being nihilistic. The idea produced by political violence, that it is better that no one has power than that anyone has power because such power would reveal the powerlessness of the state, can be seen to parallel the idea of nihilistic violence in de Beauvoir's work discussed earlier. According to de Beauvoir, the nihilist turns to violence in order to protect himself from having to confront reality (i.e. the loss of childhood and the freedom from responsibility that came with it). According to Arendt, the state likewise turns to violence in order to protect itself from having to confront reality (i.e. the loss of authority and the power to command willing obedience that came with it).

One might object that what we are discussing here is not actually a parallel but a contradiction. For if the state becomes violent in order to attain power, that seems like the opposite of the nihilist who becomes violent in order to avoid freedom. In other words, the nihilist uses violence to become nothing, whereas the state uses violence in order to avoid becoming nothing. However, against this objection, it is important to remember that the nihilist becomes a nihilist, according to de Beauvoir, because the nihilist fails in the attempt to find an authority figure who could protect the nihilist from the anxiety of freedom in the same way that a parent protects a child. Thus, both the nihilist and the state can be viewed as turning to violence because of an absence of authority. Or to be more precise, it is the absence of authority that leads both individuals and states toward behavior that is nihilistically self-destructive.

7 Conclusion

If we bring together the analyses of de Beauvoir and Arendt, we can reach the following conclusion about the relationship between nihilism and violence: it is the absence of authority that can turn both individuals and states toward nihilism. This turn toward nihilism takes place when either individuals or states are unwilling to face the reality of this absence of authority. And it is their self-defensive attempts to desperately avoid confronting this reality that leads both nihilistic individuals and nihilistic states to pursue violence that is destructive, both to oneself and to others.

We can view this conclusion as fittingly returning us to where we began, with Nietzsche. The idea that the absence of authority produces nihilism is already present in his famous pronouncement that "God is dead." Though in keeping with our theme it is important to remember that Nietzsche makes this pronouncement twice in the *Gay Science*, and both times there is an indication of the relationship between the absence of authority and violence.

When Nietzsche first announces the death of God, he adds that, though God is dead, the idea of God will nevertheless remain very much alive. Echoing Plato, Nietzsche writes, "God is dead; but given the way of men, there may still be caves for thousands of years in which his shadow will be shown" (GS 108). Because of the persistence of God's shadow, Nietzsche concludes that God is not truly dead until we "vanquish his shadow, too." When Nietzsche repeats this pronouncement later in the *Gay Science* by famously putting it in the mouth of a "madman" (*"Der tolle Mensch"*), Nietzsche reveals that not only is God dead, but that "we have killed him," making us the "murderers of all murderers" (GS 125).

For Nietzsche, it is the absence of authority created by the death of God that should have liberated humanity from its childlike worship of the "Father," allowing us to grow up and become truly human. But instead of growing up, instead of looking for authority within ourselves rather than in sources outside of ourselves, we sought out new Gods to worship, according to Nietzsche, even choosing to worship shadows if necessary, rather than confront reality. In other words, we created God in order to give ourselves the ultimate authority figure, but when we became so dependent on that authority that we "killed" God, we chose to embrace nihilism rather than become authorities unto ourselves.

This choice, as Plato, Heidegger, de Beauvoir, and Arendt have now shown us, is a choice that leads to violence. The prisoners in the cave do not want to accept that they are prisoners in a cave worshipping shadows, and so they choose to respond to their would-be liberator by trying to kill him so they can go back to worshipping shadows. The serious man who is disappointed in his attempts to find an authority figure who could serve as a surrogate parent gives up the fantasy of returning to the freedom from responsibility found in childhood, only to choose to pursue a new violent fantasy of becoming nothing by destroying everything. The state that discovers its authority has disappeared and refuses to accept this loss of power turns to violence to try to hold on to power and so becomes incapable of governing except through violence, which ultimately leads to the destruction of the very possibility of power.

Yet the true danger that exists in this relationship between authority, nihilism, and violence is that which arises when individuals who are unwilling to face the "death of God," or the "death of childhood," seek out the authority, not of a new God, but of an authoritarian "Leader" (Arendt 1958, p. 364). According to de Beauvoir, it is the serious man, the not-yet-nihilist, who would seek to replace the Father with the Fatherland, and it is only when he becomes "disappointed" in this choice of authority figure that he would become a nihilist (de Beauvoir 1948, p. 52).

Nihilists are often regarded as anarchists bent on the destruction of the state. For this reason, we discussed at the outset the assumption that nihilistic violence would reside with active nihilists rather than with passive nihilists. Yet if we return to Arendt's description of the dynamic of a classroom where the majority chooses not to use their power to stop a surge of violence, but who instead become the latent ally to the violence by watching it unfold, we can see how passive nihilists could be just as, if not more, violent than active nihilists by becoming the latent ally to the violence of an authoritarian political party. This possibility becomes especially likely if the party is using violence to give itself the authority that the passive nihilist craves. In other words, the nihilistic individual who is looking for an authority figure and the nihilistic party that is using violence to prop itself up as an authoritarian regime, could each find what they are looking for in the other.

This is why the relationship between authority, nihilism, and violence is so dangerous as it can create the conditions for the rise of fascism, or even of totalitarianism. In her *Origins of Totalitarianism*, Arendt makes clear that the offer of an "escape from reality" is one of the major appeals that totalitarianism offers to the masses. Arendt writes:

> Before they seize power and establish a world according to their doctrines, totalitarian movements conjure up a lying world of consistency which is more adequate to the needs of the human mind than reality itself; in which, through sheer imagination, uprooted masses can feel at home and are spared the never-ending shocks which real life and real experiences deal to human beings and their expectations. (Arendt 1958, p. 353)

According to Arendt, the "uprooted masses" would feel more "at home" in a "lying world of consistency" than in the disordered chaos of the real world, and so would support totalitarian movements trying to "seize power." In other words, the more the real world is experienced as disordered and chaotic, the more likely it is that large numbers of people will nihilistically seek to flee from the real world and will thus find the fantasy world envisioned by totalitarian movements to be increasingly appealing.

Consequently, we can see why the answer to the question of how to stop the violent rise of totalitarian movements cannot simply be "the old saying that the cure for ills of democracy is more democracy" (Dewey 1927, p. 144). For if there is a sufficient number of people in the "uprooted masses," then they can democratically usher in totalitarianism. Instead, the answer has to be that we need to find ways to prevent the experience of uprootedness that leads people to embrace nihilism and violence.

In a work that she did not finish before she died, Arendt warns against the danger of the "modern growth of worldlessness, the withering away of everything *between* us," which Arendt likened to the "spread of a desert." Arendt continues:

> That we live and move in a desert-world was first recognized by Nietzsche, and it was also Nietzsche who made the first decisive mistake in diagnosing it. Like almost all who came after him, he believed that the desert is in ourselves, thereby revealing himself not only as

> one of the earliest conscious inhabitants of the desert but also, by the same token, as the victim of its most terrible illusion. (Arendt 2005, p. 201)

Arendt criticizes Nietzsche for mistakenly diagnosing nihilism as an individual phenomenon that requires an individual solution. As we discussed earlier, Nietzsche thinks that we should have responded to the death of God by becoming individual authorities unto ourselves. In this way, we could, Nietzsche hoped, avoid the "herd mentality" that he is so famous for attacking because he saw it as a symptom of nihilism. Contra Nietzsche, Arendt argues that the only way to stop the growth of this "desert-world" is not through independence, but through politics. By seeing politics as a never-ending communal project for the creation of a "human world" we can avoid the desert-making danger of treating politics as merely something to be left to bureaucrats to worry about so that we can pursue individualistic projects that nihilistically only aim at self-improvement.

Simone Weil similarly sees the need for other people as what makes us human. Weil likewise worries about the rise of uprootedness, which she likens, not to a desert, but to a disease. In her *The Need for Roots*, Weil writes:

> To be rooted is perhaps the most important and least recognized need of the human soul. It is one of the hardest to define. A human being has roots by virtue of his real, active and natural participation in the life of a community which preserves in living shape certain particular treasures of the past and certain particular expectations for the future. This participation is a natural one, in the sense that it is automatically brought about by place, conditions of birth, profession and social surroundings. Every human being needs to have multiple roots. It is necessary for him to draw wellnigh the whole of his moral, intellectual and spiritual life by way of the environment of which he forms a natural part. (Weil 2002, p. 40)

According to Weil, it is necessary for humans to have "roots" in the sense of not only belonging to a community, but to a community that is oriented both toward its past and its future. This is why Weil warns that "the disease of uprootedness" can occur when a community is cut off from its past or loses the ability to create a future for itself, such as occurs in "military conquest," in "deportations on a massive scale," or in "money-power and economic domination" (Weil 2002, p. 41).

So, if we bring Arendt and Weil together, we can see that we should not worry only about the nihilistic violence of the anarchist or of the fascist. Because to do so is to ignore the nihilistic violence of the individualist and of the capitalist. And it is perhaps precisely because our concerns about nihilism and violence have largely been so focused on anarchy and on fascism that we have allowed individualism and capitalism to continue to make our world so nihilistic and so violent.

Bibliography

Arendt, Hannah (1958): *The Origins of Totalitarianism*. Cleveland, New York: The World Publishing Company.
Arendt, Hannah (1969): *On Violence*. San Diego, New York, London: Harcourt Brace & Company.
Arendt, Hannah (2005): "Introduction *into* Politics." In: Jerome Kohn (Ed.): *The Promise of Politics*. New York: Schocken Books, pp. 93–200.
de Beauvoir, Simone (1948): *The Ethics of Ambiguity*. Translated by Bernard Frechtman. New York: Citadel Press.
Dewey, John (1927): *The Public and Its Problems*. New York: Henry Holt and Company.
Dostoevsky, Fyodor (1995): *Demons: A Novel in Three Parts*. Translated and annotated by Richard Pevear and Larissa Volokhonsky. New York: Vintage Books.
Gertz, Nolen (2018): *Nihilism and Technology*. London: Rowman & Littlefield International.
Gertz, Nolen (2019): *Nihilism*. Cambridge, London: The MIT Press.
Heidegger, Martin (2002): *The Essence of Truth*. Translated by Ted Sadler. New York, London: Continuum.
NBC News (2003): "Transcript for Sept. 14." https://www.nbcnews.com/id/wbna3080244, visited on November 25, 2020.
Nietzsche, Friedrich (1967): *The Will to Power*. Edited by Walter Kaufmann. Translated by Walter Kaufmann and R. J. Hollingdale. New York: Vintage Books.
Nietzsche, Friedrich (1974): *The Gay Science*. Translated by Walter Kaufmann. New York: Vintage Books.
Nietzsche, Friedrich (1989): *On the Genealogy of Morals and Ecce Homo*. Edited by Walter Kaufmann. Translated by Walter Kaufmann and R. J. Hollingdale. New York: Vintage Books.
Plato: *Apology*.
Plato: *Republic*.
Tartaglia, James (2016): *Philosophy in a Meaningless Life: Nihilism, Consciousness and Reality*. London, New York: Bloomsbury Academic.
Turgenev, Ivan (1991): *Fathers and Sons*. Translated by Richard Freeborn. Oxford, New York: Oxford University Press.
Weil, Simone (2002): *The Need for Roots: Prelude to a Declaration of Duties towards Mankind*. Translated by Arthur Wills. London, New York: Routledge Classics.

George Pattison
Kierkegaard's Aesthetic Stage and the Ideology of Nihilism

Abstract: In the first part of *Either/Or*, Kierkegaard presents a collection of papers composed by an unidentified person (A) that sets out the elements of an aesthetic view of life. This is often seen in terms of a general lack of self-commitment and the pursuit of more or less sophisticated forms of pleasure. This paper argues that, in reality, A's papers present the existential outworking of a consistent metaphysical nihilism. Amongst the features of a life lived in full consciousness of the ultimate meaninglessness of the world adduced by A are: (1) distraction, restlessness and a penchant for 'the interesting'; (2) the absence of any basis for mutual respect in relations between persons; (3) an underlying orientation towards violence in human relationships; and (4) the role of art as the maximum form in which life can be justified. This paper concludes by indicating how the analysis of the aesthetic in *Either/Or* I might be seen to anticipate Kierkegaard's later view of the essentially violent and persecutory nature of society.

1 Introduction

The relationship between affective states and the way in which we perceive the world has been the focus of considerable interest amongst philosophers in recent years.[1] Some scholars, such as Mark Wynn, argue that emotions have cognitive significance in the sense that emotional dispositions enable us to see features of the world that would otherwise remain obscure.[2] Positive feelings put us in a better position to see the positive aspects of others' personalities and actions.[3] Conversely, an attitude of chronic suspicion might, on the one hand,

---

[1] For the purpose of this essay, I am not pausing to distinguish between such terms as 'affections', 'passions', 'feelings' or 'emotions' and following popular usage in treating them as near-synonyms. Naturally, each has its own history and distinctive application. See, for example, the work of the Centre for the History of Emotions at Queen Mary's University (London): https://projects.history.qmul.ac.uk/emotions/.
[2] See Wynn (2013).
[3] See, e.g., Troy Jollimore's discussion of 'love's friendly eye', summed up in his comment that 'a just and loving gaze can be a route to a cognitive grasp of the world deeper and more profound than any that might be achieved from the standpoint of a more detached perspective' (Jollimore 2013, p. 73).

open our eyes to the darker motives that the positive person might fail to see but, on the other hand, blind us to what is good in the world. Either way, such feelings will play a significant role in shaping our overall attitude to life and informing our view of the world. I do not wish to enter into this discussion in detail but add only that it is most likely that there is a complex system of two-way traffic in operation here. That is to say, not only is it the case that affective states influence how we perceive our world but what we believe to be the case about ourselves, about others and about the world as a whole will in turn influence how, in any given situation, we feel. If this is the case, then affective states – even those that might seem entirely spontaneous – can be revelatory of deeper ideological commitments.[4]

These comments have particular importance for the philosophy of religion, since religious life is clearly a sphere in which beliefs and feelings are both deeply and extensively involved and equally deeply and extensively intertwined. As Augustine's *Confessions* already made clear, the search for knowledge of God is inseparable from the heart's desire for God, where desire is understood in a sense that we would describe in terms of affection, emotion, feeling or passion. This is also the territory in which Kierkegaard developed his innovative psychological or subjective approach to the question of becoming a Christian. In doing so, he contributed to an understanding of "mood" that would be further developed by Martin Heidegger in the twentieth century, best exemplified in Heidegger's reworking of Kierkegaard's concept of anxiety. This interface between how we feel about the world (inclusive of ourselves and our relations to others) and how we believe the world to be is already thematized in Kierkegaard's first major work, *Either/Or* (1843) and is especially significant in considering the relationship between aesthetics and nihilism that is the specific focus of this paper. Although elements of my analysis may carry over into other parts of Kierkegaard's authorship, I should stress from the outset that my argument here is limited to the relationship between aesthetics and nihilism as that is presented in *Either/Or*, together with a brief and merely suggestive application to his later, more radically Christian writing.[5] Apart from the fact that this already gives us more than enough to be getting on with, it also respects the conceptual distinctiveness of the world-view that this work proposes. In other words, the primary issue here

---

[4] The interaction between affective states and fundamental philosophical views is a defining theme of Martha Nussbaum's *The Therapy of Desire* (Nussbaum 1994), an approach that is applied specifically to Kierkegaard in Furtak (2005). A similar dialectic is evidenced in many of Dostoevsky's novels and is theoretically developed in Bakhtin's paradigmatic study of Dostoevsky's poetics (Bakhtin 1984).

[5] See Section 6 below.

is not 'Kierkegaard', but the distinctive life-view presented by the fictional aesthete A of *Either/Or* I.

Either/Or stages a confrontation between two forms of life that Kierkegaard calls the aesthetic and the ethical. The aesthetic is represented by a collection of papers gathered together in Part 1 and ascribed to an unnamed author referred to as A, while the ethical is set out in two long letters to A by a character called Assessor (or Judge) Vilhelm. In a third letter, Vilhelm encloses a sermon by a friend of his, who is priest to a remote community on the Jutland heath. This sermon can be read as indicative of a form of life that has a more radically religious tenor than the Assessor's own life-view. In this way, *Either/Or* also offers a first sketch of what, in later works, will be treated as the three 'stages' of life: the aesthetic, the ethical and the religious.

The place of feeling in determining the character of the aesthetic stage is already flagged on the title page by a motto taken from the eighteenth-century English poet Edward Young: 'Are passions, then, the pagans of the soul / Reason alone baptized?'.[6] This might further suggest that feeling or passion will play an especially prominent role in the aesthetic stage, whereas (to anticipate) the ethical will be defined more by volition or choice. Such a view would, of course, reflect a classic distinction between the affections and the will and the development from the aesthetic to the ethical might then be understood as moving from a life driven by emotional needs to a life based on choice or decision. There are many precedents for this in classical and Christian thought.

I do not think this way of seeing it is entirely absent from *Either/Or*. It certainly features in the Assessor's view of the situation, since he persistently represents A's problem in terms of the latter's emotional immaturity and a constant failure to commit to a definite vocation. The Assessor's complaint is, in one respect, that A quite simply lacks any life-view whatsoever and needs to grow up. However, if it is the case that affective states may reflect ideological commitments (as well as vice versa) it is at least worthwhile considering whether that might be the case here. The argument of this paper is, quite simply, that it is and that A's approach to life is not (as the Assessor at one point says) like that of a jellyfish carried backwards and forwards on tides of emotion (Kierkegaard 1987b, p. 38): instead,

---

[6] Although not widely read today, Young's advocacy of a passionate rather than a merely rational engagement with fundamental questions of life and death exerted considerable influence on the *Sturm und Drang* movement in Germany. His best-known work, from which Kierkegaard quotes, is the poem usually referred to as *Night Thoughts* (1742). See Edward Young, *The Complaint or Night Thoughts on Life, Death, and Immortality* (London: A. Millar, 1751), p. 66 (from the Fourth Night).

it reflects a definite view regarding the nature of things.[7] Consequently, it is not just immaturity that makes A resistant to the Assessor's urgings, it is also his commitment to a view of life that renders the Assessor's insistence on self-choice meaningless. Even more disturbingly, it implies that the desire to live a meaningful and valuable life in the world that motivates the Assessor is entirely worthless: the world is such that there is neither meaning nor value, leaving only a strategy of self-assertion. A's widely-noted nihilism, then, is not just the absence of goal or purpose but the resolute denial of all goals and purposes. Furthermore, this entails that A's life in the world is not merely given over to aesthetic experiences (however, these are more closely defined) but also involves a hostile and implicitly violent attitude towards others.[8]

This view of what is going on in Kierkegaard's aesthetic stage is, I should say, a minority view. "The aesthetic" is defined in various ways in the secondary literature, amongst which 'pleasure', 'immediacy' and 'contemplation' (in the sense of passively observing life rather than taking up an active role in it) are frequently encountered candidates.[9] Some note that the matter is more complex,

---

[7] One of the relatively few articles to see this as Kierkegaard's aim is the brief contribution of Charles I. Glicksberg (1960). Karsten Harries (2010) offers a reading of *Either/Or* in which the theme of nihilism is strongly to the fore, but he discusses this largely in terms the subjective world-experience of the aesthete, the Assessor and the Jutland pastor. He does not thematize – though he does quote (Harries 2010, p. 63) – the passage in which A writes about the cosmic vortex in a way that gives a cosmological underpinning to his nihilistic worldview. By way of contrast, this passage is central to the interpretation of A's nihilism offered in the present essay.

[8] It is very possible that the Assessor's own strategy of moulding his argument in an ad hominem manner has itself been largely responsible for obscuring this aspect of A's life-view. Indeed, the Assessor explicitly denies that A has or is capable of having an actual life-view. In view of this, I shall develop my argument here solely on the basis of A's own writings and shall not use the filter provided by the Assessor's letters (though I will from time to time refer to them).

[9] In what was the first anthology of Kierkegaard's writings to appear in English, Lee M. Hollander writes that the aesthete 'has but one desire which is, to enjoy the sweets of life—whether its purely sensual pleasures or the more refined Epicureanism of the finer things in life and art, and the ironic enjoyment of one's own superiority over the rest of humanity' (Hollander 1960 [1923], pp. 12–13). That A is concerned primarily with pleasure is often reflected in popular views of Kierkegaard, as in *Kierkegaard for Beginners*, where we read that '"aestheticism" is a form of hedonism. People who find themselves in the aesthetic realm have their lives governed by the principles of sensuousness' (Palmer 1996, p. 83). 'Immediacy' is the category favoured in Hampson 2013, while Patrick Sheil speaks of the aesthetic as 'the mindset of just watching, absorbing and witnessing, and of mere knowing' (Sheil 2011, p. 4). None of these are entirely misleading but (to my mind) they do not identify the main point. While giving a dominant role to immediacy, C. Stephen Evans notes that the aesthetic stage includes reflective as well as immediate forms. See Evans 2009, pp. 72–74 (on immediacy and reflection see also the following note). These are,

since 'The Seducer's Diary' (the last document in *Either/Or* I) reveals a reflective form of aestheticism that is far removed from the simple immediate enjoyment of life.¹⁰ Scholars also note that the designation 'aesthetic' itself can be read as indicating not only an affinity with sensuous experience (as opposed to volition or cogitation) but also with the world of artistic production and reception. Since Kierkegaard's view of art was to a very large extent shaped both positively and negatively by the aesthetics of both Romantic and Hegelian idealism, this further implies that 'the aesthetic' has a distinct ideological dimension. At its simplest, this suggests that 'the aesthetic' as a form of life is the adoption of the idealist model of artistic production and reception as a project for life in the world.¹¹ However, this also means that the negative implications of this model flagged in Kierkegaard's thesis *On the Concept of Irony* (from two years before *Either/Or*) now become existential and not merely theoretical vices.¹²

I shall now set out key elements of the evidence for this claim from *Either/Or* Part 1 itself and explore further how the defining nihilism of A's position is manifest in several of his aphorisms and essays.¹³ I will then further show how this is also an explicitly violent view of human relationships, as becomes evident both in A's theoretical formulations and in the life-situations that he uses to illustrate his position. In conclusion, I briefly indicate how this view anticipates what Kierkegaard's later writings increasingly depict as the violent and conflictual relationship between Christianity and the world. In this way, I believe we get an insight into the radical cultural and (potentially) political implications of the critique of the aesthetic in Kierkegaard's writings. When the aesthetic is understood primarily in terms of pleasure or immediacy, then the negative outcomes of living an aesthetic life may seem only to affect the individual concerned. By

---

of course, only a small selection of views from a large literature, but I take them to be characteristic with regard to their omission of what I take to be the fundamentally metaphysical nature of A's nihilism.

10 It is not only the aesthetic that shows itself as having both immediate and reflective forms, since these purely formal categories are in fact manifest in any given range of phenomena. This, indeed, is part of Kierkegaard's complaint against Hegelianism, namely, that it tries to define faith in terms of a dialectic of immediacy and mediation (reflection), but this involves abstracting from the specificity of the content of (in this case) faith. If it were plausible to think of a life of pure immediacy, it would not be what we see in A's papers but something akin to the childlike naivety described in some of the early upbuilding discourses. See, e.g., Kierkegaard 1992, p. 33.
11 See, amongst others, Vetter 1963, pp. 101–132, Pattison 1991, pp. 140–151, and Walsh 1994, pp. 63–98.
12 This is the thrust of Kierkegaard's criticisms of Schlegel and the early Romantics. See Kierkegaard 1989, pp. 272–323.
13 Given the wealth of material, this is necessarily a small, but I hope representative selection.

way of contrast, the interpretation being offered here shows that what is at issue is of a potentially more far-reaching cultural and ontological character. That being said, I emphasize again that this essay is essentially limited to identifying the basic character of A's nihilism as it is represented in *Either/Or* 1. Demonstrating its further application is essentially a task for another day.

2 A's Nihilism

The clearest expression of A's fundamental metaphysical position comes in the essay 'Shadowgraphs', imagined as a speech delivered to an association calling itself the 'Symparanekromenoi', a term translated by Walter Lowrie (*Either/Or*'s first English translator) as 'the fellowship of buried lives' (Kierkegaard 1944, p. 450). Early on in his address, A sets out what he regards as a view on cosmic origins shared by members of the fellowship:

> Yes, would that the vortex, which is the world's core principle, even if people are not aware of it but eat and drink, marry and propagate themselves with carefree industriousness, would that it might erupt with deep-seated resentment and shake off the mountains and the nations and the cultural works and man's clever inventions; would that it might erupt with the last terrible shriek that more surely than the trumpet of doom announces the downfall of everything; would that it might stir and spin this bare cliff on which we stand as light as thistledown before the breath in its nostrils (Kierkegaard 1987a, p. 168).[14]

We shall return to the violence implicit in this imagery, but I emphasize now the essential claim that the world is without any defining telos or purpose. This cannot be read as a mere expression of feelings of aimlessness or purposelessness on A's part but involves a clear statement regarding his view of the fundamental nature of the universe. But can we really live with such a conviction as to the ultimate futility of it all? If this is what the world is like, how can we bear to live in

---

14 As the commentators to the standard Danish edition note, this could be taken as referring to the teaching of Anaxagoras, who nevertheless believed that the movement of the primordial vortex was directed by *nous* or mind (Cappelørn et al. 1997, pp. 156–157). However, Kierkegaard's phrasing suggests that the closest model is the atomism of Democritus and Leucippus. The vortex reappears in *Fear and Trembling* in the panegyric over Abraham, where it is suggested that it is only the combination of hero and poet that is able to redeem existence from the eternal extinction of meaning that is implied in such a cosmology (Kierkegaard 1983, p. 15). Pursuing what this entails for a broader reading of that work and the depiction of Abraham that it contains must be a task for another day, though it would surely problematize the reliability of *Fear and Trembling*'s Abraham as an authentic representative of faith.

it and how can we be motivated to engage in common social activity? What is the point?

In the various parts of *Either/Or* 1, we see a range of explorations of these questions, but the basic commitment to an atomistic cosmology is, I believe, implicitly accepted across the board, together with the acceptance that human lives are therefore governed by chance. Amongst the features of a life lived in full consciousness of its ultimate meaninglessness adduced by A are: (1) distraction, restlessness and a penchant for 'the interesting'; (2) the absence of any basis for mutual respect in relations between persons; (3) an underlying orientation towards violence in human relationships; and (4) the role of art as the maximum form in which life can be justified.

3 Distraction, Restlessness, and the 'Interesting'

The conviction that the world as a whole is ultimately meaningless and random may provoke a range of existential reactions, including avoidance and absorption into what Heidegger would call the everyday world of 'das Man' – or, in Kierkegaard's own terms, 'the crowd' (see Heidegger 1927, pp. 113–114, Kierkegaard 1998, pp. 123–124). Whether or not we think it to A's credit, he (like Sartre) does at least aim at living in a manner that reflects this basic insight. Nothing is ultimately of any value, so why delude ourselves that anything is? This view comes to clear expression early on in the 'Diapsalmata', a series of aphorisms collected at the start of A's papers:

> I don't feel like doing anything. I don't feel like riding—the motion is too powerful; I don't feel like walking—it is too tiring; I don't feel like lying down, for either I would have to stay down, and I don't feel like doing that, or I would have to get up again, and I don't feel like doing that either. Summa summarum. I don't feel like doing anything (Kierkegaard 1987a, p. 20).

The accidental and contingent nature of existence is further underlined in many other Diapsalmata. For instance, A sees himself as resembling a printing error that, as he puts it, is not to be despised since it can be made into something in its own right (Kierkegaard 1987a, p. 20). Or, he likens himself to the word "Schnur", which, as he explains, can equally well mean 'string', 'daughter-in-law', 'camel' or 'whisk broom' (Kierkegaard 1987a, p. 36) – and there are many other aphorisms of this ilk.

Clearly, these could be understood merely as expressive of A's particular and peculiar swings of mood, a sign that (as the Assessor claims) he has no deeper life-view. Many 'Diapsalmata' could certainly suggest the common malaises of adolescence. But while recognizing that we are not dealing with any simple one-way causal relationship, if we believe that A does indeed have a defining commitment to metaphysical nihilism, then it seems plausible that these are also to be understood as grounded in and reinforced by this basic view and not just to be ascribed to growing pains. There is no all-embracing causal nexus holding together the myriad elements of the universe and therefore nothing can achieve any abiding or meaningful state of being.

Of all the essays in *Either/Or* I, it is in 'The Rotation of Crops' that the principle of randomness finds its most clearly stated articulation, together with further hints as to the social consequences of this principle (the subtitle is 'A Venture in a Theory of Social Prudence'), to which we shall return later. The essay sets out from the principle that all people are boring, a statement that is subsequently qualified by dividing the population between those who bore themselves (but entertain others) and those who bore others (while, often, remaining satisfied with themselves).[15] Those who belong to the former category are the aristocrats, the latter make up the mediocre multitude. Without developing the point very extensively, A also offers a few hints as to the metaphysical situation that makes boredom's universal sway over humanity possible. It is, he says, 'demonic pantheism', a statement that finds some explanation a page later, when it is said that 'Pantheism ordinarily implies the qualification of fullness; with boredom it is the reverse: it is built upon emptiness, but for this very reason it is a pantheistic qualification. Boredom rests upon the nothing that interlaces existence; its dizziness is infinite, like that which comes from looking down into a bottomless abyss' (Kierkegaard 1987a, p. 291). Boredom, therefore, is (in A's view) an effect of the lack of any fundamental ground of being or universal telos. Given (again) the consequent meaninglessness of all human activity, the best that can be achieved is simply to look away and pursue a policy of distraction. As A continues, 'That the eccentric diversion [as can be seen amongst the English] is based upon boredom is seen also in the fact that the diversion sounds without resonance, simply because in nothing there is not even enough to make an echo possible (Kierkegaard 1987a, p. 291). In other words, those forms of behaviour that are without any ground in being leave no real effects behind them. They are arbitrary, occasional, inconsequent – and, if A is correct, this is the true character of all human action.

But – on this occasion – A does not succumb to melancholy. Instead, he proposes making a virtue of necessity by means of what he calls 'the rotation of crops' (Kierkegaard 1987a, p. 292). The multitude seek to escape boredom by end-

---

15 Kierkegaard takes this distinction from Byron.

lessly changing their environment – travelling abroad when they grow bored at home, fantasizing about interstellar travel when 'abroad' is no longer enough, eating from silver when they grow bored with porcelain and from gold when they get bored with silver – a dynamic that A sees as a practical equivalent to Hegel's 'bad infinity' (Kierkegaard 1987a, p. 292). A's alternative is not for people to vary their external surroundings but to vary their approach to where they are. The secret, as he explains, is in arbitrariness. One should not watch a play or read a book from end to end but watch only the middle section or read the third part. Attending a philosophical lecture, we should focus not on the content of what is said but on some accidental feature of the speaker, such as the sweat dripping down his nose (Kierkegaard 1987, p. 299).[16]

Crucial to A's development of his theme is his claim that such a pursuit of arbitrariness will necessarily be hindered by long term commitments such as friendship, marriage, or accepting some socially useful (but binding) vocation. To maintain the principle of arbitrariness one must remain one's own master, always deciding for oneself what policy to pursue or what attitude to take.

It is not hard to see that this segues into the restlessness that is another feature of A's personality and writings. As the 'Diapsalma' 'I don't feel like doing anything' already suggests, A is not committed to investing long-term energy in any particular undertaking and must consequently move from one thing to the next. At the same time, he has a distinctive interest in personalities and situations defined in terms of restlessness. This is part of the reason why he believes that the figure of Don Giovanni is best represented in operatic form, since, as he argues in relation to the final scene, a drama would need to be as brief as possible in representing the 'inner unrest in the situation' if it was not to become tedious. Music, however, can exploit it, letting it become 'the wilder' as it 'resonates in the abyss over which Don Giovanni hovers' (Kierkegaard 1987a, p. 134).

In a very different way, restlessness is also definitive of the three abandoned women who are the subject of 'Silhouettes' (one of them abandoned by Don Giovanni himself). What A finds fascinating in these women is precisely the fact that their abandonment is not unambiguous and that each has the possibility of believing that 'he' will return or was 'really' faithful all along. However, the evidence of their abandonment cannot be ignored, with the result that they are tossed backwards and forwards between faith and doubt: he was faithful, he

---

[16] For a fuller discussion of the treatment of boredom in this essay and in *The Concept of Anxiety*, together with consideration of similarities to and differences from the analyses of boredom given by Schopenhauer and Heidegger, see Pattison 2013, pp. 58–85.

is a deceiver. In a further twist, A suggests that it is this compulsive indecision that makes them conceal their grief, since any external expression would mean committing to one interpretation or the other. Only a psychological observer such as himself (he believes) can see beneath the surface to the anguish below.

'The Unhappiest Man' (another address to the 'Symparanekromenoi') offers a meditation on an inscription found on a grave somewhere in England, identifying the man who is buried beneath it as 'the unhappiest man' (Kierkegaard 1987a, pp. 217–230). This gives A occasion to think what such a man's life must have been like. He concludes that it would have been a life torn between memory and hope, unable to find security in either and still less to find enjoyment in any present moment of existence – a situation that is confirmed by A's notion that perhaps the grave is in fact empty: the epitome of a life in which there is no rest.[17]

If no personality and no topic merits our attention for long, then on what basis ought we pay attention to anything at all? A's answer is condensed in what becomes a key term in Johannes the Seducer's journal, namely, 'the interesting', a principle that the fictional editor of *Either/Or*, Victor Eremita, had already flagged up in the Introduction as defining the Seducer's modus operandi.[18] Johannes explains how Cordelia, the object of his desire, is interesting to him, not so much because of her beauty or because of any personal qualities she may possess (at this point he does not yet know her socially at all). Rather, it is a collage of personal circumstances and possibilities, especially the possibility that she may already have a suitor who falls short of what she expects from love, that makes her interesting – or, to be more precise, that makes the prospect of seducing her interesting. As his further comments go on to show, the category of the interesting only ever relates to one aspect of life at a time. It never encompasses the whole person in such a way as to allow for full and mutual recognition. 'The strategic principle, the law for every movement in this campaign is always to encounter her in an interesting situation. The interesting it is that is the domain in which the battle is to be fought [and] the potential that is in the interesting is to be exhausted' (Kierkegaard 1987a, pp. 345–346).[19]

---

17 This makes a notable pendant to Kierkegaard's later religious writings, where the search for the 'sabbath rest' becomes a pervasive theme.
18 The idea of the interesting was given currency by Friedrich Schlegel, who understood it as distinctive of modern aesthetics; Kierkegaard's contemporary, the influential critic and dramatist J. L. Heiberg also incorporated this idea into his own aesthetics.
19 There seems to be a certain affinity between A's idea of 'the interesting' and Augustine's view of curiosity, which he regarded as both sinful in itself and as luring us on to further

4 Respect and Violence

Johannes' fascination with the interesting is indicative of the fact that he has no intention of entering into relationships that involve full and mutual recognition. The interesting is focussed solely on what is occasional and accidental. The same holds true across the range of arbitrary and random moods, actions and reflections that are represented in *Either/Or* 1. Because these never allow a whole person to come to view – neither A himself nor those with whom he interacts – genuine personal relationships based on recognition of what is of abiding value in the other can never get off the ground. And, as we have seen in 'The Rotation of Crops', A is also determined that they *should not* get off the ground. In this respect the difference between Don Giovanni and A's Seducer that comes to expression that comes to expression in the former's '1003' in Spain and the latter's more limited though more carefully manipulated Scandinavian seductions is not so significant. The Spaniard wins out quantitatively, there is no doubt of that. But even if Johannes takes several months to secure a result that Don Giovanni could gain in just a few minutes he is no more essentially interested in the person of his temporary beloved than the famed Latin lover.

Clearly – and for reasons that anyone in the post-Kantian era will immediately understand – such a strategic lack of respect for others undermines the possibility of having a morally commendable relation to them, since respect for the personal integrity of the other is the basic condition of such relations.[20] This does not of itself mean that relationships with others will be actively hostile. Custom or *Sittlichkeit* might still be able to ensure a modicum of social order. Where each knows what they are expected to do and what will be socially advantageous to themselves, it may be possible to achieve an ensemble of relatively stable relationships between individuals. However, such a situation provides no persuasive rationale for such relationships, which are simply a matter of 'what we do' or 'what suits us'. There therefore seems to be little by way of protection against those who, however motivated, do not care to do 'what we do' or act according to social expectation.

In fact, the human condition as perceived by A is much darker than a logic of *Sittlichkeit* might allow. Even in a cursory overview of his subject-matter we can see that there is a fascination with violence. The opening metaphor of the

---

sins. See Augustine, *Confessions*, X.34–5, the themes of which are taken up in Heidegger 1927, pp. 170–173.
20 This is further developed in Hegel's notion of mutual recognition, a notion that 'A' expressly disavows (Kierkegaard 1987a, p. 295).

Ox of Phalaris sets the tone by envisaging the life of the artist in terms of a horrendous and sadistic punishment. But *Don Giovanni*, too, for all the sparkle of champagne bubbles and the exhilarating bravura of Mozart's music, is a story of violence. In the opening scene, the Don arrives on stage having just raped Donna Anna and, shortly afterwards, murders her father. The quasi-comic asides of Leporello should not blind us to the brutal reality of what the Don is about. His treatment of Zerlina (and, we might add Masetto) does not have the same fatal outcome, but she is ultimately forced rather than charmed, while Masetto ends by being beaten up. This, at the very least, is an abuse of power by a social superior who can cruelly impose his will on those of lower social status in the assurance that they have no recourse against his depredations. Don Giovanni is no loveable moustache-twirling rogue, but a sociopathic rapist and killer. Even where his seductions do not involve coercion, as in the case of Donna Elvira, they still typically (as far as we learn) involve deceit and the entire disavowal of any responsibility for the consequences.

If we turn to the 'Silhouettes', the violence is not in every case so overt. Yet Clavigo's behaviour leads to Marie Beaumarchais' death; here, too, we again meet Elvira from Don Giovanni, and then, finally, Margareta from *Faust*. As in the case of Don Giovanni and Zerlina, the social imbalance in the relationship between Margareta and her seducer bespeaks anything but a free meeting of equals and, of course, the story ends with Faust killing her brother and her imprisonment and death.

Fast-forwarding to the 'The Seducer's Diary', we have already noted that although Johannes' strategy is aimed at manipulating Cordelia to giver herself to him 'freely', this supposedly free consent is in fact the outcome of his systematic and covert manipulation of her emotions. His age, experience and social power make her a victim that #MeToo would recognize.

However, my point here is not simply to make explicit the violence that runs through large swathes of *Either/Or* 1, but to show that this is a result of A's basic metaphysical nihilism. The connection is made by A himself, most explicitly in 'The Rotation of Crops'. Here he writes that 'There is so much talk about man being a social animal, but basically he is a beast of prey, something that can be ascertained not only by looking at his teeth' (Kierkegaard 1987a, p. 288), a comment that the editors of relate to Plautus' saying that 'man is a wolf to man' (Cappelørn et al. 1994, pp. 194–195).[21] What he calls his 'doctrine of social skill' (Kierkegaard 1978a, p. 296) might be paraphrased as a 'doctrine of social

---

[21] The editors also note that, as such, it proposes a direct refutation of Aristotle's dictum that 'man is a political animal'.

cunning', aimed at securing his own maximum advantage in relation to others whilst making it impossible for them to take advantage of him.

Here we see that the lack of respect inherent in a life lived in pursuit of randomly interesting situations and accidental conjunctions of events is not simply a by-product of such a life. What it reveals is a basically hostile attitude towards the other, a conviction that human relationships are fundamentally adversarial. Intimacy such as is found in friendship or marriage is at all costs to be evaded, since intimacy would bring us face to face with this disturbing truth, manageable only by maintaining a logic of non-involvement. Nevertheless, this is not the non-involvement of the ascetic who removes himself from social interaction, but a non-involvement that manifests as a sustained attitude of contempt for others. 'A's boredom is not, as many of the bored complain, a result of not having anything to do. It is rather a basic refusal of the possibility of love and mutual recognition. Kierkegaard here touches on a logic that links boredom and criminality and to which Pushkin's Eugen Onegin, Dostoevsky's Svidrigailov and contemporary crime fiction all testify. Boredom, we may say, is a latent or passive form of violence and, as such, offers neither rational nor psychological grounds for permanent abstention from being transformed into violent action.[22]

5 Art and the Justification of Life

The opening paragraph of the long essay on Mozart's *Don Giovanni*, which follows on the opening 'Diapsalmata', might seem to contradict my claim that 'A's cosmos is not merely accidentally or psychologically disordered but metaphysically chaotic, the product of pure chance. In this essay, A begins by explicitly denying that it is mere chance that has enabled a series of great artists to find a subject-matter appropriate to their talents – Axel and Valborg, Homer and the Trojan War, Raphael and Catholicism, and Mozart and *Don Giovanni*. On the contrary, he says, this is the expression of the essential Greek view that the world is a well-ordered whole, a *kosmos* in the fullest sense of the word. It bespeaks a 'guiding wisdom' that is constantly at work in 'a higher order of things, in the world of ideas' (Kierkegaard 1987a, p. 47). However (as on many other occasions), there are reasons to approach A with a hermeneutics of suspicion.

---

[22] For further discussion of the specific connections between boredom and violence, see Pattison 2013, pp. 58–85.

Firstly, here, as throughout the essay, his focus is exclusively on works of art.[23] It is, in fact, axiomatic for Kierkegaard that art is to be seen in terms of ideality, but this leaves entirely open whether the ideality in question has any purchase on the reality of life. It will indeed be central to the Assessor's criticism of A that the reconciliation with existence proposed by him is purely aesthetic, that is to say, that it is solely and exclusively a reconciliation within the sphere of art that is incapable of any wider extension. But we do not need to read on to *Either/Or* II to discover this. Several of the 'Diapsalmata' preceding the essay on *Don Giovanni* suggest an unbridgeable gap between art and life. The very first aphorism of all is characteristic, likening the poet to a victim of the Sicilian tyrant Phalaris who had his prisoners roasted alive in a bronze ox fitted out with a system of pipes that made their screams sound like music. This, he suggests, illustrates how 'people crowd around the poet and say to him: sing again soon, which is to say, 'may new sufferings torture your soul, and may your lips continue to be formed as before, because your screams would only alarm us, but the music is charming' (Kierkegaard 1987a, p. 19). The illusion of art is not simply a piece of entertaining magic since its true meaning is the opposite of what it appears to be. In this regard, the poets are in a similar situation as the philosophers of whom A writes that their works are like a shop-sign that says 'Ironing done here' whereas it is only the sign itself that is for sale (Kierkegaard 1987a, p. 32). Actuality – the real world – is beyond their reach. In a more poignant image, A describes himself as the solitary inhabitant of a remote castle in which he lives like a dead man but from which, from time to time, he swoops down into the world to find an image that he can weave into a tapestry that he contemplates in endless solitude, forgetting 'everything finite and contingent' (Kierkegaard 1987a, p. 42).

Secondly, the actual exposition of *Don Giovanni* presents us with something of a paradox. Although A affects to provide an argument for the classic status of the opera, the way in which he interprets this seems to subvert the idea of the classical as that was understood in Kierkegaard's time. For the classical was then taken to refer not solely to antiquity but to a kind of balance between form and content in art that moved the recipient to a deep sense of harmony or contentment, a sense of rest or repose – the sculptures of Thorvaldsen, for example. However, in this case the correspondence of form and content relates to Don Giovanni's erotically sensuous character and what the musical form expresses is precisely the restlessness of the Don's amatory desire. This is not art

---

[23] The reference to Axel and Valborg is to a play by the contemporary Danish playwright Adam Øhlenslæger.

that brings us to a state of quiet and benign contemplation but art that carries us out onto a turbulent stream of desire. It is in this connection that we are to understand A's insistence that the quintessential moment of the opera is in the champagne aria of the final scene in which we hear Don Giovanni give untrammelled voice to his lust for life even in the face of impending death, an artistic moment in which we, the listeners, find ourselves drawn out over the abyss above which the Don himself now hovers (Kierkegaard 1987a, p. 134). Far from being the expression of a well-ordered whole, this so-called 'classic' therefore sets in motion the chaotic world of A's more metaphysically articulated atomism. There is no meaning here, only a certain rapture of the deep.

This view is reinforced if, thirdly, we note how A defines music's relation to Christianity, namely, as that which Christianity excludes. Of course, we presume that A was well aware that human beings made music long before Christianity and have continued doing so ever since. In the most general sense, music is a natural and spontaneous expression of human beings' sensuous nature. As such it is entirely innocent. However – and this is A's point – once Christianity had set before the world the challenge to strive for a higher spiritual existence, sensuousness received a different meaning. To persist in or to return to forms of life characterized by sensuousness is no longer innocent but now appears as sin (Kierkegaard 1987a, pp. 64–65). The organ may or not be 'the devil's bagpipes' (Kierkegaard 1987a, p. 72) but insofar as it is a salient manifestation of the power of sensuousness, music becomes spiritually dangerous. This association of music and spiritual danger is precisely what A brings to the fore by matching the character of music as artistic form to the personality of Don Giovanni as the supreme musical subject-matter. For Don Giovanni's sensuous lust for life is certainly by no means innocent. As we have seen, it is a lust that is entirely amoral, sociopathic even, allowing no person or law to obstruct its fulfilment: if Don Giovanni cannot get what he wants, he kills, rapes or uses whatever violence he needs— and this is as true in Mozart's opera as in other versions of the legend.

The celebration of *Don Giovanni* as a 'classic' work of art is therefore paradoxically the revelation of a view of life as governed by violent and purposeless passion, redeemable or meaningful only in the transient medium of musical art. Or, to put it in conventional philosophical language, it is a purely aesthetic justification of life, devoid of any ontological substance.

Nevertheless, we might say that even if the essay on Don Giovanni does in its own way arrive at the same nihilistic position as the teaching on the primordial vortex, it does offer a relatively coherent position. Minimally, it allows for the kind of investment of cultural energy that is required for the composition, production and reception of a grand opera. In Rilke's sense, it is a contribution to the ensemble of those 'things' that make up humanity's cultural inheritance, achieving a certain level of perdurance and universality. However, albeit on a grand scale, it is 'ontologically' no more than a distraction from the abyss that opens up beneath the Don himself in the closing scene. In this sense, A's long and involved essay on why this is such a classic work of art is not essentially different from those many other passages where he finds gratification in random or arbitrary actions or events (a feature of A's life that is also commented on at several points by the Assessor). Art 'redeems' life in the sense that the mirroring of life in art allows us (in this case) to enjoy the violence and cruelty of a Don Giovanni while forgetting the terror we might experience if confronted with such a personality in real life – and forgetting (if ' is right) that 'real life' is defined more by personalities such as the Don than it is by the sweetness of artistic form.[24]

6 'A's Nihilism and Kierkegaard's Later Authorship

Either/Or I sets out the life-view of the aesthete. Both here and in *Either/Or* as a whole, he is presented as an outsider figure, despite the best efforts of the Assessor to draw him into the orbit of bourgeois society. Yet, several years down the line, when Kierkegaard offers an explanation for why it was necessary to introduce the Christian themes of his mature authorship by resorting to a series of aesthetic deceits, he tells us that a major reason was the fact that society as a whole was living in essentially aesthetic categories (or, as he puts it, 'at most' in aesthetic-ethical categories; see Kierkegaard 1998, p. 43). In this situation, this meant adopting the pedagogical principle of starting where the learner is – thus the sequence of pseudonymous books for which Kierkegaard is best-known. But, as he tells us, these were designed to lead the reader via a kind of negative dialectic to see the emptiness of such a life and the desirability of the Christian alternative (Kierkegaard 1998, pp. 39–56). However, if the argument of this paper is correct, then a further implication of the strategy that he now outlines is that the basic assumptions of everyday life in bourgeois Denmark is that human relationships were fundamentally violent, a violence moderated only by the desire for self-preservation.Strikingly, the image of 'the vortex'

---

[24] To apply Kierkegaard's point to more contemporary forms, many people (perhaps a majority) throughout the developed world voluntarily choose to spend several evenings a week watching televisual dramas involving multiple and often sadistic murders or other crimes that they would go to great lengths to avoid in actual life.

itself recurs in Kierkegaard's letters to the jurist J. L. A. Kolderup-Rosenvinge with whom he several times discussed the political issues of the day during 1848 and, especially, the threat of revolutionary violence (Kierkegaard 1978), pp. 260–261).

This is, in effect, what Kierkegaard himself experienced when he was made the butt of a series of cruel satires in the journal *The Corsair*. Even though, as he acknowledged, his 'martyrdom' was only a 'martyrdom of laughter', it was no less cruel for that (Kierkegaard 2011, p. 289). This reinforced a view that, as he tells us, he had already learned in childhood, namely, that the crowd will always turn on Christ and on those who bear witness to Christ. Increasingly in his last years, he approaches the view that martyrdom 'unto death' is not just an exceptional fate but what every Christian must expect. The hostility between a world built on the principle of mutual antagonism and a new world developed on the principle of love cannot be mediated but only suffered. At the same time, he believed that the new democratic reforms introduced in 1848 involved the institutionalization of popular will as the ultimate power in the state – and that, he believed, meant empowering the implicit violence of the majority against the minority. Anticipating the teaching of Carl Schmitt, this meant that the internal unity of the state was premised on the existence of enemies against whom this implicit violence could be released, whether these were external enemies (such as Prussia) or internal enemies, such as those solitary individuals who bore witness to the crowd's 'untruth'.[25]

Kierkegaard's later writings engage less extensively with examples drawn from art and literature and focus more on the Church, but what he says of the Church is applicable also to the world of culture – not least as he says that the Church itself has now become no more than a kind of theatrical entertainment. What the Church (and by extension the world of culture) does is to give the public a good conscience they have not earned. Abstracting from the actual violence that is endemic in social life and periodically war and revolution, religion and culture provide a mirror in which we see ourselves as the virtuous, noble and refined citizens of a harmonious and well-governed social order. All the while, the vortex rages beneath the surface, and wilfully ignorant of our true condition, we are dragged towards the abyss, numbed by the spectacle of a disaster for which we persistently refuse to take responsibility.

These last remarks make clear why it is that many see Kierkegaard's later thought as exaggeratedly pessimistic and it is true that there are passages in which he indulges a kind of dualism that is scarcely compatible with historic

---

[25] On Carl Schmitt's reading of Kierkegaard, see Ryan 2012 and Ryan 2014.

Christianity. At the same time, it is also clear why, in 1914, many could see him as a prophet of Europe's then 'present age'.[26] Perhaps our time requires a greater leap of interpretative imagination, since the catastrophe that we now face is by no means a solely human catastrophe but an extinction event involving the whole biosphere. Yet here, too, it is the human refusal to confront, to acknowledge, and to transform our mutual antagonism and rapaciousness so as to bring about a community of authentic love and responsible planetary stewardship that is the main agent of the doom we confront. It would require another kind of essay to argue the next step, namely, that an essential condition of such a transformation would be a metaphysical revolution in which the chaotic maelstrom that A sees as the sole ground of being would be supplanted by the movement of love. Such a love would not only be capable of moving the sun and other stars but also of moving human hearts to be reshaped in its own image and likeness – arguably a still more difficult and demanding task.

Bibliography

Augustine (1912), *Confessions*. Translated by William Watt Cambridge MA: Harvard University Press.
Bakhtin, Mikhail M. (1984): *Problems of Dostoevsky's Poetics*. Translated by Caryl Emerson. Minneapolis: University of Minnesota Press.
Cappelørn, N. J., Garff, J., Kondrup, J., McKinnon, A., and Mortensen, Finn Hauberg (1997): Søren Kierkegaards Skrifter. Kommentarbind til Enten-Eller.Copenhagen: Gad.
Furtak, Rick Anthony (2005): *Wisdom in Love: Kierkegaard and the Ancient Quest for Emotional Integrity*. Notre Dame: Notre Dame University Press.
Glicksberg, Charles I. (1960): "The Aesthetics of Nihilism". In: *The University of Kansas City Review* 27, pp. 127–130.
Hampson, Daphne (2013): *Kierkegaard: Exposition and Critique*. Oxford: Oxford University Press.
Harries, Karsten, (2010): *Between Nihilism and Faith: A Commentary on* Either/Or. Berlin: de Gruyter.
Heidegger, Martin (1927): *Sein und Zeit*. Halle: Max Niemeyer.
Jollimore, Troy (2011): *Love's Vision*. Princeton: Princeton University Press.
Kierkegaard, Søren (1978): *Letters and Documents*. Translated by H. Rosenmeier. Princeton: Princeton University Press.
Kierkegaard, Søren (1987a): *Either/Or* Part I. Edited and translated by Howard V. and Edna H. Hong. Princeton: Princeton University Press.

---

[26] In 1914, Theodore Haecker entitled his translation of the section 'The Present Age' from Kierkegaard's 1846 work *Two Ages*, *Kritik der Gegenwart*—'Critique of the Present', making it clear to readers that it was this present, the crisis of 1914, that Kierkegaard's words addressed. See Kierkegaard 1914.

Kierkegaard, Søren (1987b): *Either/Or* Part II. Edited and translated by Howard V. and Edna H. Hong. Princeton: Princeton University Press.

Kierkegaard, Søren (1983): *Fear and Trembling/Repetition*. Edited and translated by Howard V. and Edna H. Hong. Princeton: Princeton University Press.

Kierkegaard, Søren (1989): *On the Concept of Irony: with Continual Reference to Socrates*. Edited and translated by Howard V. and Edna H. Hong. Princeton: Princeton University Press.

Kierkegaard, Søren (1998): *The Point of View on my Work as an Author*. Edited and translated by Howard V. and Edna H. Hong. Princeton: Princeton University Press.

Kierkegaard, Søren (1960 [1923]): *Selections from the Writings of Søren Kierkegaard*, Translated and edited by Lee M. Hollander. New York: Anchor.

Kierkegaard, Søren (2011): *Kierkegaard's Journals and Notebooks*, vol. 5. Translated and edited by Bruce Kirmmse et al. Princeton: Princeton University Press.

Kierkegaard, Søren (1914): *Kritik der Gegenwart*. Translated by Theodore Haecker. Munich: Brenner.

Nussbaum, Martha (1994): *The Therapy of Desire: Theory and Practice in Hellenistic Ethics*. Princeton: Princeton University Press.

Palmer, Donald D. (1996): *Kierkegaard for Beginners*. New York: Writers and Readers Publishers.

Pattison, George (1991): "Kierkegaard: Aesthetics and 'the Aesthetic'". In: *The British Journal of Aesthetics*. 31. No. 2, pp. 140–51.

Pattison, George (2013). *Kierkegaard and the Quest for Unambiguous Life*. Oxford: Oxford University Press.

Ryan, Bartholomew (2012): "Kierkegaard and Carl Schmitt: Zones of Exception and Appropriation". In: Jon Stewart (Ed.): *Kierkegaard's Influence on Social-political Thought*. Farnham: Ashgate, pp. 177–208.

Ryan, Bartholomew (2014): *Kierkegaard's Indirect Politics: Interludes with Lukács, Schmitt, Benjamin and Adorno*. Amsterdam: Rodopi.

Sheil, Patrick (2011): *Starting with Kierkegaard*. London: Continuum.

Vetter, August (1963): *Frömmigkeit als Leidenschaft: Eine Deutung Kierkegaards*. Freiburg, Munich: Alber.

Walsh, Sylvia (1994): *Living Poetically: Kierkegaard's Existential Aesthetics*. Pennsylvania: Pennsylvania University Press.

Wynn, Mark R. (2013): *Renewing the Senses: A Study of the Philosophy and Theology of the Spiritual Life*. Oxford: Oxford University Press.

Luca Lupo
"To smear his boots with the other's fat": Conscious and Unconscious Violence

Abstract: This chapter centers on three vivid images as a means of focusing on and philosophically grasping the roots of nihilism, that is, its primordial manifestations. Through the examples that will be examined, it will be possible to observe the tormented path that leads from the ego, as an original point of condensation of drives in search of release, to a subjectivity endowed with conscience. Forming the background of this chapter is the mysterious space in which human and non-human lives intertwine.

An attempt will be made to answer some decisive ethical questions on which the troubled emergence of conscience turns: do we know what we are doing when we act? What does "knowing what one is doing" mean?

The subject who becomes aware of the centrality of such questions, partly thanks to the other, opens the way to a new form of subjectivity and can enter into a constructive relationship with the other.

1 Smeared Boots

When Nietzsche opens his philosophical reflections on nihilism, he immediately emphasizes the extent to which nihilism manifests itself first and foremost as a "will to destruction" (*Wille zur Zerstörung*) rooted in the biology and physiology of the living. This will in turn contains the "will of an even deeper instinct, the instinct of self-destruction, the will to nothingness" (*Wille eines noch tieferen Instinkts, des Instinkts der Selbstzerstörung, des Willens ins Nichts*) (NL 1886, 5 [71], KSA 12, p. 215, my translation). Such a will precedes, founds, and feeds nihilism in its more refined, spiritualized forms. A nihilistic tendency runs through every age,[1] and "in the end, everything takes place as if the world affected and perme-

---

Note: This chapter is dedicated to the memory of Emilio Sergio (1968–2020), a dear and unforgettable friend and colleague, irreplaceable reviewer and reader, and to Kim Ki Duk (1960–2020), who was able to express the essence of ethics in a few images.

[1] "Every age—and in the end, none is worth more than any other—has its own figure of nihilism. The names change, but always under these names ('ethics,' for example) we find the articulation of conservative propaganda with an obscure desire for catastrophe" (Badiou 2001, p. 38).

ated itself with a death drive that soon would have nothing else to destroy than the world itself" (Nancy 2007, p. 34). The Freudian hypothesis of the existence of a death drive at work in the organic world helps us to grasp and understand the persistence of nihilism as a constitutive phenomenon that, in the form of the death drive, makes its appearance together with life itself. It also explains why it can take such extreme forms, before becoming an epoch-making event.[2] In the light of such an event, it is possible to read the entire destiny of being retrospectively.[3]

The death drive expresses the living being's tendency to return to the state of quiescence that characterizes the inorganic world.[4] Death thus appears as the destiny of all drives and life, an elaborate diversion by which we reach the goal of inorganic quiescence from which it arose long ago.[5] Even though Freud does not explicitly refer to nihilism, his hypothesis therefore represents a decisive and illuminating stage in the development of thought on this issue, following in the footsteps of Nietzsche and Schopenhauer.[6]

It is from Schopenhauer that we will follow the *peripeteia* of what we might call the "perennial nihilism" of the death drive in some of its most relevant manifestations, such as egoism and gratuitous violence. We will then see what elements stand in opposition to the primacy and prevalence of the latter.

"Being minded to characterize the magnitude of egoism at a single stroke, to express the strength of this anti-moral power without long-windedness, and so seeking after some really emphatic hyperbole," Schopenhauer "finally arrived at this one: many a human being would be ready to strike another dead simply to smear his boots with the other's fat." "But," Schopenhauer concludes with bit-

---

2 Cf. Heidegger 1982.
3 See Heidegger 1982.
4 Cf. Freud 1955. Likewise, "Schopenhauer maintains not only that death is not an evil, but also that it often appears like a good thing, for 'everything that runs up against an insurmountable obstacle in its existence or its endeavours, anything that suffers from incurable diseases or inconsolable grief, has as its last resort ... a return to the womb of nature' (*WWR* II: 486)" (Stellino 2020, p. 99). As Paolo Stellino points out, "Schopenhauer defines this 'return to the womb of nature' as '*cessio bonorum* [surrender of goods]' (*WWR* II: 486), an expression derived from Roman Law" (Stellino 2020, p. 99).
5 Cf. Freud (1955.
6 In a letter to Lou Salomé of 1 August 1919, Freud explicitly states that he first felt the need to read texts on the subject of death, including Schopenhauer, when writing *Beyond the Pleasure Principle*, the work in which he presents the hypothesis of the death drive and whose title, moreover, clearly alludes to Nietzsche's *Beyond Good and Evil*. Freud ends the letter by stating that he is "not fond of reading," although it is unclear whether this refers to Schopenhauer or to reading in general (Pfeiffer 1972, p. 99).

ter and harsh irony, "a scruple still remained in me as to whether it really is a hyperbole" (Schopenhauer 2009, p. 192).

Cleaning one's boots is unnecessary; one's life is not at stake if one fails to do this. Schopenhauer emphasizes the futility of the end to amplify the absurdity and gravity of the action he describes. This image is both striking and powerful. The disproportion between the grounds of the action and the gravity of its consequences seems absurd. The gratuitousness of violence is especially evident here. The argumentative objective for which Schopenhauer uses this image is essential: "to characterize the magnitude of egoism."

In the relationship between mother and child, the egoistic perspective is already clearly visible: even before she has affective value for the child, before being an end (an object of attachment and love), the mother is a means of nourishment and enjoyment for the child.[7]

Schopenhauer's image represents the most radical form of reducing the other to a simple means:[8] the other is not only reduced to a simple means but is also annihilated. In this sense, this example represents the absolute negation of the categorical imperative in the form of the principle of humanity.[9] Schopenhauer establishes a very close link between egoism and violence. Egoism is essentially a negation of all that is non-ego,[10] and violence is one of the most extreme ways in which this negation takes place: "The organism preserves its own life, so to say, by destroying an extraneous one" (Freud 1964b, p. 211). In this sense, when violence appears as a side effect of affirming an individual's life in the natural world, it seems partly justified. In the non-human animal world, the predator must kill the victim if it wants to feed itself. At the level of the organism, antibodies must eliminate pathogens so that the individual in whom they operate can remain intact. Again, violence appears as a justified attitude when it functions as a defense mechanism against the endless occasions on which the outside world, in the form of non-human and human otherness, appears threatening and destructive.

---

[7] "Children love themselves first, and it is only later that they learn to love others and to sacrifice something of their own ego to others. Even those people whom a child seems to love from the beginning are loved by him at first because he needs them and cannot do without them—once again from egoistic motives. Not until later does the impulse to love make itself independent of egoism. It is literally true that his egoism has taught him to love" (Freud 1961, p. 204).
[8] Arendt rightly points out that "Violence is by nature instrumental; like all means, it always stands in need of guidance and justification through the end it pursues. And what needs justification by something else cannot be the essence of anything" (Arendt 1970, 51).
[9] "So act that you use humanity, in your own person as well as in the person of any other, always at the same time as an end, never merely as a means" (GMS 4: 429; Kant 2011, p. 87).
[10] In Arendt's words: "The extreme form of violence is One against All" (Arendt 1970, p. 42).

In relations between humans, at least from a certain point of ontogenetic development onwards (as we saw in the case of the child), violence can lose its character of natural necessity. It does leave its trace on us, however, like the mark of Cain. Violence is rooted in the ego that thinks it is separate and unique, cultivating the false belief that it can remain isolated and unrelated. However, it is manifestly impossible for any living being to do without the outside world and the other, both non-human and, even more so, human. This impossibility shows the extent to which this belief is unsupported. The relationship with the other is necessary even in its negative form, that is, if one considers the other merely as a means.

When violence loses its character of natural necessity, it also loses its natural innocence and becomes gratuitous.[11] It becomes gratuitous when one *can* avoid it. When humans experience the fact that they can avoid violence, the feeling that they *should* avoid it also arises. However, this feeling arises and becomes apparent only when humans become able to say to themselves, through language, that non-violence is possible. Therefore, there is a connection between the possibility of containment, the containment of violence, and the presence of language.

Language manifests itself as an interval that stands between the stimulus and the response, unhinging the automatism and immediacy that is constitutively and habitually inherent in the relationship between the two moments.[12] Language interrupts and disrupts the rigid necessity of blind repetition at work in the stimulus response scheme, just as the organic springs from the inorganic and the living from the non-living. The interference of language in the relationship between stimulus and response makes consciousness of the "in-fans" utterly different from animal consciousness, transforming it into a subject in the proper sense.

Thus, the presence of language determines a fundamental leap in the quality of the relationship between humans. This presence marks the transition of the

---

[11] The *Dizionario della lingua italiana Treccani* immediately links the meaning of the term 'violence' to the concept of gratuitous violence: the first definition of the Italian word *violenza* (violence) is, in fact, "A habitual tendency to use physical force *brutally or irrationally* [*tendenza abituale a usare la forza fisica in modo brutale o irrazionale*]" (emphasis added) (https://www.treccani.it/vocabolario/violenza/, visited on February 7, 2022).

[12] Put in the theoretical frame of Freud's *Beyond the Pleasure Principle*, language appears as the most refined and sublime form through which the living person amplifies, complicates, dilates, and changes in a virtual yet real way, through representation (that is to say, symbolically), the achievement of the quiescence from which life arose thanks to the accidental intervention of an original, unknown force.

natural universe's relationship to the cultural and properly human universe. When the mother teaches the child to use words, this gradually enables the latter to finally see the mother as something other than a mere means. Thus, one could say that it is language, above all, that enables the passage from simple animal attachment to what we can appropriately define as real love.

In light of this, in analogy with Kant, we might say that if love appears as the *ratio essendi* of a word endowed with meaning, that is, a full and therefore truthful word, the word is the *ratio cognoscendi* of a love that would otherwise be difficult to distinguish from simple animal attachment.[13] Thanks to language, the child learns that the mother is not merely a means but much more. The presence of language also determines a leap in the quality of knowledge, which only takes on its proper form through language. Perhaps it is in this prodigious passage from the pre-linguistic dimension to the linguistic that we can locate the birth of conscience.

When language opens up the possibility of seeing the other beyond the latter's primitive function as a mere means and, despite this possibility, one *still cannot see* the other, such blindness paves the way to gratuitous violence. Thus, it begins with not seeing the other. After all, egoism consists in not knowing about the other—or more accurately, in *not wanting to know* about the other. Here, 'knowing' means taking an interest in what the other is, an interest that is not only cognitive but also emotional, affective, and above all relational: an interest guided by a deep feeling and intuition that the other is our concern, that it has to do with us. As an unwillingness to know the other, egoism is closure. It is a defensive closing off from the other as an expression of the external world in general: a defensive closing off from the other as another, potentially dangerous, human.

To be able to use brute violence against the other, as in Schopenhauer's example, it is necessary to have produced the other, to have represented an image of the other as already reduced to a simple thing, usable and ultimately eliminable. It is necessary to be blind to the meaning of humanity and the sensitivity of the other. In this sense, it is possible to say (to a certain extent) that to be able to

---

[13] In a famous footnote to the preface of the *Critique of Practical Reason*, Kant remarks that "whereas freedom is indeed the *ratio essendi* of the moral law, the moral law is the *ratio cognoscendi* of freedom. For, had not the moral law already been distinctly thought in our reason, we should never consider ourselves justified in assuming such a thing as freedom (even though it is not self-contradictory). But were there no freedom, the moral law would not be encountered at all in ourselves" (KpV 5:4fn; Kant 2015, p. 3). Similarly, without love, every word would sound empty.

commit violence, one must either lack awareness of the value of the other's humanity or have suspended or repressed one's awareness of that value.

Alternatively, it is a necessary part of doing evil that it must never emerge from the unconscious (never become conscious). Egoism and ignorance overlap and merge. Violence is accompanied by the denial of violence: that is, by telling oneself that what one is doing is not, in the end, a form of violence. An excellent example of this kind of denial is the typical fable told by the rapist, who is convinced of the fact (and openly declares) that the victim enjoyed what happened or was a willing participant.

The basis that makes violence possible is, after all, not knowing what one is doing, or belittling it, denying its ethical weight, as long as one—as an agent—can comprehend its gravity.

2 The Lamb of God

"One of the toughest roots of all evil is unconsciousness," writes Jung:

> and I could wish that the saying of Jesus, "Man, if thou knowest what thou doest, thou art blessed, but if thou knowest not, thou art accursed, and a transgressor of the law,"[14] were still in the gospels, even though it has only one authentic source. It might well be the motto for a new morality. (Jung 1969, p. 197)

Here, Jung quotes an interpolation present in the Gospel of Luke.[15] The quotation recalls another fundamental (although philologically controversial) text from this source: the passage in which Jesus, just crucified, asks for forgiveness for those who "know not what they do."[16] Let us consider this passage in its context:

---

[14] Ειπεν αυτω/ ανθρωπε ει μεν οιδας τι ποιεις/ μακαριος ει ει δε μη οιδας επικαταρατος/και παραβατης ει του νομου (*Codex Bezae* 205v, see the note *infra*); et dixit illi/homo si quidem scis quod facis/beatus es si autem nescis maledictus/ et trabaricator legis (*Codex Bezae* 206r, see the note infra).

[15] After Luke 6:4, according to the *Codex Bezae*, one of the most ancient Codices in the philological tradition of the Gospels. The digitalized Codex can be found on the University of Cambridge website. The bilingual (Greek and Latin) version is on Folios 205v and 206r, along with further information on the *Codex Bezae* by David Parker, Edward Cadbury Professor of Theology and Director of the Institute for Textual Scholarship and Electronic Editing at the University of Birmingham: http://cudl.lib.cam.ac.uk/view/MS-NN-00002-00041/391, visited on 31 December 2020.

[16] Luke 23:34a. Here, it is impossible to provide even a partial account of the enormous complexity of the centuries-long philological, exegetical, and theological debate connected with this

When they came to the place called the Skull, they crucified him and the criminals there, one on his right, the other on his left.
[Then Jesus said, "Father, forgive them, they[17] know not what they do."][18]

---

text, and such a task is beyond the scope of this chapter. Among the most salient references, however, are Brown 1994, King 2010, and Strahan 2012.

17 "The 'they' for whom Jesus is praying includes both the Romans and the Jews in proportion to their respective roles in Jesus' death" (Brown, 1994, p. 973). J. Rendel Harris has argued vigorously that the prayer was excised from the text because of "an early and violent anti-Judaic polemic ... involving an actual abrenuntiation of all fellowship with the Jews" (Harris). For a philological survey of the originality of this Gospel passage, see Eubank 2010.

18 According to René Girard, this sentence defines "the unconscious persecutor at the very heart of the Passion story" (Girard 1986, p. 110). "Christians insist here," according to Girard, "on the goodness of Jesus. This would be fine were it not that their insistence eclipses the sentence's real meaning, which is scarcely ever recognized. The commentary on this sentence implies that the desire to forgive unpardonable executors forces Jesus to invent a somewhat trifling excuse for them that hardly conforms to the reality of the Passion. Commentators who refuse to believe what this sentence says can only feel faint admiration for it, and their devotion imbues the text with the taint of their own hypocrisy. The most terrible distortion of the Gospels is our ability to project our own hypocrisy on them. In reality the Gospels never seek lame excuses; they never speak for the sake of speaking; sentimental verbiage has no place in them. If we are to restore to this sentence its true savor we must recognize its almost technical role in the revelation of the scapegoat mechanism. It says something precise about the men gathered together by their scapegoat. *They do not know what they are doing.* That is why they must be pardoned. This is not dictated by a persecution complex or by the desire to remove from our sight the horror of real violence. *In this passage we are given the first definition of the unconscious in human history*, that from which all the others originate and develop in weaker form: the Freudians will push the dimension of persecution into the background and the Jungians will eliminate it altogether" (Girard, 1986, p. 110–111, emphasis added). Epp discusses the so-called "ignorance motif" (Epp 1962, p. XX), i.e. the traditional argument that the Jews put Jesus to death because they were ignorant of his divine nature (in other words, they did not know what they were doing). Among other things, Epp analyses the argument, especially in *Codex Bezae*, and refers to the literature dealing with textual variants of the codex (see Epp 1962, p. 52). What is striking is the difference between the position Jesus takes in the face of those "who know not what they do" in the interpolation after Luke 6.4 and in the passage from Luke 23.34a: whereas in the apocryphal text he says that those who do not know what they are doing incur a curse, in the integration of the canonical version he invokes forgiveness for them. As far as the interpolation at Luke 6.4 is concerned, among the commentaries it is worth mentioning an article by Bammel (Bammel 1986). Bammel attempts to account for the confessional context of the Jewish tradition in which the apocryphal *logion* is inscribed, especially regarding the religious meaning of observance of the Sabbath. On the *Codex Bezae*, see the studies from the Lunel Colloquium of June 1994, edited by Parker and Amphoux (Parker and Amphoux 1996). There seem to be no studies specifically highlighting the recurrence of the topic of "not knowing what one is doing" both in the interpolation after Luke 6.4 and in Luke 23.34a, and likewise no studies on the interesting fact that this interpolation is present in the *Codex Bezae*, while Luke 23.34a is absent.

> [ὁ δὲ Ἰησοῦς ἔλεγεν Πάτερ, ἄφες αὐτοῖς, οὐ γὰρ οἴδασιν τί ποιοῦσιν.]
> They divided his garments by casting lots.
>
> The people stood by and watched; the rulers, meanwhile, sneered at him and said, "He saved others, let him save himself [σωσάτω ἑαυτόν] if he is the chosen one, the Messiah of God."
>
> Even the soldiers jeered at him. As they approached to offer him wine they called out, "If you are King of the Jews, save yourself [σῶσον σεαυτόν]."
>
> Above him there was an inscription that read, "This is the King of the Jews."
>
> Now one of the criminals hanging there reviled Jesus, saying, "Are you not the Messiah? Save yourself and us [σῶσον σεαυτὸν καὶ ἡμᾶς]." (Luke 23: 33–39)

With the crucifixion, we encounter the paradigm of gratuitous violence par excellence. Crucifixion was one of the most painful ways to die and was preceded by scourging. The purpose of the torture was precisely to increase the suffering of the condemned person by prolonging his agony.

When John the Baptist first meets Jesus, he apostrophizes him and exclaims, "Behold the Lamb of God!" [καὶ ἐμβλέψας τῷ Ἰησοῦ περιπατοῦντι λέγει Ἴδε ὁ ἀμνὸς τοῦ θεοῦ] (John 1:35–36). With the crucifixion, the words of John the Baptist become real: the humanity of Christ fades away, and what remains is what the human shares with the living non-human, the pure animal essence of the suffering body, the mute, wordless suffering of the lamb.

Whereas in Schopenhauer's image there was at least one reason to kill, even if macabrely futile, in the case of Christ a well-founded reason is missing: Christ is innocent.[19] All who surround him, friends and enemies, know it. Christ, the man, transforms himself into the lamb of God and goes to meet violence in all its gratuitousness. Two aspects are at stake here: on the one hand, the link between the problem of the motives of the executioners (who do not know what they are doing) and gratuitous violence; on the other hand, the fact that the suffering of the victim—and, more generally, sentience—is what the human victim shares with the non-human victim.[20] Crucified as a sacrificial victim, as a

---

[19] See Girard 1986.
[20] According to Peter Singer, If a being suffers, there can be no moral justification for refusing to take that suffering into consideration. No matter what the nature of the being, the principle of equality requires that its suffering be counted equally with the like suffering—insofar as rough comparisons can be made—of any other being. If a being is not capable of suffering, or of experiencing enjoyment or happiness, there is nothing to be taken into account. So the limit of sentience (using the term as a convenient if not strictly accurate shorthand for the capacity to suffer and/or experience enjoyment) is the only defensible boundary of concern for the interests of others. To mark this boundary by some other characteristic like intelligence or rationality would be to mark it in an arbitrary manner. Why not choose some other characteristic, like skin color?" (Singer 2015, p. 38).

"lamb,"[21] in the words of John, Jesus takes the form of the absolutely other from the human, of the absolutely other as an animal, even before taking the form of the absolutely other as divine.

In the Isaac episode, precisely at the moment Abraham is about to sacrifice his son, an angel stops him: "look[ing] about, he spied a ram caught by its horns in the thicket. So he went and took the ram and offered it up as a holocaust in place of his son" (Gen. 22:13 [New American Bible]). A significant inversion occurs between the Old and the New Testament: The son of God takes the ram's place in the Isaac episode. The human occupies the sacrificial position in the New Testament – a position that was occupied by the non-human in the Old Testament. Unlike Isaac, the human in the form of Jesus cannot escape the animal's destiny of torture and death. It is emblematic that Jesus takes on an animal form, even symbolically—the living form of the lamb, harmless and innocent—to sacrifice himself for the salvation of humanity.

The assumption of an animal position by the "son of man," even if only symbolically, divinizes the animal dimension, representing life before the advent of sin, before evil. Jesus becomes the paradigm of a man who learns, through his body, how it feels to be an animal led to slaughter, and John's symbolic attribution of the animal form to Jesus emphasizes the absurdity and gratuitousness of the sacrifice of an innocent and, at the same time, the immaculate purity of the victim. Therefore, in the most extreme suffering, Jesus embodies the nature of the animal led to slaughter, allowed no rebellion, no escape, and above all, no speech.[22] At the moment of the sacrifice, an extraordinary event occurs: the

---

21 John calls Jesus "the Lamb of God." This reference allows us to grasp the correlation between the sacrifice of Christ and the sacrifice of Isaac. Moving from a survey of the hermeneutical tradition on the topic, Abraham Oh rightly notes that, from the perspective of a New Testament interpretation of the episode narrated in Genesis 22, it is not so much the figure of Isaac that overlaps with the figure of Jesus, but rather the ram that is offered as a sacrifice in Isaac's place (Oh 2016, *passim*).

22 Recently, in her *On Body and Soul*, Hungarian director Ildikò Enyedi effectively portrayed the victimized dimension of the animal subjected to the logic of industrial slaughter. Enyedi presents images of cattle awaiting their death in the concentrated space of the slaughterhouse. She succeeds in making us appreciate the meaning of Rilke's verses on the animal's gaze as an opening to the unspeakable, an opening that allows them to be one with the world: "All other creatures look into the Open / with their whole eyes. But our eyes, / turned inward, are set all around it like snares, / trapping its way out to freedom. / We know what's out there only from the animal's / face; for we take even the youngest child, / turn him around and force him to look / at the past as formation, not that openness / so deep within an animal's face. Free from death" (Rilke 1977, p. 55). From the slits in their enclosures, the animals look at their uniformed, human executioners: the allusion to other, more brutal exterminations is explicit. One seems to be able to read the humans' thoughts as they talk about this and that. Deep down, they know they could prevent the holocaust, but this moral scruple is vague; it is like a fleeting, almost disturbing thought that barely touches them and that they prefer to set aside, perhaps so as not to be overwhelmed by it. They choose not to look at the non-human other, aware, perhaps, of the fact that only by looking away does it become possible for them to deny this "other": "Emmanuel Levinas once said that the face of the other says, Don't kill me. This is the language that we must learn to read, and the language that is denied by people who defend the right to treat animals as things, through a self-serving tautology. Elizabeth Costello [see below in this note] speaks of animals that refuse to speak, that keep the dignity of the silence. I disagree: they speak, and we refuse to grant them the dignity of *listening* to them" (Wendy Doniger in Coetzee 1999, pp. 104–105). The negation of the non-human other appears as a kind of training given the more demanding negation of the human self, and this negation, in turn, can be the premise of a more extreme form of negation, oblivion, denial of self. Our human guilt, both anthropomorphically projective and speciesist, hypocritical and compassionate, prompts us to read into the non-human gaze a mixture of uncanny awareness of impending doom, resignation, and mute condemnation. The alertness emanating from the victim's gaze contrasts with the indifference of the executioners, who smoke and chat, apparently quiet. Both concentration camp literature and daily experience teach us that only blindness to the other, not meeting its gaze, is the fundamental condition that makes denial of the other possible. Meeting the gaze, the other living person's face, human or non-human, would make mirroring and recognizing oneself, finding oneself and loving oneself, problematic. Comparing extermination camps to industrial meat production is of course disturbing (see the awkward position taken by John Coetzee through his literary alter ego, Elisabeth Costello). Given the theme's tricky nature, it is no coincidence that Coetzee adopts the rhetorical strategy of giving the Princeton Tanner Lecture from behind the mask of one of his characters. Prima facie, it may appear that Coetzee/Costello unacceptably equate the two forms of annihilation, when in fact they reveal the unprecedented fact that the spirit of the camps has survived in essence in a form accepted by all, swamped and hypocritical, in the industrial practice of the systematic destruction of life as an end in itself. The camps' spirit remains intact; it is put into practice in a socially acceptable way, through the orientation of annihilating aggression towards the non-human. Nevertheless, despite this change in direction, the deviation, the atrocity of the acts remains unaltered. What connects the two forms of extermination, from a transcendental ethical point of view, lies in a typical attitude towards life, an attitude that allows for the transformation from life to bare life, to being a pure means, a transformation grounded in a total disregard for the suffering of the other who is put to death, whether human or non-human: "The horror is that the killers refused to think themselves into the place of their victims, as did everyone else. They said, 'It is they in those cattle-cars rattling past.' They did not say, 'How would it be if it were I in that cattle-car?' They did not say, 'It is I who am in that cattle-car.' They said, 'It must be the dead who are being burnt today, making the air stink and falling in ash on my cabbages.' They did not say, 'How would it be if I were burning?' They did not say, 'I am burning, I am falling in ash.' In other words, they closed their hearts" (Coetzee 1999, p. 34). Of course, putting an innocent non-human to death has a very different ethical meaning than putting a human to death, yet this does not give us license to ignore the absolute gratuitousness, in principle, of the very act of taking any life and the constitutive innocence of the victim. Industrial slaughter goes entirely beyond the archaic logic of sacrifice, at the core of which lies an awareness of the intrinsic value of the victim's life. The ancients had elaborate rituals to justify the sacrifice itself and to silence the guilt of the executioners. The essence of Coetzee/Costello's argument lies in considering the value of

victim takes the floor. By speaking, Christ gives voice to the non-human within the human: like a mother who reveals the existence of love to her child through her words, Jesus gives meaning to the piercing and silent cry of every victim, all the more piercing because he is silent.

Jesus's exclamation is disorienting and scandalous. It does not matter whether the sentence was actually uttered. Historical truth does not matter here. What matters is the ethical meaning and the evocative power of the mythical representation that the sacrificial scene proposes. One must be a god (or a mother) to say those words at such a time. At the moment of his greatest suffering caused by gratuitous violence, with a superhuman impetus, Christ nails us to humankind's fundamental ethical problem: the problem of the absolute, solitary responsibility of the individual at the moment prior to action. Christ identifies in "not knowing what one does" the essence of the problem of acting and, in this case, of committing gratuitous violence. At the same time, in carrying out the (superhuman) act of forgiveness,[23] Christ testifies to his faith in the law to which he referred in the text quoted by Jung: not the old Hebrew law of observance of ritual but the (new) law of love.[24]

If we leave aside the historical and exegetical problems regarding the possible addressees of Jesus's invocation,[25] the ethical meaning of the statement seems to be: humans do not know the origin of (or the reasons for) their actions; egoism and violence depend on this "not knowing." Whereas the effects of not knowing are clear, it is less clear what "knowing what one is doing" entails. The account in the Gospel of Luke tells us that Jesus speaks the words "Father, forgive them for they know not what they do." *Who* speaks these words? It is the

---

life as inclusive of all life and as a supreme ethical category that embraces all living forms insofar as they can suffer. For Coetzee/Costello, human rationality is insufficient to justify our alleged ethical primacy over non-humans. —Instead, the body and the experience of sensitivity linked to the body unites humans and non-humans: "fullness, embodiedness, the sensation of being—not a consciousness of yourself as a kind of ghostly reasoning machine thinking thoughts, but on the contrary the sensation—a heavily affective sensation—of being a body with limbs that have extension in space, of being alive to the world" (Coetzee 1999, p. 33).
23 Fergus J. King rightly remarks that "in Luke 23:34a, a picture is given of forgiveness in which even apparently clearly motivated sins can be categorized as 'unintentional.' They stem from a basis in ignorance (they think they know what they are doing, but they really do not)" (King 2010, p. 148).
24 It is surprising to read Freud's words to Einstein on the possibility of overcoming the violence of war: "There is no need for psycho-analysis to be ashamed to speak of love in this connection, for religion itself uses the same words: 'Thou shalt love thy neighbour as thyself'" (Freud 1964b, p.212).
25 See n. 10 above.

man-God who speaks them; they are therefore divine words. Whatever this utterance means, the incarnate God experiences its effects on his human flesh, effects that are revealed to those who witness his life at the very moment it is ending. From this testimony, then, we can grasp, *ex negativo*, what knowing what one does consists in, that is, from the effects of suffering that any failure to know what one does always brings with it.[26] Nevertheless, the suffering of Christ is "only," as it were, a paradigm of the suffering of *every* creature, human and non-human, who suffers gratuitously at the hands of another and who, like Jesus, can therefore exclaim: "Father forgive them."

What Jesus says at the point of death shows other humans the path that should be taken toward the end of violence. Jesus's divinity manifests itself in the abandonment of the egoist perspective. If we stick to the word of the Gospel, the divinity of Jesus has nothing to do with transcendence and instead manifests itself as an entirely immanent and human project of liberation from egoism. Jesus seems to provide us with a lay[27] concept of what divinity means: the one who can see beyond the confines of individuality, in this way overcoming them, can be conceived of as divine. The example of Jesus seems to say that if it was once possible for *one* man to be genuinely free, then this is possible for *all* men. In contrast to Jesus's project, there is the "temptation," the danger, of continuing to follow the principle of egoism. This temptation is expressed in the thrice-repeated suggestion that Jesus simply "save himself," voiced mockingly by the executioners and the spectators. In response, we can imagine that Jesus is saying: What do I matter! *Was liegt an mir!*[28] Ask yourselves instead, why do *you* do what you do?

3 Fish, Frog, Snake

At first glance, Schopenhauer's hyperbole seems to have nothing to do with the non-human sphere. On closer inspection, however, the scene sinisterly recalls

---

[26] One could object that there are countless everyday examples of those who do evil knowing full well that they are doing evil: Those who say they are (or were) fully aware that they are doing (or have done) evil perhaps say so without really knowing what it means; they just *believe* they know. They might not know because they are blind to the meaning of their actions. What is meant to be argued is that the very act of doing evil shows that one does not know what one is doing, for if one knew, one would not do it, or at least one would *try* not to.

[27] For a lay interpretation of the figure of Jesus, see Perrella 2018.

[28] Nietzsche used this phrase on several occasions in his writings, starting from the late 1880s and returning to it several times until 1888. On this subject, see above all Brusotti 1997, p. 206.

the fate of an animal. Schopenhauer lets us imagine a human being, gutted for fat like a cetacean or a seal. In this image, as in the crucifixion scene, human and non-human are implicitly identified and overlap. It is the animal essence of the human that Schopenhauer emphasizes. Human and non-human are united under the sign of the cruelty and violence that accompany the transformation of life into a simple usable means via the exclusive activity of the human being. As we have seen, it is necessary for the value of the other to be repressed, to be thrown back into the unconscious so that violence can take place. Alternatively, we must not have the slightest conscience; we must be children so as not to perceive the meaning of violence. One can remain fixed in an infantile affective stage even as an adult.

In his *Spring, Summer, Autumn, Winter … and Spring*, Kim Ki Duk tells the story of a child and his teacher, a Buddhist monk.[29] In a typically Asian, almost dreamlike landscape, a man and a child live alone in a small pagoda, surrounded by a lake. As a sort of living metaphor, the man and the child must cross the water every time they wish to leave the retreat. Water appears as a dominant element: stagnant, running—it recalls the omnipresence of transformation, of an unending becoming.

The child seems to have a cheerful spirit as he follows and observes the master. The child gathers medical herbs, and the master teaches him to distinguish healing herbs from poisonous ones.[30] Like all children, the pupil also loves playing: he lets a small dog chase him and cuddles him; he shoots stones into the water with his sling.

One morning, the child walks to a crystal-clear stream where a fish is darting around. The child grabs it with his hands, laughing, his expression suggesting that he is enjoying himself as he ties a stone to the animal's tail before placing

---

29 On Kim Ki Duk's work, see Sofair 2005, Cho 2014, and Bartashius 2017.

30 Child: "'I have picked a lot of herbs, Master.' Master: 'Really, You've picked a lot? Careful! Stop! Throw this away, my child.' C: 'Why? It looks the same.' M: 'Even though it looks the same, this is a deadly plant. The other one can save lives.' C: 'It looks the same. How can I know?' M: 'Look closely here at the tip: you can see a white line. If you ate this plant you'd die'" (Kim Ki Duk 2003). Simplicity is the sign of the highest forms of mastery: Kim Ki Duk condenses the essential meaning of the act of teaching into a single scene. After all, this act always has to do with judgment: practicing the act of distinguishing (discriminating) allows one to understand the difference between healing and poisonous herbs. This act is the fundamental act of theoretical knowledge based on recognizing the difference between entities. It is also the fundamental act of moral knowledge based on recognizing the difference between good and evil. What is always at stake in both is life and death. Having to do with them, it has to do with truth. Beyond appearances, even in the simplest acts, being aware of what one is doing is always a matter of life and death.

it back in the water, where it is visibly suffering and unable to move.[31] The same fate befalls a frog and a snake. The child betrays an evident satisfaction and sense of fun. After torturing the animals, he bathes in the stream and seems to be in a happy and carefree mood. The teacher observes the child's behavior from a distance and does not intervene, even though his face expresses disappointment and bitterness at what his pupil has done. Evening comes. The child returns to the retreat on the lake and falls asleep. While the child is sleeping, the teacher ties a large stone to his back. When the child awakens, he realizes with surprise and dismay the presence of the stone and asks the master for help:

> Child: Master, there is a stone on my back. Please take it off.
> Master: Does it torment you?
> C: Yes, Master
> M: Didn't you also do it to the fish?
> C: Yes, Master
> M: Didn't you also do it to the frog?
> C: Yes, Master
> M: Didn't you also do it to the snake?
> C: Yes, Master
> M: Stand up! Walk around!
> C: I can't walk, it's too heavy
> M: How do you think the fish, the frog and the snake endured it? It was wrong to do it. Go and find all the animals and release them from the stones. Then I will release you too. But if any of the animals, the fish, the frog or the snake is dead, you will carry the stone in your heart for the rest of your life.

Weighed down by the stone on his back, the child returns to the stream. First, he paddles; he climbs over the rocks; finally, he descends to the point where the water flows. There, he finds the fish floating, dead. In tears, he buries it, as one would a human. The snake is also dead, likely following much suffering: its head is bloody and its body twisted. Only the frog has miraculously survived. At this point, the child bursts into a loud cry, which mingles with the roaring of the stream.

4 Wo Es war ...

In the middle of the scene there is the action of the child. The action of the child expresses pure possibility, experience, experimentation with enjoyment. What

---

[31] See n. 33.

we see is what the child does, left to himself. The world of the child is a world of usable objects subordinated exclusively to the child's desire; it is a world of object-means. The child tries to satisfy his desire, both cruel and innocent, in different ways. He is a natural born offender-tormentor. In his action, we clearly observe how the intertwinement of the life drive and the death drive marks the essence of the human. Even if violence is destructive, its vitality is undeniable, and stillness and peace evoke proximity to death.

The first thing the child does is to try to catch the butterflies, but he cannot. His drives then guide him to the fish, the frog, and the snake. The child jumps from one thing to another. The pleasure principle is not focused on a single object but throws itself on everything it encounters. The drives do not move toward a defined goal but only seek their satisfaction. The child gives us a striking example of the meaning, in a moral sense, of the Freudian expression "polymorphous perversion." Perversion occurs wherever the means becomes the end. Polymorphous perversion is a freedom that does not know the limit of the law, and thus, strictly speaking, we cannot even define it as freedom.[32]

---

[32] Freud limits the use of the expression "polymorphous perversion" to the sphere of the libido: "What in adult life is described as 'perverse' differs from the normal in these respects: first, by disregarding the barrier of species (the gulf between men and animals), secondly, by overstepping the barrier against disgust, thirdly that against incest (the prohibition against seeking sexual satisfaction from near blood-relations), fourthly that against members of one's own sex and fifthly the transferring of the part played by the genitals to other organs and areas of the body. None of these barriers existed from the beginning; they were only gradually erected in the course of development and education. Small children are free from them. They recognize no frightful gulf between human beings and animals; the arrogance with which men separate themselves from animals does not emerge until later. To begin with, children exhibit no disgust at excreta but acquire this slowly under the pressure of education; they attach no special importance to the distinction between the sexes, but attribute the same conformation of the genitals to both; they direct their first sexual lusts and their curiosity to those who are nearest and for other reasons dearest to them—parents, brothers and sisters, or nurses; and finally, they show (what later on breaks through once again at the climax of a love-relation) that they expect to derive pleasure not only from their sexual organs, but that many other parts of the body lay claim to the same sensitivity, afford them analogous feelings of pleasure and can accordingly play the part of genitals. Children may thus be described as 'polymorphously perverse,' and if these impulses only show traces of activity, that is because on the one hand they are of less intensity compared with those in later life and on the other hand all a child's sexual manifestations are at once energetically suppressed by education" (Freud 1961 pp. 208–209). Here I suggest an extension of polymorphous perversion to the ethical sphere, an extension that is nonetheless anchored in the Freudian vision: "The ego, freed from all ethical bonds, also finds itself at one with all the demands of sexual desire, even those which have long been condemned by our aesthetic upbringing and those which contradict all the requirements of moral restraint. The desire for pleasure— the 'libido,' as we call it—chooses its objects without inhibition, and by preference, indeed, the

Paradoxically, the child feels satisfaction in exercising his "freedom" to deprive animals of their own freedom of movement, which is the fundamental, the most basic, raw, form of freedom.[33] The opening of the space of possibilities with regard to the executioner's actions corresponds to the restriction of possibilities for the victim.

The master observes for a long time without intervening. When he finally intervenes, he does not punish the pupil but leads him to live out the same experience as the other, induces him to feel, to experience what it means to feel what the other feels, what it is like to be another who suffers: a fish, a frog, a snake. This is precisely what it means to see meaning and not to be ethically blind to meaning. The teacher pushes the child to "be moved," as Hannah Arendt would say, the opposite of which is not a state of being "'rational,' whatever that may mean, but either the inability to be moved, usually a pathological phenomenon, or sentimentality, which is a perversion of feeling" (Arendt 1970, p. 64).[34]

The non-speciesist attitude of the master is a crucial point here. With his intervention, the master implicitly puts the suffering of the child on the same level as the suffering of the animals: not only should no human be offended, harmed, but indeed no living being deserves such treatment. The mere fact of being sentient makes every living thing sacred and dignified.

The act of the master also tells us what the function of being a master consists in. Being a master means, above all, performing significant acts, not only transmitting information—acts that embody openness to what is other than one-

---

forbidden ones: not only other men's wives, but above all incestuous objects, objects sanctified by the common agreement of mankind, a man's mother and sister, a woman's father and brother…. Lusts which we think of as remote from human nature show themselves strong enough to provoke dreams. Hatred, too, rages without restraint. Wishes for revenge and death directed against those who are nearest and dearest in waking life, against the dreamer's parents, brothers and sisters, husband or wife, and his own children are nothing unusual. These censored wishes appear to rise up out of a positive Hell; after they have been interpreted when we are awake, no censorship of them seems to us too severe" (Freud 1961, pp. 142–143).

33 "The freedom of the body to move in space is targeted as the point at which reason can most painfully and effectively harm the being of the other. And indeed it is on creatures least able to bear confinement—creatures who conform least to Descartes's picture of the soul as a pea imprisoned in a shell, to which further imprisonment is irrelevant—that we see the most devastating effects: in zoos, in laboratories, institutions where the flow of joy that comes from living not in or as a body but simply from being an embodied being has no place" (Coetzee 1999, p. 34). It is significant that the Jewish tradition refers to the sacrifice of Isaac with the term "akedah," which means "binding" (Oh 2016, p. 2).

34 On the other hand, "It is the use of reason that makes us dangerously 'irrational,' because this reason is the property of an 'aboriginally instinctual being'" (Arendt 1970, p. 62).

self, the opposite of egoism. In the scene set out above, the master performs two decisive acts: at first, he lets the child freely live out his experience of enjoyment, which, despite his enjoyment, is a destructive experience for the other. The master acts without acting. In a second moment, he ties the stone to the child's back. This is not an act of punishment. In reality, the master is merely showing the child *the limits* of acting freely. These limits cannot be recognized if there is no one to help us to do so. We observed it in the case of the mother who, through her words, gives the child a first chance to become human; similarly, Jesus gives voice to the silent sorrow of every victim, human and non-human, and recalls the importance of ethical knowledge; we see it again, finally, in the figure of the teacher. Emerging from the state of minority—the conquest of autonomy and freedom, becoming subjects who can know what they are doing—consists in opening up space between oneself and the possibility of committing gratuitous violence. Becoming and remaining human has to do with, and indeed depends on, this space, this distance.

If violence finds expression in the negation of the other, the rejection of violence can only occur thanks to the intervention of the other. The teacher, not unlike Jesus speaking from the cross, limits himself, as it were, to returning the burden of personal responsibility to the child, metaphorically signified by the stone loaded onto his back. In other words, the teacher allows the child *to learn by himself* to become aware of what he is doing.

The final cry of the child accompanies the painful birth of conscience and, at the same time, the discovery of the limits of the pleasure principle. The final cry contrasts with the child's laughter in the first part of the fable, an expression of the pleasure of cruelty which that adult humans try to conceal and which that they are ashamed of in public yet enjoy in private.

Wo Es war soll Ich werden. With this formula, Freud indicates the ultimate ethical task of psychoanalysis: Where the *Es* was, it should (*soll*) become I.[35] We can read this Freudian formula as saying that where gratuitous violence was, non-violence should become possible. The crying of the child faithfully re-

---

35 Strachey translates this as "Where id was, there ego shall be" (Freud 1964a, p. 80). I propose a modified version of the German, following Lacan and the spirit of the original. On the translation of this Freudian sentence, Lacan states: "*Wo es war, soll Ich werden.* This does not mean, as some execrable translation would have it, *Le moi doit deloger le ça* (the ego must dislodge the id). See how Freud—and in a formula worthy in resonance of the pre-Socratics—is translated in French. It is not a question of the ego in this *soll Ich werden*; the fact is that throughout Freud's work—one must, of course, recognize its proper place—the *Ich* is the complete, total locus of the network of signifiers, that is to say, the subject, *where it was*, where it has always been" (Lacan 1981, p. 44).

flects the exhausting transition from the blind violence of drives, *Wo Es war*, to the duty of becoming an I, *soll Ich werden*, the becoming I of an Ego that no longer lives in the service of drives, in the cocoon of its self-referential isolation, but attempts to learn, on its own, to go beyond itself, not without stumbling.

Bibliography

Arendt, Hannah (1970): *On Violence*. Orlando: Harvest Book Harcourt Inc.
Badiou, Alain (2001): *Ethics: An Essay on the Understanding of Evil*. London, New York: Verso.
Bammel, Ernst (1986): "The Cambridge Periscope. The Addition to Luke 6.4 in Codex Bezae." In: *New Testament Studies* 32. No. 3, pp 404–426.
Bartashius, Jason (2017): "Subverting patriarchal Buddhism in Spring, Summer, Fall, Winter … and Spring." In: *Culture and Religion* 19. No. 1, pp. 127–138.
Brown, Raymond E. (1994): *The Death of the Messiah: A Commentary on the Passion Narratives in the Four Gospels*, 2 vols. New York: Doubleday.
Brusotti, Marco (1997): *Die Leidenschaft der Erkenntniss*. Berlin, New York: De Gruyter.
Cho, Francisca (2014): "The Transnational Buddhism of Spring, Summer, Fall, Winter … and Spring." In: *Contemporary Buddhism* 15. No. 1, pp. 109–124.
Coetzee, John (1999): *The Life of Animals*. Princeton: Princeton University Press.
Epp, Eldon Jay (1962): "The 'Ignorance Motif' in Acts and Anti-Judaic Tendencies in Codex Bezae." In: *Harvard Theological Review* 55. No. 1, pp. 51–62.
Eubank, Nathan (2010): "A Disconcerting Prayer: On the Originality of Luke 23:34a." In: *Journal of Biblical Literature* 129. No. 3, pp. 521–536.
Freud, Sigmund (1955): *Beyond the Pleasure Principle, Group Psychology and other Works*. In: James Strachey (Ed.): *The Complete Psychological Works of Sigmund Freud, Standard Edition*, vol. XVIII. London: the Hogarth Press and the Institute of Psychoanalysis, pp. 3–64.
Freud, Sigmund (1961), "Introductory Lectures on Psycho-Analysis (Parts I and II)". In: James Strachey (Ed.): *The Complete Psychological Works of Sigmund Freud, Standard Edition*, vol. XV. London: the Hogarth Press and the Institute of Psychoanalysis, pp. 3–228.
Freud, Sigmund (1964a): "New Introductory Lectures on Psycho-Analysis." In: James Strachey (Ed.): *The Complete Psychological Works of Sigmund Freud, Standard Edition*, vol. XXII. London: the Hogarth Press and the Institute of Psychoanalysis, pp. 3–184.
Freud, Sigmund (1964b): "Why War? (1933[1932]) (Einstein and Freud)". In: James Strachey (Ed.): *The Complete Psychological Works of Sigmund Freud, Standard Edition*, vol. XXII. London: the Hogarth Press and the Institute of Psychoanalysis, pp. 195–215.
Girard, René (1986): *The Scapegoat*. Baltimore: The Johns Hopkins University Press.
Heidegger, Martin (1982): *Nietzsche. Volume IV: Nihilism*. San Francisco: HarperSanFrancisco.
Jung, Carl Gustav (1969): *Psychology and Religion: West and East*. 2nd ed. In: Gerald Adler, R. F. C. Hull *The Collected Works of Carl Gustav Jung*, vol. 11. Princeton: Princeton University Press, 3–199.
Kant, Immanuel (2011): *Groundwork of the Metaphysics of Morals*. Edited by Jens Timmermann. and translated by Mary Gregor. Translation revised by Jens Timmermann, Cambridge: Cambridge University Press.

Kant, Immanuel (2015): *Critique of Practical Reason*. Edited and translated by Mary Gregor. Cambridge: Cambridge University Press.

King, Fergus J. (2010): "'Father, forgive them, for they know not what they do.' Reflections on Luke 23:34a, Kol Nidre and the Atonement." In: *Australian Journal of Jewish Studies* 24, pp. 134–160.

Lacan, Jacques (1981): *The Seminar of Jacques Lacan Book XI. The Four Fundamental Concepts of Psychoanalysis*. Edited by Jacques-Alain Miller and Alan. Sheridan. New York, London: W. W. Norton & Company.

Nancy Jean-Luc (2007): *The Creation of the World* or *Globalization*. Albany: State University of New York Press.

Nestle, Eberhard, and Kurt Aland (Eds.) (2012): *Novum Testamentum Graece*. 28th ed. Peabody: Hendrickson Publishers.

Oh, Abraham (2016): "Canonical understanding of the sacrifice of Isaac: The influence of the Jewish tradition." In: *HTS Teologiese Studies/Theological Studies* 72. No. 3, pp. 1–7.

Parker, D. C. and C. -B. Amphoux (Eds.) (1986): *Codex Bezae. Studies from the Lunel Colloquium, June 1994*. Leiden, New York, Koln: Brill.

Perrella, Ettore (2018): *L'uomo Gesù e la nascita dell'etica laica*. Roma: Nep Edizioni.

Pfeiffer, Ernst (Ed.) (1972): *Sigmund Freud and Lou Andreas Salomé Letters*. New York: A Helen and Kurt Wolff Book, Harcourt Brace Jovanovich, Inc.

Rilke, Maria Reiner (1977): *Duino Elegies and the Sonnets to Orpheus*. Boston: Houghton Mifflin Company.

Schopenhauer, Arthur (2009): "On the Basis of Morals." In: Schopenhauer: *The Two Fundamental Problems of Ethics*. Edited by Christopher Janaway. Cambridge: Cambridge University Press, pp. 113–258.

Singer, Peter (2015): *Animal Liberation*. New York: Open Road Integrated Media.

Sofair, Michael (2005): "Spring, Summer, Fall, Winter … and Spring." In: *Film Quarterly* 59. No. 1, pp. 36–44.

Stellino, Paolo (2020): *Philosophical Perspectives on Suicide: Kant, Schopenhauer, Nietzsche, and Wittgenstein*. Cham: Palgrave Macmillan.

Strahan Marshall, Joshua (2012): *The Limits of a Text: Luke 23:34a as a Case Study in Theological Interpretation*. Winona Lake: Eisenbrauns.

Filmography

Enyedi, Ildikò, director. (2017): *On Body and Soul*.
Kim Ki Duk, director. (2003): *Spring, Summer, Autumn, Winter… and Spring*.

Luís Aguiar de Sousa
Cruelty, Bad Conscience, and the Sovereign Individual in Nietzsche's *Genealogy of Morality*

Abstract: In this paper, I argue that, although for Nietzsche the cruel character of our instincts is an ultimate fact of nature and the foundation of all culture and civilization, his ideal human being corresponds not to a return to pre-civilized humanity, to the human beast, but rather to a rational, autonomous, and self-affirmative human being. I will base this argument on an interpretation of relevant passages from the second essay of *On the Genealogy of Morality*. First, I will show that Nietzsche identifies the instinct for cruelty with the will to power and that, as such, it constitutes our primordial drive and instinct and is the foundation of culture and civilized society. I will then focus on Nietzsche's account of bad conscience as internalized cruelty, arguing that he takes a profoundly ambiguous stance toward bad conscience. To the extent that it develops into a consciousness of guilt, it lies at the basis of what he calls the "sickness" of the human being. Nonetheless, I will claim that conscience can have more positive functions. To illustrate this, I conclude by presenting an interpretation of the "sovereign individual" as a case study of the nature of Nietzsche's ideal human being.

1 Introduction

There is a tendency to think that nihilism, understood as a complete lack of belief in moral values or meaning, may be the underlying cause of acts of violence, especially when these are extreme and apparently unmotivated. Since Nietzsche often describes himself as an "immoralist" (HH I Preface 1; D Preface 4; GS 346; BGE 32, 226; TI Arrows 36, Morality 3, 6, Errors 7, Skirmishes 32; EH Books, Untimely 2, Human 6; EH Destiny 2, 3, 6) and sometimes as a "nihilist" (NL 1887, 9[123], KSA 12, p. 407), seeming to extoll the virtues of the strong, masters, birds of prey, the ferocious pack of blond beasts over the herd, it is only natural to assume that if any value is left for him, it seems to lie in the notion of power and of willing power. In this way, even if he does not fully embrace it, one might read Nietzsche's philosophy as legitimizing all kinds of violent acts. Although several passages from both his published works and his *Nachlass* may suggest this picture, in this paper, I will show that Nietzsche's view on these matters is not only far more complex, subtle and considerably different, but also, to a certain extent, the exact opposite. Although Nietzsche describes humans as radically cruel and violent, he thinks that peaceful and civilized society is built on these brutal foundations. Moreover, even though Nietzsche describes European civilization and modern societies as sick and *décadent*, his conception of the ideal human being does not entail a return to pre-civilized, pre-societal life–to the "human beast." The ideal human being as envisaged by him can only be a product of modern civilization; rather than being a thoroughgoing species of nihilism, his philosophy corresponds to an attempt to overcome it.

2 Cruelty and the Will to Power

Let us begin by considering the details of Nietzsche's understanding of cruelty. In the course of the second essay of the *Genealogy*, Nietzsche says, quoting Prosper Mérimée, that cruelty consists in *"faire le mal pour le plaisir de le faire* [doing evil for the pleasure of doing it]" (GM II 5), by which he means not only the pleasure of doing evil, but also the pleasure of seeing evil or harm being done to others. In other words, cruelty involves taking pleasure in the suffering of the other for its own sake.

Right off the bat, we should note that Nietzsche thinks of cruelty as a manifestation or an aspect of his broader notion of the will to power. In *Daybreak* 18, for example, Nietzsche writes that the practice of cruelty is "the highest gratification of the feeling of power." Further in *Daybreak* 113, he shows that barbarism and asceticism, although seemingly completely opposite phenomena, are just "rungs" in the same "ladder" (D 113). In this early text, he links this "ladder" to different degrees of what he calls the "striving for distinction," the essentially cruel nature of which Nietzsche emphasizes and that here appears to be an earlier version of what he would later call the will to power. In later passages, Nietzsche does not shy away from emphasizing the cruel aspect of the will to power: "life itself is *essentially* a process of appropriating, injuring, overpowering the alien and the weaker, oppressing, being harsh, imposing your own form, incorporating, and at least, the very least, exploiting" (BGE 259). In the same passage, he goes on to write that

> "exploitation" does not belong to a corrupted or imperfect, primitive society: it belongs to the *essence* of being alive as a fundamental organic function; it is a result of genuine will to power, which is just the will of life.—Although this is an innovation at the level of theory,—at the level of reality, it is the *primal fact* of all history.(BGE 259)[1]

---

[1] See also GM II 11: "life functions *essentially* in an injurious, violent, exploitative and destruc-

Nietzsche even seems to straightforwardly identify the will to power with cruelty, referring to cruelty as "that very *instinct for freedom* (put into my language: the will to power)" (GM II 18).

Assessing the meaning and status of the notion of the will to power in Nietzsche's oeuvre and thinking, especially concerning the question of whether it is supposed to be a metaphysical, a biological, or a merely psychological notion, is beyond the scope of this paper. Although there may be other compelling interpretations, I will presuppose that, at least in the *Genealogy*, Nietzsche does think that all biological and cultural processes can be explained as manifestations and developments of the will to power.[2] Furthermore, I will presuppose that with his thesis of the will to power, Nietzsche wants to say that, above all else, the human being wants "power," the most basic and crude manifestation or expression of which is inflicting suffering on others.[3] As we will see, however, Nietzsche does not think that all our actions are meant to hurt or harm others (something that any everyday example can prove false). To begin with, Nietzsche thinks that there is a species of cruelty that remained hitherto unaccounted for, namely, cruelty toward oneself:[4]

> We clearly need to drive out the silly psychology of the past; the only thing this psychology was able to teach about cruelty was that it originated from the sight of *another's* suffering. But there is abundant, overabundant pleasure in your own suffering too, in making yourself suffer. (BGE 229)

---

tive manner, or at least these are its fundamental processes and it cannot be thought of without these characteristics."

2 In BGE 36, Nietzsche plays with the idea of tracing "all organic functions back to this will to power" and of designating "*all* efficacious force as: *will to power*". Furthermore, in BGE 23, he claims "to grasp psychology as morphology and the *doctrine of the development of the will to power*".

3 For Reginster (2006, pp. 139–143), in accordance with his interpretation of the will to power as the "will to overcome resistance," the reason the will to power manifests itself in acts of cruelty toward others (and oneself) in opposition to merely controlling or exercising dominion over the other is that the other upon whom cruelty is exerted offers resistance. According to this interpretation, what draws us to cruel acts is not the suffering of the other for its own sake but rather his or her resistance to suffering. Although this interpretation helps us to make sense of the plastic character of the will to power, it does not explain why Nietzsche thinks cruelty was so pervasive among primitive humans at the expense of other forms of overcoming resistance.

4 As far as we know, Nietzsche was not acquainted with the work of Sacher-Masoch. The only mention of Sacher-Masoch in Nietzsche's writings is in a letter (Bf. To Constantin Georg Naumann, 02.08.1886, KGB III/3, Bf. 726) to Naumann, in which Nietzsche asks the former to send copies of *Beyond Good and Evil* to several people, among them Sacher-Masoch.

Nietzsche goes on to cite as examples of self-inflicted cruelty ascetic practices (such as self-mutilation), remorse, and the "vivisections" of conscience (among others). This can also be explained by the fact that, for Nietzsche, the will to power has a plastic character: – it seeks its ultimate goal, power, via different means and by attaching itself to different objects.[5] Thus, although the will to power manifests itself primarily in taking pleasure in the suffering of others or in acts of aggression, this is far from constituting its sole and most widespread manifestation—at least for us civilized human beings. In other words, the will to power need not manifest itself in explicit acts of cruelty; it can also manifest itself in a sublimated form.

3 Practical Reason, Morality of Custom, and Punishment

Nietzsche does not limit himself to asserting that humanity has a brutal, cruel core. He traces the genesis of humanity, civilized society, and reason as we know it back to the exertion of cruelty and its consequences, employing the instinct for cruelty as an explanatory device throughout the second essay of the *Genealogy* to trace the origin of practical reason, responsibility, legal systems, punishment, justice, moral conscience, and guilt, etc., thus overturning our habitual, self-evident, and most entrenched ways of thinking.

At first, it may come as a surprise to the reader of the *Genealogy*'s second essay that Nietzsche does not oppose cruelty to rationality: "Ah, reason, solemnity, mastering of emotions, this really dismal thing called reflection, all these privileges and splendours man has: what a price had to be paid for them! How much blood and horror lies at the basis of all 'good things'!" (GM II 3). When Nietzsche speaks of reason in this context, he is referring more specifically to what is usually called practical reason. For Nietzsche, not only is the human being a primordially practical being, but in particular, as we will see, what distinguishes humans from animals, their "humanity," consists in part in their ability to commit themselves to certain courses of action with fellow members of the human species—that is, as Nietzsche puts it, the ability to make and keep promises: "to breed an animal with the prerogative to *promise*—is that not precisely the paradoxical task which nature has set herself with regard to humankind?

---

[5] On the plastic character of drives, see Richardson (2004, pp. 28–29, 39, and 74–75); Katsafanas (2016, pp. 111–113). On the notion of power as self-overcoming, see Kaufmann (1974, pp. 260–261).

Is it not the real problem of humankind?" (GM II 1). According to Nietzsche's brief indications in the second essay of the *Genealogy*, practical reason, the ability to make plans, to deploy certain means to achieve certain ends, is not something with which we are naturally endowed. In order to make plans and calculate the means by which they can be accomplished, it is necessary to create a "will's memory: so that a world of strange new things, circumstances and even acts of will may be placed quite safely in between the original 'I will,' 'I shall do' and the actual discharge of the will, its *act*, without breaking this long chain of the will" (GM II 1). For Nietzsche, in our pre-human, merely animal state, one of the prevailing forces of our psyche is "forgetfulness." Contrary to common belief, forgetfulness is not a merely passive condition but rather "an active ability to suppress, positive in the strongest sense of the word" (GM II 1). In order for the human being to make (and especially to keep) promises, it is necessary for the latter to be well engraved in memory. For that, our natural forgetfulness must be counterbalanced. Far from being a natural endowment, memory must have been created or, as we will see, forced upon us to counterbalance the active force of forgetfulness. For this to occur, it is necessary that the individual be made to suffer for his broken promises: "'A thing must be burnt in so that it stays in the memory: only something that continues *to hurt* stays in the memory'—that is a proposition from the oldest (and unfortunately the longest-lived) psychology on earth" (GM II 3). Admittedly, it is difficult to make sense of how these proto-humans are supposed to have memorized their plans and promises in the first place if they had no memory at all.[6] If they were utterly lacking in mnemonic abilities, it would surely be impossible to expect them to remember their promises. One who inflicts suffering in retaliation for a broken promise must be able to remember that a promise was broken. Further, the very act of making a promise presupposes that we already have some kind of mnemonic ability, even if we are unable to abide by it. For this reason, it is more reasonable to suppose that when Nietzsche speaks of the ability to "make a promise," he has in mind the capacity to control one's urges or impulses and to act in a reflected manner in view of the goal one has set oneself. Thus, when Nietzsche writes of creating a memory, he is referring, more specifically, not to memory as a general cognitive capacity to remember past events, but rather to the ability to carry out one's promises and general plans for action, that is, of not yielding to the present impulse. When it comes to these early humans, Nietzsche is basically describing beings who are unable to abide by their plans and keep their promises because,

---

[6] On the problem of the circularity of Nietzsche's account of the origin of memory, see Ridley (1998, p. 18).

just like non-human animals, they live largely in the present and yield easily to their impulses. Thus, rather than being unable to make plans—how else could they be able to make promises and pledges?—at this stage humans are unable to carry them out.

The creation of a "memory of the will" is part of a larger process that Nietzsche calls the "morality of custom [*Sittlichkeit der Sitte*]" and that generally results in the human being's becoming, in Nietzsche's words, "*reliable, regular, necessary*" (GM II 1). Nietzsche first introduces the notion of "morality of custom" in *Daybreak*. The morality of custom corresponds to "*the actual and decisive eras of history which determined the character of mankind*" (D 18). This is the "pre-historical" period in which morality was first created (D 18). On Nietzsche's view, morality is intrinsically tied to socialization. In its early stages, morality was first and foremost the morality of custom insofar as it consisted in the customs of a certain community. Being moral, at least at this stage, equated to complying with the customary way things were done in a certain social setting. At this stage, morality consisted entirely in compliance with custom (*Sitte*): "morality is nothing other (therefore no more!) than obedience to customs, of whatever kind they may be; customs, however, are the traditional way of behaving and evaluating" (D 9).[7] Customs, moreover, are closely related to the conditions of the preservation of a particular community (HH I 97; GS 116; and Z I Goals). Even customs that seem absurd or arbitrary in hindsight serve to reinforce the community (HH I 96; D 16; GS 43).

Whereas without its social existence, without the morality of custom, the human species would be quite unpredictable and a slave of the moment, of the passions, the human being as transformed by the morality of custom has become quite regular and predictable, has adapted him- or herself to social constraints, that is, to the usual way of acting. This process corresponds to what Nietzsche calls the "long history of the origins of *responsibility*" (GM II 2). Practical reason, the ability to make promises, to engage one's future self, is tantamount to being responsible for one's actions.

The social context in which the human being creates a "memory" is one that pre-exists the creation of the state and where social relations are mainly those of trade (GM II 8). It is in the context of these commercial relations that Nietzsche locates the first promises: "precisely here, *promises are made*; precisely here, the

---

[7] Nietzsche also expresses this idea in *Human, All Too Human*: "to be moral, to act in accordance with custom, to be ethical means to practice obedience towards a law or tradition established from of old" (HH I 96).

person making the promise has to have a memory *made* for him" (GM II 5). For this the debtor must pledge something in case he does not keep his word:

> The debtor, in order to inspire confidence that the promise of repayment will be honoured, in order to give a guarantee of the solemnity and sanctity of his promise, and in order to etch the duty and obligation of repayment into his conscience, pawns something to the creditor by means of the contract in case he does not pay, something that he still 'possesses' and controls, for example, his body, or his wife, or his freedom, or his life. (GM II 5)

If the debtor who has broken his contract has nothing more to offer in return, he can still repay his debt by letting the creditor enact cruelty toward him:

> The equivalence is provided by the fact that instead of an advantage directly making up for the wrong (so, instead of compensation in money, land or possessions of any kind), a sort of *pleasure* is given to the creditor as repayment and compensation,—the pleasure of having the right to exercise power over the powerless without a thought, the pleasure '*de faire le mal pour le plaisir de le faire*,' the enjoyment of violating. (GM II 5)

The fact that the creditor accepts the right to impose suffering on the debtor as a form of compensation for the debt points to the fact that cruelty toward others is one of our most basic drives. (This also confirms the idea that cruelty toward others is a manifestation of the will to power.) As a matter of fact, Nietzsche explains the pleasure the creditor takes in enacting cruelty against others as a way in which "the creditor takes part in the *rights of the masters:* at last he, too, shares the elevated feeling of being in a position to despise and maltreat someone as an 'inferior'" (GM II 5).

For Nietzsche, what is vital is that the practice of cruelty is at first not done with any further end in view, such as improving the debtor morally. Further, as we saw above, the enactment of cruel acts as retribution for breaking a contract developed in a way that, according to Nietzsche, was entirely independent of the presupposition of freedom of the will, understood as the ability to act otherwise.[8] According to Nietzsche, what leads someone to make the other suffer for his broken promises is not revenge either, because the latter already presupposes what, for Nietzsche, is the more primordial phenomenon that must be posited as the foundation of all others: the fact that, at least in its more primitive stages, the human being took pleasure in the suffering of others as such: "and anyone who clumsily tries to interject the concept 'revenge' has merely obscured and darkened his own insight, rather than clarified it (—revenge itself just leads us

---

[8] "Or that punishment, as *retribution*, evolved quite independently of any assumption about freedom or lack of freedom of the will?" (GM II 4).

back to the same problem: 'how can it be gratifying to make someone suffer?')" (GM II 6). With the emergence of the state, the prerogative of exerting cruelty passes from the individuals to the state. In addition to debts that relate to commercial affairs, one incurs further debts, namely, those regarding the advantages of living under the state's protection. The creditor-debtor relationship is transferred to the relation between the members of the community and the community as a whole: "the community has the same basic relationship to its members as the creditor to the debtor" (GM II 9). Now it is the state that has the privilege of inflicting pain on its members when promises are not kept. Furthermore, individuals owe the state for the protection it affords against possible offenders. When an individual breaks the law, he breaks a promise made to society as a whole (the contract) (GM II 9). By breaking the contract that tied him to the community, he forfeits the advantages of being its member. From that point on, the community treats him as external, as an enemy: "the anger of the injured creditor, the community, makes him return to the savage and outlawed state from which he was sheltered hitherto: he is cast out—and now any kind of hostile act can be perpetrated on him" (GM II 9).

Nietzsche also points out that, to the extent that the community becomes more powerful, it ceases to expel lawbreakers and becomes more lenient toward them (GM II 10). Legal systems start to isolate the wrongdoer from his deed, and punishment becomes a way of paying the community back for the injury. The state protects the agent from the rest of the community, in particular from the anger of the injured party (GM II 10). This corresponds to the phenomenon of justice, which, according to Nietzsche, manifests itself in the impersonal manner in which the state deals with the criminal and the crime, as opposed to the mere will to revenge on the part of the injured side (GM II 11). Nonetheless, Nietzsche argues that "justice" must be interpreted in terms of power and power relations. The "legal system" is a temporary restriction of the will to power and has an exceptional character (GM II 11). On Nietzsche's view, justice exists insofar as a legal system within a community exists. There is no justice in what the contractualist tradition calls the "state of nature," just as there is no justice in relations between different states: "Therefore 'just' and 'unjust' only start from the moment when a legal system is set up. ... To talk of 'just' and 'unjust' *as such* is meaningless" (GM II 11).

As the state becomes more self-assured and certain of its power, punishment can become more lax. This culminates in what Nietzsche calls the "self-sublimation of justice [*Selbstaufhebung der Gerechtigkeit*]" (GM II 10), that is, the state's becoming so powerful that it can show criminals mercy (*Gnade*) for their crimes. In this context, *Selbstaufhebung* could also be translated as "self-supression." Nietzsche's idea is that even though "justice" has its origin in the establishment of equivalences between the breach of the contract and punishment, it can develop in such a way that the creditor, in this case the state, may forgive the breaching of the contract, the breaking of the promise, on account of its excess power.

4 Bad Conscience, Guilt, and the Ascetic Ideal

The first sections of the second essay of the *Genealogy* trace the origin and development of practical reason and responsibility—that is, of our ability to make plans and carry them out—back to the activity of making promises in a social framework characterized by commercial relations. As we have seen, Nietzsche wants to make clear that this ability developed independently of any feeling of guilt and bad conscience and of any sense of our having the ability to act differently than we do.

Nietzsche introduces the notions of guilt and bad conscience for the first time in a rather abrupt manner at the beginning of the fourth section: "how, then, did that other 'dismal thing,' the consciousness of guilt, the whole 'bad conscience,' come into the world?" (GM II 4). Nietzsche's clue to investigating the origin of our feeling of guilt lies in the fact that *Schuld*, the German word for "guilt," also means "debt." For this reason, it is up to the interpreter and translator to judge which option is appropriate in a given passage. In any case, what is most important is the fact that, from a substantive and philosophical point of view, Nietzsche sees guilt and feeling guilty as somehow having developed out of the notion of having debts and the feeling of indebtedness. Nietzsche thus concludes that consciousness of guilt must somehow be traced back to the relation between creditor and debtor (GM II 4). However, Nietzsche is far from thinking that the feeling of guilt develops in a straightforward way out of this relation. Nor does guilt ensue from the fact that debtors, those who break their promises, are punished. Nietzsche emphasizes emphatically that bad conscience or guilt is not the outcome of punishment (GM II 14–15).[9] In this regard, Nietzsche famously distinguishes the origin of punishment from the purpose of punishment (GM II 12). He criticizes those who posit the origin of punishment in the purpose and deduce the former from the latter (GM II 12

---

[9] As we will see below, the idea that punishment does not bring forth a bad conscience must be qualified. It is true that a bad conscience is not the direct outcome of punishment, but it can certainly be seen as resulting from it indirectly.

—13).[10] This is why, according to Nietzsche, punishment displays a "whole synthesis of meanings," although its origin lies in none of them but instead in an "act" or "drama," "a certain strict sequence of procedures", which is a permanent element in contrast to purpose or meaning, which is "fluid" (GM II 13). In the case at hand, we can presuppose that the cruel ritual of inflicting pain upon the other for its own sake functions here as a permanent element. The fact that this procedure was later interpreted as having a certain aim is thoroughly accidental or contingent, as new meanings and purposes can always be projected onto the procedure. Even "punishment as payment of a debt to the creditor in any form (even one of emotional compensation)" is included in the list of the possible aims of punishment, which points to the fact that the permanent element in punishment is rooted in our inextricable instinct for cruelty—which finds its expression in a "procedure" the aim of which is reinterpreted time and again and that consists in the very act of inflicting pain on the other (GM II 13).

As we saw, Nietzsche claims that punishment does help to develop reason, especially in the sense of instrumental reason, that is, anticipating possible outcomes for different courses of action, calculating the means to achieve them etc., but it does not in any way improve human beings "morally": "What can largely be achieved by punishment, in man or beast, is the increase of fear, the intensification of intelligence, the mastering of desires: punishment *tames* man in this way but does not make him "better,"—we would be more justified in asserting the opposite" (GM II 15). Instead of positing the origin of bad conscience as a consequence of punishment, Nietzsche locates its emergence in the moment at which human beings began to live in peace in a more or less organized society: "I look on bad conscience as a serious illness to which man was forced to succumb by the pressure of the most fundamental of all changes which he experienced,—that change whereby he finally found himself imprisoned within the confines of society and peace" (GM II 16). According to Nietzsche, this transition from a Hobbesian state of war of all against all to civilized society was abrupt and coincided with the creation of a tyrannical proto-state (GM II 17). The

---

[10] This is a particular application of a more general "principle": "that the origin of the emergence of a thing and its ultimate usefulness, its practical application and incorporation into a system of ends, are *toto coelo* separate" (GM II 12). Nietzsche consistently insisted, from at least *Daybreak* on, that an organ should not be explained by its function. See, for example, D 122.

state originated not in a contract, but rather in the actions of a ferocious pack of "blond beasts" upon a "shapeless" population (GM II 17).¹¹

Nietzsche's description of the onset of bad conscience suggests that the merciless and ruthless tyranny of the blond beasts generated not only bad conscience but the morality of custom. As we saw in the previous section, however, Nietzsche presents trade relations as the most primitive form of social organization and as preceding the state ("no form of civilization has been discovered which is so low that it did not display something of this relationship" [GM II 8]). For this reason, it seems that, in Nietzsche's story, the blond beasts might have come after the beginning of the morality of custom, although there is no denying that the formation of the state strongly reinforced the power of the morality of custom.¹²

Closely related to the previous problem is the fact that Nietzsche's description of the origin of bad conscience seems to contradict the idea that bad conscience did not originate in punishment. Nietzsche even seems to explicitly concede this point when he writes: "punishments are a primary instance of this kind of bulwark" (GM II 16). Matthias Risse argues that, when Nietzsche says that punishment does not bring about bad conscience, he is referring to bad conscience as a feeling of guilt (*Schuld*) and not to the primitive stage of bad conscience (*schlechtes Gewissen*) (Risse 2001, p. 58). Even though this solution may serve to dissipate any semblance of a contradiction in Nietzsche, what the latter might have had in mind is the notion that bad conscience was not a direct outcome of punishment. After all, as we will see, bad conscience manifests itself not in outward acts of cruelty but in the cruelty that we perpetrate against ourselves.

As a result of the repression resulting from the creation of the state, instincts and drives, which, according to Nietzsche, have a violent, aggressive, and cruel nature—after all, they are the will to power, at least in its more raw, pure manifestation—were precluded from being discharged outwardly.¹³ As a consequence, they were turned inward, toward the very being who harbored them.

---

11 As Leiter (2002, p. 205n17) and Janaway (2007, p. 95n3) point out, for example, when Nietzsche employs the term "blond beast," he is referring not to the Aryan race but to the lion species.

12 In GM 19, Nietzsche suggests that these "blond beasts" were the ancestors of the "noble races," the "aristocratic race" from the first essay of the *Genealogy*.) For an interpretation along these lines, see Richardson (2004, p. 83n33).

13 Katsafanas (2016, p. 57) argues that not all drives are internalized and repressed in this way, but only the aggressive, cruel ones. However, we should assume that most of the drives he cites as being non-aggressive, such as the drive for food or sex, must have had a violent expression, such as that of killing other human beings to take their food or committing rape, such that even those drives were severely repressed with the entrance into civilized society.

It is this instinct of cruelty directed toward oneself that defines bad conscience for Nietzsche:

> Those terrible bulwarks with which state organizations protected themselves against the old instincts of freedom—punishments are a primary instance of this kind of bulwark—had the result that all those instincts of the wild, free, roving man were turned backwards, against man himself. Animosity, cruelty, the pleasure of pursuing, raiding, changing and destroying—all this was pitted against the person who had such instincts: that is the origin of "bad conscience." (GM II 16)

As we saw, socialization led to the development of practical reason—humans began to postpone the immediate satisfaction of their impulses. Until that point, human beings had relied on their drives, but from that moment on the human being had to rely on intelligence, on calculating the means to achieve certain ends, in sum, on consciousness and practical reason (GM II 16). However, even when they were not immediately discharged, these drives did not simply cease to influence us: "and meanwhile, the old instincts had not suddenly ceased to make their demands!" (GM II 16). Since these drives could not vent their "energy" outwards, they became internalized and sought substitute gratifications: "but it was difficult and seldom possible to give in to them: they mainly had to seek new and as it were underground gratifications" (GM II 16).[14]

When Nietzsche describes the formation of the proto-state, he refers to its members as the raw material that is given shape by the "blond beasts of prey" and compares the community to a living being. Because of their formative function regarding the members of the community, Nietzsche likens the blond beasts to "artists" (GM II 17). At the same time, as a result of the repression of the cruel instincts (the raw will to power) of the members of the community, something similar takes place at an internal level:

> Fundamentally, it is the same active force as the one that is at work on a grand scale in those artists of violence and organizers, and that builds states, which here, internally, and on a smaller, pettier scale, turned backwards, in the "labyrinth of the breast," as Goethe would say, creates bad conscience for itself. (GM II 18)

---

14 Preceding Freud, Nietzsche develops the idea of the sublimation of drives. For example, since Nietzsche holds that our drives originally had a mainly cruel nature, he takes phenomena such as our aesthetic enjoyment of tragedy as a sublimated form of cruelty: "this is my claim: almost everything we call 'higher culture' is based on the spiritualization and deepening of *cruelty*" (BGE 229). Furthermore, in GM II 18, Nietzsche claims that the pleasure in "selflessness, self-denial, self-sacrifice ... belongs to cruelty." See also GM II 7–8. On Nietzsche's notion of sublimation, see Kaufmann (1974, pp. 218–223) and Richardson (1996, pp. 23 and 25).

With bad conscience "evolves in man what will later be called his 'soul.' The whole inner world, originally stretched thinly as though between two layers of skin, was expanded and extended itself and gained depth, breadth and height in proportion to the degree that the external discharge of man's instincts was *obstructed*" (GM II 16). The human being's entrance into civilized society thus led to a kind of splitting of the self between the natural, animal self and the reflective, conscious self. One part of the self (consciousness, reason) began to censor the other (the animal self, the instincts), thereby venting our primordial instinct for cruelty.[15] This was manifest in the fact that, for example, our rational part began to feel bad about our "old" animal self and to criticize, and even condemn it. As we will see in the last section, selfhood, for Nietzsche, is intrinsically tied to the capacity not only to restrain our instincts but to give them a certain order, organization, and hierarchy, just as the founder of the community gave order and meaning to its different parts. For Nietzsche, not only does the self have a social origin, but its structure is intrinsically social, even political, a "society constructed out of many 'souls'" (BGE 19), or a "society constructed out of drives and affects" (BGE 12).

What we have analyzed thus far is, as Nietzsche never tires of pointing out, only "bad conscience in its beginnings" (GM II 17), or what he also calls "animal 'bad conscience'" (GM III 20). Bad conscience would still go through a further major development, which consisted in its being interlaced with consciousness of debt. This took place in the following manner. As time passed, the community began to feel indebted to its forefathers, its founders (GM II 19), for its successes. In order to redeem this debt, it began to make sacrifices to them and to bring them all kinds of offerings. After some time, the founders of the most successful communities began to be worshipped and treated like gods. The origin of the gods can be traced precisely to this point, according to Nietzsche (GM II 19). As religious feeling became stronger and the gods more universal, the feeling of indebtedness grew as well, so that by the time Christianity entered the picture, the feeling of debt toward God reached its maximum: "the advent of the Christian God as the maximal god yet achieved, thus also brought about the appearance of the greatest feeling of indebtedness on earth" (GM II 20). However, Chris-

---

[15] Although Nietzsche does not identify them explicitly, bad conscience (*schlechtes Gewissen*) can be seen as identical to consciousness (*Bewusstsein*), or at least, as Richardson (2004, 93–94) points out, as a moralized version of self-consciousness. On the relation between conscience and self-consciousness, see also Ridley (1998, p. 19). The idea that the self is a complex structure whose parts can entertain various types of relations was a recurring motif in Nietzsche at least since *Human, All Too Human*. See, for example, HH I 57 and 137; D 113 and 119; and BGE 12, 19, 225, and 257.

tianity also brought another major change in our feeling of debt. Before Christianity, this debt was devoid of moral meaning; it was literally a material form of debt. With the arrival of Christianity, consciousness of debt was "pushed back" into bad conscience and became interlaced with it (GM II 21). The latter was moralized (resulting in what we can translate as the feeling of guilt) and deployed by bad conscience as an instrument of self-punishment.[16] As we will see, this resulted from the intervention of the ascetic priest, who first turned the idea of a debt toward God against us, the "debtors," and then conceived of the idea of an unredeemable debt/guilt (GM II 21). From this, Nietzsche manages to trace the origin of almost everything that is characteristic of the Christian doctrine, such as the idea of the inherently guilty, sinful, character of all existence, that is, original sin, and the idea of God as sacrificing himself for our sin:

> with the impossibility of paying back the debt, is conceived the impossibility of discharging the penance, the idea that it cannot be paid off ('*eternal* punishment'); ultimately, however, against the 'creditor,' and here we should think of the *causa prima* of man, the beginning of the human race, of his ancestor who is now burdened with a curse ('Adam,' 'original sin,' 'the will in bondage'), or of nature, from whose womb man originated and to whom the principle of evil is imputed (diabolization of nature), or of existence in general, which is left standing as *inherently worthless* (a nihilistic turning-away from existence, the desire for nothingness or desire for the 'antithesis,' to be other, Buddhism and such like)— until, all at once, we confront the paradoxical and horrifying expedient through which a martyred humanity has sought temporary relief, *Christianity's* stroke of genius: none other than God sacrificing himself for man's debt, none other than God paying himself back, God as the only one able to redeem man from what, to man himself, has become irredeemable—the creditor sacrificing himself for his debtor, out of love (would you credit it?—), out of *love* for his debtor! (GM II 21)

As a result, humans began to view their animal selves as inherently sinful, something for which they must atone, longing for an existence that was the opposite of the one they had "on this earth" (GM II 22). This longing for a completely different kind of existence is the gist of what Nietzsche calls the "ascetic ideal." The latter prevailed because it answered the human longing to know why we exist by giving meaning to the suffering that is inherent to the human

---

16 Reginster (2011) presents an alternative account of what the "moralization" of the consciousness of debt entails. According to Reginster's interpretation, Christianity did not create the feeling of guilt, but only the feeling of unredeemable guilt. By contrast, I think that debt and promises, at least before the advent of Christianity, do not have any moral status for Nietzsche in the sense that he does not think that agents felt any guilt when they failed to keep their word. This is why Nietzsche distinguishes debt towards the Christian God from debt towards other gods not only quantitatively but also qualitatively.

condition (GM III 28). According to Leiter, this suffering resulted from this existential *malaise*, but it also had more prosaic sources such as the physical suffering human beings inflict on each other, that is, precisely in cruelty (Leiter 2002, p. 256). Schopenhauer, too, recognized that the latter was one of the greatest sources of human suffering:

> we found above that suffering is an essential and unavoidable part of life, and as soon as it actually emerges in a particular form, one major source of suffering is *Eris*, the struggle between all individuals, the expression of the contradiction that afflicts the will to life from within, and which becomes manifest through the *principium individuationis*: fighting between beasts is an immediate and conspicuous, albeit cruel way of visualizing it. (Schopenhauer 2010, p. 360)

However, I take it that what Nietzsche means when he speaks of the suffering of the human being is to a great extent the result of the entrance of the human being into civilized life, that is, the notion that suffering results mainly from the "internal wound" of bad conscience. This finds support in the fact that Nietzsche describes the existence of the human beings prior to the creation of the state as much happier than ours and in the fact that his insight into the cruelty prevailing in primitive human relations should not be used as an argument in favor of pessimistic views of life (GM II 7).

According to Nietzsche, bad conscience is a sickness that is constitutive of or defines the human being as opposed to non-human animals: "with it, however, the worst and most insidious illness was introduced, one from which mankind has not yet recovered; man's sickness of *man*, of *himself*" (GM II 16).[17] It is to this disease that the ascetic priest is supposed to provide a cure, although the latter is, on Nietzsche's view, a mere palliative and only manages to make the human being sicker (GM III 17). As we learn in the third essay of the *Genealogy*, the ascetic priest created the idea of irredeemable guilt toward God and the inherently sinful character of earthly existence as a way to help the sick to deal with their suffering. He succeeds in this by making use of the fact that every sufferer looks instinctively for someone to hold accountable and to blame for her suffering (GM III 15). In turn, he achieves this by inverting the direction of *ressentiment* and imparts the idea that it is our wretched, human self who is to blame for our inherently suffering condition (GM III 15 and 20).

Although the concept of God and transcendence may have existed prior to the invention of the feeling of guilt or the development of bad conscience into

---

[17] See GM II 19: "bad conscience is a sickness, there is no point in denying it." See also GM II 16 and 22; GM III 13, 14, 15, 17, and 28; and *A* 14.

guilt, the appearance of the latter marked the beginning of the domination of the ascetic ideal, inasmuch as this is characterized by the devaluation and negation of this life and the positing of a completely different kind of existence as an ideal by which the former is judged, condemned, and negated. According to the ascetic ideal, our present existence only has value in relation to the idea of this other-worldly existence. The ascetic ideal negates this life by affirming an otherworldly life: "inasmuch as he affirms this 'other world,' must he not therefore deny its opposite, this world, *our* world, in doing so?" (GM III 24; see also GM III 11 and 13). We should keep in mind, however, that the domination of the ascetic ideal does not entail that the world beyond is necessarily viewed as existing. The beyond can simply be nothingness, the pure negation of this world (as is the case with the Buddhist notion of Nirvana or in Schopenhauer's philosophy). As Nietzsche so often emphasizes, the ascetic ideal asserts its domination even when belief in God is discredited, even after the death of God. All it takes is for existence in this world to be seen as an error, as morally condemnable or reproachable, as something that should not be in light of this otherworldly, ideal existence.

Despite all this, bad conscience has a profoundly ambiguous status, for Nietzsche.[18] Even if it is true that it lies at the core of the ascetic ideal, it is not necessarily an instrument of the negation of life. As Nietzsche makes clear at the end of the second section of the *Genealogy*, even if it remains problematic, a reversal of the intertwining of bad conscience with consciousness of debt/guilt is conceivable to the effect that bad conscience becomes intertwined with the ascetic negation of life, or what he calls the "will to nothingness":

> a reverse experiment should be possible *in principle*—but who has sufficient strength?—by this, I mean an intertwining of bad conscience with *perverse* inclinations, all those otherworldly aspirations, alien to the senses, the instincts, to nature, to animals, in short all the ideals which up to now have been hostile to life and have defamed the world. (GM II 24)

Following this passage, Nietzsche refers to his mythical figure of Zarathustra as an example of someone who can bring about this reversal. In the following, final section of this chapter, I will turn to the figure of the "sovereign individual" as a case study of what a Nietzschean ideal might look like and of how a more affirmative use of conscience might be made.

---

[18] On the ambiguity and the different meanings of bad conscience and Nietzsche's ambivalent stance towards it, see Ridley (1998, pp. 17–26).

5 The Sovereign Individual

As we saw above, the interlacing of bad conscience with the feeling of indebtedness toward God, resulting in what has often been translated as the feeling of guilt, is presented as contingent and as something that, at least ideally, could be reverted. In this last section, I would like to point to one of the possible ways in which we might overcome bad conscience on Nietzsche's view, or at least put it to more positive and affirmative use. This is the case when it comes to the figure Nietzsche calls the "sovereign individual." Nietzsche introduces this enigmatic figure in the second section of the second essay:

> Let us place ourselves ... at the end of this immense process where the tree actually bears fruit, where society and its morality of custom finally reveal what they were simply *the means to:* we then find the *sovereign individual* as the ripest fruit on its tree, like only to itself, having freed itself from the morality of custom, an autonomous, supra-ethical individual (because 'autonomous' and 'ethical' are mutually exclusive), in short, we find a man with his own, independent, enduring will, whose *prerogative it is to promise*—and in him a proud consciousness quivering in every muscle of *what* he has finally achieved and incorporated, an actual awareness of power and freedom, a feeling that man in general has reached completion. (GM II 2)

The sovereign individual is presented as the final outcome of the "morality of custom." For Nietzsche, this means that he is the one who is able to promise to the highest degree, that is, to pledge himself, his future, because he stays true to his word; he is the farthest away from being a slave to mood and desire (GM II 3). He thus corresponds to the ideal of a truly responsible human being and is distinguished by the consistency of his character—what he wants now is also what he will want in the future.

As we can see from this short characterization, if we take the sovereign individual as one of the embodiments of his ideal human being, Nietzsche is far from urging a return to a pre-societal, purely animal condition.[19] It is true that Nietzsche describes the sovereign individual as supra-ethical "because 'autonomous' and 'ethical' are mutually exclusive" (GM II 2). In a certain way, Nietzsch-

---

[19] In taking the sovereign individual to be an embodiment (of sorts) of Nietzsche's ideal human being, I follow what is still the mainstream of Anglophone Nietzschean scholarship, represented by the likes of Ridley (1998 and 2009), Richardson (2004), Gemes (2009), Owen (2009), and Katsafanas (2016), among others. In taking this position, I am also arguing against a smaller number of scholars, such as Acampora (2006) and Hatab (2008), who hold that the sovereign individual in no way represents or exemplifies Nietzsche's ideal human being, as well as those like Leiter (2002 and 2011), who, to say the least, have highly deflationary readings of it.

e's sovereign individual lives above morality (*übersittlich*), if we understand morality as the "herd-instinct in the individual" (GS 116), that is, as tied to actions that are usual and expected in a certain community.[20] However, this does not mean that the sovereign individual is amoral, or even supra-moral. Although he has freed himself from the 'morality of custom,' he "has his own *standard of value*" (GM II 2). This standard seems to consist precisely in the ability to "keep his word," that is, in being able to carry out plans or projects without yielding to the circumstances. In this respect, he seems to correspond to the apex of practical rationality and thus to be closer to a Kantian model of agency and autonomy than, for example, a Schopenhauerian model. Concerning this point, I agree with Reginster that, contrary to the individual who is not allowed to promise, the sovereign individual sees keeping his word as an end in itself and as a sign of his moral worth and standing (Reginster 2011, pp. 71–73).[21] From this we can conclude that, for Nietzsche, just like Kant, freedom in the sense of autonomy is the supreme (and perhaps unique) value.[22] What distinguishes Nietzsche from Kant in this regard is the way in which each specifies the content of this value. For Nietzsche, practical reason is not "pure," a priori, and for that reason it does not provide a universal moral law (*GS* 335). The sovereign individual's injunction is to act always according to the values he himself has created. Thus, Nietzsche radicalizes Kant's notion of autonomy in that for the former, being autonomous entails individual agency and precisely *not* acting as every rational agent would.[23]

What distinguishes the sovereign individual from ordinary human beings is that his actions display coherence over time, manifesting a stable hierarchy of drives. Just as the blond beasts managed to give shape to a primitive society, the sovereign individual has fully given shape to himself as an individual, such that there is no longer any dissonance between his animal and his cultural self. This does not mean that he has been totally socialized—as we saw, the sovereign individual asserts himself, to a certain extent, by standing out from others

---

20 In *Daybreak* 9, Nietzsche refers to the free individual as the one who has freed himself from the fetters of tradition. On morality as the herd instinct in the human being, see, for example, BGE 191, 199, 201, and 202.

21 According to Reginster (2011, pp. 70–73), the difference between the sovereign individual and the one who is not allowed to promise is that what drives the former to keep his promise is not fear of pain but rather a feeling of power.

22 According to Gemes (2009, pp. 46–47), there is a normative dimension to free will that concerns the value of being a self, that is, the value of freedom. On the idea that freedom is Nietzsche's ultimate value, see Richardson (2004, pp. 95–132).

23 On the differences between Kant's and Nietzsche's views of autonomy, see Owen (2009) and Katsafanas (2016, pp. 232–256).

or society—but rather that he has overcome the tension between nature and culture.[24] Although Nietzsche does not expand on this in the passage on the sovereign individual, we can surmise that, in place of being constituted by an anarchic plurality of drives, the sovereign individual has integrated and unified them into a coherent whole.[25] For Nietzsche, not only does the self have the character of an achievement, but this achievement consists in large part in attaining some kind of individuality, or even singularity, that distinguishes it from the masses, the herd, the community. At least regarding his ideal of selfhood, Nietzsche was still partly indebted to the Romantic tradition.[26]

Just like the pre-societal human beast, the sovereign individual is affirmative —he says "'yes' to himself" (GM II 2). Contrary to the former, however, he does this self-consciously, and like the civilized human being he is capable of self-control to the highest degree. For this reason, although retaining the egoism that is characteristic of the pre-societal beast and being more concerned with himself than with others, Nietzsche's ideal agent as expressed in the figure of the sovereign individual is not defined by the exercise of violence against others (as the creators of the state were).[27] His instinct of cruelty has been completely internalized. It is perhaps for this reason that Nietzsche calls "conscience" his "dominant instinct" (GM II 2). Note that Nietzsche does not use the adjective "bad" to qualify conscience here. This implies that conscience is now working as an affirmative, positive force. Ridley distinguishes between "bad bad conscience," "neutral bad conscience," and "good bad conscience" (Ridley 1998, pp. 21–22). I also think that the sovereign individual's conscience is an instance of "good bad conscience."

---

[24] The idea that the sovereign individual overcomes the schism between nature and culture was already put forth by Ridley: "in the sovereign individual, culture has, as one might put it, become nature. He is borne up rather than oppressed by his socialization, and his capacities and dispositions are once again in harmony—as the sea animals' were—with the conditions of his existence" (Ridley 2009, p. 183).

[25] Gemes explores the notion that Nietzsche's idea of the self entails a certain order, hierarchy, and unity of the drives: "To have a character is to have a stable, unified, and integrated, hierarchy of drives. This is a very demanding condition that most humans fail to meet" (Gemes 2009, p. 38; see also p. 44). On the issue of unity and harmony among the drives, see also Richardson (2009, p. 133). For a critique of the conception of the self as consisting in a relation of drives, see Katsafanas (2016, pp. 199–200).

[26] On Nietzsche's idea of the self as an achievement, see Gemes (2009) and Katsafanas (2016, pp. 197 and 200). On the relation between the Romantic conception of selfhood and Nietzsche's conception, see Katsafanas (2016, pp. 209–219).

[27] Ridley (1998, p. 145) argues that the sovereign individual corresponds not to a return to a beastly condition, but rather to the self-overcoming of bad conscience.

Despite all that has been said, there is no getting around the fact that Nietzsche's description of the sovereign individual is rather vague, and for that reason there is much discussion in the secondary literature concerning its meaning. To complicate things further, there are no other occurrences of the notion of "sovereign individual" in Nietzsche's published and unpublished writings (Hatab 2008, p. 76; and Leiter 2011, p. 108). One of the main points of contention in the literature is the question of when, exactly, the sovereign individual is supposed to have existed in Nietzsche's story (Janaway 2007, p. 116; Gemes 2009, p. 37; and Ridley 2009, p. 181). Has he or she already existed at some point in world history? Is he or she yet to come? Is he or she an ideal? Or a mere fantasy? Given that the sovereign individual bears some resemblance to the "masters" of the first essay or the founders of the state of the second essay, and given that he is described as the "late fruit" of the morality of custom, one could argue that he may have already existed at some point. However, the latter line of inquiry does not seem to hold much water. As we saw in the previous section, even if it is unclear from Nietzsche's text whether the blond beasts gave rise to the morality of custom, there is no doubt that they contributed to it in some form and even intensified it by creating the state, whereas the sovereign individual purportedly corresponds to its culmination. In addition, Nietzsche says that the first founders of the state "do not know what guilt, responsibility, consideration are" (GM II 17). Moreover, Nietzsche says that conscience "has already a long history before it" (GM II 2) and that it is "a ripe fruit, but also a *late* fruit" (GM II 3). I believe that this passage is intended to link the discussion of the sovereign individual with the discussion of bad conscience that is introduced many sections later in the same essay.

One could argue for something along these lines against the idea that the sovereign individual corresponds in any way to the masters of the first essay (who, in turn, must be descendants of the blond beasts who founded the state). It is true that Nietzsche describes the sovereign individual in a way that recalls his description of the masters of the first essay inasmuch as both are presented as models of self-affirmation (GM II 3; cf. GM I 10). However, contrary to the masters' brute affirmation, the sovereign individual's affirmation has a different character insofar as the latter is self-aware. The sovereign individual has a "proud consciousness quivering in every muscle of *what* he has finally achieved and incorporated, an actual awareness of power and freedom, a feeling that man in general has reached completion" (GM II 2). By contrast, the "noble tribes" belong to a "*middle* period" (GM II 19). Thus, the sovereign individual is not the master of the first essay; if he is supposed to have existed at all in Nietzsche's narrative, he must come after the master and noble, who first created the values of good and bad.

That the sovereign individual presupposes the creation of bad conscience should come as no surprise if we recall from the previous section that Nietzsche presents the emergence of the latter as profoundly ambiguous. On the one hand, bad conscience is a profound illness, and as a result the human being is a "sick animal" (GM III 13) On the other hand, Nietzsche says that bad conscience is a sickness but one "rather like pregnancy" (GM II 19). He thinks that bad conscience makes the human being "profound" (GM II 18), "interesting" (GM Preface 6), and that it brings him a certain promise:

> Since that time, man has been *included* among the most unexpected and exciting throws of dice played by Heraclitus' 'great child,' call him Zeus or fate,—he arouses interest, tension, hope, almost certainty for himself, as though something were being announced through him, were being prepared, as though man were not an end but just a path, an episode, a bridge, a great promise. (GM II 16)[28]

It could very well be that the sovereign individual corresponds to those extraordinary figures, for whom Nietzsche professed admiration at one point or another in his life, individuals like Goethe, Beethoven, Napoleon, etc., and in an earlier phase, Wagner and even Schopenhauer. The topic of the conditions of the emergence and creation of exceptional individuals that constitute the meaning of culture permeated Nietzsche's thought since its beginnings. In this case, the sovereign individual would be an exceptional figure who appears every once in a while. Another reason to think that the sovereign individual may have already existed is the fact that Nietzsche describes him as the necessary outcome of the morality of custom ("let us place ourselves, on the other hand, at the end of this immense process where the tree actually bears fruit, where society and its morality of custom finally reveal what they were simply *the means to*" [GM II 2]). This last quote must be qualified, however. If the sovereign individual corresponds to the culmination of the whole process of the morality of custom, then the history of western civilization is, for Nietzsche, a history of a falling away from that goal. It is as if something went wrong after the upsurge of bad conscience due to the latter's becoming intermingled with consciousness of guilt/debt, or, in other words, with the ascetic ideal in its Christian form. For this reason, it makes more sense, given Nietzsche's description, to think that the sovereign individual has a merely ideal status and that he is yet to come. As a result of Christianity and the ascetic ideal, far from being a necessary out-

---

28 See also A 14: "comparatively speaking, humans are the biggest failures, the sickliest animals who have strayed the most dangerously far from their instincts—but of course and in spite of everything, the most interesting animals as well!"

come of human evolution throughout history, the sovereign individual is only an ideal that may (or may not) be possible in the future, according to whether the ascetic ideal is defeated and the pervasive feeling of guilt or sinfulness, that is to say, what Nietzsche calls the will to nothingness is eradicated from the world.[29] How Nietzsche thinks this might be possible and the more precise nature of his alternative to the ascetic ideal are beyond the scope of this paper and must be left for another occasion.[30]

Bibliography

Acampora, Christa Davis (2006): "On Sovereignity and Overhumanity: Why It Matters How We Read Nietzsche's *Genealogy* II:2." In: Christa Davis Acampora (Ed.): *Nietzsche's* On Genealogy of Morals: *Critical Essays*. Lanham: Rowan & Littlefield, pp. 147–161.
Gemes, Ken (2009): "Nietzsche on Free Will, Autonomy, and the Sovereign Individual." In: Ken Gemes and Simon May (Eds.): *Nietzsche on Freedom and Autonomy*. Oxford: Oxford University Press, pp. 33–49.
Hatab, Lawrence J. (2008). *Nietzsche's* On the Genealogy of Morality: *An Introduction*. Cambridge: Cambridge University Press.
Janaway, Christopher (2007): *Beyond Selflessness: Reading Nietzsche's* Genealogy. Oxford: Oxford University Press.
Katsafanas, Paul (2016): *The Nietzschean Self: Moral Psychology, Agency, and the Unconscious*. Oxford: Oxford University Press.
Kaufmann, Walter (1974): *Nietzsche. Philosopher, Psychologist, Antichrist*. 4th ed. Princeton: Princeton University Press.
Leiter, Brian (2002): *Nietzsche on Morality*. London: Routledge.
Leiter, Brian (2011): "Who Is the Sovereign Individual? Nietzsche on Freedom." In: Simon May (Ed.): *Nietzsche's* On the Genealogy of Morality: *A Critical Guide*. Cambridge: Cambridge University Press, pp. 101–119.
Nietzsche, Friedrich (1994): *On the Genealogy of Morality*. Edited by Keith Ansell-Pearson and translated by Carol Diethe. Cambridge: Cambridge University Press.
Nietzsche, Friedrich (1996): *Human, All Too Human. A Book for Free Spirits*. Translated by R. J. Hollingdale. Cambridge: Cambridge University Press.
Nietzsche, Friedrich (1997): *Daybreak: Thoughts on the Prejudices of Morality*. Edited by Maudemarie Clark and Brian Leiter and translated by R. J. Hollingdale. Cambridge: Cambridge University Press.
Nietzsche, Friedrich (2001): *Gay Science: With a Prelude in German Rhymes and an Appendix of Songs*. Edited by Bernard Williams and translated by Josefine Nauckhoff and Adrian del Caro. Cambridge: Cambridge University Press.

---

[29] On the "will to nothingness" see GM I 24; GM III 14 and 28.
[30] This work was funded by national funds through the FCT – Fundação para a Ciência e a Tecnologia, I.P., under the Norma Transitória – DL 57/2016/CP1453/CT0035 and UIDB/00183/2020.

Nietzsche, Friedrich (2002): *Beyond Good and Evil*. Edited by Rolf-Peter Horstmann and Judith Norman and translated by Judith Norman. Cambridge: Cambridge University Press.

Nietzsche, Friedrich (2005a): *The Anti-Christ: A Curse on Christianity*. In: *The Anti-Christ, Ecce Homo, Twilight of the Idols, and Other Writings*. Edited by Aaron Ridley and Judith Norman and translated by Judith Norman. Cambridge: Cambridge University Press, pp. 1–67.

Nietzsche, Friedrich (2005b): *Ecce Homo: How to Become What you Are*. In: *The Anti-Christ, Ecce Homo, Twilight of the Idols, and Other Writings*. Edited by Aaron Ridley and Judith Norman and translated by Judith Norman. Cambridge: Cambridge University Press, pp. 69–151.

Nietzsche, Friedrich (2005b): *Twilight of the Idols or How to Philosophize with the Hammer*. In: *The Anti-Christ, Ecce Homo, Twilight of the Idols, and Other Writings*. Edited by Aaron Ridley and Judith Norman and translated by Judith Norman. Cambridge: Cambridge University Press, pp. 155–229.

Nietzsche, Friedrich (2006): *Thus Spoke Zarathustra: A Book for All and None*. Edited by Adrian del Caro and Robert Pippin and translated by Adrian del Caro. Cambridge: Cambridge University Press.

Owen, David (2009): "Autonomy, Self-Respect, and Self-Love: Nietzsche on Ethical Agency." In: Ken Gemes and Simon May (Eds.): *Nietzsche on Freedom and Autonomy*. Oxford, Oxford University Press, pp. 197–221.

Plato: *Republic*.

Reginster, Bernard (2006): *The Affirmation of Life: Nietzsche on Overcoming Nihilism*. Cambridge: Harvard University Press.

Reginster, Bernard (2011): "The Genealogy of Guilt." In: Simon May (Ed.); *Nietzsche's* On the Genealogy of Morality. Cambridge: Cambridge University Press, pp. 56–77.

Richardson, John (1996): *Nietzsche's System*. Oxford: Oxford University Press.

Richardson, John (2004): *Nietzsche's New Darwinism*. Oxford: Oxford University Press.

Richardson, John (2009): "Nietzsche's Freedoms." In: Ken Gemes and Simon May (Eds.): *Nietzsche on Freedom and Autonomy*. Oxford: Oxford University Press, pp. 127–149.

Ridley, Aaron (1998): *Nietzsche's Conscience: Six Character Studies from the* Genealogy. Ithaca: Cornell University Press.

Ridley, Aaron (2009): "Nietzsche's Intentions: What the Sovereign Individual Promises." In: Ken Gemes and Simon May (Eds.): *Nietzsche on Freedom and Autonomy*. Oxford: Oxford University Press, pp. 181–195.

Risse, Matthias (2001): "The Second Treatise in the *Genealogy of Morality:* Nietzsche on the Origin of the Bad Conscience." In: *European Journal of Philosophy* 9. No. 1, pp. 55–81.

Schopenhauer, Arthur (2010): *The World as Will and Representation*, vol. 1. Edited by Christopher Janaway and translated by Judith Norman, Alistair Welchman, and Christopher Janaway. Cambridge: Cambridge University Press.

Agata Mergler
Walter Benjamin's Media Theory in the Times of Platform Nihilism

Abstract: This chapter uses Benjamin's understanding of nihilistic temporal structure of modernity as commodity and his theoretical readings of mass media to assess the ability of two online phenomena, memes and NFT (non-fungible token) art/crypto art, to resist platform nihilism and provide profane illuminations that are able to disrupt the progress of history seen as the eternal return. The chapter follows the understanding of platform nihilism as a contemporary situation of globalized digital social networks presented by Geert Lovink and Nolen Gertz, and the roots of this recognition found in Walter Benjamin's and Friedrich Nietzsche's thoughts on nihilism, respectively. The focus on the phenomenon of crypto art and the meme culture demonstrates how these may be expressions as well as subversions of the platform nihilism online. Furthermore, using network culture research and opinions of digital art stakeholders, the chapter reveals that current nihilism is again part of a capitalist commodity structure. Thus Benjamin's cautiously optimistic view of mass media's revolutionary abilities and pessimistic views of fascist takeover of mass media of his time lend themselves to an assessment of the current moment in development of memes and NFT art. Again, Benjamin's questioning of the socio-historical entanglement of media as conditions of possibility of change proves its relevance.

1 Introduction

The Internet has been decried as a nihilist medium for over thirty years.[1] The offline romanticism of Web 1.0 in the digital platform's current moment, where there appears to be no "in real life" outside the online, seems irrelevant. I would like to present here a reading of platform nihilism that is not meant to call into question various identifiable issues with mediated and networked life, starting with issues raised in early days of the web: a lack of bodily presence, impoverished sensual perception, the flattening of connections and meaning. The most profound effect of nihilism is the realization of the senselessness of life: the lack of meaning previously found in transcendence and prescribed

---

1 That is, since around 1989/1990, when commercial dial-up Internet access, and the invention of World Wide Web popularized the use of the Internet.

moral values. Nihilism connected with information technologies has profoundly influenced our structure of meaning; it was already the case with mass communication, as Barbara Stiegler interprets Nietzsche's observations on newspapers (Stiegler 2009, p. 127). Now, "Facebook, Google, Twitter, [and] YouTube … exist to generate information," and because most of their editorial work is done by "proprietary algorithms—automated agnosticism, digital nihilism," they claim a lack of bias, but "bias is about meaning, whereas social media platforms are fundamentally nihilistic" (Seymour 2020, p. 142).

Geert Lovink elevates Walter Benjamin's profound, nihilistic "melancholy" above "today's children of Saturn," nihilist "unbearable lightness of the social" media platform-oriented life—spreading FOMO (fear of missing out) and worries about "responses to a selfie" (Lovink 2019, p. 54–55). However, platform nihilism needs to be recognized as more than an individual being "tired because we're wired" (Lovink 2019, p.150). Rather, one has to remember that the extreme side of nihilism has always been the aesthetic pleasure derived from self-annihilation (Benjamin 2008f, p. 42). If one takes suicide and planetary crisis as nihilism's avatars, the stakes become incontrovertible. The extractivist platform economy has a growing ecological impact that depends on both our digital addiction and the aestheticization of politics the digital enables. Moreover, it may be building toward a new planetary crisis due to unknown threats around AI.

In returning here to Benjamin and following the research of scholars who work to understand media from the inside, not simply by offering empty criticisms based on nostalgia for previously dominant media forms, I propose a less individualizing take on the nihilism connected to digital technologies. For Benjamin, politicizing art is the key to revolution, but how can we "politicize our own distraction" when platforms monopolize and commodify our attention so successfully (Lovink 2019, p. 43)?

What I wish to demonstrate is how two contemporary media phenomena connected to platform nihilism invite a Benjaminian reading as a way of thinking about overcoming nihilism. First, I look at memes: a phenomenon with an avant-garde-like, but mass-produced, character. In the laughter that memes induce, "Benjamin would have sensed a flash of liberation" (Lovink and Tuters 2018, para. 19). My analysis demonstrates how the virality-laughter-politicization of memes could follow Benjamin's "Reproducibility-distraction-politicization" triad (Benjamin 2008e, p. 57), and how we might end up with aestheticized politics—and appropriation of the memes-sphere by the alt-right—instead.

Next, I consider non-fungible tokens (NFTs) and crypto art, and explain how an initially welcomed revolution for digital artists promised seizing the means of making "actual money" from their artistic work by making it irreproducible online revealed itself as part of the capitalist structure of commodification (Connor

2021, para. 4). The questions surrounding NFTs as guarantees of authenticity and originality direct my reading back to Benjamin's research on cult value and the loss of aura, and his struggle with nihilism in his time, posing the following question: why are we returning to a nineteenth-century view of art? The answer might demonstrate that, despite the decentralized character of NFTs and crypto art, NFTs reification of media art might prove to be only the eternal return of the same in the "new" (Benjamin 1999, p. 546), as the temporality and structure of modernity and capitalism seeking to control any object as an economic asset has not been disturbed in any significant way.

In the first section, I will sketch the functioning of platform nihilism. Then, I will apply Benjamin's media theory and his weak messianism stemming from his confrontation with Nietzsche's legacy of nihilism (McFarland 2013, p. viii) to memes and crypto art. Benjamin does not offer an easy way out of nihilism, a historical-materialist revolution as part of inevitable historical progress, rather he describes a non-synthetic view of the dialectic, offering a weak hope—a revelation—that might appear for a moment, for an undetermined future breaking out of the eternal return (Ponzi 2017, p. 255). What technological and media development provides, and memes and NFTs illustrate, is a dialectic between the revolutionary and reactionary, or, characteristic of modernity—dialectics at a standstill (Benjamin 1999, p. 462), where active nihilism (Löwith 1997, p. 50) may only provide weak messianic hope for its disruption.

2 Platform Nihilism

"We are in the Age of Indifference, also known as the Nietzschean Century," states Lovink (Lovink 2017, p. xiii). Is it possible to discuss the nihilism of contemporary media culture without devaluing this culture from the outset? Critique of platform nihilism is the effect of a cultural, social, and philosophic work where media-specific knowledge is crucial, not for offering empty criticisms based on nostalgia, nor as a form of elitism, but rather for demonstrating the conditions of the human-platform relations. That is, this critique posits at its center that no side is neutral in these society-media-technology relations. For Benjamin, distraction and new forms of media are what brings mediality and technology into focus (Kang 2014, p. 20). Since the old functions of art, spirituality, ritual, and the moral with their reduced aura were not adequate to the needs of mass society, the new media assumed the function of addressing this new social reality. As a result, how the various sides of this equation shaped and expressed the contemporary (historical) moment required discussion (Benjamin 2008f, p. 36). Similarly, contemporary research oscillates between both sides of human-technology relations. With focus on social media conditions of cultural practices, Tero Karppi summarizes the issue at hand thus: "neither the human who becomes and interacts with the system nor the system ... where we operate should be taken as given," but "the relations between the two should be seen as actively forming, taking place in various affective encounters" (Karppi 2018, p. 50).

In evaluating platform nihilism, we must understand that nihilism is not simply meant as a pejorative, as it has a productive side as well. Nietzsche's distinction of nihilism's possible meanings as presented by Löwith seems to best illustrate this. And it is Löwith who mediated the understanding of Nietzsche for Benjamin. Löwith clarifies Nietzsche's nihilism as, on the one hand, "a symptom of the enervation of the will of an emptied existence, but on the other hand ... a first sign of the strengthening of the will and of a willed destruction—a nihilism of passive weakness or of active strength" (Löwith 1997, p. 50). When one is confronted with the death of God and collapse of all values, empty, transcendenceless existence, nihilism is either a symptom of the will becoming passive and weak, or a symptom of its activation, when its strengthening *through* nihilism promises the overcoming of it. One is passive, while the other is active nihilism.

The detrimental influence of media on the public has been discussed since Plato's *Phaedrus* and assessment of writing's nature as obscuring the truth which is accessible without mediation in speech and dialogue. Nietzsche also criticizes "the hammering of the telegraph" (NL 1877, 22[76], KSA 8, p. 392) and mass printing press, the new media of his time.² According to Stiegler in Nietzsche's view, the media-created age of machines imposes upon us a new responsibility of "organizing ourselves in organizing mediatically our own modes of perception of the flux" taking place across the disorganized bodies of a mass society (Stiegler 2009, p. 137). Nietzsche's question regarding the intimate connection between mass media and nihilism had an impact on Benjamin's history and media research. As his diagnosis of "loss of aura" is not a rejection of mass media, so are Nietzsche's remarks not a condemnation of those either. Stiegler proclaims Nietzsche as the first philosopher to recognize "the necessity of media" as "organs of remote love," notwithstanding that the development of new media also functions as "catalyst of nihilism" in our time's new, accelerated history, which Nietzsche foresaw (Stiegler 2009, pp. 127–128).

Internet critics like Lovink focus on the "signs of existential midlife crisis" regarding Internet culture as well as expressions of the passive nihilism of users (Lovink 2019, p. 4), while the technology ethicist Nolen Gertz makes de-

---

2 See Stiegler 2009, p. 125.

tailed use of Nietzsche's theory of nihilism in his analysis of the digital sphere. Discussing tools from wearable digital technology such as FitBit to various social media and search engine platforms, Gertz translates the different forms of passive nihilism proposed by Nietzsche into their corresponding digital age manifestations. One common focus of these critiques is that we project our responsibility for being human onto digital platforms, similar to the way we previously projected it onto a transcendent being (Lovink 2021, para. 7). We make these platforms into safe places "in which fluid comfort is preferred over dragging complexity" (Lovink 2021, para. 7), where we happily drop into an empty trance, disappointed with the real world (Seymour 2020, p. 212). And so, the various human-nihilism relations such as Nietzsche's self-hypnosis turned now into techno-hypnosis, (Gertz 2018, pp. 61–62), or into a capitalist trance of gamification, permeate all forms of platform nihilism (Seymour 2020, p. 215). In Gertz's vision of online life, it is saturated with Nietzschean forms and language: "Herd networking" is a new form of the "herd instinct," with followers that gather on Facebook, Instagram, or Twitter where "orgies of feeling" have become "orgies of clicking" (Gertz 2018, pp. 138 and 162). The guilt-inducing method of dealing with nihilism through releasing and acting through emotions without regard for consequences also appears to be present on almost all digital platforms. These expressions of nihilism have to do with psychopolitics (see Han 2017), that is, the ways that our attention is corralled through manipulation (Seymour 2020 p. 119) which uses attention as "a type of distraction" (Pettman 2015, p. 48). Distraction in new media is connected to what Benjamin develops following Nietzsche according to McFarland, that is, understanding the temporality of modernity, that modernity's "temporal deep structure" is one of commodity (McFarland 2013, p. 260). This is demonstrated in platform media as hypersynchronization: an evolution of the synchronicity of industrial worker's time, for example, as visualized in films like *Metropolis*, which was aesthetically different but politically and economically represented the same form of temporality and exploitation of time (Pettman 2015, p. 27–28).

Lovink suggests that designers, administrators, marketers, and tech entrepreneurs are today's shepherds and priests, though they are unaccountable ones because "their guidance…[is] experienced [only] as algorithmic governance" (Lovink 2021 par. 10). Karppi paints a more nihilistic picture of social media users as *dividuals* – a Deleuze's description of machinic subjectivities deprived of agency (Karppi 2018, pp. 21–22). Byung-Chul Han presupposes our inherent nihilistic will to "unfreedom" as a basis for Web 2.0's entry into "the age of digital psychopolitics," or, presenting this description as a religious category, the era of Big Data is a "time of devotion" with the active submission of users to active steering (Han 2017, pp. 8–9 and 12).

Within these various research approaches, one can discern that either the subject's resignation from responsibility for their existence when faced with platform nihilism (like in Han's cultural critique), or that elements of the media, machine, software, the background coding, and the legal codes (terms of use, service, privacy, etc.), that dispossess or limit users' agency become the focus (like in the more posthuman perspective of Karppi). Expanding on the religious and moral angles, thanks to Google, the issue of good and evil has gained a specific meaning in this epoch of (in)visible codes (digital and legal). With Google's well-known motto, and only "commandment" in its employee code of conduct, "don't be evil," Gertz follows Ian Bogost's claims that this simple prescription makes evil into a "matter of serviceability," that is, no longer a moral category, but an engineering one: evil is what stands in a way of progress, not virtue (Gertz 2018, p. 200). Progress, then, becomes a more important value than virtue, or at least synonymous with it. Technology companies creatively destroy traditional moral values exactly as, through hypersynchronization, they destroy traditional temporality that enables an authentic collective "we" through their aim of self-perpetuation (Pettman 2015, p. 70). As Gertz remarks, they do not seek to create "new values but new humans, posthumans" (Gertz 2018, p. 209). This follows the internal logic of modernity as recognized by Nietzsche and Benjamin: that progress is fundamentally nihilistic. For Benjamin, capitalism is an "extreme cultic religion" (Benjamin 2002, p. 288), and in its aimless madness of mechanism, and due to historical conditioning, it is effectively nihilist (Ponzi 2017, p. 4).

In making our moral, spiritual, social, and emotional needs engineering problems, they are not addressed. Our sadness is "flatly distributed across our plateau" (Lovink 2019, p. 55), simultaneously covering the violence that is inherent to the technology that is mediating our humanity. The development of the networked computer, a result of military and intelligence efforts during World War II and the Cold War period was not innocent (Lovink 2019, p. 77), and so the Internet that resulted is not guiltless either. In *The Message is Murder*, Jonathan Beller states that "Digital culture is built on and out of material and epistemological forms of racial capitalism, colonialism, imperialism, and permanent war. This violence is literally inscribed in machine architectures" (Beller 2018, p. 2).

Thus, platform nihilism is not an individual user issue, and as all machines are social before being technological, talking about technology means talking about society itself (Seymour 2020, p. 23). Furthermore, for Benjamin, research into society and culture requires historical reflection, indicating to us that all of the developments discussed here are part of modernity's temporality of eternal return of the new (and the same) and the capitalist structure of commodity. Dominic Pettman describes the experience of social media obsession with "real time" temporal standard: "you never step in the same live stream twice. And yet the digital river is tediously familiar" (Pettman 2015, p. 16). Digital platforms are capitalist media ventures as the mass media were before them—the Big Four (Google, Facebook, Amazon, and Apple) like newspapers owned by Axel Springer or Rupert Murdoch are advertising platforms and marketplaces (Seymour 2020, p. 142). However, what is new is the way in which this monopolistic power takes over consumers themselves, making their very attention into a commodity. This attention economy is what most researchers—whether lamenting on or proposing corrections to media platforms—point to when describing the network condition in which "God is not ... the Google guys, but the imperative to make money" (Pettman 2015, p. 17). Users are always on some platform, techno-hypnotized, as Karppi demonstrates in his research on disconnection in the context of Facebook; for this platform's privacy settings there is no outside, only "off-Facebook" (Karppi 2021, p. 53), and its monetizing powers of observing our habits go beyond the particular platforms it owns—beyond online, and even beyond death itself (Karppi 2018, p. 94). Lovink develops Jodi Dean's claim about platforms being doubly extractive, that is, platform users in addition to creating the content that populates networks, also pay via the collection of their data (Lovink 2021, para. 13). On such a platform producers and users are "the entreprecariat" without productivity or satisfaction[3]. Bringing this to a planetary perspective, McKenzie Wark writes that this accelerated, abstract form of commodification "enables all of the earth to appear as a resource to be mobilized under the control of information" (Wark 2019, p. 37).

There is no innocence. The contemporary democratization of sadness through digital media follows from the massification of nihilism in the mass media of the film and television era that led away from the heroic personal suicide of Nietzsche's time through to the mass suicide of two World Wars, the possibility of accelerated global suicide through nuclear holocaust during the Cold War, and on to the current crisis of climate change. Internet activities, like mining Bitcoin, cloud computing, entertainment streaming, as well as online video conferencing, are examples of flatly spreading responsibility for the latest emissions heating our planet. As disconnection or rejection of technology is not viable, we need other options. Mauro Ponzi sees Benjamin's calls for the improbable perspective of happiness as an attempt of overcoming the mythology of capitalism (Ponzi 2017, p. 15), that with a weak messianic hope for an indeterminate fu-

---

3 The term "entreprecariat" has been coined by Silvio Lorusso, and it is used by network culture scholars connected to Institute of Network Cultures and Geert Lovink, see: https://networkcultures.org/entreprecariat/

ture we might break free from the nihilist temporality of eternal return (McFarland 2013, p. 247).

3 Memes

Memes provide an insight into the conditions, as well as revolutionary possibilities, of the current moment, due their homemade now-time character guaranteeing authenticity of message and immunity from direct appropriation by capitalism (Wershler and Surman 2001, p. 255). Following Nietzsche's rejection of history as progress and discovery of nihilism, Benjamin understands the avant-garde as resulting from industrial modernization. Thus, in times of digital reproducibility and transmissibility, nihilism becomes expressed via the avant-garde in niche net art, before being transformed into the creative mass product of a global online community—the Internet meme (Wiggins 2019, p. 46). Memes were initially mostly text based viral content, for example, ads for a physical zine that Darren Wershler created for the mailing lists in 1989 (Wershler and Surman 2001, p. 248–249). In 2001 at the dawn of Web 2.0, Wershler wrote that the process of spreading ideas fast online was uncontrollable and hard to build "artificially" from the ground up because of the "public commons" character of the Internet (Wershler and Surman 2001, pp. 250–255). Since then, the Internet has become mostly a platform media ecosystem, and the following analysis focuses on the Internet memes as genre within that ecosystem (Wiggins 2019, pp. 37–56).

Now, memes are part of the platform capitalism while, as dialectical images, still being able "to dissipate the semblance of eternal sameness, and even of repetition, in history" (Benjamin 1999, p. 473). Despite the monolithic landscape that the Big Four have created online, there has been a play-space (Benjamin) for the "virality" of memes: their rhizomatic proliferation that is not tied to a specific platform. Memes are "artifacts of digital participatory culture" that are "produced, reproduced, and transformed to reconstitute the social system" (Wiggins 2019, p. 40). Memes are not elitist by construction, which is fairly effortless, and all are potentially viral. Memes appear to be art that the masses are in control of, a place where they rule the whole of production, and thus can use it as a means for self-understanding, as Benjamin wished (Benjamin 1991, p. 488).

In "Some Remarks on Folk Art," Benjamin discusses the connection of folk art with kitsch and how it differs from fine art: "Art teaches us to see into things. Folk art and kitsch allow us to see outward from within things" (Benjamin 2008d, p. 255). The internal force, which appears to be detonating kitsch, or reframing recent political, social, or cultural events, is the humor of memes. They often present ludic, absurdist, or ironic qualities, sometimes nonsensically playing with meaning in a manner reminiscent of Dadaism (Wiggins 2019, pp.130 – 131). That kind of humor "can only arise from the machine" (Salzani 2018, p. 173).

The "reproducibility-distraction-politicization" triad that Benjamin introduces in "The Work of Art", removed fragment titled "Theory of Distraction," might be reintroduced as virality-laughter-politicization in discussing the revolutionary possibilities of meme production (Benjamin 2008e, pp. 56–57). According to Jeaho Kang, Benjamin views media as creating a new public through novel forms of experience and perception, and that "politics is primarily concerned with identifying ways of organizing experience" (Kang 2014, p.130). His claim that "art begins at a distance ... [while] in kitsch, the world of things advances on the human being" is a promise of kitsch's political potential (Benjamin 2008b, p. 238). Memes work similarly: they approach the viewer, and by proximity, "awaken the imagination ... that leads in turn to a recognition," in which the situation presented has been experienced before and is brought forth from the unconscious (Doherty 2008, p. 209). Kitsch represents "artistic volition," a will not toward art but toward more urgent concerns: to the understanding of the political needs of the present in the previously unconscious past (Doherty 2008, p. 209). Memes as folk art and dialectical image, "that emerges suddenly, in a flash" (Benjamin 1999, p. 473), might bring profane illumination and "the energies of intoxication for the revolution" (Benjamin 2005a, p. 216). Despite regard for Surrealism, Benjamin does not see the avant-garde as a truly revolutionary force, as no one will "win the massed over to a higher art ... only film can detonate the explosive stuff ... which is kitsch" (Benjamin 1999, pp. 395–396). Videos and photographs, the raw material of memes, might be viewed as the "explosive stuff" of digital folk art.

One of the most popular memes of 2020 (Zach 2021), "Cat Vibing,"[4] depicts a cat moving rhythmically to music while displaying an appreciative visage. The most successful version of this meme is "Cat Vibing to Street Musician's Levant Polkka," which in turn became a meme where next to the vibing cat, Donald Trump is seen dancing to a face-swapped Joe Biden playing a drum. This version, though created during the 2020 presidential campaign, appears to have no political undertones as both candidates are equally ridiculed. Playing with gesture (swaying back and forth to music), brought on by the spontaneity of carnivalesque distraction, nonsense, and joyful repetition connects to Benjamin's pedagogical ideas regarding building habits toward overcoming bourgeois culture (Kang 2014, pp. 96–97).

---

[4] For visuals of the memes mentioned, type the titles provided here in an online image search engine.

One habit that may develop within meme culture is that of viewing the world through a "meme structure," that is, seeing the absurdity and juxtapositions of real-life events, thus revealing their complicity in the structure of commodity. Thus, the absurd meme of two presidential candidates "vibing" might suggest to us that whoever wins the election, we can at least laugh. Instead of passive mass spectators, this habit might bring about active, "distracted examiners" who are critical, though not in the strict sense of critical reasoning, which requires distance between an object (art) and the examining subject (critic) (Kang 2014, p. 126). The task of the criticism—similar to the task of history—is to get truth from objects or images through their unveiling, and, if necessary, through the destruction of the aura encompassing them, leading to revelation (A. Benjamin 2005, p.155–156). That is, truth is in the world of material objects, and critical destruction might bring the object's history *and* present state to the fore revealing the object's nature; that nature points to the future potentiality of the object and the hope of redemption through this potential. In a meme, the negativity and destructiveness of (distracted) criticism are covered with irony, comedy, and sarcasm, but always with affective power. Through their "close-up character," enabled by ubiquitous "optic" technologies that allow one to zoom in on a specific part of a scene (as with the "Bernie Sanders Mittens" meme), they might produce "profane illuminations, glimpses of a sur-reality within the banal experiences of everyday life" (A. Benjamin 2005, p. 158). Thus, memes might become tactical media while also affording cultural researchers to be historical critics of the present.

Meme structure could be called dialectical, as the imagery in memes tends to work through juxtaposition: an axis is found in the original appropriated picture or video along which one value is contrasted with an opposite one, as seen in the recent "Boat Stuck in the Suez Canal" memes. In the photographs, one of the biggest transporting ships in the world, the Ever Given, is juxtaposed in size either with the canal or with the excavating machine trying to dig it out from the shore. In other instances, the axis is a constructed visual division between two or more pictures, structurally reminiscent of the early net art works or of storyboards and comic books, as in "Drakeposting" memes. Sometimes cinematic scenes are context-reinterpreted in order to reveal tension. The popular older meme, "One Does Not Simply," is comprised of a single screenshot from the first *Lord of the Rings* film with the character Boromir making a meaningful hand gesture. With a divided text, one part positioned atop the image while the other sits below Boromir's gesture, the context lends itself to dialectical juxtapositions and humor. What started with "one does not simply walk into Mordor," a quote from the film, splintered into myriads of memes creating layers of meaning via various references and "memetic" history.

Benjamin's dialectical images juxtapose utopian potential with the betrayal of that potential in a now-time of "catastrophic and barbaric present reality" according to Susan Buck Morss' discussion of *The Arcades Project* (Buck-Morss 1989, p. 251). The structure of dialectical images is the "fore-history and after-history" between the facticity of things and their utopian potential (Benjamin 1999, p. 470). This is represented in memes through a montage-like structure, and by the temporal effect of the scrolling gesture, creating the conflict of "temporal nucleus of the dialectical image" (Lovink and Tuters 2018, para. 14). Sometimes the image chosen for the meme provides this dialectical juxtaposition. The "Boat Stuck in the Suez Canal" meme reveals multiple historical and economical contextualizations. The utopian promise of the capitalist push for faster shipping and larger quantities has its conditions revealed for Internet users who may be realizing their own participation in global shipping acceleration. A single image, then, might provoke the awakening that Benjamin hoped for, or the weak messianic moment as a slight adjustment (McFarland 2013, p. 165). Since the dialectical images function as "politically charged monads" (Buck-Morss 1989, p. 221) able "to ignite the explosive materials that are latent in what has been" (Benjamin 1999, p. 392), memes might reveal a glimpse of an unexpected future—a destruction of the eternal sameness.

The reproduction of a meme, and the exchangeability of its parts demonstrate elements of humor structuring similar to that of early Mickey Mouse films. Portions of the material featured in memes are exchangeable. In the "Drakeposting" meme series, the left side contains two emotional reactions, one negative and one positive, of the rapper Drake that are screen captured from one of his music videos. On the right side is an empty space continuously re-filled with textual quotes, or pictures that depict events, political figures, or celebrities, to be evaluated. Mickey Mouse's body reflects the commodification of workers and their work: the extension and interchangeability of body parts, their durability and survival, all of which is taken up with a (eerie) smile (Salzani 2018, p. 164). Similarly, memes reveal the commodification of content creators and users in the context of the Internet: the exchangeability and continuous flow of content. In this revelation, absurdist laughter is the release of affective energies expressing the "dialectical correlation" between horror and humor that is especially well demonstrated in memes like "This Is Fine."[5] This correlation may either become creative or destructive.

---

[5] This meme consists of two panels of an anthropomorphized dog sitting casually amongst the flames of a house on fire, with the dialog "this is fine" added in a second panel.

Confronted with alt-right meme appropriation, Lovink follows the Benjaminian approach to mass media in "working on memes as myths" (Lovink 2019, pp.136–137). Nihilism expressed through the automated content agnosticism of platforms (Seymour 2020, p. 142), became the basis for the rise of alt-right memes. Lovink and Tuters use Benjamin's theory to discuss the appropriation of concepts such as "woke," "awakening," and "blue pill/red pill" (a concept drawn from the progressive science-fiction film, *The Matrix*), as well as meme production previously connected to progressive and anarchist net circles now usurped to express sexist, racist, and violent views of the alt-right "awaken" (Lovink and Tuters 2018, para. 7). Whereas outrageousness, playfulness, and sometimes vulgarity would be pedagogically useful for Benjamin (Kang 2014, pp. 77–82), Lovink and Tuters view them as a mechanism of only limited freedom (Lovink and Tuters 2018, para. 19): limited by individualized platform world. Memes are not conservative or progressive by default; rather, they express "an aesthetic that suits those who believe in nothing but the liberation of the individual and the id" (Lovink 2019, p. 121). As demonstrated in the "Punching the Nazi [Richard Spencer] in the Face" affair and its subsequent memes, the only universal rule of memes is that there is no master of meme-fication (Hardesty et al. 2019, p. 3).

Still, this is the new, aestheticized politics that was once connected to "the nihilist-heroic World War-technological syndrome" (Hillach 1979, p. 107), and now is linked to an apocalypse-technological syndrome. As war was once the "solution" to tensions through the use of "technological resources while maintaining property relations" (Benjamin 2008f, p. 41), now rather than liberation, the alt-right evokes the same aesthetic pleasure that is connected to the experience of annihilation (Benjamin 2008f, p. 41), "seeking" solutions through an accelerationist vision of a technological singularity, brought on by AI, that will clear the field and make way for survival of the fittest.

Memes present a genuine possibility of bringing into existence a revolutionary collective of those who "get it" (Lovink and Tuters 2018, para.17). This is both their power and their weakness since they are in need of mass appeal in order to live longer, and their makers are guided by a weak hope for "seizing the memes of production" (Hardesty et al. 2019, p. 18). James McFarland writes that "a temporary conjunction of Benjamin and Nietzsche [suggests]: to produce with the tools of the dominant culture a cultural product that accelerates the destruction of that culture" (McFarland 2013, p. 247), as it could be cathartic. Benjamin's belief in laughter's revolutionary power, and its bringing about a different barbarism, is limited by the realization that the same elements for mass self-expression could be used opposite to revolutionary goals (Salzani 2018, p. 174). Regarding that ambiguity Benjamin writes that it is "the law of dialectics at a standstill.

This standstill is utopia and the dialectical image, therefore, [is] dream image." (Benjamin 2006, p. 40) This kind of image description, one that is "afforded by the commodity per se: as fetish," is true of many online cultural products offered by platforms in such a way that the user is "seller and sold in one" (Benjamin 2006, p. 40). The utopian ideas of the early internet culture that memes are heirs of, with the online public commons, are unattainable in a platform economy; however, messianic moments, a tiger's leap afforded by the current folk art of the meme, might bring about an interruption of "the consequentiality of time" of the modern (Ponzi 2017, pp. 253–256).

4 Crypto Art

What began as a move toward reproducible art through mass media technologies and became (new) media art has now come full circle: back to an auratic understanding of art. As I am writing this chapter on the emergent phenomenon of NFTs or crypto art, it is developing further after its recent rise in prominence.[6] Crypto art lies at the crossroads of crypto currency development, memes as a digital folk art, and net art as an established genre in media art world.

At the heart of once-revolutionary media art (and its consequent incarnations: digital art and net art) is their ephemerality, their reproducibility, their dependence on mediatic infrastructures and contexts. Media art in its emergent forms resisted reification by the museum-gallery complex, which focused on aura of the art objects (Benjamin 2008e, p. 27). This resistance has also been typical for many net artists since the net.art movement in the '90s. Memes as simply viral content were not that different from net art. Initially, both shared an avant-garde character: the use of kitsch or the profane (e. g. *Deep ASCII* by Vuk Čosić), of found and appropriated footage, remixes, hacking (e. g. *Super Mario Clouds* by Cory Angel), repetition, collage, montage, amateur graphic aesthetics, issues with authorship, as well as resistance to commercialization. Most net artists, like meme-makers, embraced the ephemeral character of their work, akin to street art, due to copyright issues and the unstable character of the net itself: its protocols, coding, and website domains. Memes and net art depended on an Internet commons, that is, specific mailing lists, forums, social media, and hosting platforms where these creative pieces were shared and co-produced.

---

[6] Thus, I am citing mostly sources that are direct reactions to the early 2021 success of crypto art: three interviews from *Hyperallergic*, texts from *Rhizome*, *Network Cultures*, and *Coindesk*, etc.

There were many efforts to legitimize and situate net art as contemporary art,[7] differentiating it from the folk art of memes, but it proved hard to present net art works outside of their media milieu until recently. Hence for the public, memes do not seem to differ from "net art."

The first signs of seeking originality while retaining the viral appeal of digital cultural products can be recognized in the paintings of memes such as "Grumpy Cat" by Lauren Kealin a decade ago. She "provided aura and originality, where none previously existed" (Grossman 2013, para. 3). Now crypto art's "second wave" of sales, like Beeple's enormous sale of *Everydays: The First 5000 Days* at Christie's for $69 million on March 11, 2021, brings the apparently awaited genius artist cult to the digital art world (Beller 2021, para.7).

The beginnings of NFTs are connected to the issue that the virality of memes underscores: their ephemeral digital form dependent on the platforms they spread on. For net artists trying to live off their digital art, and users who wanted to "collect" some of their favorite works, it was a practical issue. Silvia Dal Dosso traces the creation of NFTs in, what could be called, the digital vernacular realm to the moment when the "Pepe the Frog Rare Memes" needed a way to guarantee their uniqueness in 2016 (Dal Dosso 2021 paras. 2–4). Her history of NFTs goes through the first sales, which were connected to *CryptoKitties*, a collecting and trading game, to the "normalization" of NFT sales through the legitimacy of sales at Christie's (Dal Dosso 2021 para. 13). In the world of "established" net art, curators and gallerists tried selling and collecting digital works online and offline for years (such as Steven Sacks's gallery, *Bitforms*). The first successful sale of NFT art happened in 2014 at *Rhizome* gallery, an institution of net art since its beginning, where digital artists also experimented with Bitcoins since 2011.[8] In short, NFTs are not especially novel; what is new is the hype, and the buyers who are neither gallery art buyers nor net art collectors, but rather mostly "crypto bros" speculating on cryptocurrencies (Sacks and Vartanian 2021).

So, despite the traditional auction houses joining the crypto game, the NFTs art market is far from being domesticated. More likely the old art players have joined the new market under a looming threat that an accelerating crypto market could render them obsolete. The problem of NFTs technical-economic structure requires a deeper analysis, but what it suggests is the key critique that NFTs are furthering the commodification of art and capitalist reterritorialization of the Internet creative play-space, and thus are the return of the same.

---

7 Like during Dokumenta X.
8 See also https://ostachowski.com/about/what-is-crypto-art-or-nft-art/history-of-crypto-art/

NFTs use blockchain technology to assure the authenticity and uniqueness of the sold work (like a notary certificate) through encoded protocols. They are also non-interchangeable, unlike Bitcoins, with which they share protocols of offering guarantees that would usually be provided by banks. Both crypto entities require mining and minting since most cryptocurrency follows standard money mechanisms (Wagenknecht and Vartanian 2021). The Ethereum cryptocurrency platform that is now the main guarantor for Christie's, secures transactions through a "proof of work" protocol, which makes computers run purposeless calculations so they can secure data before putting it into a blockchain (Connor 2021, para. 18). This requires immense energy and, like Bitcoins (which also run on Ethereum), the ecological impact of one transaction is extremely high.[9] Encoding protocols may ensure the author's rights and enforce rules regarding the use of an artwork. But as the artistic director of *Rhizome* claims, "we've found that immutability is not necessarily beneficial to the long-term stewardship of digital art" (Connor 2021, para. 16). History, authorship issues, and restorations of art works were part of their identity even in times of the artist cult. In his discussion of aura, Benjamin's realization was that immutability, originality, and authenticity come from treating a cultural artifact as a fetish (Benjamin 2008f, p. 23), and despite NFTs non-interchangeable character, crypto art works are ultimately exchangeable as economical assets like other collectibles such as "sports memorabilia" (Connor 2021, para. 22). Such a digital art object is entirely abstract, but with the lack of referents that are characteristic of the crypto world, it is just a product of exchange automation and attribution of value (Berardi 2017, p. 155).

The NFT art leaves behind the replicable and re-interpretative character of memes and net art—their relatives—because the artworks guaranteed by NFTs are original, unique, and authentic, as the mentioned artwork of Beeple illustrates[10]. His work is "exclusively and without a shadow of a doubt created by a single author" (Dal Dasso, para. 21), but its topics, sense of humor, and aesthetic—a certain vulgarity mixed with political messaging—are very meme-like. Originality is not the case with all such works that are sold. Dal Dosso mentions the case of the *Nyan Cat* GIF sale, auctioned a month before Beeple's sale, for almost $600,000, as complicating the authorship or prosumerist character of memes. *Nyan Cat* was sold for so much because of its history, popularity, and nostalgia, qualities not produced by the meme's original authors, argues Dal

---

[9] The emissions value of one crypto art sale: 163 486 KgCO2, equals 1.5 thousand hours of flight. https://memoakten.medium.com/the-unreasonable-ecological-cost-of-cryptoart-2221d3eb2053 .
[10] https://www.behance.net/beeple

Dosso (Dal Dosso 2021, paras. 20–21). The sale of memes remains problematic. Meanwhile, with such a successful sale like Beeple's entirely original work, the crypto crowd can follow an artist cult (Beller 2021, para. 18).

For Benjamin, Eduard Fuchs embodied a revolutionary figure of a collector who was not just interested in the objects as commodities, but understanding their materiality and history (Kang 2014 p. 188), he was also interested in reviving their use value for the collective (Benjamin 1999, p. 908). The collector is an "aesthetic engineer" of the spectacle of history, a media practitioner who uses "media technology's mimetic possibilities" politically (Kang 2014, p. 197). The collectors of digital art and memes could be revolutionary. But the focus on authenticity and irreproducibility in an NFT object and thus fetishization (A. Benjamin 2005, p. 113), says otherwise. Then, despite the messaging about empowering artists and providing recognition to net art, NFTs markets are creating object-value; furthermore, they have actually turned the process into a casino-like speculative value exchange. Commentators stress that, unlike the traditional market where collecting comes first and flipping artworks comes later, crypto art seems to be mostly about the secondary market (Connor 2021, para. 11), as the existence of digital bots buying and reselling NFTs in split seconds proves (Sacks and Vartanian 2021).

Collectors of cryptocurrency and crypto art are not motivated by profane illumination or dephantasmagorization, or by "awakening through collective remembering" to the truth about the (crypto) platform nihilist spectacle (Kang 2014, pp. 188–197). Quite the contrary, what might have been a nostalgic need to collect artifacts from the history of memes, is now, with the NFT boom, cult creation for the crypto platform to further economic interests.

The self-referentiality of crypto art provides the term "crypto art," as Sacks points out (Sacks and Vartanian 2021), with a truer meaning—this is art about itself being sold through NFTs (some pieces on the Nifty platform are just slogans like "Don't Miss Out"). Cryptocurrencies are self-referential and based on a system of faith (Berardi 2017, p. 160). This lack of referents demotes the world to its appearance, to its *Schein* in Benjaminian terms (McFarland 2013, p. 77). Within the crypto world it is *l'art pour l'art*; a cult formation where the outside world is bracketed out (Benjamin 2002, pp. 288–291). Everything can be encoded and determined in NFTs without the need for mediation from the outside world—the terms of use of the artwork, its presentation, the reproduction and artist's rights, etc. Thus, it is an example of the "techno-linguistic automation of relations among people," and morality as a "matter of serviceability," that is, where no ethical or political negotiations are necessary, no law is enacted and no judgment is needed (Berardi 2017, pp. 158–159). Benjamin would raise objections against that aestheticization similar to the ones against aestheticizing tragedy by turning it away from its moral stakes (McFarland 2013, p. 77). The automatism of technology, the "second technology" (Benjamin 2008, p. 26), requires governing by "liberty, which contrasts politics as intrinsically anti-automatic art" (A. Benjamin 2005, p. 110).

To explain the recent appeal of NFTs and cryptocurrencies during the pandemic, Wagenknecht suggests a humane mechanism behind it: in a moment of uncertainty people turn to crypto art for hope about the future (Wagenknecht and Vartanian 2021). While this hope could be akin to the weak messianic belief that a disruption of the old will be "leading to salvation" (Ponzi 2017, pp. 248–249), it is rather what Benjamin describes as a reaction to a social order crisis that makes the creative become a fetish (Benjamin 2008, p. 293). The relations of technology, society, and revolution come to fruition for Benjamin when "all the bodily innervations of the collective become revolutionary discharge" (Benjamin 2005a, pp. 217–18). But in the frenzy around NFTs, as with Bitcoin and the GameStop "short-squeeze rebellion," innervation is taken over by the cult of money, the individual, and fetishization. Beller describes the Beeple's very "of the moment" work, (Beller 2021, para. 21) with Benjamin's evoking Marinetti's "Fiat ars, pereat mundus" in "The Work of Art" (Benjamin 2008f, p. 42). For Beller, this art is destructive, because its basis—its code and its focus—money are covered in blood; and its use does not solve any of the pressing issues (such as ecological ones) (Beller 2021, para. 20). This illustrates the failed reception of technology by capitalist regimes that Benjamin prophetically suggested in 1930 would lead from aestheticization to fascism and annihilation in their fruition (Kang 2014, p. 193; see Benjamin 2005b, pp. 320–321). Similarly, Beller summarizes his position: "NFT does not stand for Non-Fascist Token, but it should. Let's not get fooled again" (Beller 2021, para. 23).

Is there then a way out *through* the nihilism embedded in crypto platforms? "Cryptocurrency does offer some opportunity to define terms anew" (Connor 2021, para. 22). Howard mentions several niche projects by artist-activist groups based on "proof of stake" instead of "proof of work" that use significantly cleaner power sources while also trying to create more inclusive, decentralized cryptocurrencies (Howard and Vartanian 2021). For Benjamin, the artist's task was to be a producer (Kang 2014, p. 106), but now they must also become economists and coders for the micropolitics of grassroots movements diversifying crypto ecology. Addie Wagenknecht calls these attempts ways to get out of the "white (male), walled-off world of the market" (Wagenknecht and Vartanian 2021), since NFTs "are rooted in material infrastructures, politics of nation states, deep-seated societal power relations" (Connor 2021, para. 23). To achieve something truly revolutionary, artists like Wagenknecht see the need for NFTs to be an instrument stemming from existing social realities in order to foster new collaborations. This is rather hard to achieve with automated speculation, addiction to gambling, and collecting all effectively sustained by crypto platforms that use the same techniques as the Big Four media platforms.

5 Conclusion

Dealing with platform nihilism does not cure the illness itself (Karppi 2018, p. 2–3) since it has been absorbed by the digital religious functions (Gertz 2018, p. 183) and the business planning of platform economy (Karppi 2021, pp. 52–53). Whatever is subversive can be commodified; this is the hell of the eternal return of "the new and the same," in which the community's perception of new events does not provide any historical awareness (Benjamin 1999, p. 546) because history as progress does not recognize death or moral stakes (Benjamin 1999, p. 66). The search for bliss, Nietzsche's self-hypnosis, and current techno-hypnosis coined by Gertz, are all hostile toward the real, bringing about the negative manifestation of the absence of happiness: destruction (McFarland 2013, p. 237). Faced with the danger of fascism and lost hope for a communist revolution, Benjamin, in Mauro Ponzi's interpretation, proposes something different than Nietzsche, the (improbable) "perspective of happiness" (Ponzi 2017, p. 15). Furthermore, according to Ponzi, in *Theses on the Concept of History*, Benjamin calls to follow the "weak messianic power," a belief that the continuum of history can break and lead to an unexpected future (Ponzi 2017 pp. 248–249), resulting in a self-destructive or a creative force.

Against the aestheticization of politics, "the World War-technology syndrome" of fascism (Hillach 1979, p. 107), a sacrificial tragic hero who "drops to his knee with such violence that the throne begins to totter" can appear (Benjamin 1999, p. 111), not as a symbol of individual survival, but of the idea this defiance expresses. This is agonistic, historical thinking in face of possible annihilation, when no neutrality is possible (MacFarland 2013, p. 232). Messianism might allow for "an absolutely indeterminate future," with a "tiger's leap" interrupting "the consequentiality of time," and thus momentarily promoting the messianic force (Ponzi 2017, pp. 253–255). Therefore, against a theory of neutrality and the aestheticization of media, art, and technology, Benjamin proposes politicization (Benjamin 2008f, p. 41). As technology is social, so media creating new habits are politically charged (Kang 2014, p. 130). Politicization is more than the instrumental use of technology toward a specific goal: "Just as the Greek *pharmakon* is both poison and antidote … technology can signify either the destruction of human nature or its potentiation (and … salvation)" (A. Benjamin 2005, p. 109).

Ponzi suggests that because Benjamin is aware that what one can do is only represent (*The Task of the Translator*) and is disappointed with communist visions of liberation, Benjamin intends to represent, in a "messianic sense," the overturning of the modern (Ponzi 2017 p. 259 and 256). Thus, the task of revolutionary writers is to functionally organize through critical writing (Benjamin 2008, pp. 89–93). Namely, attentiveness to how digital tools influence nihilism-human relations (Gertz 2018, p. 211), engaging in "talking about the Internet" (Lovink 2021, para. 3), or understanding the conditions of the current media ecology are crucial, but it is not enough to just provide content. The revolutionary subject should reorganize, providing an apparatus such that consumers and the public become collaborators and co-producers (Benjamin 2008a, p. 89). Thus, what examples of mass, reorganized media—memes and NFT art—present is a vision of contemporary revolutionary potential.

Memes could fit into Benjamin's vision of "anthropological materialism" (Kang 2014, p. 196), leading to the politicization of aesthetics. The NFT market is a capitalist-accelerationist takeover of a tool that some artists claim could have the potential to decentralize the crypto market and change it into something that is inclusive, community building, and equity-based. For the moment, it remains extractive and wasteful, a continuance of capitalist commodification. We need ways to disrupt the nihilistic, accelerated temporality of our digital age more urgently than ever.

What could be an expansion of Benjamin's proposal in view of recent media developments? Options like sabotage, proposed by autonomist and vitalist Hartmann (Lovink 2019, p. 80), resemble Benjamin's anarchist "utopia of self-determining community" (Ponzi 2017, p. 15). The necessity of network community building and Berardi's suggestion of an alternative rhythm to the acceleration of social media as an alternative temporality are useful (Lovink 2019, p. 137), but the task seems to first be to ask: "Revolution or reform of the platform-as-form? ... Should platforms be dismantled or appropriated?" (Lovink 2021, para. 14).

Bibliography

Beller, Jonathan (2021): "Fascism on the Blockchain? The Work of Art in the Age of NFTs." In: *Coin Desk*, March 23, 2021. https://www.coindesk.com/fascism-blockchain-art-nfts?fbclid=IwAR2GD-t_wQQjTQzC1BdUH0h7zLNV-l6PdtSiQyll-1bkZ2xKaIKDOYuOljk, visited on 31 March 2021.

Beller, Jonathan (2018): *The Message is Murder*. London: Pluto Press.

Benjamin, Andrew (2005): *Walter Benjamin and Art*. London: Continuum.

Benjamin, Walter (1999): *The Arcades Project*. Translated by Howard Eiland and Kevin McLaughlin. Cambridge: Harvard University Press.
Benjamin, Walter (2008a): "The Author as Producer". In: Benjamin, Walter: *The Work of Art in the Age of Its Technological Reproducibility and Other Writings on Media*. Edited by Michael W. Jennings, Brigid Doherty, and Thomas Y. Levin. Cambridge: The Belknap Press of Harvard University Press, pp. 79–95.
Benjamin, Walter (2002): "Capitalism as Religion". In: *Selected Writings 1913–1926*, vol.1. Edited by Michael W. Jennings, Gary Smith and Howard Eiland, Cambridge, London: Harvard University Press, pp. 288–291.
Benjamin, Walter (2008b): "Dream Kitsch". In: Benjamin, Walter: *The Work of Art in the Age of Its Technological Reproducibility and Other Writings on Media*. Edited by Michael W. Jennings, Brigid Doherty, and Thomas Y. Levin. Cambridge: The Belknap Press of Harvard University Press, pp. 236–239
Benjamin, Walter (2008c): "Little History of Photography". In: Benjamin, Walter: *The Work of Art in the Age of Its Technological Reproducibility and Other Writings on Media*. Edited by Michael W. Jennings, Brigid Doherty, and Thomas Y. Levin. Cambridge: The Belknap Press of Harvard University Press, pp. 274–298.
Benjamin, Walter (1991): "Pariser Brief I. Andre Gide und sein neuer Gegner" 1936. In: *Gesammelte Schriften*, Band 3. Edited by Hella Tiedemann-Bartels. Frankfurt am Main: Suhrkamp Verlag, pp. 482–496.
Benjamin, Walter (2006): "Paris, the Capital of the Nineteenth Century". In: *Selected Writings*, vol. 3. Edited by Howard Eiland and Michael W. Jennings. Cambridge, London: Harvard University Press, pp. 32–49.
Benjamin, Walter (2008d): "Some Remarks on Folk Art". In: Benjamin, Walter: *The Work of Art in the Age of Its Technological Reproducibility and Other Writings on Media*. Edited by Michael W. Jennings, Brigid Doherty, and Thomas Y. Levin. Cambridge: The Belknap Press of Harvard University Press, pp. 254–256.
Benjamin, Walter (2005a): "Surrealism". In: *Selected Writings 1927–1931*, vol. 2, part 1. Edited by Michael W. Jennings, Gary Smith and Howard Eiland. Cambridge, London: Harvard University Press, pp. 207–221.
Benjamin, Walter (2008e): "Theory of Distraction". In: Benjamin, Walter: *The Work of Art in the Age of Its Technological Reproducibility and Other Writings on Media*. Edited by Michael W. Jennings, Brigid Doherty, and Thomas Y. Levin. Cambridge: The Belknap Press of Harvard University Press, pp. 56–57.
Benjamin, Walter (2005b): "Theories of German Fascism". In: *Selected Writings 1927–1931*, vol. 2, part 1. Edited by Michael W. Jennings, Gary Smith and Howard Eiland. Cambridge, London: Harvard University Press, pp. 312–321.
Benjamin, Walter (2008f): "The Work of Art in the Age of Its Technological Reproducibility: Second Edition". In: Benjamin, Walter: *The Work of Art in the Age of Its Technological Reproducibility and Other Writings on Media*. Edited by Michael W. Jennings, Brigid Doherty, and Thomas Y. Levin. Cambridge: The Belknap Press of Harvard University Press, pp. 19–55.
Berardi, Franco 'Bifo' (2017): *Futurability: The Age of Impotence and the Horizon of Possibility*. Brooklyn NY, London: Verso.
Buck-Morss, Susan (1989): *Dialectics of Seeing: Walter Benjamin and the Arcades Project*. Boston: MIT Press.

Connor, Michael (2021): "Another New World." In: *Rhizome*, Mar 03, 2021. https://rhizome.org/editorial/2021/mar/03/another-new-world/, visited on 20 March 2021.

Dal Dosso, Silvia (2021): "Cats, Frogs, and Cryptoartists." In: *Network Cultures Longform*, Mar 11, 2021. https://networkcultures.org/longform/author/silvia-dal-dosso/, visited on 22 March 2021.

Doherty, Brigit (2008): "Painting and Graphics". In: Benjamin, Walter: *The Work of Art in the Age of Its Technological Reproducibility and Other Writings on Media*. Edited by Michael W. Jennings, Brigid Doherty, and Thomas Y. Levin. Cambridge: The Belknap Press of Harvard University Press, pp. 195–217.

Gertz, Nolen (2018): *Nihilism and Technology*. London, New York: Rowman & Littlefield.

Grossman, Samantha (2013): "The Meme as Art: Painter Sophisticates Cyberculture". In: *Time*, June 16, 2013. https://newsfeed.time.com/2013/06/16/the-meme-as-art-painter-sophisticates-cyberculture/, visited on 24 February 2021.

Han, Byung-Chul (2017): *Psychopolitics: Neoliberalism and New Technologies of Power*. Translated by Erik Butler. London, New York: Verso.

Hardesty, Robby, Jess Linz, and Anna J. Secor (2019): "Walter Benja-Memes." In: *Geohumanities* 5. No. 2, pp. 496–513.

Hillach, Ansgar (1979): "The Aesthetics of Politics: Walter Benjamin's 'Theories of German Fascism.'" In: *New German Critique* 17, Special Walter Benjamin Issue, pp. 99–119.

Howard, Lindsay and Hrag Vartanian (Host) (2021): "The Bourgeoning Market for NFTs," 9 March 2021. *Hyperallergic* Podcast, *Spotify*, 52:40. https://open.spotify.com/episode/6HttWutpmLXbSLbw9v0yAQ?si=GQHxCQhjQoGIM2OBUkORlg , visited 20 March 2021.

Kang, Jeaho (2014): *Walter Benjamin and the Media*. Cambridge, Malden: Polity Press.

Karppi, Tero (2018): *Disconnect: Facebook's Affective Bonds*. Minneapolis: University of Minnesota Press.

Karppi, Tero (2021): "Undoing the Outside: On Defaults and Off-Facebook Activity". In: *Undoing Networks: in Search of Media*. Karppi, Tero, Urs Stäheli, Clara Wieghorst, and Lea P. Zierott, Minneapolis: University of Minnesota Press, pp. 51–78.

Lovink, Geert (2017) "Foreword". In: Apprich, Clemens (2017): *Technotopia: a Media Genealogy of Net Cultures*. London, New York: Rowman & Littlefield, pp. xiii–xix.

Lovink, Geert (2021): "Notes on the Platform Condition." In: *Making & Breaking* 2. https://makingandbreaking.org/article/notes-on-the-platform-condition/, visited on 20 March 2021.

Lovink, Geert (2019): *Sad by Design on Platform Nihilism*. London: Pluto Press.

Lovink, Geert, and Mark Tuters (2018): "Rude Awakening Memes as Dialectical Images." In: *Non.Copyriot.Com*, 2018–04–03. https://non.copyriot.com/rude-awakening-memes-as-dialectical-images/, visited on 05 June 2020.

Löwith, Karl (1997): *Nietzsche's Philosophy of the Eternal Return of the Same*. Translated by J. Harvey Lomax. Berkeley: University of California Press.

McFarland, James (2013): *Constellation Friedrich Nietzsche and Walter Benjamin in the Now-Time of History*. New York: Fordham University Press.

Pettman, Dominic (2015): *Infinite Distraction*. Oxford: Polity Press. ProQuest Ebook Central https://ebookcentral.proquest.com/lib/york/detail.action?docID=4334753.

Ponzi, Mauro (2017): *Nietzsche's Nihilism in Walter Benjamin*. New York: Palgrave Macmillan.

Sacks, Steven and Hrag Vartanian (Host) (2021): "After Decades of Selling New Media Art," 30 March 2021. In: *Hyperallergic* Podcast, Spotify, 52:40. https://open.spotify.com/episode/6HttWutpmLXbSLbw9v0yAQ?si=tbkPtrv5T9Stbp7nda8JXA, visited on 31 March 2021.

Salzani, Carlo (2018): "Surviving Civilization with Mickey Mouse and a Laugh: A Posthuman Constellation." In: Nassima Sahraoui and Caroline Sauter (Eds.): *Thinking in Constellations: Walter Benjamin and the Humanities*. Newcastle Upon Tyne: Cambridge Scholars Publishing, pp. 161–183.

Seymour, Richard (2020): *The Twittering Machine*. Brooklyn: Verso.

Stiegler, Barbara (2009): "On the Future of Our Incorporations: Nietzsche, Media, Events." Translated by Helen Elam. In: *Discourse*, 31. No. 1 & 2, pp. 124–139.

Wagenknecht, Addie and Hrag Vartanian (Host) (2021): "The World of NFTs Explained," 9 March 2021. *Hyperallergic*, Podcast, *Spotify*, 48:28. https://open.spotify.com/episode/66XeOqClbpLVgyKu9YZICX?si=d08808c6285445aa, visited on 20 March 2021.

Wark, McKenzie (2019): *The Capital is Dead*. Brooklyn NY, London: Verso.

Wershler, Darren, and Mark Surman (2001): *Common Space: Beyond Virtual Community*. Canada: FT.com A Pearson Company.

Wiggins, Bradley E. (2019): *The Discursive Power of Memes in Digital Culture*. New York: Routledge.

Zach (2021): "KYM Review: The Top 10 Memes Of 2020." In: *Know Your Meme*. https://knowyourmeme.com/editorials/meme-review/kym-review-the-top-10-memes-of-2020, visited on 28 March 2021.

Gianfranco Ferraro
'Like ants': The Mafia's Necropolitics as a Paradigm of Nihilistic Violence

Abstract: The aim of this chapter is to develop the claim that the cultural meaning of the Mafia's violence is intrinsically nihilistic. I will attempt to show how the violent annihilation practiced by the Mafia can be situated in the field of nihilism, as a cultural phenomenon. I begin with the presentation of a back story, useful for approaching the semantics of violence and nihilism at work throughout the Mafia's history. Second, I summarize the forms of nihilism to which I will be referring in this chapter, and, thirdly, I sketch a short history of the Sicilian Mafia. Drawing on Foucault's conception of power and Mbembe's notion of necropolitics, I then attempt to identify the Mafia's semantics of power as a paradigm of those forms of violence and power that are hidden by traditional conceptions of western power – in particular, forms of violence that are characteristic of colonial and postcolonial contexts. Finally, through literary, cinematographic and historical examples, I examine the connections between the Mafia's symbolic semantics of violence and the emergence of nihilistic forms of power. The main hypothesis of the chapter is that studying the Mafia's paradigm gives us an understanding of the contemporary compromises between illegal and legal powers.

The word "Mafia" was used throughout the twentieth century, spreading into the first decades of the twenty-first century and referring to specific forms of criminal organization characterized by ritual brotherhood, territorial control based on extortion and the use of violence and, *lato sensu*, a form of power based on a semantics in which explicitly violent attitudes are accompanied by specific uses of words, silences and gestures. Nevertheless, far from being mere criminal organizations, mafias 'are economic organizations that derive their strength from the fact that they sell protection and services (often forcibly imposed) that someone buys' (Catino 2019, p. 2). In short, the term Mafia seems to stand for a paradigm – an archetype, a discourse – that is embodied in forms of living originating in southern Italy, and in Sicily in particular, and that is now recognizable in several phenomena that belong to our current globalized context.[1] Taking into account

---

[1] Paoli describes the Sicilian Cosa Nostra and the Calabrian 'Ndrangheta as follows: 'Cosa Nostra and the 'Ndrangheta are confederations of mafia families, which create ritual brotherhood

Nietzsche's diagnostic of nihilism in particular, conceived of as a form of behaviour and of orienting life conduct, the violence of the Mafia can be approached as a manifestation of a nihilistic paradigm: as a political form of nihilism. How does the Mafia, as a historical paradigm of violence and power, help us to approach and to define nihilism today? And conversely, how might nihilism help us to understand the cultural phenomena that are integrated within the archetype and discourses of the Mafia?

On 29 July 1983, a bomb exploded in the centre of Palermo, Sicily. The victim, killed in the attack, was the anti-Mafia judge Rocco Chinnici. This was the first attack in the new strategy of the Cosa Nostra, which focused on bomb attacks. Before that fateful day, in the centuries-old history of the Sicilian Cosa Nostra, Mafia attacks had exclusively involved guns and rifles.[2] Some years later, in 1992, two other anti-Mafia judges, Giovanni Falcone and Paolo Borsellino, as well as their bodyguards, were killed in separate attacks. The former's car exploded on the motorway connecting Palermo to the airport. The second was struck down in the doorway of his mother's home. The TV images of the burned-out cars, the damaged streets and buildings, the ripped-apart bodies, deeply shocked the Italian public and, given the international relevance of the investigations carried out by the two judges, were met with dismay around the world. In fact, the judges were the authors of the famous Maxi Trial (*Maxiprocesso*), which, in the late 1980s, resulted in the conviction of hundreds of Sicilian

---

ties among their members through rites and symbols. They are clearly distinct from the blood families of their members—so much so that they have their own ruling bodies. The two associations resort systematically to violence and secrecy to defend themselves from state repression and to pursue their aims, and they have a plurality of functions within their social environment' (Paoli 2003, p. 19). For an overview of the Mafia throughout history, see Romano (1966), Hess (1974), Falcone and Padovani (2004), Dickie (2004), Sifakis (2005), Santino (2006) and Lupo (2010a). I use the terms 'paradigm' and 'archetype' in Kuhn's sense, the first signifying the operational rules and practices that permit a scientific community to study a specific phenomenon, and the second consisting of specific phenomena that acquire greater meaning within a paradigm (see Kuhn [1996, pp. 10 and 103]). When examining literary, cultural and political phenomena, Foucault preferred to use the notion of "discourse", aiming to approach the practical connections and consequences of the use of an exemplary category or an exemplary phenomenon. As I will demonstrate, as a social and political phenomenon, the Mafia gave rise to a new historical and juridical paradigm: in this context, Sicilian local phenomena continued to function as meaningful archetypes. At the same time, both are perfectly approachable through Foucault's category. See Foucault (2004, p. 131).

2 Before the bombing attacks against the judges, in 1963, the Mafia did use bombs in Ciaculli. According to the informant Buscetta, however, in that case the Mafia did not intend to attack the state directly and was not pursuing a 'terroristic' strategy. Indeed, those responsible were punished by other Mafia bosses.

mafiosi, including top bosses, and in the legal definition of the Mafia as a unitary and pyramidal organization. The attacks were therefore not unexpected. Nevertheless, these bombings emerged as an exercise of violence that brought back memories of war in the minds of the Italian public, as well as memories of the tensions that had afflicted the country throughout the 1970s. As in the long string of attacks, responsibility for the murder of the two judges was not established in court. What was established, however, was the role played by the Corleonesi clan in the latter attack, in particular by the bosses Salvatore "Totò" Riina and Bernardo Provenzano.

With the introduction of bombs, a new term was thus added to the Mafia's semantics. It was as if the Mafia expressly sought to include within its semantics of violence a specific reference to war and terrorism.[3] As many investigations and studies have shown, the Mafia is a secret association characterized by specific codes of conduct and rituals. Consequently, because of its direct connection to the expression of power, it has always paid particular attention to semantics. In this semantics, the corpses become surfaces on which specific signs are inscribed so as to menace others or to reveal the motivation behind the crime.[4] This semantics of violence corresponds to a political lexicon of sorts, the entries of which are shared by the members of the organization and by the population that lives in fear of it. The method preferred by the Corleonesi clan involved the complete concealment of the corpse, either by dissolving the body in acid or by burying it in a cave or on a construction site (known as a "white shotgun", or *lupara bianca*, murder). The bombings and the destruction of bodies can thus be interpreted as specific examples of this semantics of violence, based on annihilation and terror. But how are we to understand their meaning according to this semantics of violence, and how might we approach them as cultural phenomena, that is, phenomena that can be revealed as paradigmatic of a specific culture or age?[5] In a recording taped in 2013, while the Sicilian Mafia boss Totò Riina (the "boss of bosses" of the Corleonesi clan) was in the prison yard, he recalls the 'scene' of the 1992 attack against Borsellino, which took place in the centre of Palermo, describing himself as "Someone that makes you dance the

---

[3] Between 1969 (the Piazza Fontana bombing) and 1980 (the Bologna massacre), Italy was stricken by a series of bomb attacks and coup attempts, the instigators of which were not decisively identified. These terrorist events provoked Pier Paolo Pasolini's reaction in an article titled "What is this coup d'état? I know" on 14 November 1974.

[4] The Mafia's semantics of violence includes, for instance, specific rituals such as the 'incaprettamento', where the victim is bound like a young goat ('capretto'), or the delivery of a beheaded animal as a threat or warning.

[5] See Dickie (2004, pp. 311–338).

samba this way, that makes you climb up the buildings and climb down, like ants."⁶ In these metaphoric words, we perhaps find a first key to approaching this semantics: the expression of unlimited power, exercised as a power of life and death over victims who are reduced to the smallest of animal existences.

1 Nihilism as Pessimism and the Will to Destruction

Nietzsche's approach to nihilism allows us to investigate the specificity of modern nihilism and to understand the multiple forms of nihilism as inheritances of multiple forms of modernity. In particular, Nietzsche makes clear that nihilism must be brought back to its social and historical roots: rather than having a merely psychological, individual meaning, nihilism's relation to *ressentiment* also represents a social feeling and contains a direct connection to the question of power.⁷ Nietzsche's distinction between active and passive nihilism allows us, finally, to approach the psycho-social moods we encounter when we face the Mafia's nihilistic influence on society. This approach thus proves to be particularly useful when speaking of the Mafia. In particular, in the *Genealogy of Morals*, Nietzsche refers to the origin of nihilism – 'the "last will" of man, his will to nothingness' – to the encounter between the 'great nausea at man' and the 'great compassion for man' (GM III 14) In this sense, he describes the genesis of nihilism through the feeling of ressentiment:

> Here, the worms of revenge and rancour teem all round; here, the air stinks of things unrevealed and unconfessed; here, the web of the most wicked conspiracy is continually being spun, – the conspiracy of those who suffer against those who are successful and victorious, here, the sight of the victorious man is *hated*. And what mendacity to avoid admitting this hatred as hatred! (GM III 14)

While in this way, on the one hand, he highlights the content of violence regarding ascetic ideals, on the other hand, he explains how they manifest a reaction

---

6 See "Il capo dei capi Salvatore Totò Riina una delle ultimi immagini e intercettazione del boss mafioso." YouTube video. https://www.youtube.com/watch?v=WlbuD3AI_dY, visited on 26 September 2021.
7 According to Nietzsche, ressentiment is a key-feeling of decadent forms of living, characterized by the inability of weaker individuals to face a stronger enemy through a symmetric action. Because of this, the impossibility of using violence becomes a hidden violence, directed at the enemy or – in case it cannot be discharged outwards – against the individual himself (see GM II 11).

on the part of 'the whole herd of failures, the disgruntled, the under-privileged, the unfortunate, and all who suffer from themselves' (GM III 13). A sick, wounded animal, man remains 'master of destruction, self-destruction' (GM III 13): therefore, the roots of *ressentiment* – 'that most dangerous of blasting and explosive materials' (GM III 15) – and of revenge must be sought in a yearning 'to *anaesthetize pain through emotion*' (GM III 15). Nevertheless, this shifting of the direction of *ressentiment*, which provokes the feeling of guilt, does not erase the fact that behind the will to nothingness, such a will remains, threatening to explode if left ungoverned.[8]

Following Nietzsche, what happens when a cultural system based on ascetic ideals collapses? In his unpublished notes on European nihilism,[9] Nietzsche approaches the *maladie du siècle* as a natural consequence of the collapse of Christian morality: 'Skepticism regarding morality is what is decisive…. "Everything lacks meaning" (the untenability of one interpretation of the world, upon which a tremendous amount of energy has been lavished, awakens the suspicion that *all* interpretations of the world are false)'. For Nietzsche, the core of European nihilism consists in the fact that the values that orient the world are lacking. More precisely, Nietzsche clarifies how 'social distress', 'physiological degeneration', 'or, worse, corruption' should not be assumed as the causes of nihilism (NL 1886, 2[127], KSA 12, p. 125). In themselves, they cannot produce nihilism. Here, Nietzsche's paradigm of nihilism can be summarized as follows: 'The faith in the categories of reason is the cause of nihilism. We have measured the value of the world according to categories *that refer to a purely fictitious world*' (NL 1887, 11[99], KSA 13, p. 49). The origin of nihilism is thus derived via a mechanism of production of the values that orient life conduct, placed into a historical plan. When this production fails, the mechanism goes around in circles: 'What does nihilism mean? *That the highest values devaluate them-*

---

[8] On the influence of Dostoevsky's psychology on Nietzsche's notion of *ressentiment*, see Stellino (2015, pp. 45–55). More generally, on the direct – or via Bourget and via Brunetière – influence of Russian authors on Nietzsche, see Stellino (2015, pp. 89–92). On the emergence of the legal system as a way of controlling social and individual *ressentiment*, see Nietzsche (GM II 11).
[9] Nietzsche writes on nihilism in several fragments, the most distilled of which is the "Lenzer Heide" fragment, written in 1887. Most of these were published by Nietzsche's first editors as the first part of a book that had been announced in the third part of *The Genealogy of Morals* (1987) as *The Will to Power: Attempt at a Revaluation of all Values* but which was abandoned by Nietzsche in the last years before his breakdown (see GM III 27). A pivotal source for Martin Heidegger's examination of nihilism, the book was translated into English by Walter Kaufmann (I will use his translations of the relevant fragments in what follows). On Nietzschean forms of European nihilism, see Van Tongeren (2018, pp. 44–102). See also Levin 1988, Weller 2018, Tartaglia 2016, Ansell-Pearson and Morgan 2000, Cunningham 2002 and Baker 2020.

selves. The aim is lacking; "why?" find no answer' (NL 1887, 9[35], KSA 12, p. 350). In this case, Nietzsche stresses that the deep metaphysical mechanism in search of a cause, when those causes are not reachable, results in a loss of the meaning of the entire plan of conduct. For this reason, when this occurs, the whole 'universe seems to have lost value, seems "meaningless"' (NL 1887, 11[100], KSA 13, p. 50). In this way, Nietzsche diagnoses nihilism as a cultural phenomenon, stressing the relevance of metaphysical values for orienting individual and social life. Nihilism thus implies radical pessimism about truth: no true world exists, and so 'every considering-something-true, is necessarily false' (NL 1887, 9[41], KSA 12, p. 354). Truths must be redirected to forms of practices.

Nietzsche also argues that nihilism is based on the connection between morality and truthfulness: *radical* nihilism is precisely described as deriving from the cultivation of truthfulness, consisting in the moral interpretation of truth. Nevertheless, through the forces defined by moral truthfulness – which are always practical forces – the teleological lines of morality are ultimately revealed to be mendacious and unfounded.[10] Granting man an absolute value, Christian morality assumed his ability to appreciate absolute values and to apply this knowledge to how he ought to live. In this sense, as Nietzsche explains in the *Genealogy*, this morality is also an '*antidote* against practical and theoretical *nihilism*' (NL 1886, 5[71], KSA 12, p. 211). What accompanies the collapse of that morality is thus the appearance of nihilism as a 'belief in valuelessness' (NL 1886, 7[8], KSA 12, p. 292). At the same time, this implies an antinomy: on the one hand, one is unable to reach the previous field of values; on the other hand, there are no longer any meaningful plans by which to live one's life: 'we are *weary* because we have lost the main stimulus' (NL 1886, 7[8], KSA 12, p. 293). From here, pessimism emerges as a preliminary form of nihilism. Within pessimism, Nietzsche recognizes both a strength and a decline: the strength is given by 'the energy of its logic, as anarchism and nihilism, as analytic', the form of decline appears through the aptitude of '*tout comprendre*', 'a sort of cosmopolitan fingering' (NL 1887, 9[126], KSA 12, p. 410). For Nietzsche, this pessimistic view of morality ultimately reveals the will to existence, itself rooted in morality.

As we will see a little further, the social forms of life in which the Mafia's violence and power emerged are characterized by the same pessimistic view about truth and morality. For Nietzsche, as a form of passive nihilism, pessimism involves the conviction that 'all that happens is meaningless and in vain; and that there ought not to be anything meaningless and in vain' (NL 1887, 11[97],

---

10 See NL 1886, 5[71], KSA 12, p. 211.

KSA 13, p. 45). Nevertheless, modern pessimism involves a sense of the uselessness not of the entire world of existence, but rather 'of the *modern* world' (NL 1885, 1[194], KSA 12, p. 54). The whole of modern society appears as a conglomerate of illness: 'criminals' and 'anarchists' represent the scum that society now lacks the strength to excrete (NL 1888, 16[53], KSA 13, p. 504). Nietzsche goes on to explain how nihilism manifests the fact that 'there is nothing to life that has value, except the degree of power – assuming that life itself is the will to power' (NL 1886, 5[71], KSA 12, p. 215). No morality or code of laws governs this instinct. As a direct consequence, this implies a loss of faith in any self-declared normative field ('Justice as will to power' [NL 1885, 2[122], KSA 12, p. 122]), the position of '*ourselves* as value-positing' (NL 1886, 7[64], KSA 12, p. 318) and a 'Basic contradiction in civilization and the enhancement of man' (NL 1885, 2[128], KSA 12, p. 127). This corresponds to a *political* ('*in politicis*') view of life: the things that exist must be interpreted as 'problems of power, of one quantum of power against another'. Therefore, 'we do not believe in any right that is not supported by the power of enforcement: we feel all rights to be conquests'[11] (NL 1887, 10[53], KSA 12, p. 483).

This is not the only aspect of nihilism at work in the context of the Mafia, however. In fact, as Nietzsche makes clear, nihilism does not correspond to a simple lack of action. In this sense, Nietzsche identifies an inner ambiguity in nihilism, and thus two main forms of active nihilism, on the one hand, ('Nihilism as a sign of increased power of the spirit'), and passive nihilism, on the other hand, ('as decline and recession of the power of the spirit') (NL 1887, 9[35], KSA 12, p. 351). Nihilism, as 'the highest degree of powerfulness of the spirit', manifests 'the over-richest life – partly destructive, partly ironic' (NL 1887, 9[39], KSA 12, p. 353). As active nihilism, it manifests its 'maximum of relative strength as a violent force of destruction' (NL 1887, 9[35], KSA 12, p. 351), as '*great passion*' (NL 1887, 9[107], KSA 12, p. 398). A destructive strength is thus contained in active nihilism, as a 'will to destruction', manifested 'as the will of a still deeper instinct, the instinct of self-destruction, the will for nothingness' (NL 1887, 5[71], KSA 12, p. 215). Destruction thus appears as the manifest effect of a force addressed to and outside of the subject, without any further question about its 'aim': nihilism 'does not only contemplate the "in vain!"' (NL 1887, 11[123], KSA 13, p. 59). Destruction appears precisely as a third effect of nihilism, alongside contempt and pity. Far from being illogical, this will to destruction 'is

---

[11] Precisely according to this view, in the *Genealogy*, Nietzsche dismisses the 'fantasy' that the state began 'with a "contract"' (GM II 17). This is particularly clear in the case of the Mafia's point of view, in which the legal power of the state appears as just one will to power among others.

the condition of strong spirits and wills, and these do not find it possible to stop with the No of "judgment": their nature demands the No of the deed. The reduction to nothing by judgment is seconded by the reduction to nothing by hand' (NL 1887, 11[123], KSA 13, p. 60). Nietzsche's diagnosis helps to explain the practical element of both pessimistic and active nihilism. His method implies that this cultural phenomenon should be approached not merely from a metaphysical perspective but through an analysis of concrete forms of living. Nevertheless, Nietzsche explores the real meaning of the death of God through the ways in which people live: clearly, the most relevant consequence of his analysis implies the discovery of the main structure of being as a confrontation between wills to power. The second consequence is the distinction between active nihilism, visible even in the forms of a will to destruction, and pessimism, as the feeling of the unutterable vanity of things and of human actions.

As we will see, both appear when we consider the cultural roots of the Mafia and its function as a paradigm of nihilistic violence. In particular, as Sicily's history shows (including in literature), the emergence of cosmic pessimism, the forms of living imposed by the Mafia, its semantics of violence, its approach to reality as a play of forces, all belong to the nihilistic paradigm described by Nietzsche, connecting social and individual *ressentiment* to active and passive violence. But how can a specific, criminal phenomenon, born in Southern Italy, be conceived of as paradigmatic of European nihilism or the nihilism at work in our global civilization? According to Nietzsche, a partial answer to this question emerges when we consider this phenomenon as paradigmatic of a conception of society as a collection of wills to power. Furthermore, the political way of exercising power and violence appears in this case, on the one hand, as the dark side of the foundation on which normative fields are defined.[12] On the other hand, its countless victims manifest the loneliness in which many of those who tried to resist were left in the name of an indescribable *raison d'État* that was more inclined to keeping a segment of society in a state of warfare and emergency than to protecting loyal citizens. As Falcone and Borsellino discovered, their battle was only formally supported, but in truth opposed, by a part of the Italian deep state.[13] In this sense, an investigation into the Mafia's

---

[12] 'The lawbreaker is a debtor who not only fails to repay the benefits and advances granted to him, but also actually assaults the creditor' (GM II 9).

[13] As recently confirmed by the trials related to Borsellino's death. The investigations into the so-called State–Mafia pact resulted in two opposite sentences, the last of which (See Corte di Assise di Appello di Palermo – Sezione Seconda (2021): *Dispositivo di Sentenza*, 23 Settembre 2021. In: *Giurisprudenza Penale*. www.giurisprudenzapenale.com/wp-content/uploads/2021/09/dispositivo-trattativa.pdf, visited on 12 February 2022) recognized the historical attempt at a pact

forms of power confirms its standing as a form of nihilism as political practice, on the one hand, and truth as a practical attempt to resist that power, on the other. The latter is at the heart of Michel Foucault's lectures at the Collège de France, *The Courage of the Truth*, which focused on the connections between practices of truth and Western nihilism. In this sense, for Foucault, 'The question of nihilism is not: if God does not exist, everything is permitted. Its formula is rather a question: how to live if I must face up to the fact that "nothing is true?"' (Foucault 2011, p. 189).

2 A Postcolonial History

The Mafia's history closely follows the history of the Mediterranean island of Sicily. There is no consensus on the origin of the term Mafia; what is certain, however, is that it emerged in popular slang in Palermo and in criminal contexts in the middle of the nineteenth century. The term acquired a juridical sense following the political and administrative union of Sicily and the Kingdom of Italy in 1861. Literary proof of its use first appeared in the popular theatrical piece *I mafiusi della Vicaria* [*Vicaria's mafiosi*], written in 1863 by Giuseppe Rizzotto and Gaspare Mosca.[14] In this piece, the term 'mafioso' is used to describe the minor local bosses that held power in certain criminal gangs. The *Mafiusi* are characterized as being guided by a positive ethics: they are brave and defend the local population from the arrogance and oppression of institutional powers. At the time, according to the Sicilian ethnologist Giuseppe Pitrè, the term *Mafia* was connected to the idea of beauty.[15] On the institutional side of the Mafia's roots, we meet the popular myth of secret sects that arose in Sicily as early as the Middle Ages and spread throughout the Spanish world, the aim of which was formerly that of protecting the poor from the abuses and mistreatment of

---

but did not rule that the police officers involved had committed a crime. See Dickie (2004, pp. 230–237) and Fiandaca-Lupo (2014). See also Schneider and Schneider (2003). Fiandaca (2012) had already clarified the legal difficulty of clearly identifying as a crime the attempts of politicians and police officers to stop the Mafia's attacks through dialogue, calling attention to the risk that anti-Mafia investigations could be used as a form of political self-promotion, following Sciascia (2004, pp. 862–869). Although not legally punishable, attempts to negotiate with the Mafia were an application of the doctrine of *raison d'État*. The same doctrine had been employed, although the state chose not to negotiate, in the case of the abduction and murder of the politician Aldo Moro by the terrorists of Brigate Rosse in 1978.

14 It was partially re-written by Leonardo Sciascia. See Sciascia (2004b).
15 See Pitrè (1978, pp. 180–294). As late as 1989, the Corleone boss Luciano Liggio referred to this connection in an interview.

the landowning aristocracy. This was the basis of the origin myth of the 'Beati Paoli' (an alleged secret association in Palermo's underground), on which Luigi Natoli based his novel (1910). Until recently, members of the Mafia used this myth to justify their membership: the 'pentito' Tommaso Buscetta, for example, consistently appealed the admirable ethical aims of the association, as a protector of the most humble social classes.[16]

The Mafia's development into its twentieth-century manifestation must be approached through the forms of secrecy and control over territory and populations that emerged at the end of the nineteenth century. When considering the origins of the Mafia, it is thus important to understand the context in which it arose: a society marked by inner class conflict and perpetually dominated by external powers. Both the founding myth and the concrete, secret organization of its membership can be viewed through these categories: Sicily has been a colony for the greater part of its history, characterized by the extreme polarization of a powerful upper class and a poor, humble lower class.[17] This progressively unified association began to act almost as a sovereign power, providing protection to the population where public institutions failed to do so and holding power and privilege through the possession of weapons.

The growing power of the Mafia was also due in part to the Orientalism through which external powers viewed the Sicilian way of life.[18] The most practical effect of this perception was a policy of non-interference with conditions in Sicily and of simply forming agreements with the existing powers in order to ensure the integration of the region's otherness into the new systems of power.[19] The leadership of the new liberal, post-unitary Italian state, which represented

---

[16] Buscetta also discussed a religious ritual of affiliation practiced by the clan in which a new member would cup a sacred image smeared with his own blood in his hands, which another member would then set alight. These ancestral traditions testify to the popular origins of this criminal phenomenon. See Paoli (2003, pp. 67–70). See Catino (2019, 66–72), who explains the three steps of initiation, based on an archetype, an initiatory death and the new birth. On Buscetta's role in our understanding (and the downfall) of the Mafia, see Arlacchi (2000). See also Dickie (2004, p. 237). Worthy of mention in this sense is also the recent film by Marco Bellocchio, *The Traitor* (2019). On the secret associations at the heart of the Mafia, see Crisantino (2000) and Lupo (2010b). On the recovery of the myth of Beati Paoli's sect, see Benigno (2015). On the Mafia's religious traditions, see Dino (2010).

[17] During the Second Mafia war, the Corleonesi clans represented their own rise to power as the rising up of the people against the 'civil' mafia that was the bourgeoisie of Palermo. See Dickie (2004, pp. 284–291).

[18] On 'latent' and 'manifest' kinds of Orientalism, see Said (2003, p. 216). On the type of Orientalism that has as its object Sicily and Southern Italy, see Schneider (1998).

[19] On the Mafia as 'instrument of local government', see Dickie (2004, pp. 69–86). See also Oliveira and Guerriero (2018).

a modern conception of government based on a division of powers and free elections, conceived of Sicily as a "lost land" of sorts that ultimately had to be governed by force and violence. In this sense, its approach to the South was not markedly different from the way it had governed territories and populations conquered in colonial wars.[20] The Italian central state was thus perceived by poor Sicilian peasants as a mere continuation, in all practical respects, of the previous Bourbonic rule: its presence was made known to them through the two forms of taxation and conscription. This provoked revolts and violence that made Sicily one of the most dangerous territories in Europe at the time. General Govone, sent by the government to control Sicily by force, declared a state of emergency in the region, giving him the power to detain, torture and execute people without trial. As he declared before Parliament, no other methods are available to control a population which had not yet passed from barbarism to civilization.[21] In 1866, Palermo suffered yet another insurrection, which was used by the Mafia as a way to increase its power over the public authorities.

Following the unification of Italy, hopes that the previous structures of power would crumble were dashed: the new state was not interested in redistributing the great *latifundia* of the Church and the aristocracy, instead choosing to repackage them and sell them to the highest bidder. In this way, the Mafia began to form a new, violent, predatory bourgeoisie that acquired land through fear. It had an interest, shared by the public authorities, in preventing the lower classes from changing conditions in the region. In the first decades of the twentieth century, the Mafia was a strong organization that began to extend its power to America (while maintaining its connections to the homeland) through the roads of emigration (with over one and a half million people leaving Sicily in a 25-year period).[22]

After the Fascist 'iron prefect' Cesare Mori's attempt to destroy the Mafia, in World War II the Allied forces decided to attack the Axis powers in Sicily, and the necessity of controlling the territory and population with the least effort again prompted the rise of the Mafia's power. With the substantial support of the Mafia, the Allied landing in Sicily took place without great losses. In return

---

[20] The phenomenon of the Mafia was approached through the new criminal theories of Cesare Lombroso, as in the case of Giuseppe Alongi's book *The Maffia in its factors and Manifestations*. See Dickie (2004, p. 84). On the emerging 'Southern Question' in the early history of unitary Italy, see Moe (2002, pp. 224–249).

[21] Just some years before, Garibaldi's Lieutenant, Nino Bixio, welcomed as a liberator by the population, did not hesitate to commit war crimes against the same population, including by declaring a state of emergency.

[22] See Dickie (2004, pp. 161–189). See Lupo (2015).

for this support, the first Allied administration entrusted the mafiosi with managing the first local administrations in Sicily.[23] Once again in the history of Sicily, it was an external power that decided to entrust local elites with governing the population and the territory.[24] In this sense, the origins of the Mafia are rooted in colonial forms of power that have been imposed on Sicily for generations. Since the Allied landing, the Mafia has conducted itself as a sovereign power in Sicily, aware of its power to control and negotiate with other powers. Immediately following America's decision to integrate the whole of Italy within its geopolitical sphere of influence as a buffer between the West and the new enemy represented by the Soviet Union, the Mafia's interests would become progressively integrated within Italian politics through the manipulation of votes, the exchange of favours, extortion and other forms of protection.[25]

At the end of the 1980s, two episodes signified a turning point in the Mafia's history. On the one hand, at the international level, the end of the Cold War made control over Sicilian (and Italian) territories less important to the American strategy. On the other hand, the rise of a new Mafia elite, based on the international cocaine trade and characterized by dictatorial forms of leadership, began to destroy the inner unity of the Mafia, resulting in a bloody episode that came to be known as the Second Mafia War.[26] The consequences of these two events were, on the one hand, a break in the continuity between the political interests of the ruling powers and the Mafia's own interests and, on the other hand, the appearance of the 'pentitismo', criminals who decided to collaborate with the state's forces. The revelations of the first and most important of these, Tommaso Buscetta, arrested in Brazil on 14 July 1984, helped investigators to understand the main characteristics of the Mafia as an organization. Prior to that time, the Mafia had simply been thought of as one criminal organization among others, without any specific distinguishing qualities. It soon became clear that the Mafia needed to be recognized for what it was, a unified, organized power. In 1982, the new penal code finally made clear that Mafia membership is character-

---

[23] Sciascia underplays the impact of the Fascist attack against the Mafia. See Sciascia (2004a, p. 840). Lucky Luciano's friend Vito Genovese, wanted by the FBI, appeared in Sicily as an interpreter for the American Army. Don Calogero Vizzini, the 'boss of bosses', and Genco Russo were made mayors of their villages under the Allied administration of the island. See Dickie (2004, pp. 157–158 and 191–216).

[24] On the Orientalist view of Southern Italy as an origin of specific forms of government, see Moe (2002, pp. 156–183).

[25] See Gambetta (1993). On the use of common criminals by Napoleon III and the Mafia by Americans to control and defend the status quo, see Foucault (2001, pp. 1610–1611).

[26] On the origins of the Second Mafia War, see Dickie (2004, pp. 259–291).

ized by the 'force of intimidation provoked by the associative obligation' and by the 'condition of subjugation and of *omertà* derived from it in order to commit crimes, to acquire, directly or indirectly, the management or control of economic activities ... or to realize undeserved profits or advantages'.[27] Based on this legal apparatus and on Buscetta's deposition, a team of Sicilian judges, including Giovanni Falcone and Paolo Borsellino, convicted hundreds of 'honoured men' during the Maxi Trial in Palermo. Finally, in 1992, the Court of Cassazione (the Supreme Court of Italy) confirmed for the first time that the Mafia consisted not in a variegated collection of local gangs but in a single organization, bound by an oath of loyalty until death. One and a half centuries after its emergence, this legal verdict thus defined the Mafia as a 'unitary, centralized, hierarchical organization based on fixed, territorial structures corresponding to the local context of each group' and governed by a 'unique body called the "Cupola" or the "Commissione", made up of representatives of the most important "families", who were in charge of the general governance of the organization and were thus responsible for making the most relevant decisions'.[28] On the other hand, the court also described details regarding how members of the Mafia conducted themselves: membership in the association was initiated through a solemn ritual that included entering into an unbreakable personal vow to pursue and protect the group's interests.[29] These legal dispositives thus gave form, for the first time, to a legal paradigm that was extremely useful for approaching similar kinds of organized power.[30]

In this short history of the Mafia, I have attempted to trace its main characteristics as a violent, secret organization that acts through violence in a territory governed by rules that do not correspond to those of the sovereign state. The Mafia emerged as a power that was itself generated by a type of power relation found in postcolonial territories. Characterized as a secret organization based on a specific code of conduct and a specific form of control over territory and populations, the Mafia's power is revealed through the main principles it shares with modern sovereignty, as Foucault conceives of the latter: the power of life and

---

[27] Art. 416-bis, codice penale, "Associazione di tipo mafioso". This article was promulgated by the Italian Parliament through the law 'Rognoni-La Torre' in 1982. Leonardo Sciascia did not share this monolithic image of the Mafia: see Sciascia (2004a, p. 884).
[28] Corte Suprema di Cassazione – Prima Sezione Penale (1992): *Sentenza Generale 30 gennaio 1992, n. 80* (reg. gen. n. 23501/91), pp. 97–98.
[29] See Corte Suprema di Cassazione – Prima Sezione Penale (1992): *Sentenza Generale 30 gennaio 1992, n. 80* (reg. gen. n. 23501/91, p. 104).
[30] For the paradigmatic meaning of the Maxi Trial, see Paoli (2003, p. 13). See also Sales, Isaia, "La sfida di Falcone che tolse ai boss l'impunità". In: *La Repubblica*, May 22, 2021.

death. In this sense, certain of Foucault's theories on power help us to approach the Mafia as a phenomenon based on specific forms of living and exercising power. Although the paradigm of the Mafia was based on violence, however, what remains to be clarified is whether and how this violence can be defined as 'nihilistic'.

3 Power, Politics, Necropolitics

In his short history of Sicily, English historian John Julius Norwich explains why, in his eyes, Sicily is a sad island. His view of Sicily is very helpful for understanding how Sicily and its phenomena have continued to be approached – even in recent times – from an Orientalistic point of view: as an enigma.[31] As part of Sicilian history, the Mafia also contributed to giving shape to the island's forms of living, creating values and defining the Orientalistic perspective through which Sicily's history and forms of life were viewed. In Norwich's words, the entire island appears to be destined to a melancholic, 'pessimistic' form of life, in a sense comparable to Nietzsche's diagnosis of nihilism. With our short history of the Mafia in hand, we can now consider how, according to the Nietzschean conception of power, the Mafia's forms of power and violence can be clarified as paradigms of nihilism. In particular, through the conceptions opened up by Michel Foucault and Achille Mbembe, we can better understand the Mafia's emergence as a species of a broader kind of colonial and post-colonial power that is intrinsic to western modernity. The Orientalistic gaze produced by the Mafia's paradigms and the incorporation of those paradigms within legal procedures, first within state power and then globally, will reveal the Mafia's paradigm as a reverted image produced by and revealing the real mode of operation of power in an age of nihilism. In this sense, through the history and the evolution of the Mafia's nihilism (itself derived from colonial power), what emerges as having been objectified as a paradigm and discourse is the very mode of production of western nihilism as a form of power and violence. More than a peripheral paradigm of power, the Mafia reveals a 'dialectic of anti-modernity', based on Beck's distinction – one that defines our global society as a society at risk – between 'basic principles' and 'basic institutions' (see Beck 2009, pp. 223–234).

Throughout the 1970s, Michel Foucault devoted many studies to power and the forms in which structures of power are organized. Moved by 'the suspicion

---

[31] See Norwich (2015).

that power as such does not exist',[32] Foucault's approach to power focuses on forms of rationality that imply a specific type of conduct. More precisely, more than 'a mysterious substance that one avoids interrogating in itself, no doubt because one prefers *not* to call it into question' (Foucault 2002d, p. 336), he prefers neither 'to analyze the phenomena of power, nor to elaborate the foundations of such an analysis' (Foucault 2002d, p. 326). Power must instead be approached through *power relations*, as something that can be studied through the concrete ways in which populations are governed and in connection to forms of resistance to this governance. Power 'exists only as exercised by some on others, only when it is put into action' (Foucault, 2002d, p. 340). This appears to be particularly important given the Mafia's main characteristic as being 'deeply embedded in the economy, in politics, and in society' (Catino 2019, p. 2).

When formalized, these relations indeed seem to exclude violence: 'A relationship of violence acts upon a body or upon things; it forces, it bends, it breaks, it destroys, or it closes off all possibilities' (Foucault 2002d, p. 340). The exercise of power involves both violence and consent, although violence and consent do not constitute the basic nature of power. This is because power relations necessarily imply, according to Foucault, a form of freedom: 'In itself, the exercise of power is not a violence that sometimes hides, or an implicitly renewed consent.' (Foucault 2002d, p. 341). This relates to what Foucault calls 'government', a term that refers not to specific political structures but to the structure of 'the possible field of action of others' (Foucault 2002d, p. 341). Neither fully reducible to violence or struggle nor reducible to negotiation, Foucauldian power relations cannot be understood in isolation from the constitutive freedom of the subject:[33] In power relations, at every moment, the opposed forces can be subverted by the action of the other. What happens when this game comes to a close and this confrontation achieves its aims? For Foucault, the destruction of all opposition or resistance, of all 'points of insubordination' (Foucault 2002d, p. 347) – when 'stable mechanisms replace the free play of antagonistic reactions' (Foucault 2002d, pp. 346–347) – corresponds to the end of the power relationship, and thus to the end of power itself.[34]

In this moment, as occurs when the Mafia pretends to dominate economic relations, the field of struggle becomes a cemetery. Of course, 'every strategy of confrontation dreams of becoming a relationship of power and every relation-

---

[32] See also Foucault (1988, pp. 103–104).
[33] See Foucault (2002d, p. 342) and Foucault (2002d, p. 326).
[34] Institutions, for Foucault, can certainly be approached through this conception: in this sense, the state appears not simply as a crystalized power but rather as a situation to which much of the form of power relations refers.

ship of power tends, ... to become a winning strategy' (Foucault 2002d, p. 347), but when this really happens, the power is transformed into pure domination.

For Foucault, two different meanings of the term 'subject' correspond to two different forms of power relation: on the one hand, one is 'subject to someone else by control and dependence'; on the other hand, the subject is 'tied to his own identity by a conscience or self-knowledge' (Foucault 2002d, p. 326). In this sense, 'truth' is also a practice, 'no doubt a form of power' (Foucault 1988, p. 107). Governmentalization (see Foucault 2002a) thus consists in the progressive appropriation – by an organized field of powers – of types of power relations among subjects. Historically, this corresponds to the appearance of the modern state, conceived of as a complex form of techniques that orient power relations. Foucault calls the 'strategy' of this progressive incorporation 'pastoral power'.[35] The political reason for the rise of the modern state begins when the boundaries of the state are determined through control over the population that inhabits it. Pastoral power is thus characterized in terms of overseeing a flock, a population, rather than a territory; it is also characterized as a form of control over individuals and the population taken as a whole: the shepherd determines whether the flock lives or dies, and his aim is its salvation. This figure is thus characterized by a specific duty, consisting in keeping and guarding each individual member. The inevitable effects of pastoral power are thus 'both individualization and totalization' (Foucault 2002b, p. 325). In this sense, politics becomes aimed at defining power relations through the care of forms of living: a biopolitics. But while this form of power is legitimated by the care of lives, it does not hesitate to sacrifice them if a superior danger requires it: 'So the reverse of biopolitics is thanatopolitics' (Foucault 2002c, p. 416). Foucault develops his conception of sovereignty in line with this ambivalence between biopolitics and thanatopolitics. In his lecture *Society must be defended*, he explains that while sovereignty is based on the right of life and death, 'Sovereign power's effect on life is exercised only when the sovereign can kill' (Foucault 2003, p. 240). In this sense, the very essence of this right consists in the right to kill: no real symmetry exists in the right of life and death, 'Nor is it the right to allow people to live or to leave them to die. It is the right to take life or to let alive' (Foucault 2003, pp. 240–241). For Foucault, the great transformations that permeated nineteenth-century sovereignty correspond precisely to the progressive transformation of this right from a right 'to take life or let live' into a power 'to "make" live and "let" die' (Foucault 2003, p. 241). The rise of the Mafia's power can in this sense be interpreted as integrated within the development of pastoral and

---

35 See also Foucault (2002d, p. 333) and Foucault (2002c, p. 222).

biopolitical forms of modern power: alongside the power to take life or to let live, the Mafia follows the evolution of sovereignty as an economic power to make live, to biopolitically control *omnes et singulatim*. By contrast, Foucault's notion of subjectivation helps us to approach the opponents of the Mafia, who embodied an attitude that makes truth and public frankness instruments for eroding the culture of silent control that is typical of the Mafia's biopolitics.

This new kind of sovereignty, focused on biopower and on the definition of mortality as a new field in the exercise of power, was taken up by Achille Mbembe through the notion of 'necropolitics'. Mbembe's point of departure is no longer the living subject, but rather the relation between the murderer and his victim. What Mbembe prefers to explore in the field of sovereignty is, more than the right to let live, the right to put to death. For him, this right clearly also provokes a deep transformation of the relation between the governed and the governors: the subject of this right can only be an enemy. In exercising this power, sovereignty's effect thus reveals its own similarity to war.[36] Mbembe's investigations focus in this sense on 'those figures of sovereignty whose central project is not the struggle for autonomy but *the generalized instrumentalization of human existence and the material destruction of human bodies and populations*' (Mbembe 2019, p. 68). Contemporary experiences of human destruction suggest to Mbembe that a different reading of politics and sovereignty must be pursued. He highlights two key concepts that are pivotal to Foucault's notion of biopower: the state of exception and the state of siege. In this sense, for Mbembe, power always produces exceptions, emergencies, and even a fictionalized notion of the enemy. If biopower, for Foucault, is a function that divides people into those who must live and those who must die, Mbembe's question becomes 'What is the relationship between politics and death in those systems that operate only through a state of emergency?' (Mbembe 2019, p. 70). Among the examples Mbembe gives are colonies, archetypes of a form of violence inscribed in modernity. Modernity is inhabited by forms of terror that manifest themselves in the concatenation of biopower, the state of exception and the state of siege (Mbembe 2019, p. 76). In this sense, the state of exception, typical of the colonies, divides the population into subgroups. What the rise of violence in the civilized West during World War II manifests is thus 'an extension of methods previously reserved for the "savages" to the "civilized" peoples of Europe' (Mbembe 2019, p. 76). The colony is a space in which sovereignty is manifested in an exercise of power that is completely outside of the law, where an absolute exercise of violence is interrupted by a peace that 'is more likely to assume the face of "'end-

---

[36] See Mbembe (2019, p. 66).

less war"' (Mbembe 2019, p. 76). The *jus publicum europaeum* thus seems to be based on a distinction between those parts of the world where power relations are determined by terror and those parts where they are defined juridically.[37] In this sense, 'the colony is thus the site par excellence where controls and guarantees of judicial order can be suspended – the zone where the violence of the state of exception is deemed to operate in the service of "civilization"' (Mbembe 2019, p. 77).[38] Not subject to legal rules, in the colony 'the distinction between war and peace does not hold' (Mbembe 2019, p. 78): 'Invisible killing is added to outright executions' (Mbembe 2019, p. 83). Against appearances, Mbembe clarifies how types of power relations and violence in the colonies appear clearly in the contemporary world. As concretely evidenced by postcolonial geopolitics in many parts of the globalized world, 'many Urban militias, private armies, armies of regional lords, private security firms, and state armies all claim the right to exercise violence or to kill'. Mbembe identifies these types of power relations and violence through the Deleuzian notion of war machines 'involved in constituting highly transnational local or regional economies' (Mbembe 2019, p. 86): 'War machines are made up of segments of armed men that split up or merge with one another, depending on the tasks to be carried out and the circumstances involved. Polymorphous and diffuse organizations, war machines are characterized by their capacity for metamorphosis' (Mbembe 2019, p. 85). Mbembe concludes that the contemporary world is characterized by an increase in weapons and, clearly, in forms of power that are oriented towards 'maximally destroying persons and creating *death-worlds*' (Mbembe 2019, p. 92).

As we saw above, the Mafia was born historically in a certain territory: Sicily, a region that was subjected to forms of colonial occupation. This resulted in the generation of specific forms of power. Sects and organizations, power relations determined both through secret agreements with public powers and through terror, control over the population defined as control over life conduct, violence for the sake of preventing all resistance: these characteristics appear to render the Mafia a product of those forms of power that are typical of colonial occupation, a violent power generated by a state of emergency and siege that inaugurated an endless state of war. In times of peace, the Mafia engaged in a type of violence that was invisible; outside of the controlled territories they acted as camouflaged war machines, laundering dirty money through legitimate investments and act-

---

[37] Mbembe (2019, p. 77).
[38] From this perspective, the roots of power appear to lie outside of right, constituting what the German jurist Carl Schmitt and, more recently, Jacques Derrida define as the force of law: nihilism then appears as a governmental, 'katechontic' force. See Prozorov (2012).

ing as normal businesses.³⁹ Nevertheless, far from being unrelated to normal, political forms of power, the violence that is ostensibly monopolized by the state, the Mafia reveals the dark side of western legal institutions and western rules. As testified by the many pentiti, the Mafia comes into play when decision-makers must circumvent public rules in order to guarantee the execution of dirty deeds.⁴⁰ Acting as a necropower, the Mafia displays the violence inherited by external policies, exhibiting the extreme, nihilistic bases in which western forms of power are rooted. This post-colonial approach to the Mafia's paradigm allows us, finally, to understand current globalized powers as the heirs to 'multiple modernities' (Bhambra 2013, p. 301), as opposed to a more stable notion of Eurocentric modernity: even the latter must be understood as containing multiple forms, as demonstrated by the presence of colonial powers within Europe.

4 The Mafia as a Paradigm of Nihilistic Violence

> In Sicily it doesn't matter whether things are done well or done badly; the sin which we Sicilians never forgive is simply that of "doing" at all. We are old, Chevalley, very old. For more than twenty-five centuries we've been bearing the weight of superb and heterogeneous civilizations, all from outside, none made by ourselves, none that we could call our own. We're as white as you are, Chevalley, and as the Queen of England; and yet for two thousand and five hundred years we've been a colony. (Lampedusa 1961, p. 182)

Giuseppe Tomasi di Lampedusa's *The Leopard* portrays the tragic pessimism that Nietzsche describes as a manifestation of passive nihilism. This is particularly evident within the metaphysics of history represented in a speech by *The Leopard*'s main character, the Prince of Salina Don Fabrizio. In this speech, what emerges is the disenchanted spiritual attitude of the ancient, feudal aristocracy regarding the possibility of the new Italian state, of disrupting and reconfiguring the present games among powers and the engine of human history. His appreciation of the vanity of ancient values makes Don Fabrizio completely disillu-

---

39 See Sergi 2017.
40 In Sicily, Mafia-owned companies have succeeded in securing building contracts for public works. In addition, those responsible for the Palermo attacks against Falcone and Borsellino have yet to be brought to justice. Finally, in Campania and Calabria, Camorra and 'Ndrangheta became involved in waste disposal, illegally filling their own homelands with chemical and nuclear waste from legitimate companies and states that preferred to dispose of their toxic waste illegally to avoid huge costs. For an analysis of the compromises between legal powers and the Cosa Nostra, see Dickie (2004, pp. 319–325).

sioned about his role and, furthermore, about the idealistic attempt by the royal mandatory, Chevalley, to involve him in the new system of power, inaugurated by the Kingdom of Italy's annexation of Sicily. Don Fabrizio recommends installing the bourgeois Calogero Sedara as representative of the new emerging class. Whereas Don Fabrizio represents a form of immutable power that is passively resistant to all change, even embodying a will to nothingness – like other characters written by Sicilian writers (such as Verga) – the values of the new class are precisely defined by a will to power and by *ressentiment*.[41] Their representatives are aware of the groundlessness of all values: furthermore, they use values merely to obtain power. In this sense, they perfectly represent the spiritual attitude that inaugurates Sicilian history as belonging to the new state's periphery. Precisely at the end of the nineteenth century, another Sicilian writer, Federico De Roberto, represented this attitude with the character of Consalvo Uzeda di Francalanza, whose progressive quest for power is marked by a complete indifference to values.[42] The truth of history appears in this sense as a theatre in which the only true characters are wills to power.[43]

On the ironic side of this tragic pessimism, we find the Sicilian writer Leonardo Sciascia's essays and novels, which depict forms of life in contexts dominated by the Mafia. In the novel *The Day of the Owl*, Sciascia depicts a typical Mafia murder in a Sicilian village. The effect not only of the violent episode itself but of the biopolitical control exercised over the population is the adoption of an attitude of 'omertà' and fear on the part of the witnesses. The murder is narrated in the first scene of the novel. A bus is just about to leave the square when the conductor asks the driver to wait for a passenger, who is killed before his very eyes.[44] The same scene is then played out again from the perspective of a policemen, who, after having interviewed witnesses of the event, reports, absurdly,

---

41 I am referring to Verga's "Ciclo dei vinti" ("The Cycle of Won people"), including the novels *I Malavoglia* (1881) and *Mastro don Gesualdo* (1889), in which Verga studies the psychology – consisting of feelings of revenge, the will to power and *ressentiment* – of Sicily's lower classes. The characters of 'Ntoni Malavoglia and Mastro don Gesualdo, in particular, share the same characteristics as Lampedusa's Calogero Sedara. The same influences (mainly Bourget and Dostoevsky) that informed Nietzsche's notion of resentment can be found in the works of many Sicilian authors. See Ferraro (2020). On Verga's geographical poetics, see Moe (2002, pp. 250–295).
42 See De Roberto (1984, p. 1263).
43 Pirandello's plays also testify clearly to the theatricalization of power relations throughout history. His novel *The Old and the Young* (1913) is particularly relevant here, connecting the beginning of a social nihilism with the disappointment provoked by the new Italian regime. See Sciascia (2004c).
44 See Sciascia (1984, p. 9).

that no one has seen anything.⁴⁵ In another episode in which the investigator attempts to maintain a rational attitude in the face of the absurd, itself the result of deep fear provoked by a system of power, he muses: 'All right, then, no flights of fancy. But Sicily is all a realm of fantasy and what can anyone do there without imagination? Nothing but plain facts.' (Sciascia 1984, p. 35). This absence of proof, evidence or witnesses becomes the driving force of the investigation. The detective, the northerner Bellodi, is foreign to the Sicilian context and thus to the codes of living and surviving in the village. He is thus forced to replace his normal strategies with a totally logical approach based on conjecture. In other words, the brutal facts cannot speak for themselves: Mafia violence is protected by implicit understandings and the silences of a disempowered people. What is revealed is a specific form of power that simply emerges through violence when it cannot avoid emerging via a simple exercise of power. At the limit, this power is simply identified with silence.⁴⁶ As testified by the most recent sentences imposed in the State-Mafia pact,⁴⁷ legal truth can differ significantly from historical truth.⁴⁸ Sciascia reveals the ways in which the Mafia operates as a paradigm of power: even non-criminal forms of power can behave as the Mafia does. Hence the relevance of a continuous effort of resistance that must operate at the level of logic.⁴⁹ This same manifestation of power is intrinsically nihilistic from Sciascia's perspective, no different from Nietzsche's conception. Sciascia's realism in this sense manifests itself in an attempt to reveal the connections between the forces that struggle to define a scenario, precisely as Foucault observed. Any narration is thus seen, nihilistically, as the fruit of this struggle. The intellectual's role instead coincides with the search for truth, and, precisely according to Nietzsche's diagnosis of the relation between morality and truthfulness, the pressure to arrive at truth reveals the unfounded basis of

---

45 Ivi (1984, p. 14).
46 Sciascia stresses the way in which the informer Contorno spoke at the *Maxitrial:* his 'Sicilianism' demonstrated his genuine will to tell the truth (see Sciascia 2004a: pp. 852–854).
47 See Corte di Assise di Appello di Palermo – Sezione Seconda (2021): *Dispositivo di Sentenza*, 23 Settembre 2021. In: *Giurisprudenza Penale.* www.giurisprudenzapenale.com/wp-content/uploads/2021/09/dispositivo-trattativa.pdf, visited on 12 February 2022.
48 See also Foucault 2002e.
49 In different circumstances, as is the case in *L'Affaire Moro*, Sciascia himself interprets his ethical and political role as an intellectual as resembling that of a private detective – one who, by connecting facts, interpretations and partial truths, arrives at a reasonable understanding of a problematic event the causes of which, rooted in struggles among different powers, are partly determinable juridically and historically. Based on the real-life event of the kidnapping and murder of the Italian politician Aldo Moro, in this study Sciascia applies the investigating model of his novels to real-life historical events. See Castagnino 2014.

morality. Rather, it resembles a pessimistic approach to truth, based precisely on research that aims merely to resist the given conditions of power. Sciascia's notion of enlightenment is precisely observable not as a value, but rather as a pessimistic practice of enlightening the darkness in which mankind is trapped, due to the forms of governance (and values) it has produced.[50]

Mafia violence acts in silence and outside of the public sphere. The semantic code that renders the Mafia a 'transformational object' (Pine 2019) has been paradigmatically reproduced, again and again, by cinema.[51] Perhaps surprisingly, cinema has had a deep effect on the behaviour of Mafia bosses.[52] As Roberto Saviano stresses, 'it's not the movie world that scans the criminal world for the most interesting behavior. The exact opposite is true' (Saviano 2007, p. 250). We might therefore argue that Mafia movies contribute to spectacularizing the Mafia as a paradigm of power and self-government.[53] Even in the case of Francis Ford Coppola's *The Godfather*, Don Corleone's power is not based on a manifest exercise of violence: violence is often merely promised (in the case of *Scarface*, directed in 1983 by Brian De Palma, we can also highlight a parresiastic moment in the life of the criminal Tony Montana, revealing, by contrast, the false values of society).[54] The Mafia became a popular cinematographic subject and a paradigm to be imitated in part because its values were desirable to an underprivileged part of society. Once the old values have disappeared, violence emerges as the only force that can legitimate power.[55] Nevertheless, as a genre, Mafia movies do not follow the real history of the Mafia, although they create semantic codes, in some cases giving form to Orientalistic views by separating criminal

---

[50] On Sciascia's approach, see Chu (1998). See also Olujić and Fioretti (2018).

[51] For a recent and detailed approach to Mafia movies and to the relevance of such films in regard to the Mafia as a phenomenon, see Morreale (2020). Sciascia's *The Day of the Owl* was meaningfully adapted for the cinema by Damiano Damiani in 1968.

[52] On the development of Mafia movies as a genre, see Morreale (2020, p. 33). See Renga (2011). A relevant topic in this sense is also the representation of Italians and the Mafia in videogames: see Pitroso (2019).

[53] Saviano's Mafia bosses live in houses that resemble those of the bosses in films such as *Scarface*. Morreale highlights Mafia bosses Riina and Brusca's fascination with mafia movies: see Morreale (2020, p. 14–16). In addition to *The Godfather* and *Scarface*, Tarantino's films and the recent *The Irishman* are also worthy of mention in this context, as is Martone's *Gomorrah*. See Morreale's list of Italian Mafia movies from 1949 to 2019 (2020, pp. 313–316), among them popular tv series like *La Piovra*. See also Massari and Martone 2019.

[54] Something similar occurs in Sciascia's *The Day of Owl*, where, in the moments just preceding his arrest, Don Mariano voices his anthropological point of view on human nature, which he confesses to captain Bellodi. See Sciascia (1984, p. 102).

[55] See Sergi (2017, pp. 32–36).

phenomena from daily life, in others by creating an image that the bosses could enjoy and identify with.[56]

According to Foucault, any power relationship that descends into complete dominion – or in Mbembe's terms, the *unthought* of modern politics – corresponds to a necropolitics. What the Mafia seems to reveal is the archetypal violence of power, a paradigm of the unfounded soil on which all power settles and the danger of what can occur when society descends into a state of warfare: the proliferation of a nihilistic will to destruction. The proliferation and evolution of the Mafia's forms of criminality around the world, on the one hand, and the level of destruction caused by the Mafia's necropolitics on landscapes and natural resources, on the other, now embody the unsolvable compromise inherited from biopolitical modernity: governance based on a distinction between those populations and territories that must live, or survive, and those populations and territories that can die. Understanding the Mafia can thus help us to understand how nihilism reveals itself in the world. Having inherited the violence of the colonial period, the Mafia developed new forms of power that were perfectly suited to governing both their global trade and the local population, the 'glocal' dimension of nihilism always a part of their DNA (see Sergi and Lavorgna 2016).[57] As Beck writes, '*a changed reality presupposes a changed perspective.* Politics emerges from and consists in the way it itself interprets given situations historically' (Beck 2005, p. 278). The evolution of the Mafia's power was particularly explanatory in this sense: in order to better defend its interests, after the bomb attacks in 1992, the Sicilian Mafia, led by the boss Bernardo Provenzano and then by Matteo Messina Denaro, preferred to return to a semantics of silence. In fact, this strategy allowed its power to adapt to the new political conditions, redefining itself as a 'grey thing' in which bosses share strategic decisions on investments with unscrupulous managers (Di Girolamo 2012, p. 20).[58] Even more adaptive than the Sicilian Mafia were the other mafias, however, such as 'Ndrangheta and Camorra, which lacked hierarchical structures and were thus better suited to an amphibious kind of action. What is more, the Mafia's financial liquidity allowed it to penetrate legal businesses, such that there was no longer a distinction between legal and illegal forms of economy, especially in times and contexts of crisis.[59]

---

56 Morreale argues that 'today, to make a film on the Mafia is, more than ever, to narrate something that is similar to us' (Morreale 2020, p. 9, my translation).
57 See Sergi and Lavorgna (2016).
58 See also Santino (2006, p. 12).
59 As stressed by Hellyer (2014) and Catino (2019, p. 283). See also Dickie 2011 and Serenata 2014.

According to Nietzsche's and Foucault's conceptions of power, only an opposing form of power can prevent power from becoming complete domination. As Foucault and Sciascia show, this must be embodied by specific attitudes. If one dies – as Giovanni Falcone observed – this is because one is left alone. Mafia violence is no longer signified by the semantics of bombings, but the biological catastrophes of our anthropocentric world risk bringing us back to these realities. As illustrated by the success of new criminal sects that replay Sicilian colonial paradigms, for example the Nigerian Mafia,[60] it is not only the people of Sicily and Naples who must now resist the perverted effects of a will to destruction that intersects with a will to nothingness: the Mafia represents a paradigm of power at work in a risk society that is precisely like our own, in which, as Beck argues, 'a state of normalcy and a state of exception overlap' (Beck 2009, 76).[61] In this sense, we are all like ants. What the Mafia's nihilistic violence paradigmatically seems to reveal is the origin and fate of our global culture should it fail to choose 'the fresh fragrance of freedom' over 'the stink of moral compromise, indifference, contiguity, and thus connivance'.[62]

Bibliography

Ansell-Pearson, Keith, and Diane Morgan (Eds.) (2000): *Nihilism Now! Monsters of Energy.* Basingstoke: Palgrave.

Arlacchi, Pino. (2000): *Addio Cosa Nostra. I segreti della mafia nella confessione di Tommaso Buscetta.* Milano: BUR.

Baker, Gideon (2020): *Nihilism and Philosophy: Nothingness, Truth and World.* London, New York: Bloomsbury.

Beck, Ulrich (2005): *Power in the Global Age: A New Global Political Economy.* Cambridge: Polity Press.

---

60 See Ellis (2016).

61 On ecocide as applied nihilism, see Gare (1996, pp. 1–31). O'Leary uses the Mafia as a paradigm of the perverted effects of the present environmental management. See O'Leary (2013). See also the post-colonial perspective of Ben-Shai and Lebovic (2014) and Lebovic 2015. For the global dimension of mafia paradigms, cf. Hill (2003), Falcone (2010) and Wang (2017). For a comparative study on global mafias see also Varese (2011).

62 These words are quoted from the last, public intervention by Judge Paolo Borsellino. See Lotta alle mafie. Osservatorio su criminalità e malapolitica. "Borsellino ricorda Giovanni Falcone a 28 giorni dalla strage di Capaci." YouTube video. https://www.youtube.com/watch?v=l9dHNYASqZk, visited on 12 February 2022.

This work is funded by national funds through the FCT – Fundação para a Ciência e a Tecnologia – under the project DFA/BD/5403/2020. The revision was supported by IFILNOVA – FCSH, Portugal.

Beck, Ulrich (2009): *World at Risk.* Cambridge: Polity Press.
Ben-Shai, Roy, and Nitzan Lebovic (2014): *The Politics of Nihilism: From the Nineteenth Century to Contemporary Israel.* New York, London: Bloomsbury
Bhambra, Gurminder K. (2013): "The Possibilities of, and for, Global Sociology: A Postcolonial Perspective". In: *Political Power and Social Theory* 24, pp. 295–314.
Castagnino, Angelo (2014): *The Intellectuals as a Detective: From Leonardo Sciascia to Roberto Saviano.* New York: Peter Lang.
Catino, Maurizio (2019): *Mafia Organizations: The Visible Hand of Criminal Enterprise.* Cambridge: Cambridge University Press.
Chu, Mark (1998): "Sciascia and Sicily: Discourse and Actuality". In: *Italica* 75. No. 1, pp. 78–92.
Crisantino, Amelia (2000): *Della segreta e operosa associazione: Una setta all'origine della mafia.* Palermo: Sellerio.
Cunningham, Connor (2002): *Genealogy of Nihilism: Philosophies of Nothing and the Difference of Theology.* London: Routledge.
De Roberto, Federico (1984): "L'Imperio". In: Carlo Alberto Madrignani (Ed.): *Romanzi, novelle e saggi.* Milano: Mondadori.
Dickie, John (2004): Cosa Nostra. *A History of the Sicilian Mafia.* Basingstoke: Palgrave.
Dickie, John (2011): *Mafia Brotherhoods: Camorra, Mafia, 'Ndrangheta: The Rise of the Honoured Societies.* London: Sceptre.
Dino, Alessandra (2010): *La mafia devota: Chiesa, religione, Cosa nostra.* Roma-Bari: Laterza.
Di Girolamo, Giacomo (2012): *Cosa Grigia.* Milano: Il Saggiatore.
Ellis, Stephen (2016): *This Present Darkness: A History of Nigerian Organized Crime.* Oxford: Oxford University Press.
Falcone, Giovanni, and Marcelle Padovani (2004): *Cose di Cosa Nostra.* Milano: BUR.
Falcone, Giovanni (2010): *La posta in gioco: Interventi e proposte per la lotta alla mafia.* Milano: Rizzoli.
Ferraro, Gianfranco (2020): "Demoni di Sicilia. Il nichilismo europeo di Federico De Roberto". In: *Oblio*, No. 38–39, pp. 155–175.
Fiandaca, Giovanni (2012): "La trattativa Stato-mafia tra processo politico e processo penale". In: *Criminalia. Annuario di Scienze Penalistiche*, pp. 67–93.
Fiandaca, Giovanni, and Salvatore Lupo (2014): *La Mafia non ha vinto: Il labirinto della trattativa.* Roma, Bari: Laterza.
Foucault, Michel (1988): "On Power". In: Lorenz D. Kritzman (Ed.): *Politics, Philosophy, Culture: Interviews and other writings 1977–1984.* New York: Routledge, pp. 96–109.
Foucault, Michel (2001): "Entretien sur la prison: le livre et sa méthode". In: Foucault, *Dits et écrits I. 1954–1975.* Gallimard: Paris, pp. 1608–1621.
Foucault, Michel (2002a): "Governmentality". In: James D. Faubion (Ed.): *Power: Essential works of Michel Foucault 1954–1984*, vol. 3. New York: New Press, pp. 201–222.
Foucault, Michel (2002b): "'Omnes et singulatim'. Toward a Critique of Political Reason". In: James D. Faubion (Ed.): *Power: Essential works of Michel Foucault 1954–1984*, vol. 3. New York: New Press, pp. 298–325.
Foucault, Michel (2002c): "The Political Technology of Individuals". In: James D. Faubion (Ed.): *Power: Essential works of Michel Foucault 1954–1984*, vol. 3. New York: New Press, pp. 403–417.

Foucault, Michel (2002d): "The Subject and Power". In: James D. Faubion (Ed.): *Power: Essential works of Michel Foucault 1954–1984*, vol. 3. New York: New Press, pp. 326–348.

Foucault, Michel (2002e): "Truth and Juridical Forms". In: James D. Faubion (Ed.): *Power: Essential works of Michel Foucault 1954–1984*, vol. 3. New York: New Press, pp. 1–89.

Foucault, Michel (2003): *"Society Must Be Defended". Lectures at the Collège de France 1975–1976*. Edited by Mauro Bertani and Alessandro Fondana and translated by David Macey. New York: Picador.

Foucault, Michel (2004): *The Archaeology of Knowledge*. London: Routledge.

Foucault, Michel (2008): *The Birth of Biopolitics: Lectures at the Collège de France (1978–1979)*. Edited by Michel Senellart. Translated by Graham Burchell. Basingstoke: Palgrave MacMillan.

Foucault, Michel (2009): *Security, Territory, Population: Lectures at the Collège de France (1977–1978)*. Edited by Michel et al. Translated by Graham Burchell. New York: St. Martin's Press.

Foucault, Michel (2011): *The Courage of the Truth: The Government of the Self and of the Others II: Lectures at the Collège de France 1983–1984*. Edited by Frédéric Gros and translated by Graham Burchell. Basingstoke: Palgrave.

Gambetta, Diego (1993): *The Sicilian Mafia: The Business of Private Protection*. Cambridge, London: Harvard University Press.

Gare, Arran (1996): *Nihilism Inc.: Environmental Destruction and the Metaphysics of Sustainability*. Sydney: Eco-logical Press.

Hellyer, Paul T. (2014): *The Money Mafia: A World in Crisis*. Walterville: Trine Day.

Hess, Henner (1973): *Mafia*. Con prefazione di Leonardo Sciascia. Roma-Bari: Laterza.

Hill, Peter B. E. (2003): *The Japanese Mafia: Yakuza, Law and the State*. Oxford: Oxford University Press.

Kuhn, Thomas S. (1996): *The Structure of Scientific Revolutions*. Chicago, London: The University of Chicago Press.

Lampedusa, Giuseppe Tomasi di (1961): *The Leopard*. Translated by A. Colquhoun. New York: Signet.

Lebovic, Nitzan (2015): "The History of Nihilism and the Limits of Political Critique". In: *Rethinking History*, 19. No. 1, pp. 1–17.

Levin, David Michael (1988): *The Opening of Vision: Nihilism and the Post-Modern Situation*. New York, London: Routledge.

Lupo, Salvatore (2010a): *Potere criminale. Intervista sulla storia della mafia*. Edited by G. Savatteri. Roma, Bari: Laterza.

Lupo, Salvatore (2010b): *Il tenebroso sodalizio: La mafia nel rapporto Sangiorgi*. Roma: Edizioni XL.

Lupo, Salvatore (2015): *The Two Mafias: A Transatlantic History. 1888–2008*. Basingstoke: Palgrave MacMillan.

Massari, Monica, and Vittorio Martone (2019): *Mafia Violence: Political, Symbolic, and Economic Forms of Violence in Camorra Clans*. London: Routledge.

Mbembe, Achille (2019): *Necropolitics*. Translated by S. Corcoran. Durham, London: Duke University Press.

Moe, Nelson (2002): *The View from Vesuvius: Italian Culture and the Southern Question*. Berkeley, Los Angeles: University of California Press.

Morreale, Emiliano (2020): *La mafia immaginaria: Settant'anni di Cosa Nostra al cinema (1949–2019)*. Roma: Donzelli.

Nietzsche, Friedrich (1968): *The Will of Power*. Edited by Walter Kaufmann and translated by Walter Kaufmann and R. J. Hollingdale. New York: Vintage Books.

Nietzsche, Friedrich (2014): *On the Genealogy of Morality*. Edited by Keith Ansell-Pearson and translated by Carol Diethe. Cambridge: Cambridge University Press.

Norwich, John Julius (2015): *Sicily: An Island at the Crossroads of History*. New York: Random House.

O'Leary, Richard (2003): *The Environmental Mafia: The Enemy is Us*. New York: Algora Publishing.

Oliveira, Guilherme de, and Carmine Guerriero (2018): "Extractive States: The case of the Italian Unification". In: *International Review of Law and Economics* 56 (C), pp. 142–159.

Olujić, Elis Deghenghi, and Fabrizio Fioretti (2013): "*I mafiosi* di Leonardo Sciascia. Analisi di una riscrittura". In: *Tabula* 11, pp. 103–114.

Paoli, Letizia (2003): *Mafia Brotherhoods: Organized Crime, Italian Style*. Oxford: Oxford University Press.

Pine, Jason. (2019): "The Mafia as Transformational Object". In: *Voci: Annuale di Scienze Umane* XVI, pp. 131–141.

Pitrè, Giuseppe (1978): *Usi, costumi, usanze e pregiudizi del popolo siciliano*. Palermo: Il Vespro.

Pitroso, Giulio (2019): "Mafia and the Representation of Italians". In: *Transactions of the Digital Games Research Association* 5. No 1, pp. 45–76.

Prozorov, Sergei (2012): "The Katechon in the Age of Biopolitical Nihilism". In: *Continental Philosophical Review* 45, pp. 483–503.

Renga, Dana (Ed.) (2011): *Mafia Movies: A Reader*. Toronto, Buffalo, London: University of Toronto Press.

Romano, Salvatore F. (1966): *Storia della mafia*. Milano: Mondadori.

Said, Edward W. (2003): *Orientalism*. London: Penguin.

Santino, Umberto (2006): *Dalla mafia alle mafie*. Soveria Mannelli: Rubbettino.

Saviano, Roberto (2007): *Gomorrah*: London: Macmillan.

Schneider, Jane (Ed.) (1998): *Italy's "Southern Question". Orientalism in One Country*. Oxford-New York: Berg.

Schneider, Jane C., and Peter T. Schneider (2003): *Reversible Destiny: Mafia, Antimafia, and the Struggle for Palermo*. Berkeley, Los Angeles: University of California Press.

Sciascia, Leonardo (1984): *The Day of the Owl: Equal Danger*. Boston: D. R. Godine.

Sciascia, Leonardo (2004a): *A futura memoria (se la memoria ha un futuro)*. In: Claude Ambroise (Ed.): *Opere: 1984–1989*,. Milan: Adelphi, pp. 763–898.

Sciascia, Leonardo (2004b): *I Mafiosi*. In: Claude Ambroise (Ed.): *Opere: 1984–1989*. Milano: Adelphi, pp. 1229–1296.

Sciascia, Leonardo (2004c): *Pirandello e la Sicilia*. In: Claude Ambroise (Ed.): *Opere: 1984–1989*. Milano: Adelphi, pp. 1041–1203.

Serenata, Nicoletta (Ed.) (2014): *The 'Ndrangheta and Sacra Corona Unita: The History, Organization and Operations of Two Unknown Mafia Groups*. London: Springer.

Sergi, Anna (2017): *From Mafia to Organised Crime: A Comparative Analysis of Policing Models*. Cham: Palgrave.

Sergi, Anna, and Anita Lavorgna (2016): *'Ndrangheta. The Glocal Dimensions of the Most Powerful Italian Mafia*. Cham: Palgrave.
Sifakis, Carl (2005): *The Mafia Encyclopedia*. New York: Facts on File.
Stellino, Paolo (2015): *Nietzsche and Dostoevsky: On the Verge of Nihilism*. Bern: Peter Lang.
Tartaglia, James (2016): *Philosophy in a Meaningless Life: A System of Nihilism, Consciousness and Reality*. London, New York: Bloomsbury.
Tongeren, Paul van (2018): *Friedrich Nietzsche and European Nihilism*. Newcastle upon Tyne: Cambridge Scholars Publishing.
Varese, Federico (2011): *Mafie in movimento*. Torino: Einaudi.
Volpi, Franco (1999): *Il nichilismo*. Roma-Bari: Laterza.
Wang, Peng (2017): *The Chinese Mafia: Organized Crime, Corruption and Extra-Legal Protection*. Oxford: Oxford University Press.
Weller, Shane (2008): *Literature, Philosophy, Nihilism: The Uncanniest of Guests*. Basingstoke: Palgrave.

Francescomaria Tedesco
Against the Kinship: State, Terror, Nihilism

Abstract: This text argues that there is a very close link between terror, terrorism and sovereignty. Terrorism, usually read as an act of nihilism, is here interpreted as the other side of the coin of modern sovereignty. The idea of brotherhood that underpins modern politics is questioned here, in order to propose that political obligation is founded not so much on the community of destiny between brothers, but on a brotherhood by lot.

1 Nihilism or Sovereignty?

The orientalist scholar Olivier Roy has argued that Islamist radicalisation in Europe is the result of a nihilistic European generational revolt, or rather a radical and total revolt of the young which, in Europe, manifests itself in the terms of jihadism. It is not, therefore, a question of resentment due to the Palestinian question or to the abuses perpetrated during the season of the so-called wars on terrorism, but of a sort of crisis of presence, of inability to situate oneself within society. So, we are faced, Roy maintains, not so much with the radicalisation of Islam, but with the Islamisation of nihilistic radicalism:

> A distinction should be made here between the ISIS version of Islam, much more grounded in the methodological tradition of exegesis of the Prophet's hadith (ISIS ostensibly uses the writings of "scholars" who are well versed in the traditional sciences) and the jihadis' version, which first of all revolves around an imaginary of heroism and modern-day violence. The ISIS exegeses that fill the pages of *Dabiq* and *Dar al-Islam*, the two recent magazines written in English and French and hence accessible to volunteers from the West, are not the cause of radicalization (which began in 1995). Radicals do not undertake these long, demonstrative analyses using a string of hadith the way ISIS does. What works with them is the linkage between the radical imaginary and the theological "rationalization" provided by ISIS, and *it is based not on real knowledge but an appeal to authority*. (Roy 2017, p. 43, emphasis added)

Roy argues that violence is not a means, but an end in itself, and this is the core of what he calls nihilism. There is no rational or finalistic logic to terrorist violence, other than terror for terror's sake. But, countering Roy's point of view, terrorist violence is not just an expression of nihilism (even if not necessarily religious); it is the deformed mirror of modern sovereignty, its mirrored and teratogenic other.

Also, according to the Jesuit magazine *La Civiltà Cattolica*, the terrorist phenomenon should be interpreted in terms of a religious radicalisation, although it recognises that:

> A few decades ago, this scourge had well-defined political and ideological connotations and inspirations and was used to achieve clear and specific objectives, and only rarely was it transnational. Covertly, it was a favorite tool of many totalitarian regimes. Nowadays, an international terrorism with religious and cultural nuances has emerged, often invading the world information scene through organizations such as Boko Haram and ISIS. (Lobo Arranz 2021, p. 73)

The Islamic State's recruitment propaganda insists, according to scholars, on the theme of the absolutization of friendship, which must go hand in hand with the 'alterisation' of the enemy and the unbeliever (see Al-Dayel 2019). Al-Dayel analyses the phenomenon of terrorist propaganda in favour of emigration to the Islamic State not as an example of nihilism, but by placing it in the more complex relationship between citizens and sovereignty. Sanctions such as the cancellation of passports for foreign fighters who have emigrated to the Islamic State tend to clarify how the management of terrorism is not seen from a purely religious point of view, but in the light of the nexus between citizenship and sovereignty:

> Contrasting the oft-framing of nihilistic and irrational behaviour of the Islamic State foreign fighter – one who beheads a journalist with zest, forces his children to execute hostages, enslaves and rapes civilians and hostages – the careful stylisation of its "citizens" such as Al-Cambodi urges us to consider how to analyse discourse beyond the normal constructions of "othering" or even propaganda framings of ideology, victimisation and religious fulfilment. (Al-Dayel 2019, p. 15)

The spectacle of the executions, the fact that they were filmed like films or video clips, the aestheticization of violence, are more in keeping with a sadistically patibular logic than with a purely nihilistic perspective. The state must be able to condemn to death, otherwise history is over: the State condemns to death and war is a right of the State, since these are the chrisms of historicity and politicity.

It is precisely the case of the cancellation of citizenship, proposed in France by the then President Hollande, that shifts the question of terrorist violence, and the State's reaction to it, to a position in which both subjects have a political relationship with the State, mediated by the notion of friendship and the attempt to absolutize friendship, rather than by a nihilistic logic. The terrorist objective, rather than a nihilist objective, represented instead, in the case of the terrorists of French citizenship who have struck France in recent years, the model of a questioning of the State of belonging and at the same time the affirmation of the need for a new *State*, the so-called 'Caliphate'. Hollande's immediate reaction can be read in the *compte rendu* of the 16 November 2015 session at the National Assembly. On that occasion, the French president had stated that Article 16 and Article 36 of the Constitution (respectively governing exceptional powers for the president of the République and the state of siege) were insufficient to deal with terrorism and had proposed the constitutionalisation of the citizenship loss (already provided for in the Civil Code) and the state of emergency. Following that speech, on 10 February 2016, the National Assembly approved the bill on constitutional reform with the inclusion in the fundamental charter of the state of emergency, and the *déchéance de nationalité* measure (citizenship loss) for those with dual nationality who had attacked State security. In the meantime, on 19 February 2016, the Conseil Constitutionnel ruled on a *question prioritaire de constitutionnalité* relating to the 1955 law which established the state of emergency as amended in 2015 after the Bataclan attacks, essentially confirming the structure of the law and of the entire discipline of the state of emergency, considering that the needs of national security are not to be considered recessive with respect to the rights of individuals, and intervening only on a specific point concerning respect for privacy. In any case, shortly afterwards Hollande had to acknowledge that the constitutional reform project had stalled, in particular because of the measure of loss of citizenship provided for in Article 2. But during the session of 16 November, Hollande had stated, quite icastically for our purposes: 'France is at war. The acts committed on Friday night in Paris and near the Stade de France are acts of war. At least 129 people were killed and many were injured. They are an attack on our country, on its values, on its youth, on its way of life' (Hollande 2015, my translation).[1]

A question of public order has turned into something else that opens up a fissure through which to look at the relationship between sovereignty and terror. How can one think of the citizenship loss when it comes to war? Even if the terrorists that ISIS has claimed as its affiliates are to be considered agents or soldiers of a foreign State (which one: the so-called Islamic "Caliphate"?), how is war conceivable since they were French (or at most Belgian) citizens? Should one think of a civil war? An internal war waged by citizens of the State that was the victim of the attacks? There is something that does not add up, and not only does it denounce the fact that the interpretation of a war attack does not work, but it also highlights the fact that we are dealing with an attack

---

[1] 'La France est en guerre. Les actes commis vendredi soir à Paris et près du Stade de France, sont des actes de guerre. Ils ont fait au moins 129 morts et de nombreux blessés. Ils constituent une agression contre notre pays, contre ses valeurs, contre sa jeunesse, contre son mode de vie'.

that is entirely internal to the logic of the State. This is all the more so as the reform proposal concerned the possibility of extending loss to citizens born in France and not only those who had become (also) French. In fact, art. 25 of the Civil Code provided for the loss of nationality for non-original citizens (who had a second nationality) but not for original citizens (who would otherwise have become stateless, as in the case of non-original citizens without another nationality). The Conseil constitutionnel has expressed its opinion on several occasions that the difference in treatment between originals and non-originals is reasonable: a compression of rights made possible in view of the protection of the State's interest and mitigated by the fact that the Civil Code provides for a time limit (no more than 10 years) for the disqualification of non-originals in order to prevent them from living in limbo with the perennial threat of losing their nationality. The reform proposal, by providing that the *déchéance* could be extended to dual nationals, removed the time limit guaranteeing non-originals, while the claim of constitutionalisation should have protected the decision from constitutional doubts. It should be noted that, symbolically, the *déchéance* should have been included in Title I, *De la souveraineté*. In short, under the reform, any French person born or becoming French, but with dual citizenship, could have been deprived of French citizenship for final convictions for acts of terrorism. Indeed, as reported in the opinion of the Conseil d'État

> Moreover, the Constitutional Council has ruled that persons born French and those who have become French by acquisition are in the same situation with regard to nationality law. Consequently, by extending to persons born French the sanction of disqualification already authorised by the Civil Code for persons who have become French by acquisition, the proposed provision does not create a breach of equality between these two categories of persons. (Conseil d'État2015, p. 2, my translation)[2]

Thus, very strange contrast measures for a war: directed internally, at its own citizens, and even extended not only to those who had become French, but also to those who were French by birth. Reinforcing this inward-looking interpretation is the fact that the motivations accompanying the proposal for the constitutionalisation and extension of the *déchéance* stated that it intended to 'pun-

---

[2] 'Par ailleurs, le Conseil constitutionnel a jugé que les personnes nées françaises et celles ayant obtenu la qualité de Français par acquisition étaient dans la même situation au regard du droit de la nationalité. Dès lors, en élargissant aux personnes nées françaises la sanction de la déchéance déjà autorisée par le code civil pour les personnes devenues françaises par acquisition, la disposition envisagée ne crée pas non plus une rupture d'égalité entre ces deux catégories de personnes'.

ish those whose behaviour is aimed at destroying the social bond' (Conseil d'État2015, p. 1, my translation).³ In other words, not the enemy, but those who, participating – by birth or by acquisition, but in any case by right – in the social bond, want to destroy it from within. A civil war lexicon. A perspective in which the outside (or the partially so: he who has become French) and the inside are equal. Both are threats.

2 Terror, Fiction, Awe

The paradigm of terror is not something external, alien to the Western tradition, including the history of the foundation of the rule of law. The founding of democracy also has a close relationship with the use of force as the foundation of the State, the cornerstone of modern politics and law. But, as Norberto Bobbio wrote, 'The problem of the justification of power stems from the question: "Given that political power is the power that deploys the exclusive use of force within a definite social group, is force enough to make it accepted by those on whom it is exercised, to induce its addressees to obey it?"' (Bobbio 1989, p. 81). The answer to this classic question of political philosophy concerning the problem of legitimacy can be found in Carlo Ginzburg's enlightening essay on Hobbes, in which Ginzburg thematises the question of force by connecting it to terror and reverence:

> Hobbes believed that political power implies force, but force alone is insufficient. The State, the "Mortall God" generated by fear, inspires terror: an emotion in which fear and reverence converge. In order to present itself as the legitimate authority, the State needs the instruments (the weapons) of religion. This explains why the modern reflection on the State is based on political theology: a tradition that Hobbes inaugurated. (Ginzburg 2008, pp. 12–13)

The word used by Hobbes is '"awe"', whose 'true translation', according to Ginzburg, is precisely 'terror' (see Ginzburg 2008, p. 11). And it is Ginzburg again who, taking up the studies of Horst Bredekamp, points out the sinister connection between the foundation of the State in Hobbes and the expression Shock and Awe, which indicates in code the US war operation that started the last Gulf War in 2003: 'Bredekamp pointed at the impact of a "trivialized version" of Leo Strauss's idea on American neo-cons' (Ginzburg 2008, p. 14). There is no doubt that terror has a close relationship of mutual implication with the for-

---

3 '[S]anctionner ceux qui par leurs comportements visent à détruire le lien social'.

mation – and life – of the State: 'Terrorism is the specter of modern sovereignty, which, in turn, is always potentially terrorist' (Di Cesare 2019, p. 39). So does terror have to do with sovereign power, or is it something that is internal to the State, or is it rather a threat external to it? The question is asked with respect to the issue of Islamic terrorism, of course, which has bloodied Europe in recent years. Is it in fact useful, after what we have written, to look at the phenomenon of terrorism and the so-called 'Islamic State' as a religious and nihilistic phenomenon?

Perhaps it is appropriate to look, in the wake of what has been said about terror, reverence, death, at the theme of political obligation, that is, at the 'to die for' question,[4] which is typical of the (nationalistic?) foundation of the modern State. Irving Krisol, former US Trotskyist and spearhead of the neocons, as well as father of William, neoconservative and leader of the Project for a New American Century, wrote: 'Another (and related) consequence of the disestablishment of religion as a publicly-sanctioned mythos has been the inability of liberal society ever to come up with a convincing and generally-accepted theory of political obligation' (Kristol 1973, p. 10). So, religion as an element of affirmation and consolidation of motivations for which to die, yes, but in the name of the State. 'Fingunt simul creduntque', wrote Tacitus in the *Annals* about religion ('they feign and at the same time they believe') (the original Tacitus citation [*Annals*, VI, 10] is 'fingebant simul credebantque': 'They fabricated a tale – and immediately believed it themselves' [Tacitus 2008, p. 183]). The Hobbesian origin is itself a reworking of Tacitus based upon Francis Bacon's paraphrase in *The Advancement of Learning* (Bacon 1996, p. 142): 'Hobbes's verb *feign*, close to *fiction* and *fictive*, echoes the verb used by Tacitus: *fingebant*' (Ginzburg 2005, p. 8). 'To sum up: at the origin of religion, as well as at the origin of the State, there is fear that produces awe. In between, there is fiction, which imposes itself, upon those who make it up, as a reality' (Ginzburg 2008, p. 9). Terror and subjection as the alpha and omega of the political order, but with an operating principle in the middle, an engine: fiction. The latter serves to make the machine work, which would otherwise be forced to rely on a mere tautology: 'Why are we obeyed?' 'Because the law is the law'. As Žižek writes:

---

[4] By this expression I am referring here to the political obligation that implies death in the name of the State: 'We assert a political obligation to die only when we describe the reason for the obligation in one or more of three ways: as a function of the state's foundation or of the individual's act of adherence, or as a deduction from the collectively affirmed or (it is said) universally recognized ends of the state, or, finally, as a necessary consequence of the citizen's relations with the political community as a whole' (Walzer 1970, p. 77).

> What we call 'social reality' is in the last resort an ethical construction; it is supported by a certain *as if* (we act *as if* we believe in the almightiness of bureaucracy, *as if* the President incarnates the will of the People, *as if* the Party expresses the objective interest of the working class ...). As soon as the belief ... is lost, the very texture of the social field disintegrates... . It follows, from this constitutively senseless character of the Law, that we must obey it not because it is just, good or even beneficial, but simply *because it is the law* – this tautology articulates the vicious circle of its authority, the fact that the last foundation of the Law's authority lies in its process of enunciation. (Žižek 2008, pp. 34–35)

The law itself seems to be nihilistic, that is, hollow. However, those who, like Leibniz, accuse Hobbes of having a merely imperativistic and voluntaristic conception of law (and also of religion), à la Thrasymacus, are wrong:

> A celebrated English philosopher named Hobbes, who is noted for his paradoxes, has wished to uphold almost the same thing as Thrasymachus: for he wants God to have the right to do everything, because he is all-powerful. This is a failure to distinguish between right and fact. For what one can do is one thing, what one should do, another. It is this same Hobbes who believes (and almost for the same reason) that the true religion is that of the state and that, as a consequence, if the Emperor Claudius, who decreed in an edict that *in libera republica crepitus atque ructus liberos esse debere*, had placed the god Crepitus among the authorized gods, he would have been a real God, and worthy of worship. (Leibniz 1988, p. 47)

It is not in fact a question of placing the god Crepitus in the Pantheon of recognised deities and thus making him a 'true god'. *Fictio* works by making 'true' what is 'false', but this produces effects in terms of legitimacy: *fingunt simul creduntque*. *Fictio* legitimises tautology, whereas invention is only a deception that can be guaranteed by force but does not produce effects in terms of legitimacy. With Hobbes, with the beginning of political modernity, the foundation of the State on theological-political *fictio* takes place, and at the same time the State itself begins to fade as the lack of the foundation that afflicts it marks the beginning of the crumbling of its foundations.

To speak of "fiction", we could evoke Gaetano Mosca's notion of the 'political formula', where he argues that this 'formula' is the principle of sovereignty – I would say of legitimacy – since it answers the question of whether it is enough for the political class to justify its power with de facto possession, or whether it needs something which substantiates it. Mosca says that the fact that the political formula draws on convictions, even religious ones:

> does not mean that political formulas are mere quackeries aptly invented to trick the masses into obedience. Anyone who viewed them in that light would fall into grave error. The truth is that they answer a real need in man's social nature; and this need, so universally felt, of governing and knowing that one is governed not on the basis of mere material or

intellectual force, but on the basis of a moral principle, has beyond any doubt a practical and a real importance. (Mosca 1939, p. 71)

It should be added that, for Mosca, the principle of legitimation is not necessarily drawn from religious or transcendent convictions, but is a principle that functions to justify power and that can naturally be substantiated – he gives the example of the United States – in popular suffrage.

3 Against the Kinship

Carl Schmitt argued that if war is regulated, the partisan, as an irregular combatant, is outside that paradigm, outside the limitation – the 'formalisation' – of the war conflict: 'The modern partisan expects neither law nor mercy from the enemy. He has moved away from the conventional enmity of controlled and bracketed war, and into the realm of another, real enmity, which intensifies through terror and counter-terror until it ends in extermination' (Schmitt 2007b, p. 11). In reality, the Geneva Convention relative to the Treatment of Prisoners of War of 1949 (as well as the Additional Protocol to the Geneva Conventions of 12 August 1949 relative to the Protection of Victims of International Armed Conflicts of 1977) also recognises protection for resistant forces, but under certain conditions (e.g., organisation) that Schmitt criticised (Schmitt 2007b, pp. 15 and 23). But in truth, the exercise of internal police functions (and their extraterritorial extension) does not place the terrorist outside the jurisdiction of the State and outside the regulation of war: on the contrary, it places him within the horizon of an abnormal statehood that treats him as an emergency object to be administered. Not a belligerent, he is the object of a police State which, in the case of planetary hyper-sovereignty, becomes global. The terrorist is therefore inside and outside, he is both friend and foe.

Moreover, with regard to such hyper-sovereignties, the logic of humanitarian intervention consists precisely in the global extension of police functions beyond the sovereignty of States: 'The U.S. National Defense Strategy, for example, argues that it is unacceptable for states to invoke a sovereign "shield"' (Elden 2009, p. 172). But the extension of functions does not correspond to the idea of territorial expansion of empires, but at most to a kind of temporary hyper-sovereignty. It can be seen at work in the exercise of that raison d'état that has been invoked to justify US humanitarian interventionism. In that case, in fact, the protection of US citizens at home and abroad allowed, according to White House legal advisors, the use of violence (mostly largely illegal: 'summary executions; apprehension, rendition, and detention of terrorist suspects; and enhanced interrogation techniques, or torture' (Erlenbusch-Anderson 2013, p. 144)) both against foreigners (and outside the country) and citizens. As Verena Erlenbusch-Anderson writes, 'previously distinct spheres of internal order, or *police power*, and external peace, or *military power*, began to converge in a general peace-enforcing function of the state.... [B]oth internal and external enemies appeared as threats to the life and health of populations' (Erlenbusch-Anderson 2013, p. 148, emphasis added). Police functions (internal/external) are based on the assumption of the sacrificability of the citizen, the political obligation to which he is bound, the ultimate ideal of the 'to die for' that underpins the State. Discussing the political obligation, Habermas argued that:

> There is a remarkable dissonance between the rather archaic features of the "obligation potential" shared by comrades of fate who are willing to make sacrifices, on the one hand, and the normative self-understanding of the modern constitutional State as an uncoerced association of legal consociates, on the other. The examples of military duty, compulsory taxation, and education suggest a picture of the democratic state primarily as a duty-imposing authority demanding sacrifices from its dominated subjects. This picture fits poorly with an enlightenment culture whose normative core consists in the abolition of a publicly demanded *sacrificium* as an element of morality. (Habermas 2001, p. 101)

Even beyond Kantian-Habermasian enlightenment optimism, the quoted text grasps a fundamental point concerning the construction of that community of destiny which is always in need of new victims to establish and preserve it through sacrifice. It is the contemporary State itself that is still constituted around that moral of sacrifice that underlies and innervates it. It is probably a remnant, but one that continues to perform a unifying function, failing which the political order, at least in some of its structuring and essential functions (war, for example), would collapse on itself. And this is the point: is this remnant perhaps what makes ISIS not *archaic*, not distant, as if emerging from a past we cannot decipher, but *modern* as the construction of the national State is modern? And does religion really have that much to do with it, or does it participate – as we wrote above about Hobbes – in that same mechanism in which the construction of the political order participates, in an indistinction of secularisation of theological concepts and theologisation of secular concepts? In the end, as with the modern Western State, it is not a question of having subsumed the mechanisms of religious legitimation by transferring them into the political order, but of two levels proceeding together, in which one is a metaphor for the other, in which the borrowing is reciprocal and probably the need is one: to legitimise vertical power.

However, the third generation of the Frankfurt School re-evaluated the concept of 'fraternity', which was in fact not very well defined on a theoretical level:

Axel Honneth proposed his own model of socialism based on fraternal solidarity. But, as Eleonora Piromalli writes:

> Individuals, therefore, are free to keep their own self-interest without having to adopt the dispositions of fraternity requested in *The Idea of Socialism*. As Marx and Engels state in *The German Ideology:* 'the communists do not oppose egoism to selflessness or selflessness to egoism, nor do they express this contradiction theoretically.... They do not put to people the moral demand: love one another, do not be egoists, etc.... This contradiction is only a seeming one because one side of it, what is called the "general interest", is constantly being produced by the other side, private interest'. (Piromalli 2019, p. 5)

On the other hand, if one really looked at how Islam has theorised (not necessarily practised this theorisation) political power and the government of the people, one would discover that, in Islam, the sovereign who did not fulfil the religious dictates could well be deposed, since the obedience of the subjects is conditional on the implementation of Islamic law, and that therefore – at least on a theoretical level – 'Parliamentary democracy, monarchy, autocracy or aristocracy: everything seems to be fine, as long as Islam is respected' (Campanini 2012, p. 50, my translation). Or, that the political programme of the first Salafists was to 'Islamise' modernity through a confrontation with it and with the West that was not articulated in terms of a frontal opposition, but that thought politics through the notion of 'consultation' (of the people), in Arabic *shûrà* (see Campanini 2012, pp. 54–55). Or, more famously, that the socialism of many Arab countries was also based on religious premises: Nasser quoted a hadith according to which salt, water and pastures belong to everyone, in order to legitimise socialism (Campanini 2012, p. 49). Massimo Campanini argues that:

> If one studies Islamic history in depth and above all the evolution of Islamic political thought, it emerges that the identity, in Islam, of religion and politics is anything but immediate and obvious. Reversing the terms of the question, I think we can assume that in the Muslim mainstream represented by Sunnism there is a tradition of 'secular' Islam. (Campanini 2012, p. 58, my translation)

The frontispiece of *Leviathan*, designed by Abraham Bosse, depicts two small black men in the deserted streets of the city. If you look closely, you will recognise the profile with the typical beak nose: they are two plague doctors. Shock and Awe against the plague. Today, this paradigm – starting from the very expression just quoted – concerns the plague of terrorism. However, especially in its latest developments on European soil, as we have tried to say, it is not the external attack – the war tout court by a foreign State – but the challenge to the State by its own citizens. Sovereignty on the territory of the State or the exorbitant sovereignty exercised by States, or large States with an imperial vocation, is fuelled by the same idea of the absolutization of friendship, where it is a claim to inclusion that is always ready to exclude, inclusion that excludes. In fact, trying to take terrorists under one's own jurisdiction even outside one's own jurisdiction without any respect for the national borders of States, exercising police functions there rather than actual war actions (which therefore do not require respect for sovereignty, since war is founded on the idea of violating the sovereignty of others; whereas police functions are the prerogative of sovereign States, and therefore trespassing – like the French policemen on Italian trains in search of irregular immigrants – is a violation of sovereignty, since the exercise of police functions presupposes jurisdiction over a given territory) means thinking that everyone is subject to the jurisdiction of that State, that everyone – regardless of where they are – is a *friend*, and therefore liable to be caught in the grip of the State, to be caught in the embrace that kills, in the embrace of friendship. So, this signals the claim to make friends not only of citizens, but of everyone, wherever they may be, so that they can be caught insofar as they are friends, and insofar as the *dispositif* of friendship is an inclusion that excludes (it could not be otherwise: one must first be a friend in order to be expelled), included and at the same time excluded.

Civil war is, after all, a family war (*oikeios polemos*), a war based on blood, on the bond of blood which determines it (and resolves it, since the Greeks fight as if to reconcile themselves; in the Sicilian city of Nakone, after a stasis, the citizens were separated into groups on the basis of a lottery which divided them into *adelphoi hairetoi*, brothers by lot [see Loraux 2017, pp. 56 – 60]). The most important propaganda text of the ISIS, translated in English as *Administration or Management of Savagery* (Naji 2006) speaks of dividing the societies, that is, of necessarily calling for a polarization, a battle from which one cannot – as for the civil war in which one must participate, in ancient Greece – escape. The strategy is to accelerate the chaos in order to achieve a polarisation of the parties in the field, and thereby call 'the masses to battle':

> By polarization here, I mean dragging the masses into the battle such that polarization is created between all of the people. Thus, one group of them will go to the side of the people of truth, another group will go to the side of the people of falsehood, and a third group will remain neutral, awaiting the outcome of the battle in order to join the victor. We must attract the sympathy of this group and make it hope for the victory of the people of faith, especially since this group has a decisive role in the later stages of the present battle. Dragging the masses into the battle requires more actions which will inflame opposition and which will make the people enter into the battle, willing or unwilling, such that each individual will go to the side which he supports…. This was the policy of battle for the pioneers: *to transform societies into two opposing groups* …. This battle alone, through its vehemence and its (ability to) separate (people), is that which will enable us to polarize the largest number of individuals toward our ranks. (Naji 2006, emphasis added, § 46)

Faced with politics' attempt to absolutize friendship, ISIS calls for a battle 'to transform societies into two opposing groups'. The modern project, on the contrary, is to make friendship and enmity coexist, as well as inclusion and exclusion from the political community.

Friendship makes sense, in classical thought, either as belonging not only to a family but to a restricted group of free men, or as a relationship established through a pact, or rather an oath. In the first case, it separates from strangers and slaves, in the second case it is linked to the notion of *xénos*, the stranger.

4 Dismantling the Common Father

The terrorist war is therefore not a war between friends and enemies, but a war between friends (-enemies), between brothers, it is – in essence – a civil war. This is because the paradigm of modernity, apparently Schmittian, is, on the contrary, that of pervasive friendship, of the absolutization of friendship, of rejecting and encompassing within Europe. Politics is this continuous pendulum between *oikos* and *polis* (see Agamben 2015), family and politics, private and public (and also friendship and enmity): the theme of friendship is rooted in that of brotherhood, that is, friendship in the sense of family ties, friendship between families.

If the city tends to familiarise itself, then civil war intervenes to repoliticise it; vice versa, when the family tends to politicise itself by loosening the family bond, civil war intervenes to reconstitute the family bond (sometimes with the creation of a fake brotherhood). The only fraternity possible, therefore, is the fake one of brothers by lot. The Franco-Tunisian Lacanian psychoanalyst Gérard Haddad spoke of the Cain Complex to explain terrorism in terms of fratricide, when Cain kills the cadet Abel to re-establish universal order (see Haddad 2021). However, in Haddad's case the solution is reversed: one needs to recognise the other as a brother in order to end the war. On the contrary, here it is argued that the family relationship needs to be eliminated in order to think of oneself as a community of right, a fake brotherhood, by lot.

So, from solidarity back to the contract between fake brothers. The depoliticisation is not the end of the friend/enemy distinction, since the political is not based on it, but – as already mentioned – on the absolutization of friendship and brotherhood (contrary to Schmitt's statement that 'For the classic European state had succeeded in something quite improbable: achieving peace within its own borders and to excluding enmity as a legal concept' (Schmitt 2018, p. 40, my translation)[5]: there is no longer the other, the foreigner. Depoliticisation is actually (against Schmitt) the return of the friendship/enemy distinction, a pre-political distinction, while politicity is the coexistence of friendship and enmity. Brothers may well be enemies, and discord may be no less political, in Schmitt's sense, than war: conflict (i.e. politics, for Schmitt) and friendship are by no means incompatible. This is possible because friend and foe coincide, as demonstrated by the death penalty – the ultimate moment of sovereignty – in the modern State: it both includes in the community and excludes. In a letter to Alexandre Kojève of 7 June 1955 from Plettenberg, Schmitt writes, 'it is all over with the "state," that is true; this mortal God is dead, nothing can be changed about that; … no longer capable of war or the death penalty; and hence also no longer capable of making history' (Kojève and Schmitt 2001, pp. 101–102). But the death sentence is what properly excludes and includes in the political community at the same time. Friend/enemy is not an opposition, but a hendiadys: friend-and-enemy, and what for Schmitt is depoliticisation, is actually the ambiguous essence of politics: going from enemies to friends. For Friedrich Hayek, the term 'catallaxy' comes from the Greek *katallattein* (or *katallassein*) 'which meant not only "to exchange", but also "to admit into the community" and "to become, from enemies, friends"' (Tedesco 2004, p. 99, my translation; see also Tedesco 2004, pp. 148–149; on Schmitt and Hayek see Scheuerman 1999). The dimensions of economics and politics dance in an ambiguity that shows them to be intertwined. In his *Note on War, the Game, the Enemy*, Giorgio Agamben traces war back to its 'agonal' dimension – at least in Greco-Roman antiquity: war was a 'game', albeit with real bloodshed. As he writes, 'at the very moment of its institution, war takes the form of a contest between two parties between whom there is no enmity' (Agamben 2018, p. 307, my translation). Quoting Vernant, Agamben recalls how war in Greece was another way of trading between human groups: 'one of the forms that trade between human groups can take' (Vernant 1985, my translation; see Agamben 2018, p. 308). For Agamben, Schmitt elides this agonal dimension, which he contrasts with the seriousness of war because if he were to recognise it, it would defeat Schmitt's thesis of a circularity and mutual implication between enmity and war. We need to go even further: it would defeat the idea that the politician is opposition of friend to foe. It is clear that Hayek, by substituting catallaxy for economics and advo-

---

[5] It is necessary to mention two editions of Schmitt's *The Concept of the Political*, since the English-language edition published in 2007 by The University of Chicago Press and translated by George Schwab surprisingly does not contain the *Vorwort* written by Schmitt for the 1963 German reprint, from which this passage is taken. So, the *Vorwort* is quoted from the synoptic edition published in German in 2018 by Dunker & Humblot.

cating the idea of exchange as a procedure for resolving the relationship between friend and foe, is the litmus test of an ideological position that elides the hendiadys of politics as the coexistence of friendship and enmity. But the light thrown on the absolutization of friendship is entirely consistent with the liberal project of pacification through market and exchange. An ideological project, but one that captures a point: friend/enemy is a hendiadys, a mediation, not an opposition. It also grasps the vector orientation of politics, namely, the absolutization of friendship (to which corresponds the absolutization of enmity).

In fact, going back to Schmitt again, if he invokes the ban as an element of the distinction between friend and foe in the context of the State (Schmitt 2007a, pp. 46–47), he does not realise that the ban is not the sign of total enmity, but on the contrary is distancing and calling, *arrière-ban:* 'The *arrièreban* is ... a compulsory *Publizität* that acts uninterruptedly; everyone is summoned at every moment, every day, by secondary bans of secondary bans. In this, then, consists the "oppressive structure of society", and there are neither bandits nor persons who ban, but rather a being-there that is by now perpetually available' (Pizzingrilli 2008, p. 116, my translation). Therefore, to keep the peace it is not enough to distinguish friend from foe, both inside and outside the city – nor is it to be said that the end of the distinction between friend and foe emanates from the global total war in which there is no longer any difference between the combatant and the non-combatant. This can be deduced from Schmitt himself by an *a contrario* reasoning. He argues, in fact, for the distinction between *polemios* and *echthrós*, between the *hostis* (a term Schmitt 'was careful not to mention' [Agamben 2018, p. 308, my translation] because it is ambiguous, indicating both host and enemy[6]) in *polemos* and the enemy in *stasis*, with whom we have only private hatreds. To do so, he turns to Plato (Schmitt 2007a, pp. 28–29n9), who in the *Republic* distinguishes precisely between the struggles with the Barbarians, which are wars, and the tearing apart of brothers, which are *staseis*, 'civil discords'. The former are political, they are struggles against the political, the latter are not, and this is what Schmitt needs in order to be able to develop his discourse on the purity of the political, which instead, if the two categories are not pure, is not pure either. Actually, as Jacques Derrida points out, it is Plato himself who theorises the overcoming of the distinction between friend and foe, between Greek and Barbarian: 'far from being satisfied with the opposition on which Schmitt relies so heavily, the *Republic* indeed *prescribes* its erasure. In this

---

6 Here Agamben, in stating that Schmitt 'was careful not to mention', refers to the fact that Schmitt avoids mentioning not the term, but its ambiguity, its polysemy. Indeed, in both Schmitt (2020) and Schmitt (2006), Schmitt mentions the term *hostis*, but never in its polysemic ambiguity.

case, it is indeed recommended that the Greeks behave towards their enemies – the barbarians – as they behave today among themselves' (Derrida 2005, p. 90). In truth, one must be careful about Plato: for Derrida, Plato prescribes as a law that the Hellenes should behave towards the Barbarians as they behave towards each other, meaning, if one follows Derrida on this point, that they should behave without excessive hostility. In fact, in the passage from the *Republic*, Plato says that the Hellenes among themselves should not set fire to houses; while with the Barbarians there is war, but the Hellenes with the Barbarians must behave as enemies just "as in our day the Hellenes among themselves" (*Rep.* 471b, 6–8), alluding in truth to the fact that, in the time recalled by Plato, the Hellenes among themselves are treating each other as enemies, thus making war. In fact, shortly before, Plato had referred to wars between Hellenes in which they treat each other as enemies, make slaves, etc. (*Rep.* 469b, 8–9, but see also the sequel). All this unless Derrida too, in theorising that the Greeks behaved with the Barbarians as they behaved with each other, meant precisely this, that is, that the distinction between wars and discords was not extinguished in favour of discords (handled with less hostility) but in favour of wars. In other words, unless Derrida is also saying that the Greeks should behave with the Barbarians as they behave with the Greeks themselves today, that is, with an attitude of war. But this does not seem to be the case, since Derrida follows up the quotation with the following lines from the *Republic:* 'should we then lay down another law for our guardians, forbidding them to devastate land or burn houses?' (*Rep.* 471c, 1–2; cf. Derrida 2005, p. 90). As if the two points were connected: let us make the Greeks behave towards the Barbarians as they behave towards each other, that is, let us give them the law not to ravage the land and not to set fire to the houses; but in reality there is a gap here, a hiatus: the Greeks behave towards the Barbarians with a polemical attitude as they now behave towards each other; but for the future we have this law, not to ravage and not to set fire.

But back to Derrida, so he continues:

> this difference between the disagreements never takes place. It can never be found. Never concretely. As a result, the purity of polemos or the enemy, whereby Schmitt would define the political, remains unattainable. The concept of the political undoubtedly corresponds, as concept, to what the ideal discourse can want to state most rigorously on the ideality of the political. But no politics has ever been adequate to its concept. No political event can be correctly described or defined with recourse to these concepts. (Derrida 2005, p. 114)

Hayek represents the political in the sense of absolute friendship that finds its concretisation in the market (depoliticised, one might say), Schmitt in the sense of absolute enmity that finds its concretisation in war (the highest point of politicity together with the death sentence, hyperpoliticisation), but *stasis*,

Derrida tells us again, can well be converted into absolute war, '*absolute* hostility can aim at the brother and convert, this time, interior war into true war, into absolute war, hence absolute politics' (Derrida 2005, p. 149), when 'the friend and the enemy pass into one another through the figure of the brother' (Derrida 2005, p. 150). So, there is no difference between war and discord, both actually falling under the species of a nosology, a disease of living together. In the case of terrorism, the enemy is both the citizen, the brother, and not the radical other. And how is this disease averted? Not by distinguishing between friend and foe, not by identifying within the community a founding *ghenos*, a kinship, because even between kin there is war; but through a symbolic brotherhood. The enemy *is* the friend (the brother, the blood relative), and it is this that makes enmity and war indistinguishable, unless an artificial brotherhood is formed. One can only try to hint at the philosophical chasm we face when approaching the issue in these terms. Dismantling political theology, or rather theurgy (i.e. the idea that God, like the sovereign, is created by the doxology of the believers and the subjects) is to dismantle the common father, thus ceasing to be blood brothers, *ecclesia*, incestuous community, to become, if anything, artificial and fatherless brothers, orphans and adults: the father's place is an empty place (borrowing Claude Lefort's expression). Fatherless and landless, with conventional soil, but also – above all – motherless,[7] whereas in the epitaph of Aspasia analysed by Derrida, the symbolic dimension is based precisely on the imagination of a common motherhood (in order to constitute the aristocracy). After all, the bond with the mother is sublimated into religion, and it is this, in its symbolic dimension, that acts as a social bond, which then becomes a political obligation, always from the symbolic point of view mentioned above. All the more so since paternity is in any case already a fiction, whereas maternity cannot be (*mater natura vera*). Moreover, if for Schmitt the right comes from the land through allocation, distribution, and if Schmitt knew Bachofen, one can assume that the latter – the giving – is in connection with the giving of the mother, the fact of originating (on these themes see Berni 2014, p. 38). And it is true that all citizens are brothers and that even the *extraneus* is already a brother even without ties of consanguinity, and that therefore a certain form of artificiality is found in Crete as in Rome; and yet it is an artificiality that is based on the common birth by the mother earth, so that the killing of the other, whether brother or

---

[7] According to an etymology that is, however, considered unreliable, the word *Umma* comes from the root *umm*, 'mother'. Actually, it seems that the root is common to Aramaic and Hebrew, and that it refers to 'community': see (Mandaville [2001, p. 71]). Of course, this is a normative concept, which for centuries had no political significance, given the divisions, including geographical ones, within the context of Islam.

stranger, is always and in any case, there, a *paricidium* (from *pario*, says Bachofen: 'to give birth'), so that every killed child of a common mother is also a victim of *paricidium* (see Bachofen 2007).

Bibliography

Agamben, Giorgio (2015): *Stasis: Civil War as a Political Paradigm*. Translated by Nicholas Heron. Stanford: Stanford University Press.

Agamben, Giorgio (2018): *Homo sacer. Edizione integrale*. Macerata: Quodlibet.

Al-Dayel, Nadia (2019): "'Now Is the Time to Wake Up': Islamic State's Narratives of Political Awareness". In: *Terrorism and Political Violence*, pp. 1–21, https://doi.org/10.1080/09546553.2019.1603145.

Bachofen, Johann Jakob (2007): *An English Translation of Bachofen's Mutterrecht (Mother Right) (1861): A Study of the Religious and Juridical Aspects of Gynecocracy in the Ancient World: "Lycia", "Crete", and "Athens"*. Lewiston: Edwin Mellen Press.

Bacon, Francis (1996): *The Advancement of Learning*. In: Bacon, *The Major Works*. Oxford, New York: Oxford University Press, pp. 120–299.

Berni, Stefano (2014): *Cultura e diritto: Alle origini dell'antropologia giuridica*. Ariccia: Aracne.

Bobbio, Norberto (1989): *Democracy and Dictatorship: The Nature and Limits of State Power*. Translated by Peter Kennealy. Minneapolis: University of Minnesota Press.

Campanini, Massimo (2012): *Democrazia e islam, valori e istituzioni*. In: Gian Paolo Calchi Novati (Ed.): *Verso un nuovo orientalismo: Primavere arabe e Grande Medio Oriente*. Rome: Carocci.

Conseil d'État (2015): "Avis sur le projet de loi constitutionnelle de protection de la nation". https://www.legifrance.gouv.fr/contenu/Media/Files/autour-de-la-loi/legislatif-et-re glementaire/avis-du-ce/2015/avis_ce_prmx1529429l_cm_23.12.2015.pdf. Visited on 21 January 2022.

Derrida, Jacques (2005): *The Politics of Friendship*. Translated by George Collins. London, New York: Verso.

Di Cesare, Donatella (2019): *Terror and Modernity*. Translated by Murtha Baca. Cambridge: Polity Press.

Ginzburg, Carlo (2008): "Fear Reverence Terror. Reading Hobbes today". In: *Max Weber Lectures Series* 5, pp. 1–15.

Habermas, Jürgen (2001): *The Postnational Constellation: Political Essays*. Translated, edited and with an introduction by Max Pensky. Cambridge: MIT Press.

Haddad, Gérard (2021): *A l'origine de la violence: D'Oedipe à Caïn, une erreur de Freud?* Paris: Salvator.

Honneth, Axel (2017): *The Idea of Socialism: Towards a Renewal*. Translated by Joseph Ganahl. Cambridge: Polity Press.

Kojève, Alexandre, and Carl Schmitt (2001): "Correspondence". Edited and translated by Erik De Vries. In: *Interpretation* 29. No. 1, pp. 91–130.

Kristol, Irving (1973): "Capitalism, Socialism, and Nihilism". In: *The Public Interest*. No. 31, pp. 3–16.

Lobo Arranz, Álvaro (2021): "Populism and terrorism, The Illegitimate Heirs of Nihilism". In: *La Civiltà Cattolica English Edition*. 5, pp. 71–85.
Loraux, Nicole (1997): "La guerre dans la famille". In: *Clio* 5, pp. 21–62.
Leibniz, Gottfried Wilhelm (1988): "Meditation on the Common Concept of Justice". In: Leibniz, *Political Writings*. Edited by Patrick Riley. Cambridge: Cambridge University Press.
Mandaville, Peter (2001): *Transnational Muslim Politics: Reimagining the Umma*. London, New York: Routledge.
Mosca, Gaetano (1939): *The Ruling Class*. Translated by Hannah D. Khan. Edited by Arthur Livingston. New York, London: McGraw-Hill.
Naji, Abu Bakr (2004): *The Management of Savagery: The Most Critical Stage Through Which the Umma Will Pass*. Translated by William McCants. Cambridge: John M. Olin Institute for Strategic Studies at Harvard University. https://web.archive.org/web/20170110084554/https://azelin.files.wordpress.com/2010/08/abu-bakr-naji-the-management-of-savagery-the-most-critical-stage-through-which-the-umma-will-pass.pdf, visited on 21 January 2022.
Plato: *Republic*.
Piromalli, Eleonora (2017): "Does Socialism Need Fraternity? On Axel Honneth's *The Idea of Socialism*". In: *European Journal of Political Theory*, pp. 1–21, https://doi.org/10.1177/1474885117718431.
Piromalli, Eleonora (2019): "Socialism Through Convergence, or: Why a Socialist Society Does Not Need to Be a Fraternal Community". In: *Philosophy and Social Criticism* 45. No. 6, pp. 1–8, https://doi.org/10.1177/0191453719842354.
Pizzingrilli, Clio (2008): "Aggiunte". In: Karl Marx, *Critica della filosofia hegeliana del diritto pubblico*. Translated by Galvano della Volpe. Macerata: Quodlibet.
Roy, Olivier (2017): *Jihad and Death: The Global Appeal of Islamic State*. Oxford: Oxford University Press.
Scheuerman, William E. (1999): *Carl Schmitt: The End of Law*. Lanham: Rowman & Littlefield.
Schmitt, Carl (2006): *The Nomos of the Earth in the International Law of the Jus Publicum Europaeum*. Translated by G. L. Ulman. New York: Telos Press.
Schmitt, Carl (2007a): *The Concept of the Political: Expanded Edition*. Translated by George Schwab. Chicago, London: The University of Chicago Press.
Schmitt, Carl (2007b): *Theory of the Partisan: Intermediate Commentary on the Concept of the Political*. Translated by G. L. Ulman. New York: Telos Press.
Schmitt, Carl (2018): *Der Begriff des Politischen: Synoptische Darstellung der Texte*. Edited by Marco Walter. Berlin: Dunker & Humblot.
Tacitus, Cornelius (2008): *The Annals: The Reigns of Tiberius, Claudius and Nero*. Oxford: Oxford University Press.
Tedesco, Francescomaria (2004): *Introduzione a Hayek*. Rome, Bari: Laterza.
Tedesco, Francescomaria (2006): "L'impero latino e l'idea di Europa. Riflessioni a partire da un saggio (parzialmente) inedito di Alexandre Kojève". In: *Quaderni Fiorentini per la Storia del Pensiero Giuridico Moderno*. No. 35, pp. 373–401.
Tedesco, Francescomaria (2017): "Individual Sovereignty. From Kelsen to the Increase in the Sources of the Law". In: Peter Langford, Ian Bryan and John McCarry (Eds.): *Kelsenian Legal Science and the Natural Law*. Cham: Springer, pp. 213–237.

Tedesco, Francescomaria (2020): *Sovereign Excess, Legitimacy and Resistance.* Translated by Karen Whittle. London, New York: Routledge.
Thomas, Yan (2011): Fictio legis. *L'empire de la fiction romaine et ses limites médiévales.* Paris: Seuil/Gallimard.
Vernant, Jean-Pierre (1985): "Introduction". In Jean-Pierre Vernant (Ed.): *Problèmes de la guerre en Grèce ancienne.* Paris: Éditions de l'École des Hautes Etudes en Sciences Sociales, pp. 9–30.
Walzer, Michael (1970): *Obligations. Essays on Disobedience, War, and Citizenship.* Cambridge, London: Harvard University Press.
Žižek, Slavoj (2008): *The Sublime Object of Ideology.* London, New York: Verso.

Part 2: **Literature and Film**

Derek Offord
Nihilism in Nineteenth-Century Russian Literature and Thought

Abstract: The term "nihilism" generally denotes the rejection of established beliefs and authorities, and often political violence as well. In late imperial Russia, nihilism served as a loose negative construct with which conservative thinkers and writers and government officials attacked members of the radical intelligentsia and the surging revolutionary movement. This chapter ranges over the aesthetic, ethical and metaphysical ideas associated with nihilism in Russia, the sub-culture established by disaffected members of the younger generation, and the political unrest and terrorism of the 1870s and 1880s. I focus on three aspects of the Russian debate about nihilism, in which major writers and thinkers participated. First, I consider the novel *Fathers and Children*, in which Turgenev imagined representatives of the phenomenon and gave them a name. Second, I outline the contribution of Chernyshevsky and Pisarev to the intellectual revolt, especially their hope that 'new people' might emerge who would both achieve personal liberation and bring about social and political revolution. Third, I examine the influential way in which the dangers of rejection of existing values are treated in the novels of Dostoevsky, for whom nihilism portended apocalypse.

1 Definitions and Context

The term "nihilism" has a perplexingly broad range of meaning. Although nihilism is sometimes seen as an expression of cynicism or despair, its definitions in modern English dictionaries generally associate it and its exponents (nihilists) with hostility to established beliefs, values and institutions, and with the rejection of rules, conventions, moral principles and religious and political authority.[1] The hallmarks of the phenomenon, thus defined, are its sweeping and extremist nature. Nihilism seems also to presage destruction – of institutions, physical objects, property, other people or even the self. It may drive those who preach it to

---

[1] I have consulted the following dictionaries: *Collins English Dictionary* at www.collinsdictionary.com/dictionary/english/, Merriam-Webster online at https://www.merriam-webster.com/dictionary/nihilism and *Oxford English Dictionary*, online version of September 2019 at https://www.oed.com/, all accessed on 17 January 2022.

https://doi.org/10.1515/9783110699210-010

violent political action. At the same time, we need to be aware that the capaciousness and looseness of the term endow it with great potential for the polemicist. As a label applied to ideological opponents, it offers its users an easy route to moral high ground, obviating the need for further proof of error or malign intent, just as the labels "socialist" or "communist", in certain right-wing discourses, or "bourgeois" or "fascist", in certain left-wing discourses, may seem unanswerably damning.

Entries on nihilism in many dictionaries also recognize the early manifestation of the phenomenon in Russia over the period from the 1860s, following the country's chastening defeat in the Crimean War (1853–1856), up until the outbreak of the First World War in 1914. This particular national strand of nihilism (*nigilizm* in Russian), dictionaries typically tell us, is associated with a revolutionary group determined to 'clear the way for a new state of society' by 'employing extreme measures, including terrorism and assassination'.[2] The Soviet lexicographer Sergei Ozhegov, for his part, defines a "nihilist" (*nigilist*, or *nigilistka* in the case of a woman) in the following way: 'In the 60s of the nineteenth century in Russia: a free-thinking person, an *intelligent-raznochinets*, with a sharply negative attitude towards bourgeois-noble traditions and customs and the ideology of the serf-owning order' (Ozhegov 1988, p. 334). Despite the Marxist-Leninist veneer with which this description of the nihilist's attitudes is coated, Ozhegov's definition is helpful inasmuch as it associates nihilism with the intelligentsia, a socially engaged and politically committed educated minority that was coming into being in mid-nineteenth-century Russia.[3] It is less helpful in so far as it bolsters the misleading view prevalent in Soviet historiography that the nihilist camp was exclusively or largely made up of so-called *raznochintsy*,[4] that is to say, 'men of various ranks' (many of them sons of clergymen) who were positioned below the nobility in the social hierarchy of late imperial Russia and women of similar background.

Early signs of the emergence of nihilism, conceived as rejection and destruction, are apparent in remarks made by two of the most rebellious spirits in the Russian intelligentsia in the 1840s. In a letter of 1841 in which he admitted that his nature always went to extremes, the literary critic Vissarion Belinsky declared that 'negation' was his god and that his heroes in history were 'destroyers of the past such as Luther, Voltaire, the Encyclopedists, the terrorists [i.e. the Ja-

---

[2] https://www.dictionary.com/browse/nihilism and https://www.merriam-webster.com/dictionary/nihilism, both accessed on 7 April 2021.
[3] The word used by Ozhegov, *intelligent* (or *intelligentka*, if a woman), denotes an individual member of the intelligentsia.
[4] This is the plural form of the word *raznochinets* which is used in Ozhegov's definition.

cobins of the French Revolution], Byron' (Belinsky 1956, p. 70). In a similar spirit, the future anarchist Mikhail Bakunin, who would later compete with Karl Marx for pre-eminence in the international workingmen's movement and dream of 'elemental' peasant revolt in his native land, ended an article of 1842 with the statement that the 'passion for destruction is a creative passion, too' (Bakunin 1973, p. 58). We know precisely when the term 'nihilism' began to be used to denote such passion for negation and destruction, and more generally for uncompromising refusal to accept beliefs that had previously been accepted without demur, namely, in March 1862, when Ivan Turgenev's fourth novel, *Fathers and Children*, was first published in the periodical *The Russian Herald* (*Russkii vestnik*).[5] It was at this point that the concept of nihilism seized the attention of leading Russian authors and thinkers.

However, even in the Russian setting, where "nihilism" became commonplace in public discourse at a relatively early date, use of the term throws up many problems. Although Turgenev seems to suggest in his literary memoirs, for example, that he himself coined the word *nigilist* (Turgenev 1967, p. 105), *nigilizm* had in fact been used from the 1830s to the 1850s in a variety of meanings, ranging from vacuity to scepticism (Alekseev 1928). These meanings were not much related to, or at least not identical with, those that the word acquired as a result of its use in Turgenev's novel. Again, there were differences of opinion among people to whom the term 'nihilists' was applied, as attested by the title of a polemical article of 1864, "Mr Shchedrin, or the Schism among the Nihilists", by Fedor Dostoevsky (Dostoevsky 1980), who in his fiction would offer an influential critique of the nihilist mindset as he perceived it. Nor did all or even many of those whom their critics labelled 'nihilists' embrace this description of themselves. They generally preferred to identify themselves as 'new people' or members of the intelligentsia, often adding the epithet 'radical' or 'revolutionary' (Moser 1964, pp. 19–20; Brower 1975, p. 32).

A further problem is posed by the range of meanings that the term nihilism may have in scholarship about Russian literature and thought. While widely used with reference to radical Russian thought of the 1860s (especially the outlook of the younger, more militant cohort of post-Crimean rebels, for whom Dmitrii Pisarev was a figurehead [Pozefsky 2003, p. 9]), the term may also retrospectively describe the outlook of 'people of the 40s', the 'fathers', in Turgenev's terminology, in other words, representatives of precisely that generation of the intelligentsia against whom the nihilistic 'people of the 60s' were rebelling. Victoria Frede,

---

5 I am using a more literal translation of Turgenev's title than *Fathers and Sons*, as this novel is also known in English.

for instance, in her useful recent survey of Russian nihilism, deals with both Alexander Herzen and the politically moderate Turgenev himself as well as Belinsky (who, as we have seen, was a plausible forerunner of the destroyers of the 1860s). She justifies the inclusion of Herzen and Turgenev on the grounds that they denied 'the ability of signifiers such as good and evil to capture and account for human experience, especially suffering,' and broke down faith 'in a providential God and in a beneficent plan that organizes worldly events' (Frede 2020, p. 152).

The case for associating Turgenev with the phenomenon that he was thought by many members of the radical intelligentsia to have besmirched has also been made by Aileen Kelly. Tormented by humans' insignificance in the impassive natural world (Turgenev 1964a, pp. 51–52) and paralysed by the introspection that seemed to characterize his own generation of the Russian educated class brought up in the oppressive reign of Nicholas I (1825–1855), Kelly argues, Turgenev adopted an air of scepticism, pessimism and haughty detachment. This mood led to despair and inaction and itself amounted to a form of nihilism (Kelly 1998). In characterizing Turgenev in this way, Kelly is reprising a criticism of him made by Herzen (Gertsen 1960, p. 349), who was stung by Turgenev's rejection of his hope that a Russian future superior to the present bourgeois order of Western Europe could be built on the collectivist instincts of the Russian peasant. Kelly's endorsement of Herzen's pejorative use of the word nihilism returns us, though, to the heart of the problem we have when we try to characterize the phenomenon that it is supposed to describe. From the early 1860s, this elastic term has had potency as a weapon in political disputes but relatively limited value – by comparison, let us say, with such terms as materialism, socialism and utilitarianism – as a descriptor of a set of beliefs. It tended above all to serve as a negative construct that proved useful to conservative intellectuals and government officials (see Pozefsky 2003, chs. 5 and 6).

With the problematic nature of the term in mind, I shall approach Russian nihilism in this chapter as an intellectual, political and cultural phenomenon which evolved over time in a changing historical context. The phenomenon began to be identified – by the authorities, including censors and police agencies, as well as by writers of fiction, thinkers and journalists – in the early part of the reign of Alexander II (1855–1881). It first found philosophical expression in the domains of aesthetics, ethics and metaphysics, manifesting itself in repudiation of traditional values and received assumptions, on the one hand, and in a positivistic respect for data that were thought to be verifiable by the empirical method of the natural sciences and the emergent social sciences, on the other. At the same time, Russian nihilism became associated at an early stage in its history with a generational rebellion that flared up among students in the country's higher education system. Forms of association such as self-education circles, supportive groups of students from the same region of the empire, libraries and refectories were established. The emergence of a corporate spirit among the student youth proved just as important as the reading of literature and journalism infused with radical social and political ideas for the development of political opposition after the Crimean War and helped to generate numerous outbreaks of unrest in higher education institutions, especially in 1861 and 1868–1869. While *raznochintsy* were certainly well represented in the disaffected student community, as they were in polemical journalism, they may not have been so predominant as Ozhegov's above-cited definition of a nihilist might suggest. Students who belonged to the noble estate – especially the petty gentry, in which many families, like Pisarev's, were losing wealth and social status – were also prominent in it (Brower 1975, pp. 18–19, 117–118, 122–140 and 220–226).

The radical youth, inspired by new ideas which I shall outline in the following sections and by new patterns of collective behaviour that were at odds with traditional Russian social life, settled upon their own causes and practices, particularly the habit of communal living, defence of free love and the arrangement of fictitious marriages designed to liberate women from the patriarchal family. They also developed a semiotic system intended to exhibit their group identity and shock their elders. They favoured colloquial forms of language and an informal register and refused to observe noble linguistic etiquette and noble manners more generally. They disdained the polite, refined, witty conversation (often conducted in French) that was valued in the aristocratic drawing-room. They rejected the code of conduct characterized by gallant behaviour towards women and defence of a man's honour (sometimes still by means of the ritual of duelling). They discarded traditional dress codes and wore modest clothing. Women smoked and had their hair cut short, while men wore their hair long. Both men and women often wore dark glasses. Russian nihilism therefore amounted not just to a set of ideas but also to the performance of a subculture or counter-culture. On one level, it was an 'active violation of social norms', a rejection of old practices ('deculturation' in Pierre Bourdieu's terms) and acceptance of new ones (Moser 1964, p. 44; Brower 1975, pp. 15–16 and 35–36; and Pozefsky 2003, pp. 163 and 215).

As the radical intelligentsia became disappointed with the outcomes of the reforms that Alexander II had introduced with the intention of modernizing his backward empire (especially the abolition of serfdom in 1861 and reforms of regional government and the judicial system, which were implemented from 1865), so nihilism acquired a more overt political dimension as well. It increasingly came to be associated with the developing revolutionary movement, which found many recruits in higher education institutions and took many forms, including political violence. In 1866, a former student expelled from the universities of Kazan' and Moscow, Dmitrii Karakozov, made the first attempt to assassinate the tsar. Towards the end of the decade, socialist circles proliferated in higher education institutions. In the summer of 1874, some 2,000 young men and women conducted socialist propaganda among peasants in the countryside during an ambitious 'going to the people'. In 1876, a well-organized underground revolutionary party, Land and Liberty, was formed, under the aegis of which revolutionary journals and leaflets were produced and attempts made to incite a peasant revolt. Occasional acts of terrorism, conceived as revenge for harsh treatment of peaceful activists, were directed at agents of the regime, such as police chiefs, prosecutors and prison governors. In April 1879, a further attempt was made by a lone revolutionary, Aleksandr Solov'ev, to kill the tsar himself. In the summer of 1879, Land and Liberty split into two new parties, one of which, The Black Partition, planned to continue its agitation in the countryside but the other of which, The People's Will, prioritized attempts to assassinate Alexander – an aim achieved on the bank of a St. Petersburg canal on 1 March 1881.

The intense debate about nihilism which took place in the age of Alexander II, during the latter part of the golden age of Russian literature and thought, and which it is the purpose of this chapter to survey, grew out of the intellectual reappraisal that followed military defeat in the Crimea and the end of the oppressive reign of Nicholas I. The debate was conducted in the burgeoning public sphere occupied by the literary community and the socio-politically engaged intelligentsia. Its principal media, which interacted with one another in a way that can be characterized as dialogic (Pozefsky 2003, pp. 212–213), were prose fiction (this was the age when the Russian novel came into full bloom) and literary criticism published in the periodical press. Participants in this debate tended not to make a distinction between social reality and literary representations of it, treating fictional characters as authentic humans who were often typical of their time and milieu (Pozefsky 2003, p. 18). Authors of literary texts provided models for readers' behaviour and in so doing tended to undermine the claim often made by radical critics that it was the proper function of art merely to reproduce reality. Those critics, for their part, established a utilitarian aesthetic standard, giving greater weight in their literary judgements to the writers' ability to reveal signs of the times than to conventional artistic qualities or defects, such as balance and elegance or wooden characterization and prolixity (Moser 1989).

It is notable, finally, that the anxiety of those who opposed the great reforms of the early 1860s, or who at least feared change that was revolutionary rather than evolutionary, was heightened by the fact that debate about nihilism coincided with early signs of revolutionary unrest. Turgenev ruefully reported the consequent hostility he encountered shortly after publication of *Fathers and Children* when he returned to St. Petersburg, where fires which it was widely believed had been started by revolutionaries had just broken out. "'Look what *your* nihilists are doing!', an acquaintance exclaimed; "they're burning St. Petersburg!'" No matter that his use of the word nihilist in that novel, Turgenev subsequently pleaded, was intended not as a reproach or insult but as an accurate expression of an historic mood that had seized the Russian public. It had been 'turned into an instrument of denunciation, an irrevocable condemnation, almost a stigma' (Turgenev 1967, pp. 98, 105). In this respect, nineteenth-century Russia furnishes an example that is still instructive of the way in which a term may be invented or appropriated, modified for a particular purpose and itself deployed as a weapon in a political or cultural war.

2 Turgenev's *Fathers and Children*

Even before the publication of *Fathers and Children*, Russian writers had begun to consider the clash between supporters of tradition and rebels. In *An Asmodeus of Our Time* (1858), for example, the minor novelist, historian and journalist Viktor Askochensky provided a critical portrait of the new type in his empty-headed character Pustovtsev, the evil spirit to which the title of this novel refers (Moser 1964, pp. 64, 140 and 191). They also began to focus attention on life in the non-noble milieu that was coming to be associated with radicalism. In his novellas *Bourgeois Happiness* and *Molotov* (both 1861), Nikolai Pomialovsky portrayed *raznochintsy* who could find no productive path out of the morass in which their social stratum seemed doomed to dwell. Readers would have doubted, though, whether such men would remain resigned for long to the limited, prosaic nature of the happiness open to them. Equally worrying for those who clung to conventional ethics was the 'graveyard philosophy' of Cherevanin, a companion of Pomialovsky's eponymous hero Molotov, whose deterministic views lead him to a moral relativism according to which humans have neither virtues nor vices. More menacing still, from the point of view of supporters of the established order in which the nobility occupied a privileged position, is Potesin, a character in an unfinished novel *Brother and Sister* (published posthumously in 1864), on which Pomialovsky embarked in 1862. Potesin is a young member of the gentry who becomes disenchanted with the values of his class, contemplates robbing the rich, and eventually, when he is dying after turning to drink and sinking socially, regrets that his 'useless honesty' has prevented him from carrying out this crime (Pomialovsky 1951, p. 545; Offord 1990, pp. 63–68; and Peace 2010, pp. 122–123).

It was Turgenev's *Fathers and Children*, though, that gave a name to the intellectual and cultural rebellion that was beginning in Russia after the Crimean War and helped different groups in the Russian literary community and intelligentsia of that time to plot their position. In the opening chapters of his novel, Turgenev introduces his principal male protagonists, the brothers Nikolai and Pavel Kirsanov, who are provincial nobles in their forties, Nikolai's son Arkadii, who is returning to his rural home after completing his university course in St. Petersburg, and Evgenii Bazarov, a student of medicine whom Arkadii has befriended in the capital. Whereas Nikolai and Arkadii tend to seek common ground with fellow human beings, Pavel and Bazarov are uncompromising individuals who provoke each other from the outset. On one level, this antagonism between a dyed-in-the-wool nobleman and Turgenev's conception of the new man from a lower social class is fuelled by the irritation of each at the other's modes of dress, speech and manners. Bazarov arrives at Mar'ino, the Kirsanovs' estate, wrapped in a loose-fitting outer garment associated with peasants or other poor people. His free-and-easy manner and colloquial, informal speech betray his non-noble social origin, but they also convey the disdain of radical members of the younger generation for the code of etiquette of the hereditary nobility. Pavel, for his part, is offended by the lack of deference shown by this 'hairy creature', the son of an army doctor, and is apprehensive about entertaining him as a guest (Turgenev 2009, pp. 21 and 13),[6] foreseeing that the new ideas and attitudes that Bazarov bears threaten the age-old way of life on the Russian provincial estate. As for Pavel's immaculate manners, elegant English suit, and affected French pronunciation of the loanword *printsip* ('principle') (Turgenev 2009, pp. 13 and 19), they strike Bazarov as out-of-place in this Russian rural milieu and out-of-date by 1859, when *Fathers and Children* is set, as Turgenev tells us in the first sentence of the novel.

The behavioural signals transmitted by characters in Turgenev's opening chapters imply differences of outlook and quickly give rise to a discussion of nihilism. Over breakfast the morning after the arrival of Arkadii and Bazarov at Mar'ino, and in the absence of the family's unsettling guest, who has risen early and gone out in search of frogs and beetles for scientific examination, Pavel asks his nephew to explain, as he puts it, what Bazarov actually is. 'He's a nihilist', Arkadii ventures. Each participant in the conversation then makes his own attempt to gloss the term. To Nikolai, who notes the Latin origin of the word, it denotes a person 'who ... acknowledges nothing'. For Pavel, who is already hostile towards Bazarov, it means somebody 'who respects nothing'. To Arkadii (who feels that he will gain a measure of independence by holding

---

[6] For references to and quotations from *Fathers and Children* in this chapter I have used the English translation by Michael R. Katz in the Norton Critical Edition series, which also has an extensive apparatus, including translated extracts from early Russian reviews of the novel and excerpts from over twenty scholarly essays on it.

views of which his elders disapprove), a nihilist is somebody who 'approaches everything from a critical point of view', 'doesn't bow down before authorities', and takes no principle on trust, no matter how much it is respected (Turgenev 2009, pp. 18–19). Bazarov, who joins the group when he returns from his early-morning expedition, does not himself use the term 'nihilist', but he does confirm that he does not believe in anything (Turgenev 2009, p. 22).

What specifically does the new type as Turgenev imagines him challenge, beyond those superficial behavioural signifiers of noble identity that Turgenev has taken care to describe? What authoritative principles does Bazarov repudiate, to the consternation of the older Kirsanovs? For one thing, he discards received aesthetic beliefs. In fact, formulation of the radical outlook embraced by the younger generation of the intelligentsia began with the rejection, by critics such as Nikolai Chernyshevsky and Nikolai Dobroliubov, of the then prevalent view that great artists – writers, painters, composers – strive to capture an ideal beauty not otherwise perceptible in the ephemeral, imperfect world around us. Artists were urged by such critics to enlighten the public, draw attention to topical social problems and inspire reforms that would benefit the majority of the population. Viewed from this angle, enjoyment of classical music or lyric poetry could stir up personal emotions and encourage introspection and nostalgia, distracting attention from contemporary ills. Bazarov therefore mocks Nikolai Kirsanov for his heart-felt renderings of Schubert on his cello and for his fondness for reading the verse of Alexander Pushkin, the great Russian poet of the age of Nicholas I. Arkadii, still in thrall to Bazarov, obediently confiscates Nikolai's copy of Pushkin's narrative poem *The Gypsies* (1827) and replaces it with the popular materialist tract *Force and Matter* (1855) by the German physiologist Ludwig Büchner. From the nihilist's standpoint, then, art produced for its own sake has no practical value. Judged by Bazarov's utilitarian standard, the Italian painter Raphael, one of the supreme representatives of the high Renaissance, is worthless (Turgenev 2009, p. 43).

Nor is aesthetics the only sphere in which supporters of conventional wisdom draw a distinction that members of the radical intelligentsia reject between the mundane here and now and an ideal transcendent world which may bring consolation, joy or hope to humanity. Of all the types of authority that nihilists repudiate, the most pervasive and pernicious is godhood, belief in which encourages humans to think they possess an immortal spirit separable from their perishable body. Bazarov has no expectation that part of him will continue to exist after his corpse has been buried, or that the brief life of a human being has any divinely ordained purpose. It is his lack of belief in anything beyond this physical existence that accounts for the rush of anger he experiences when his unexpected and unreciprocated passion for an aristocratic woman, Anna Odintsova, breaks down the soulless materialism (in the philosophical sense of the word) in which he has wrapped himself and reveals the insignificance of his fleeting presence in the infinite, eternal universe. Bazarov never accepts last unction when he is dying of typhus, which he has carelessly contracted from the corpse of a peasant on whom he had conducted a post-mortem, although his father pleads with him to perform this Christian duty.

Nor can nihilism as Turgenev characterizes it in *Fathers and Children* be altogether separated from debate about national identity, which looms over discussion of many a problem in mid-nineteenth-century Russian literature and thought. As far as Pavel is concerned, nihilism signifies rejection of Russian national essence, which he thinks is manifested in the pious Russian peasant. He is irritated by Bazarov's high regard for Germans (*nemtsy*, but Pavel ironically calls them *germantsy*), whom Bazarov acknowledges as Russians' teachers in the natural sciences. Not that the cosmopolitan Pavel can easily dismiss the charge that he too is influenced by alien ideas. The concepts he invokes – 'aristocratism', 'liberalism', 'progress' – are all foreign, Bazarov points out, and devoid of content that is useful to ordinary Russians in present circumstances (Turgenev 2009, pp. 20–21 and 39).

Dangerous as Bazarov's outlook certainly is to idealist aesthetics, Christian belief and conventional gentry patriotism, we cannot say that Bazarov wholly rejects everything. Some of the contours of an alternative outlook can already be glimpsed beyond the ruins of the received wisdom that he demolishes. After all, he does respect the natural sciences, which were regarded by the mid-nineteenth-century Russian radical intelligentsia as the highest example of the application of the power of reason. The immediate purpose of his life is the study of fast-developing disciplines such as physics, chemistry, zoology, botany and medicine. In this endeavour, he embraces the empirical method, dissecting the creatures he collects in order to glean knowledge that doctors may one day put to practical use. Such work has far greater utility, the radical intelligentsia had begun to argue, than the poetry, prose fiction or other artistic endeavour prized by the older generation of noble writers. A 'decent chemist', Bazarov opines in one of many such programmatic statements made in the 1860s, 'is twenty times more useful than any poet' (Turgenev 2009, p. 21).

Not that Bazarov's respect for science makes his outlook any more palatable to those who fear his nihilism, for it is conducive to a new view of nature and even the worth of the individual human being. Nikolai and Arkadii Kirsanov, and also Odintsova's gentle sister Katia, with whom Arkadii gradually realizes he wishes to share his life, find in nature a beauty to which they respond emotionally. Bazarov, on the other hand, treats nature as 'not a temple, but a workshop' which furnishes material for scientific experiments (Turgenev 2009, p. 35).

Under this clinical gaze, moreover, human beings fare no differently from frogs or trees, for they cease to be treasured for their unique personalities. Since all people are alike in body and soul, Bazarov explains to Odintsova, no individual human specimen deserves any more attention than a botanist would pay to a single birch tree (Turgenev 2009, p. 67).

Bazarov's dispassionate scientific approach to the world and all the creatures in it, together with his single-mindedness, energy and capacity for hard work, earn respect from other characters in the novel. The authority he enjoys among those who know him prompts reflection on the question – which is pertinent to revolutionary ethics – of how such exceptional people should be judged. His father doubts whether they should be measured 'by ordinary standards', although he realizes that the steely disposition that sets his son apart goes together with arrogance and lack of feeling (Turgenev 2009, p. 99). Thus, the 'self-confidence' of the new man, to which Turgenev draws attention when he first describes Bazarov's face, and which is construed as conceit by Nikolai and Pavel (Turgenev 2009, pp. 6 and 37), are of a piece with intolerance, lack of empathy and the unkindness that readers cannot help but detect in Bazarov's treatment of his doting parents. Above all, Bazarov's detachment renders him indifferent – or so he believes until he finds himself overpowered by passion for Odintsova – to the profound emotions humans experience. Being guided by cold calculation, Isaiah Berlin argued in a well-known essay, Bazarov foreshadows twentieth-century technocrats whose 'calm moral arithmetic of cost-effectiveness' obviates the need for them to 'think of the entities to which they apply their scientific computations as actual human beings who live the lives and suffer the deaths of concrete individuals' (Berlin 2008, pp. 346–347).

Does the nihilist outlook as personified in Bazarov necessarily entail the political violence to which such a purposeful and calculating individual may be able to resort without qualms? Is *Fathers and Children* in fact a prototype of the revolutionary novel, a sub-genre to which Turgenev returned in *Virgin Soil* (1877), which was written when the revolutionary movement had gained momentum through the 'going to the people'? The absence of any explicit mention of revolutionary activity in *Fathers and Children* could not have convinced readers that Bazarov would not have countenanced it. After all, proclamations exhorting people to take up axes had already begun to appear on the streets of Moscow and St. Petersburg in the years 1859–1861, causing widespread anxiety, even before the outbreak of the fires that were burning in St. Petersburg when *Fathers and Children* was published. Indeed, the novel does contain hints of revolutionary intent, conveyed in the Aesopian language that writers in tsarist Russia often employed in order to reduce the likelihood that passages would be excised from their work by the censors. What is useful at the present time, Bazarov contends, is 'rejection', that is to say destruction. Construction, the building that Nikolai Kirsanov advocates, is not the business of his contemporaries, Bazarov believes, for 'the ground must be cleared' first (Turgenev 2009, p. 40). When Pavel asks Bazarov whether he is 'preparing to take action', moreover, there is an unmistakable hint of violence in the confident reply he receives. 'There aren't as few of us as you think', Bazarov tells Pavel. When Pavel probes further, wondering whether Bazarov really believes he and those who are like-minded can 'take on, cope with a whole people', he responds cryptically with a popular Russian saying: 'Moscow, you know, burned down from a candle that cost only one copeck' (Turgenev 2009, pp. 42–43).

Nihilism, as it finds expression in Turgenev's Bazarov, thus represents a sweeping challenge to the outlook of the older generation, who risk seeming out of touch with new conditions in their backward nation. If opponents of radical ideas unconditionally ruled out the use of political violence, then they would in effect be resigning themselves to indefinite continuation of the status quo. They laid themselves open to characterization as garrulous, weak-willed 'superfluous men', of whom writers active in the age of Nicholas I, including Turgenev himself, left memorable portraits. This was the literary type that was transformed, in the age of Alexander II, when political identities became more sharply defined, into the archetypal ineffectual Russian liberal, who came under attack from both wings of the Russian intelligentsia, Romantic conservative on the right and revolutionary socialist on the left.

3 Pisarev and Chernyshevsky

Fathers and Children is the creation of an author who does not reduce human character and experience to black-and-white categories. In neither the older nor the younger generation are those characters who lean to one side of the argument or the other all alike. The good-natured Nikolai Kirsanov will adapt himself to new ways more successfully than his uncompromising brother Pavel, who will live out his days as a lonely bachelor in Dresden. Of the younger generation, Arkadii is not really a nihilist in any sense, just an amiable youth who settles down to family life as a politically moderate gentleman-landowner. Other characters who profess radical views, Sitnikov and Kukshina, also differ from Bazarov, whose seriousness and sincerity they offset. Kukshina surrounds herself with props that seem to affirm her identity as an emancipated woman, such as the so-called 'thick journals' that litter her sitting-room. Tellingly, though, the pages of these journals, in which the topical polemical writings of the intelligentsia (known as *publitsistika*) and works of Russian fiction were first published, are for the most part uncut (Turgenev 2009, p. 52), that is to say, Kukshina has not read them.

The nuances in Turgenev's treatment of nihilists and those who were shocked by them, however, would be lost in the polarized debate that followed publication of his novel. This debate oscillated between *publitsistika* and further works of prose fiction in which echoes of *Fathers and Children* can be heard. It began with reviews of the novel in which critics discussed whether Bazarov should be treated as a positive or negative figure and whether Turgenev himself was unduly sympathetic to or critical of the older or the younger generation. (Turgenev's own attitude towards Bazarov seems to have been ambivalent: 'the Lord knows whether I loved him or hated him!', he wrote to a correspondent in 1870 [Turgenev 1964b, p. 152].) On the one hand, critics of the right, including Mikhail Katkov, the editor of the journal in which the novel first appeared, rounded on Turgenev for allegedly applauding nihilists (Berlin 2008, pp. 321–322, 327–329). From the left, on the other hand, Maksim Antonovich treated *Fathers and Children* as an encomium to the 'fathers' and a merciless defamation of the 'children'. Turgenev, according to Antonovich, hated, despised, mocked and demonized his principal representative of the young generation, slandering him as a cold, heartless cynic and comprehensively discrediting contemporary radical thought in the process (Antonovich 1961, pp. 38, 42, 45, 48, 52, 82 and 87–88).

However, another critic of the left, Pisarev, accepted Bazarov as exemplary and himself became the chief standard-bearer for nihilism, although he preferred to classify Turgenev's hero as a 'realist' rather than a nihilist. In "Bazarov", an article published in *The Russian Word* (*Russkoe slovo*) in 1862, Pisarev praised his subject for treating human feelings as mere outcomes of the operation of the nervous system and for recognizing, as an empiricist, 'only that which may be attested by one of the five senses' (Pisarev 1955b, p. 9). In a second essay on *Fathers and Children*, "Realists" (1864), Pisarev used Turgenev's novel as a basis for instructions to would-be nihilists on how to conduct themselves in accordance with their principles (Pisarev 1956a; Pozefsky 2003, pp. 87–92). Besides admiring Bazarov's rejection of what realists thought were prejudices, such as recognition of a deity, Pisarev shared his utilitarian view of art and in an article of 1865 undertook his own "Destruction of Aesthetics" (Pisarev 1955b, p. 25; Pisarev 1956b). In fact, Pisarev himself had already begun before the publication of Turgenev's novel to champion the iconoclasm that Bazarov came to typify. In his early essay "Nineteenth-Century Scholasticism" (1861), he looked forward to the demolition that Bazarov would advocate. What could be broken, he argued here, should be broken, and what was worthwhile would withstand the attack (Pisarev 1955a, p. 135). In 1862, the revolutionary significance of such defiance became explicit in an illegal pamphlet (which, however, did not appear because the clandestine press on which it was to be printed was seized by the authorities). Here Pisarev looked forward to the possibility that the house of Romanov and the St. Petersburg bureaucracy would be given a 'final shove' (Pisarev 1955c, p. 126).

Pisarev's admiration for Bazarov prompted him to reflect on the question Turgenev had broached, through Bazarov's father, about whether nihilists were exceptional people who might enjoy exemption from normal moral rules. Humankind, Pisarev decided, should be divided into 'categories'. First, there is the ordinary mass of humans who live 'according to the established norm', neither making discoveries nor committing crimes. Second, there are more intelligent individuals who cannot come to terms with everything that the mass accepts but who are not themselves capable of taking their rebellion beyond a theoretical stage. Third, there are individuals who distinguish themselves from the mass 'by their acts, habits and whole way of life', achieving 'full self-liberation, full individuality and independence'. Astute readers would easily have construed humans of Pisarev's highest category as revolutionaries in the making. These exceptional individuals recognize no external regulator or principle and are governed 'only by personal whim or personal calculation'. Unlike the 'superfluous men' of earlier generations, who either had 'will without knowledge' or 'knowledge without will', they 'have both knowledge and will', and thought and action come together in them (Pisarev 1955b, pp. 20–21). Through discussion of emblematic literary types, Pisarev lays foundations for a philosophy of revolutionary action.

Much of the groundwork for the intellectual rebellion that was embodied in Turgenev's Bazarov and debated in critical reception of *Fathers and Children* had already been done by Chernyshevsky, the leader of the left wing of the intelligentsia, in the years immediately after the Crimean War. Not only had Chernyshevsky argued that art should be seen as a means of reproducing reality rather than transcending it (Chernyshevsky 1949). He had also played the leading role in attacking religion by preaching materialism and monism and introducing Russians to the utilitarianism of Jeremy Bentham (which, however, served in Russia as an ethical basis for cooperative socialism rather than for laissez-faire capitalism) (Chernyshevsky 1950c). In the political sphere, Chernyshevsky discredited liberalism, presenting it as a doctrine which demanded rights that are in practice useless if one does not have the wherewithal to take advantage of them (Chernyshevsky 1950a, pp. 215–219).

Following the publication of *Fathers and Children*, Chernyshevsky himself engaged with Turgenev's portrayal of the nihilist archetype in a highly influential novel of his own, *What Is to Be Done?*, sub-titled *A Story about New People* (1863) (Chernyshevsky 1939). (Chernyshevsky wrote this novel, which somehow escaped prohibition by the censor, while imprisoned in St. Petersburg following his arrest in July 1862 on suspicion of involvement in the production of seditious pamphlets and incitement of the unrest that coincided with the appearance of *Fathers and Children*.) Two of the positive characters portrayed in *What Is to Be Done?* are doctors who, like Bazarov, have an interest in medical research. By his choice of surnames for these characters Chernyshevsky relates them in readers' minds to Turgenev's representatives of the younger generation. Kirsanov is of course a namesake of Turgenev's Arkadii, while Lopukhov (whose surname is derived from the Russian word *lopukh*, 'burdock') brings to mind the plant which, Bazarov tells Arkadii, will grow out of him when he is dead and buried (Turgenev 2009, p. 103).

Chernyshevsky's fictitious ideal members of the younger generation, however, differed in several respects from Turgenev's Bazarov. Firstly, the rational egoism that Chernyshevsky preaches turns out to be a species of altruism. Chernyshevsky's heroes believe that their personal interests are best served by performing acts that are of use to the greatest possible number of other people. Chernyshevsky made it clear that his heroes were socialists (one of them reveres Robert Owen) and offered models of communal living which proved inspirational to the contemporary youth but which it is difficult to imagine the aloof and fiercely independent Bazarov inhabiting. Secondly, Chernyshevsky is an early advocate of the emancipation of women and stands out in retrospect as a forerunner of the feminist movement. No woman in *Fathers and Children* looks likely to play any useful role in Russian life outside provincial noble society. In *What Is to Be Done?*, on the other hand, Chernyshevsky's cast of 'new people' includes Vera Pavlovna Rozal'skaia, who liberates herself from her patriarchal society by a common-law marriage to Lopukhov. Indeed, it is Vera who sets up a cooperative of seamstresses and, in the last of a series of dreams that chart her progress towards liberation, imagines the establishment of a utopian community of the sort envisioned by the French socialist Charles Fourier. Thirdly, Chernyshevsky's most exceptional character, Rakhmetov, is a more overt prototype of a revolutionary than Bazarov. He is preparing himself intellectually for revolutionary activity by absorbing the doctrine of rational egoism and studying socialist thinkers, strengthening himself physically through diet, gymnastics, and heavy physical labour, and toughening his will through his habit of lying on a bed of nails. Rakhmetov served, incidentally, as a role model for Lenin, who read and re-read *What Is to Be Done?* and, four decades after the novel had been written, appropriated its title for an important work of his own on revolutionary organization and strategy.

There are affinities between Chernyshevsky and Pisarev, both of whom made major contributions to the task of undermining existing values and sanctioned revolutionary activity against the *ancien régime*. And yet, we should not identify the former so closely as the latter with nihilism as it has come to be generally understood. The programme put forward by Chernyshevsky and his allies such as Dobroliubov (if we can talk of programmes in an age before political parties, properly speaking, had been formed in Russia) devoted much attention to the ways in which the 'new people' imagined in Chernyshevsky's novel might construct a society of the future based on collectivism as well as to the destruction prioritized by Pisarev. Chernyshevsky (who did not embrace the word nihilism to describe the multi-faceted outlook he presented) also identified the existing Russian peasant commune – the *mir* or *obshchina* – as a promising indigenous basis for a socialist society (Chernyshevsky 1950b).[7] The difference in spirit between Chernyshevsky's thought and that of the more iconoclastic Pisarev is felt in Antonovich's review of *Fathers and Children*, which was written for *The Contemporary* (*Sovremennik*), the journal that Chernyshevsky edited until his arrest. For all the crudity of his review, Antonovich had good grounds for objecting to Bazarov's focus on negation and for insisting on the need not just to destroy but also to defend certain principles, in other words to outline a constructive agenda (Antonovich 1961, pp. 45–46).

By the end of the 1860s, nihilism as an amoral doctrine and destructive political force seemed to have found embodiment in Sergei Nechaev, a ruthless conspiratorial organizer of student circles in higher education institutions, and in the revolutionary he imagined in the notorious "Catechism of a Revolutionary" (1869) that he wrote, almost certainly together with the émigré Bakunin, whom he had captivated in Switzerland. The revolutionary as conceived in this document has a consuming interest in the 'science of destruction'. He is a self-denying figure who has suppressed all sentiments of kinship, love, gratitude and honour and broken all ties with his society. As dictated by Machiavellian or Jesuitic morality, the judgements this social outcast makes and the practical decisions he takes should be determined only by pitiless calculation about what best serves his cause (Pomper 1979, pp. 90–94). Unsurprisingly, the Russian authorities attempted to exploit the "Catechism" to arouse public opinion against the radical younger generation when they brought members of the student circles Nechaev had organized in St. Petersburg and Moscow to court in 1871, using the more open system of justice that had come into being as a result of the judicial reforms introduced a few years earlier.

---

[7] These ideas had already been put forward by Herzen in a series of essays published abroad about what he called 'Russian Socialism'. They would provide the ideological basis for the revolutionary Populists of the 1870s and their successors.

4 Dostoevsky and the Anti-Nihilist Novel

Of the many philippics against nihilism in the 1860s, the book *Nihilism in Russia* (1867) by a Baltic German nobleman, Baron Theodor Fircks, deserves special mention. Over a period of some ten years from the late 1850s, Fircks penned a series of controversial *Studies on the Future of Russia,* ranging over such topical subjects as the emancipation of the serfs and the future of Poland after the Polish rebellion against Russian rule in 1863.[8] As an arch-conservative aristocrat alarmed by the development of revolutionary activity, Fircks reckoned that he could inflict the greatest damage on the radical intelligentsia by treating nihilism as a moral infirmity rather than a political movement. He defines nihilism variously as an unhealthy expression of self-regard (the trait the older Kirsanovs had deplored in Bazarov, it will be recalled) and a sign of nihilists' sense of entitlement to reject foundations of the social contract, such as religion and the patriarchal family.

According to Fircks, nihilism affected only the Russian educated classes, not the merchants, the peasantry or the Germanic elite of the Baltic provinces to which he himself belonged. Nevertheless, it had taken a much firmer hold in Russia than in other nations, Fircks supposed, because the Russian elite had separated itself from the rest of the population to an exceptional extent by adopting foreign cultural values and habits. The principal antidote prescribed by Fircks was reform of the way in which noble women were brought up. In order to eradicate nihilism, he argued, it would be necessary to 'raise the moral level' of women by detaching them from the Gallicized *beau monde* and developing in them a love of the family hearth. To this end, legislators should reduce the importance attached to instruction in the French language (in which Fircks wrote his 'études'!) in girls' schools (Fircks 1867, pp. 2–5, 8–10, 72–73, 171–172, 193–194, 202–203, 208, 225–226 and 236–237). *Nihilism in Russia* thus reveals apprehension in conservative circles about the further westernization of Russia and about the appetite of young women there for social equality and satisfying professional roles.

Opposition to nihilism also flourished in the 1860s and 1870s in a sub-genre of the novel. Examples of the sub-genre include Aleksei Pisemsky's *Troubled Seas* (1863) and *In the Whirlpool* (1871), Nikolai Leskov's *No Way Out* (1864) and *At Daggers Drawn* (1870–1871), Vsevolod Krestovsky's *Plague* (1867), Vasilii Avenarius's *Panurge's Herd* (1869) and Ivan Goncharov's *Precipice* (also 1869).

---

8 Fircks wrote under the pseudonym Schédo-Ferroti (a near anagram of his German forename and surname).

Members of the radical intelligentsia are for the most part portrayed in this fiction as amoral, cynical, self-interested, untidy, conceited and sometimes delinquent (Moser 1964). Nowadays, much of this corpus of anti-nihilist prose fiction is forgotten, but not the contribution made to it by Dostoevsky, whose engagement with nihilism was the more intense as a result of his own youthful attraction to utopian socialism. In 1847–1849, Dostoevsky had participated in the so-called Petrashevsky circles in St. Petersburg in which numerous young men discussed the ideas of Fourier and other – mainly French – socialists about ideal communities. Having been imprisoned in Siberia for four years and exiled in Central Asia for a further five for his role in these circles, Dostoevsky returned to St. Petersburg in 1859 with his Christian Orthodox faith restored and a belief in the Russian peasant as its true bearer. In the early 1860s, he articulated his new outlook, known as Native-Soil Conservatism (*pochvennichestvo*), in two periodicals, *Time* (*Vremia*) and *The Epoch* (*Epokha*), of which he was de facto editor. Nihilism and its causes (especially loss of touch with one's Russian roots or native soil) and effects (especially loss of moral bearings and sense of purpose in life) were central preoccupations of these journals and of Dostoevsky's subsequent prose fiction.

The intellectual rebellion of the radical intelligentsia, for example, has affected Raskol'nikov, the anti-hero of *Crime and Punishment* (1866), an impoverished young man who has been expelled from university. Raskol'nikov has succumbed to 'certain strange "incomplete" ideas that are in the air', as Dostoevsky described the plan for his novel in a letter to his publisher (Dostoevsky 1985, p. 136), drawing perhaps on Pomialovsky's creation Potesin (Peace 2010, p. 123). In the early part of *Crime and Punishment*, Raskol'nikov conceives of his murder of a pawn-broker and theft of the wealth she has hoarded as an experiment in the utilitarian ethics commended by Chernyshevsky. A 'tiny little crime' of the sort he is contemplating would be cancelled out – as the issue is described by someone in a conversation Raskol'nikov overhears – by the numerous good acts that the criminal could subsequently perform with the proceeds of his crime. 'For one life – thousands of lives, saved from rotting and decay. One death and a hundred lives in exchange – why, it's arithmetic isn't it?' (Dostoevsky 1973, p. 54).

As a highly topical novel set in the mid-1860s, however, *Crime and Punishment* reflects the 'schism among the nihilists' to which Dostoevsky had already alluded in a polemical article inspired by the argument between Antonovich and Pisarev about *Fathers and Children*. Dostoevsky's crude young nihilist Lebeziatnikov, who moves into the foreground in the later parts of *Crime and Punishment*, seems to have Pisarev in mind when he claims that he would argue even with Dobroliubov (who had died in 1861 at the age of 25) if that critic were to rise from his grave. 'We have gone further in our convictions', Lebeziatnikov boasts. 'We reject more!' (Dostoevsky 1973, p. 283). Raskol'nikov himself is associated with a Pisarevan motivation, which emerges somewhat later than the Chernyshevskian motive put forward in the novel's early stages. In an article on legal matters which he had written before he murdered the pawnbroker and of which the investigating detective, Porfirii, reminds him, Raskol'nikov too had divided humans into categories, albeit with a slight simplification of Pisarev's taxonomy. His first category comprised the obedient mass. His second, higher category contained people 'of the future', 'destroyers', those who were capable of saying a '*new word*' (Dostoevsky 1973, p. 200). Conceived within a framework in which humankind was divided into ordinary and extraordinary beings, Raskol'nikov's crime represents an experiment in self-liberation, a claim to a right to transgress normal moral boundaries. The act demonstrates the arrogance and pride which, by common consent, are characteristic of the nihilist and which Raskol'nikov's loyal friend Razumikhin sees in him. Raskol'nikov has another attribute of the nihilist type too, besides his status as a man-God. As he is characterized by Razumikhin, who functions as Dostoevsky's moral compass in *Crime and Punishment* (Offord 1983, p. 47), he is a Russian 'translation' of something 'foreign' (Dostoevsky 1973, p. 130), that is to say, a being – like Bazarov, as Pavel Kirsanov sees him – who has been led astray by alien doctrines.

In *The Devils* (1871–1872), Dostoevsky's examination of nihilism is more openly political. For one thing, the novel reflects the upsurge of organizational activity and agitation among the student youth in Russia in 1868–1869 which Nechaev had helped to orchestrate. It recreates the world of the revolutionary underground, with its codes of rules, clandestine printing presses, safe houses, false documents and secret cells. There is repeated reference to the appearance of revolutionary proclamations of the sort that had caused such alarm in Russian society since the early 1860s and of which Andrei von Lembke, the ethnic German governor of the provincial town in which *The Devils* is set, has a prized personal collection. Dostoevsky's fictional revolutionaries devote attention to sections of the population that were being targeted by their real-life models: workers at a factory where employees were being laid off, soldiers who might support the revolutionary movement, students in institutions of higher education who might join protests. There are also plentiful signs in this novel of the tensions that were developing in the revolutionary camp itself, not least because of revulsion at the activities of Nechaev (Offord 1999, p. 73).

A large number of characters in *The Devils* illustrate the ways in which nihilism, in Dostoevsky's opinion, has manifested itself in political extremism. Shigalev, for example, devises a schema for a socialist society in which nine-tenths of the population will be enslaved by the remainder. Speculating on how humans will attain 'unlimited freedom', Shigalev arrives at the perplexing conclusion that there will have to be 'unlimited despotism' (Dostoevsky 1974, p. 311). Some of the 'devils' to whom the novel's title refers clearly relish the prospect of revolutionary violence. Kirillov, who is said to reject morality as such and to adhere 'to the latest principle of general destruction for the sake of good final ends', is reported as believing that more than a million heads would have to fall for the establishment of good sense in Europe. Another conspirator, Liamshin, would simply blow up the nine-tenths of humanity whom Shigalev thinks it is necessary to oppress (Dostoevsky 1974, pp. 77, 312–313).

Chief among the novel's nihilists is Petr Verkhovensky, who is plainly modelled on Nechaev, about whom Dostoevsky had informed himself by attending the trial of Nechaev's co-conspirators while he worked on *The Devils*. Petr creates a secret society that supposedly has a central committee with international connections and a pan-Russian network of small cells operating independently of one another with the aim of undermining and demoralizing society and eventually seizing political control. Like the revolutionary described in Nechaev's and Bakunin's "Catechism", he is an unscrupulous but beguiling operator, a skilled liar and dissimulator adept at manipulating and compromising people. He hopes to use rumour and arson to precipitate a major peasant revolt of the sort that had erupted four times in Russia in the seventeenth and eighteenth centuries. It is socialism of a totalitarian kind, moreover, that both Nechaev and Petr seem to envisage. In the society imagined by Nechaev, power would be concentrated in the hands of a committee that would withhold the means of livelihood from citizens who did not comply with the committee's instructions (Pomper 1979, p. 137). Petr, for his part, admires the method and discipline of the authoritarian Russian imperial regime he plans to overthrow. Most shockingly, he arranges and participates in the murder of a member of his revolutionary cell, Shatov, in circumstances strikingly reminiscent of the killing, in November 1869, of a Moscow student, Ivan Ivanov, whom Nechaev accused of betraying his network (Offord 1999, pp. 69–71).

At the same time, Dostoevsky's examination of nihilism in *The Devils* takes us beyond revolutionary politics and on to an ontological plane. His nihilists do not partake of the national essence, which for Dostoevsky is a crucial component of human personality and identity and which, in the Russian case, manifests itself in command of the Russian language, adherence to the Orthodox religion, and the apoliticism, peaceable nature and spirit of brotherhood supposedly characteristic of the Russian peasantry. Dostoevsky's nihilists therefore lack a moral compass and, in the final analysis, any reason for living. Accordingly, Kirillov, who speaks his native language awkwardly (as do Lebeziatnikov in *Crime and Punishment* and another of Dostoevsky's young nihilists, Burdovsky in *The*

Idiot [1868]), aims to prove his identity as a new man by overcoming fear of death and eventually demonstrates his triumph in this quest by shooting himself. Similarly, Dostoevsky's strong-willed but altogether amoral anti-hero, Stavrogin, who is quite unable to distinguish between good and evil, reports at the novel's end, in a letter written in slightly flawed Russian, that he has taken up Swiss citizenship and then hangs himself. Suicide, for Dostoevsky, is a possible natural outcome of nihilism.

Who, Dostoevsky asks in *The Devils*, was to blame for the insurgency he observes and for the intellectual rebellion and collapse of morals that had made it possible? His answer implicates not only the 'children', who advocate and perpetrate revolutionary violence, but also the 'fathers'. The main representative of the older generation in the novel is Stepan Verkhovensky, who is literally Petr's father, although he has been so negligent as a parent that he has only ever seen his son twice before Petr unexpectedly turns up in the town in which the novel is set. Stepan is a composite portrait of the typical Westernizer of the 1840s, but his biographical details, personal traits and scholarly interests are particularly reminiscent of Timofei Granovsky, a renowned historian and professor at Moscow University. Granovsky's public lectures on medieval European history had breathed humane ideas into the opponents of Russian autocracy during the repressive reign of Nicholas I (Offord 1999, pp. 75–76). Under Dostoevsky's malicious gaze, though, this eloquent advocate of altruistic public service is turned into a vain and vacuous orator and attention-seeking moral coward. Nor is Petr the only monster that Verkhovensky *père* has created. Stepan has also been responsible for the upbringing and intellectual development of Stavrogin, the son of the woman, Varvara Stavrogina, with whom he has been living in an apparently Platonic relationship for two decades. In the eyes of Petr, Stavrogin is a charismatic potential leader of the peasant revolt he hopes to incite.

Such fathers as Stepan and the Westernizers of the 1840s did not explicitly sanction the destruction that nihilists such as Petr hoped to unleash. And yet, their free-thinking, Dostoevsky wishes to persuade his readers, had created the moral (or rather, amoral) climate in which nihilism took root. Consequently, cosmopolitan liberals are as much to blame for the impending apocalypse, in Dostoevsky's eyes, as the socialist conspirators and agitators they have sired, tutored or indulged. Their destruction of religious and moral authority, according to Dostoevsky, does indeed lead inevitably to violence, even though they might think that the accommodations they seek with revolutionary hotheads will save their country from the worst excesses they fear. There are so many of these useful idiots too. They are to be found in the tsarist administration and polite society (the town governor von Lembke and his deluded wife Iuliia are examples), in the literary community (represented by the condescending man of letters Karmazinov, who is a spiteful parody of Turgenev) and among professional people such as barristers and teachers.

Thus, Dostoevsky re-examines in *The Devils* all the characteristics of nihilism rehearsed by Turgenev in *Fathers and Children:* the rejection of aesthetics and promotion of a utilitarian view of art; the doctrine of egoism; the denial of meaning and spiritual purpose in human life; the spurning of warmth and feeling in human relationships; rejection of the institutions of marriage and the family; and the repudiation of nationality. Unlike Turgenev, though, Dostoevsky does not attempt to offer a balanced view of his subject-matter, as attested by his numerous hostile allusions to Chernyshevsky's works, especially *What Is to Be Done?* (Offord 1999, pp. 81–86). His nihilists, like the Gadarene swine in the biblical passage (Luke 8:32–36) that Dostoevsky quotes in his novel's epigraph, are possessed by evil spirits.

Nor had Dostoevsky lost interest in the subject of nihilism when he wrote his last novel, *The Brothers Karamazov* (1879–1880), although by then he was conducting an enquiry, conceived on an epic scale, into how humans might in future either live together harmoniously in a Christian utopia or be enslaved in a totalitarian dystopia. It is significant that Dostoevsky tells us in a short foreword that the novel is set thirteen years before it is published (Dostoevsky 1976, vol. 14, p. 6) – that is to say, more or less at the time when *The Devils* had been set. On one level, *The Brothers Karamazov* too is an enquiry into morality, or the collapse of it, in a world in which humans live without belief in a god or in the immortality of the soul. In such a world, where only the gratification of immediate desires need be considered, 'everything will be permitted', as Ivan Karamazov is said to believe (Dostoevsky 1976, vol. 14, pp. 64–65), thereby granting licence to his half-brother Smerdiakov to kill their despicable father Fedor. As understanding of his guilt preys upon Ivan, the seedy devil who visits him towards the end of the novel expresses the opinion that the only thing that the 'new men' really need to destroy is 'the idea of God in humankind'. Once all humans renounce God, the entire old outlook and, crucially, the old morality will collapse and a new age will dawn (Dostoevsky 1976, vol. 15, p. 83).

5 Conclusion

Following the publication of *Fathers and Children*, the term 'nihilist' became a convenient label with which the Russian government, its supporters and, more broadly, conservatives such as Dostoevsky could demonize their opponents, among whom advocates of revolutionary terrorism were never in a majority in the late nineteenth century. The imagined nihilist embodied the anxieties of his or her creator and that creator's readers. In the Anglophone world, too, the terms 'nihilism' and 'nihilist' quickly came to be applied in a pejorative way to a large swathe of critics of Russian autocracy. No doubt this linguistic usage was partly due to the fact that western readers soon became acquainted with Turgenev's novel through a translation into English done by the American scholar and diplomat Eugene Schuyler, who noted in his preface that the Russian government exploited the label 'nihilist' 'to stigmatize all revolutionary, and ultra democratic and socialistic tendencies' (Turgenef 1867, p. vii). In *The Times*, which reported extensively on Russia during the 1870s and 1880s, the terms were often used lazily as synonyms for socialists, communists, revolutionaries and radical ideas of various complexions. An editorial published shortly after the assassination of Alexander II, for example, conceived of nihilism in the loosest terms, presenting it as not only a Russian variant of socialism but also a form of 'Byronism or Wertherism applied to politics' with 'roots in sentimentalism, in egotistical discontent, and the vagaries of vanity' (Editorial, *The Times*, March 15, 1881, p. 9)! Oscar Wilde also treated the subject in a melodramatic way in his first play, *Vera; Or, the Nihilists*, a 'tragedy' set in Moscow, where Wilde wrongly located the imperial palace.⁹

In truth, though, the Russian socialist camp included many groups and individuals who did not refer to themselves as nihilists or place such emphasis on negation and destruction as the label that was often pinned to them en bloc implied. The 193 men and women who were brought to court in 'the great Nihilist trial' on which *The Times* reported in 1878 (*The Times*, February 11, 1878, p. 5), for instance, were for the most part peaceful propagandists. To label a consciencestricken radical a 'nihilist' is not to prove conclusively that a young man or woman possessed a Nechaevan heart of darkness or planned to incite the destruction of life and property for which Bakunin longed. Nor should we equate all revolutionaries of the age of Alexander II with terrorists active in the early twentieth century in the Combat Organization of the Socialist Revolutionary Party, let alone with the narratorial persona created by one such former terrorist, Boris Savinkov, in *Pale Horse* (1909), which is the literary diary of a self-consciously Dostoevskian nihilist living a futile life in the shadow of death (Savinkov 2019).

What generalizations, then, can we safely make about nihilism as an historical concept fashioned by Russian thinkers and writers of prose fiction, both rad-

---

9 Wilde completed the play in 1880. It was staged in New York in 1883 but withdrawn after only a week.

icals and conservatives, who jousted with each other in the latter half of the nineteenth century?

Firstly, it was a product of the sudden influx of western ideas, movements and disciplines into a backward country on Europe's eastern periphery. These intellectual and cultural imports included Romanticism, utopian socialism, utilitarianism, political economy, the atheism encouraged by Ludwig Feuerbach's *Essence of Christianity* (1841), vulgar materialism (exemplified in the writings of Büchner), the positivist philosophy of Auguste Comte, Darwinism, the sociology of Herbert Spencer, the emerging social sciences more generally and the socially engaged European novel. Received in Russia in unexpected combinations and reconsidered in the light of social flux and changing political expectations there, all this nourishment for the mind affected the intense national self-examination that followed Russia's defeat in the Crimean War. Turgenev and Dostoevsky provided classic fictional records of the disorientation caused by this exposure of an educated class in a traditional society to foreign modernity.

Secondly, nihilism was a more complex and multi-faceted concept than popular use of the term as a means of stigmatization of opponents has allowed the uninformed observer to understand. As is evident from Turgenev's seminal text, it implied a world-outlook which required adherence to consistent views on many subjects. Intellectual rebels who were branded as nihilists, on the whole, were drawn into debate with their detractors about a wide range of inter-connected questions of an aesthetic, ethical, metaphysical, social, political or even geopolitical nature. Recurrent topics in the debate included the nature and function of art, egoism and altruism, the existence of a divine being, loss of faith and its consequences, social organization and political governance, the strength or weakness of a sense of nationality and the apparently superhuman powers of a human being able to live without moral restraint.

Thirdly, the rebels labelled 'nihilists' shared a belief that thinking humans should reject received wisdom which has no empirically demonstrable basis in fact. Indeed, it was liberating for rational individuals and essential for the well-being of their society, they felt, to challenge conventional assumptions and values. As men and women who refused to accept ideas and practices just because most of their contemporaries accepted them, Russia's nineteenth-century nihilists were not dissimilar to people of sceptical outlook anywhere who have doubted, before or since the mid-nineteenth century, that the Earth was flat, or that it was the centre of the universe, or that it was created by a divine being a few millennia before the birth of Christ.

Fourthly, we may also say with confidence that rebels on the spectrum ranging from followers of Chernyshevsky to those who were more attracted to Pisarev all helped to break down respect for autocracy in late imperial Russia and therefore that they prepared the ground for the revolutions that destroyed the Russian tsarist regime in 1917. They achieved these outcomes, intentionally or unintentionally, not merely by challenging ideas and beliefs on which the old order rested but also by thoroughgoing opposition to the social practices and norms of late imperial Russia's long-established noble culture. The sense of spiritual breakdown, moral chaos, social disintegration, loss of national cohesion and impending apocalypse that Dostoevsky so vividly captures in his novels is the product of this sudden wholesale challenge to tradition and authority after the Crimean War.

To go far beyond these general conclusions, though, is to risk crossing the border between academic inquiry and political advocacy. It would be problematic, for instance, to claim that the views of nihilists, in the broadest definition of the term, necessarily led to revolutionary violence, as conservative thinkers such as Dostoevsky would have us believe. In any case, to what extent is it right to pillory thinkers or artists for acts subsequently carried out by those who claim to have been influenced by their views? Still less does it seem fair or reasonable to indict Russian radical writers who hoped to dislodge autocracy by peaceful means, let alone more moderate critics of the autocratic regime, for acts of revolutionary violence in the period between the Crimean War and the October Revolution. To do so would surely be to suggest that it is irresponsible of humans to think thoughts that challenge the institutions or beliefs (an established religion, say, or the patriarchal family, or the cultural superiority of an ethnos) that are held dear by supporters of a social and political order they detest.[10]

Bibliography

Alekseev, Mikhail (1928): "K istorii slova 'nigilizm'". In: Vladimir N. Peretts (Ed.): *Sbornik statei v chest' Akademika Alekseia Ivanovicha Sobolevskogo*. Leningrad: Izdatel'stvo Akademii nauk SSSR, pp. 413–417.
Antonovich, Maksim. A. (1961): "Asmodei nashego vremeni". In: Maksim A. Antonovich: *Literaturno-kriticheskie stat'i*. Moscow, Leningrad: Gosudarstvennoe izdatel'stvo khudozhestvennoi literatury, pp. 35–93.
Bakunin, Mikhail A. (1973): "The Reaction in Germany." In: *Michael Bakunin: Selected Writings*. Edited by Arthur Lehning. London: Jonathan Cape, pp. 37–58.
Belinsky, Vissarion G. (1956): letter of 8 September 1841 (Old Style) to V. P. Botkin. In: Belinsky: *Polnoe sobranie sochinenii*, 13 vols., Vol. 12. Moscow: Izdatel'stvo Akademii nauk SSSR, pp. 65–73.

---

10 I am grateful to Victoria Frede for her useful suggestions on the content of this chapter.

Berlin, Isaiah (2008): "Fathers and Children: Turgenev and the Liberal Predicament". In: Isaiah Berlin: *Russian Thinkers*. Edited by Henry Hardy and Aileen Kelly. 2nd rev. ed. London: Penguin, pp. 299–352.

Brower, Daniel R. (1975): *Training the Nihilists: Education and Radicalism in Tsarist Russia*. Ithaca: Cornell University Press.

Chernyshevsky, Nikolai G. (1939): *Chto delat'? Iz rasskazov o novykh liudiakh*. In: Chernyshevsky: *Polnoe sobranie sochinenii*, 16 vols., Vol. 11. Moscow: Gosudarstvennoe izdatel'stvo khudozhestvennoi literatury, pp. 5–336.

Chernyshevsky, Nikolai G. (1949): "Esteticheskie otnosheniia iskusstva k deistvitel'nosti". In: Chernyshevsky: *Polnoe sobranie sochinenii*, 16 vols., Vol. 2. Moscow: Gosudarstvennoe izdatel'stvo khudozhestvennoi literatury, pp. 5–92.

Chernyshevsky, Nikolai G. (1950a): "Bor'ba partii vo Frantsii pri Liudovike XVIII i Karle X". In: Chernyshevsky: *Polnoe sobranie sochinenii*, 16 vols., Vol. 5. Moscow: Gosudarstvennoe izdatel'stvo khudozhestvennoi literatury, pp. 213–291.

Chernyshevsky, Nikolai G. (1950b): "Kritika filosofskikh predubezhdenii protiv obshchinnogo vladeniia". In: Chernyshevsky: *Polnoe sobranie sochinenii*, 16 vols., Vol. 5. Moscow: Gosudarstvennoe izdatel'stvo khudozhestvennoi literatury, pp. 357–392.

Chernyshevsky, Nikolai G. (1950c): "Antropologicheskii printsip v filosofii". In: Chernyshevsky: *Polnoe sobranie sochinenii*, 16 vols., Vol. 7. Moscow: Gosudarstvennoe izdatel'stvo khudozhestvennoi literatury, pp. 222–295.

Dostoevsky, Fedor M. (1973): *Prestuplenie i nakazanie*. In: Dostoevsky: *Polnoe sobranie sochinenii*, 30 vols., Vol. 6. Leningrad: Nauka, pp. 5–422.

Dostoevsky, Fedor M. (1974): *Besy*. In: Dostoevsky: *Polnoe sobranie sochinenii*, 30 vols., Vol. 10. Leningrad: Nauka, pp. 5–516.

Dostoevsky, Fedor M. (1976): *Brat'ia Karamazovy*. In: Dostoevsky: *Polnoe sobranie sochinenii*, 30 vols., Vols. 14 and 15. Leningrad: Nauka, pp. 5–508 (Vol. 14) and 5–197 (Vol. 15).

Dostoevsky, Fedor M. (1980): "Gospodin Shchedrin, ili raskol v nigilistakh". In: Dostoevsky: *Polnoe sobranie sochinenii*, 30 vols., Vol. 20. Leningrad: Nauka, pp. 102–120.

Dostoevsky, Fedor M. (1985): letter of 10 September 1865 (New Style) to M. N. Katkov. In: Dostoevsky: *Polnoe sobranie sochinenii*, 30 vols., Vol. 28, Bk. 2. Leningrad: Nauka, pp. 136–139.

Frede, Victoria (2020): "Nihilism". In: Caryl Emerson et al. (Eds.): *The Oxford Handbook of Russian Religious Thought*. Oxford: Oxford University Press, pp. 152–168.

Gertsen, Aleksandr I. [i.e. Alexander Herzen] (1960): "Eshche raz Bazarov". In: Gertsen: *Sobranie sochinenii v tridtsati tomakh*, 30 vols., Vol. 20, Bk. 2. Moscow: Izdatel'stvo Akademii nauk SSSR, pp. 335–350.

Kelly, Aileen M. (1998): "The Nihilism of Ivan Turgenev". In: Aileen M. Kelly: *Toward Another Shore: Russian Thinkers between Necessity and Chance*. New Haven, London: Yale University Press, pp. 91–118.

Moser, Charles A. (1964): *Antinihilism in the Russian Novel of the 1860's*. The Hague: Mouton.

Moser, Charles A. (1989): *Esthetics as Nightmare: Russian Literary Theory, 1855–1870*. Princeton: Princeton University Press.

Offord, Derek (1983): "The Causes of Crime and the Meaning of Law: *Crime and Punishment* and Contemporary Radical Thought". In: Malcolm V. Jones and Garth M. Terry (Eds.): *New Essays on Dostoevsky*. Cambridge: Cambridge University Press, pp. 41–65.

Offord, Derek (1990): "Literature and Ideas after the Crimean War: The 'Plebeian' Writers". In: Richard Freeborn and Jane Grayson (Eds.): *Ideology in Russian Literature*. Basingstoke: Macmillan in association with the School of Slavonic and East European Studies, University of London, pp. 47–78.

Offord, Derek (1999): *"The Devils* in the Context of Contemporary Russian Thought and Politics". In: W. J. Leatherbarrow (Ed.): *Dostoevsky's "The Devils": A Critical Companion*. Evanston: Northwestern University Press, pp. 63–99.

Ozhegov, Sergei I. (1988): *Slovar' russkogo iazyka*. 20th ed. Moscow: Russkii iazyk.

Peace, Richard (2010): "Nihilism". In: William Leatherbarrow and Derek Offord (Eds.): *A History of Russian Thought*. Cambridge: Cambridge University Press, pp. 116–140.

Pisarev, Dmitrii I. (1955a): "Skholastika XIX veka". In: Pisarev: *Sochineniia*, 4 vols., Vol. 1. Moscow: Gosudarstvennoe izdatel'stvo khudozhestvennoi literatury, pp. 97–159.

Pisarev, Dmitrii I. (1955b): "Bazarov". In: Pisarev: *Sochineniia*, 4 vols., Vol. 2. Moscow: Gosudarstvennoe izdatel'stvo khudozhestvennoi literatury, pp. 7–50.

Pisarev, Dmitrii I. (1955c): "O broshiure Shedo-Ferroti". In: Pisarev: *Sochineniia*, 4 vols., Vol. 2. Moscow: Gosudarstvennoe izdatel'stvo khudozhestvennoi literatury, pp. 120–126.

Pisarev, Dmitrii I. (1956a): "Realisty". In: Pisarev: *Sochineniia*, 4 vols., Vol. 3. Moscow: Gosudarstvennoe izdatel'stvo khudozhestvennoi literatury, pp. 7–138.

Pisarev, Dmitrii I. (1956b): "Razrushenie estetiki". In: Pisarev: *Sochineniia*, 4 vols., Vol. 3. Moscow: Gosudarstvennoe izdatel'stvo khudozhestvennoi literatury, pp. 418–435.

Pomialovksy, Nikolai G. (1951): "Brat i sestra". In: Nikolai G. Pomialovsky: *Sochineniia*. Moscow, Leningrad: Gosudarstvennoe izdatel'stvo khudozhestvennoi literatury, pp. 483–548.

Pomper, Philip (1979): *Sergei Nechaev*. New Brunswick: Rutgers University Press.

Pozefsky, Peter C. (2003): *The Nihilist Imagination: Dmitrii Pisarev and the Cultural Origins of Russian Radicalism:* New York: Peter Lang.

Savinkov, Boris (2019): *Pale Horse*. Edited and translated by Michael R. Katz. Pittsburgh: University of Pittsburgh Press.

Schédo-Ferroti, D. K. [i. e. Théodore de Fircks] (1867): *Études sur l'avenir de la Russie*. 9e étude: *Le nihilisme en Russie*. Berlin: E. Bock and Brussels: F. Claassen.

Turgenef, Ivan Sergheïevitch (1867): *Fathers and Sons*. Translated by Eugene Schuyler. New York: Leypoldt and Holt.

Turgenev, Ivan S. (1964a): "Poezdka v poles'e". In: Turgenev: *Polnoe sobranie sochinenii i pisem*, 28 vols, *Sochineniia*, Vol. 7. Moscow, Leningrad: Izdatel'stvo Akademii nauk SSSR, pp. 51–70.

Turgenev, Ivan S. (1964b): letter of 23 December 1869 (Old Style) to I. P. Borisov. In: Turgenev: *Polnoe sobranie sochinenii i pisem*, 28 vols., *Pis'ma*, Vol. 8. Moscow, Leningrad: Izdatel'stvo Akademii nauk SSSR, pp. 151–153.

Turgenev, Ivan S. (1967): *Literaturnye i zhiteiskie vospominaniia*. In: Turgenev: *Polnoe sobranie sochinenii i pisem*, 28 vols., *Sochineniia*, Vol. 14. Moscow, Leningrad: Izdatel'stvo Akademii nauk SSSR, pp. 76–202.

Turgenev, Ivan (2009): *Fathers and Children*. 2nd ed. Edited and translated by Michael R. Katz. New York, London: W. W. Norton and Company.

Marco Piazza
Violence, Evil and Nihilism: Nietzschean Traces in Guimarães Rosa's *Grande Sertão: Veredas*

> I am not a novelist;
> I am a writer of critical short stories
> (Rosa in Lorenz 1983, p. 70).

Abstract: Long considered a philosophical novel, João Guimarães Rosa's *Grande Sertão: Veredas* contains an analysis of the various ways in which human violence manifests itself. The theme of violence in the economy of the novel (and in the author's work more generally) is strongly linked to the theme of evil, which is often personified in Rosa's work in the form of the devil, with whom his characters have a metaphysical relationship. Rosa's reflections on violence, evil and free will in the *Grande Sertão* should be considered in relation to his reading of Nietzsche's works, which he studied before writing the novel. It is possible to reconstruct this reading, at least in part, from the books that are preserved in his library to this day, the margins of which still contain his marks and notes. It is thus possible to consider the investigation of evil, violence and free will contained in the novel against the backdrop of the tragic and nihilistic theories not only of Nietzsche but of Unamuno and Kierkegaard, philosophers who were also appreciated by Rosa.

1 Introduction: Absorbing Philosophy Without Killing the Language

Philosophical readings of literary texts always involve risk. And yet, within the field known as the 'philosophy of literature' (Lamarque 2009), scholars have proposed diverse methodological approaches over the years (Carrol and Gibson 2015; Stocker and Mack 2018). The methodological approach followed here derives substantially from the fusion of two models. On the one hand, it aims to reconstruct the philosophy of the text – which can be a novel, as in the case of the *Grande Sertão* by João Guimarães Rosa (1908–1967) (Rosa 1963) – without restricting itself to the philosophy in the text, that is, to its expressly philosophical parts, recognizable as such by citations, references to authors and other explicit signals from the author. On the other hand, to avoid engaging in a reckless deconstructionist hermeneutics, it links analysis of the philosophy of the text to a reconstruction of the philosophical readings of the author and to the cultural influences to which his work has been exposed. Behind this approach lies the conviction that it is impossible to identify a stable and objective criterion for defining a text as literary or philosophical in an absolute way, since philosophy relies on style for its expression and since literature always conveys ideas, values, models and the like (Frank 1999, p. 167).

For this reason, I view as reductive the recent proposal of a philosophy of literature, understood as the philosophical study of 'literature' (Barbero 2013). If philosophical works are themselves literary texts, philosophers cannot approach literature as something that is completely external to their field, regulated by a completely different intentionality. Instead, it must accept that texts that, due to their stylistic or rhetorical features, are not generally expected to have philosophical content may in fact offer important philosophical insights (Piazza and Vincenti 2019). The philosophical richness of Proust's *In Search of Lost Time*, for example, cannot be appreciated if we limit ourselves to investigating the aesthetic doctrine contained in the final part of the work – centred on the themes of artistic meaning, memory and time. We can only understand this by considering the philosophical content found in the rest of the work (where Proust considers personal identity, passions, moral norms, etc.), which are much more consistent and mostly to be found in the middle of the novel (Descombes 1987, pp. 14–15).

Similarly, Rosa's masterpiece, *Grande Sertão: Veredas*, is a literary work that has long been the subject of philosophical interpretation (as have several of his stories, contained in various collections published throughout his life).[1] This is not only because Rosa explicitly includes references to philosophy in his texts, as when he frames his *Tutaméia* collection with epigraphs taken from Schopenhauer or places a long quotation from Plotinus in the epigraph to the *Corpo de Baile* collection. Rather, it is largely because of the way in which the presence and metabolizing of philosophical texts emerge in Rosa's writing, revealing a familiarity with philosophy that Rosa himself has confirmed in private exchanges and public interviews. The following traces two emblematic examples.

The first is the answer that Rosa gave to Benedito Nunes when the latter asked him to identify which of Plato's dialogues he had drawn on to arrive at the transliterated Greek expression *hai prókheiroi hêdonai* (Rosa 1984, p. 126,

---

[1] For example, among the most recent works, see Nuesch (2008); Cordeiro (2008); Gregório (2010); Amorim (2011); Santiago Sobrinho (2011); and Magalhães (2017).

note **) – translated into Portuguese as 'prazeres fáceis e ligeiros', or 'easy and light pleasures' (Nunes, 2006, p. 241). The expression is contained in the notes of the story 'Cara-de-Bronze', on a meeting between Grivo, one of the two main protagonists, and the prostitute Nhorinhá (Rosa 1984, pp. 125–126):

> I wouldn't be able to tell you now. I read the philosophers and transcribe in my notebooks what interests me about them, and that can be part of a story, like the one I collect from people's mouths. I am not a scholar. I do not quote; I absorb. Those words you mentioned are from the Greek philosopher, as recorded in my novel. However, I can forge a text or excerpt from Plato. Not even the experts in the history of philosophy could distinguish them without hesitation from the true texts. (Rosa in Nunes 2006, p. 241)

Modern technology makes it easy to locate the source of this phrase in the *Philebus*, where Socrates asks, rhetorically, whether 'the commonest and greatest pleasures [αἱ πρόχειροί γε αἵπερ καὶ μέγισται τῶν ἡδονῶν]' are 'those connected with the body [αἱ περὶ τὸ σῶμά]' (*Philebus* 45a). This reveals Rosa's interest in the philosophical question, debated by Plato, on the nature of pleasure and the distinction between true and false pleasures, among which, according to Rosa, are to be counted the carnal pleasures that Grivo refuses to take part in with the beautiful Nhorinhá (Rosa 1984, p. 125) – the same Nhorinhá who plays a major role in *Grande Sertão*, representing secular love in the ideal triptych of Riobaldo's three great loves, with his girlfriend and then bride Otacília representing sacred love and Diadorim (alias Maria Deodorina) representing impossible love and the irretrievable past (Sumiya 2015, pp. 304–305).

The other example is contained in the interview Rosa gave to Günter Lorenz, in the context of the *Congresso dos Escritores Latino-Americanos* held in Genoa in 1965. Here, Rosa uses a dry and peremptory tone, typical of a writer who refuses to accept the labels that critics put on his work, such as that of 'philosophical novel' (which is often used to define *Grande Sertão*): 'Philosophy is the curse of language. It kills poetry, as long as it doesn't come from Kierkegaard or Unamuno, but then it's metaphysics' (Rosa in Lorenz 1983, p. 68).

These references to Kierkegaard and Unamuno are highly relevant to those who want to study the philosophical background of Rosa's work in detail and to the thematic issues addressed in this chapter. However, from the perspective of the relationship between literature and philosophy (which we will address in a preliminary way here), direct references to certain philosophers in the passage quoted above do not fully convey Rosa's conception of the relationship between poetry and philosophy, fully in tune with his response to Nunes. In other words, according to Rosa, when writing literature one must 'absorb' any philosophical content, or else philosophy – in its pure state, as it were – will kill literature in the sense of substituting it. Note that Rosa uses the term *idioma*, or 'language':

literature is a site of linguistic experimentation, for Rosa, where the recovery of outdated terms, the introduction of dialecticisms and the creation of neologisms form the linguistic-semantic texture of the text. This is not because of an inclination toward the Baroque or preciosity but because it is only in this way that it is possible to describe the complex framework of the world, in all its nuances. From this perspective, every apparent trifle is a place of being and must be read as such, so as not to betray the mission of the artist, who is therefore a re-inventor of reality, which is exiled in common language (Martínez Pereiro 2017, p. 334).

For Rosa, there is nevertheless a type of philosophy that does not kill poetry, one written in a literary style, such as that of Kierkegaard and Unamuno. Thus, we can deduce that he would accept the possibility of a type of literature that does not kill philosophy, in which the convergence between the poetic and the philosophical, which Rosa himself sought in his work, is manifested: a convergence of the sort that we find in *Grande Sertão* concerning the great philosophical theme of good and evil, where an original reflection on violence is placed within the broader context of a comparison, at a distance, with European nihilism.

2 The Pre-Statehood Condition

Rosa began writing the first draft of the *Grande Sertão* in Paris (Retz Lucci 2008), where he resided between August 1948 and March 1951 (Martins 2006, p. 10). Among the surviving books that belonged to Rosa are two works by Nietzsche – *Human, All Too Human* and *Beyond Good and Evil* – and an anthology of selected pages. These are translations from German into French by Henri Albert (which were very popular in France), which Rosa read in a series of reprints published by Mercure de France between 1941 and 1948 (Bonomo 2010, p. 178). All of the volumes contain Rosa's handwritten notes in the margins (Bonomo 2010, p. 178). It is therefore likely that during his Parisian period Rosa conducted a careful reading of Nietzsche's works, in particular of *Human, All Too Human* and *Beyond Good and Evil*. It is also more than likely that this reading strongly contributed to the development of his original reflections on the theme of good and evil, the origin of violence and the limits of free will – reflections that are contained in an organic way in *Grande Sertão*, which can be read as an attempt to overcome the traditional antinomies of value, taking the questions posed by nihilism seriously without surrendering to nihilism, or rather offering an anthropological perspective in which the dry alternatives of traditional morality (good and evil) are put to the test and their tragic inadequacy as tools of classification laid bare.

The terrain on which the scope of Rosa's approach can be tested is more precisely that of radical evil and its annihilating power. From the first pages of the novel on, we find emblematic examples of cruelty apparently without reason, often extreme and brutal (Ginzburg 1992, p. 90). This cruelty is represented by four secondary characters: Aleixo, Pedro Pindó, Jazevedão and Firmiano (Rosa 1963, pp. 7–16). Aleixo randomly kills an old man asking for charity; Pedro Pindó and his wife beat their son, Valtêi, to the point of killing him; Jazevedão is a government delegate who enjoys inflicting pain on those he encounters; Firmiano, an ex-*jagunço* (gunman), sick and old, reveals to the protagonist, Riobaldo, his desire to skin and castrate a soldier.

In at least two of the four cases, however, we are faced with a sort of moral dialectic, which calls into question the principle of the reversibility of good and evil (Mazzari 2008, p. 280): Aleixo becomes good and charitable after his four innocent children are blinded by an incurable form of blepharitis; conversely, Pedro Pindó and his wife are initially moved by the aim, in itself good, of correcting the malignant behaviour of their son, Valtêi, who since childhood has taken pleasure in leaving harmless animals to bleed to death (Rosa 1963, pp. 7–8). The cases of Aleixo and Pedro Pindó therefore seem to anticipate the 'case of Maria Mutema and Father Ponte' (Rosa 1963, p. 186), to which ample space is given later in the narrative. Maria Mutema kills her husband while he is sleeping (again for no reason) by pouring molten lead in his ear. She then leads her parish priest to despair, and ultimately his death, by falsely convincing the father that her passion for him is what drove her to murder her husband. When a missionary discovers the truth and asks Maria Mutema to confess to her double crime, however, the woman confesses to her crimes publicly, asks for forgiveness, is imprisoned without protest, and, thanks to her irreproachable and devout conduct, becomes a saint (Rosa 1963, pp. 186–190).

If we look carefully, these cases of moral reversal result from a rapprochement with religion, a regained spirituality, but they fundamentally allude to a ubiquitous malignancy in man that unites the inhabitants of *sertão* in different ways. It is this natural human malignancy that is manifested explicitly and fully in the condition prior to any social pact, in the condition in which coexistence is not governed by rules and laws, that is, by the state. In this condition, man must necessarily resort to violence. This is the logic pursued by the *jagunços*, groups of organized bandits who violently impose a primitive brand of justice in the *sertão* – a logic that recalls the contents of aphorism 99 of *Human, All Too Human*, where Nietzsche describes the innocence of the cruel actions perpetrated by the man who finds himself in the pre-statehood condition. These actions are neither good nor bad in themselves, and indeed are even pleasant as they return to the individual his sense of superiority over others:

> All 'evil' actions are motivated by the drive for preservation, or more exactly, by the individual's striving for pleasure and avoidance of pain; thus, they are motivated, but are not evil. 'Causing pain as such' *does not exist*, except in the brain of philosophers, just as little as 'causing pleasure as such' (pity in Schopenhauer's sense). In the condition prior to civil society, we kill the creature, be it ape or human, that wants to beat us to the fruit of a tree, if we are ourselves hungry and heading for the tree: as we would still do to an animal if we were traveling in a desolate area. – The evil actions that now infuriate us the most rest upon the error that the one who inflicts them upon us has a free will, that it therefore lay within his *freedom of choice* not to do this terrible thing to us. This belief in free will provokes hatred, vengefulness, malice, an entire degradation of the imagination, whereas we get much less angry with an animal because we do not consider it to be responsible... . In the condition that precedes civil society, the individual can treat other beings harshly and cruelly for the sake of *deterrence:* in order to make his existence secure by demonstrating his power of deterrence (HH I 99).

When Rosa came across the aphorism, he noted the keyword 'cangaceiros' in the margins of the last passage quoted above – the one that begins with 'In the condition that precedes ...' (Bonomo 2010, p. 167). *Cangaços* were rebel groups formed by *jagunços*, which appeared in the late nineteenth and early twentieth centuries in north-eastern Brazil. It is this logic, typical of the *jagunços*, that determines the fate of Riobaldo, who becomes a *jagunço* (and then chief *jagunço*) to avenge the death of the enlightened leader Joca Ramiro and to bring peace to the *sertão*, eliminating unjust violence of the sort that led to the death of Joca Ramiro at the hands of the traitor Hermógenes.

Justice and violence are thus presented as having a common origin, just as Nietzsche suggests in this and other aphorisms in the second part of the first volume of *Human, All Too Human*, entitled "For the History of Moral Sentiments". In fact, according to Nietzsche, justice is born within a relationship of equivalent but contrasting forces:

> Justice (fairness) has its origin among people of approximately equal power, as Thucydides correctly understood (in the terrible dialogues of the Athenian and Melian ambassadors); where there is no clearly discernible superiority and a struggle would lead to ineffectual damages on both sides, the thought arises of coming to an understanding and negotiating the claims of both sides: the character of exchange is the original character of justice (HH I 92).

However, certain forms of power and justice, Nietzsche argues, guarantee greater social peace, unlike those based on extreme violence, which can gratify the individual but are harmful to the community. Whence the prevalence of forms of power management based on a prudent exercise of violence, which have historically been transformed into codes and laws – norms which, because of our cultural and religious filters, we take to derive from a moral feeling innate in man, although in truth they are rooted in the struggle of the strongest against the weakest (HH I 92).

In his own way, Rosa seems to have adopted these Nietzschean conclusions, as the end of Riobaldo's existential parable suggests. The apparently placid ex-*jagunço* settled on the farm that he runs with his beloved wife, Otacília, in a *sertão* now pacified and without rebels, although he keeps a handful of *jagunços* as bodyguards and continues to shoot his carbine for practice (Sumiya 2015, p. 312). In other words, the justice operated by Riobaldo corresponds to a balance of forces that can be subverted at any time but that is marked by the prevalence of a prudent administration of power – a situation that is analogous to that imposed by politics, in which the spirit of mediation pushes one to come to terms with evil more often than one should.

3 Men 'Beyond Heaven and Hell'

Rosa read Nietzsche in the aftermath of World War II, which he experienced in part from a privileged point of view in Berlin, where together with his second wife, Aracy, he helped hundreds of Jews flee to Brazil. This reading instilled in him the pessimistic conviction – attributed to 'my *compadre* Quelemém' in the novel, that is, to Riobaldo's spiritual confidant and friend – that humans are all from hell, that is, from a place where doing harm to others causes pleasure:

> People came from hell – all of us – so says my *compadre* Quelemém. From some lower depths so monstrous-terrifying that Christ himself was able, thanks only to his radiant strength, to descend for a quick glance, in the darkness of the eve of the Third Day. Do you believe it? That in that place the normal pleasure of each one is to abuse and torment the others; that the heat and cold afflict them sorely; and in order to digest what they eat, they have to strain in the middle, with awful pangs; even to breathe hurts; and there is no rest (Rosa 1963, p. 39).

Rosa is therefore convinced that by nature we are often violent and cruel not only to defend ourselves and to ensure our survival but also without reason, simply to measure our power and to feel pleasure (Ginzburg 1992, p. 91). It is therefore cultural and social structures developed over millennia, of a mythical-religious and political-social type, that keep us from falling fully into that condition which, in the novel, is symbolized by the 'people of Sucruiú':

> It struck me that to have come across those back-landers, and talked with them, and them destroyed their warning could bring bad luck. I had a presentiment that it was the beginning of much trouble. Those were men of a different breed, crude in their ways and habits. In even small matters, they had an almost effortless capacity for deep and far-reaching hatred (Rosa 1963, p. 318).

This is echoed in a note from the diary Rosa kept during the three years he lived in Paris: 'We all come from hell; some of us still hot from there' (Rosa 2001, p. 332).

Thus, two types of violence coexist in the world: one equivalent to radical evil (Mazzari 2008, p. 283), a symptom of our original nature, and one that has as its objective justice and social peace – a relative evil, aimed at the good. In this way, social peace is simply the result of the prevalence of violence justified by non-selfish ends compared to violence motivated by purely selfish and destructive ends. Since both types of violence have a common root in human nature, however, no individual can be defined as fully evil or good; rather, each of us lies somewhere on a scale between the two opposites. Moreover, in the novel, it is Riobaldo who argues that if 'everybody were bad', then 'everybody would be good', alluding to the fact that there must be an inscrutable divine plan that uses evil to realise, along a timespan of extended duration, positive ends (Rosa 1963, p. 259, translation modified). This is one of the numerous metaphysical hypotheses expounded by Riobaldo in the broader narrative on the problem of good and evil. What is problematic for Rosa is precisely the presence of evil without reason, radical evil, which is 'mixed up in everything it is' and which is personified in the narration by the 'demon [*demo*]' or 'devil [*diabo*]' (Rosa 1963, p. 7, translation modified).

The demon in the novel assumes a human form in the figure of Hermógenes, who treacherously kills the chief *jagunço*, Joca Ramiro. Hermógenes is famous for his terrible brutality, for taking pleasure in the fear and suffering of others, and yet he too has a glimmer of humanity somewhere deep in his core. This disgusting man, who like Faust would make a pact with the devil, not only has 'a wife and children' (Rosa 1963, p. 196), but offers Riobaldo something to eat during a fight, when he had not yet betrayed their leader (Rosa 1963, p. 179).

Traces of Nietzsche once again lie behind this extreme humanity: in this case, as the author of *Beyond Good and Evil* and the transvaluation of all values. In fact, according Rosa, men are all 'beyond heaven and hell' (Rosa in Lorenz 1983, p. 86), and the question with which the novel begins, on the existence of the devil, can now, at the end, receive an answer – one that is anticipated several times in the course of the narrative. On the last page of the novel, Riobaldo affirms that the devil does not exist, that what exists is 'human man [*homem humano*]' (Rosa 1963, p. 492, translation modified). However, this does not equate to affirming that humans are essentially good or to denying the existence of evil, as is clear from Riobaldo's subsequent assertion: 'God exists even when they say He doesn't. But the devil does not need to exist to be' (Rosa 1963, pp. 48–49). In other words, even if radical evil does not exist in the form of a superior evil entity to be placed on the same plane as God, evil nevertheless shows itself in human behaviour in all its cruelty and violence, especially when men live in a dimension imbued with ignorance. In fact, Riobaldo is a pivotal figure who exists between a mythical world and a rational world, and the tragedy that he and his history represent is explained in terms of an irreconcilable opposition between myth and rationality (Sumiya 2015, pp. 299–301): an irresolvable composition of these two elements, beyond knowledge's apparent claim to be able to redeem the evil that supposedly results from ignorance. The continuous oscillation between the mythical explanation (evil as a product of the devil, but also of destiny) and the rational (the evil for which we are solely responsible) is but one of many manifestations of the natural ambivalence of the human being, which therefore originally lies beyond good and evil.

4 Conclusion: 'Nonada' and Nihilistic Temptation

Rosa's philosophical novel therefore depicts this ambivalent human condition, which reveals itself only if one immerses oneself in nihilism, understood, following Nietzsche, as the 'self-suppression of morality' and as a 'process of self-transcendence' (Vercellone 1992, pp. 65 and 70) generated by the consequences of the death of God, announced in aphorism 125 of the *Gay Science:* a nihilism that, on the one hand, denies the personification of absolute evil represented by the devil – and with it the possibility of isolating absolute evil and radically opposing it to God – and, on the other hand, asks us to accept the presence of evil within us, in a sort of tragic awareness that it shares a common root with the divine, which tends to be confused with reality. The 'devil [*diabo*]' is, by Rosa's own admission, 'nada': nothing, the negation of being, nothing other than 'evil [*o mal*]' (Bizzarri 1972, p. 54). If God exists even when He is not there, then God is everywhere, even where we do not see Him, but to see Him we must accept that He takes on the appearance of the devil.

This does not entail either taking a metaphysical salvific perspective or committing to tragic pessimism. Taking up the famous formula contained in Nietzsche's *Posthumous Fragments* of autumn 1887, beyond the 'passive nihilism' that leads to the abyss in which Nazism attempted to submerge the world, there is the 'active nihilism' of those who know how to recognize the transvaluated equivalent of both the diabolical and the divine (NL 1887, 9[35], KSA 12, p. 351).

Rosa's nihilistic view of man and the world is related to the tragic vision of life that he appreciated in Unamuno (Magalhães 2017) – whom he considered both a 'philosopher' and a 'poet of the soul', in addition to serving as a kind of 'grandfather' from whom he inherited his own existential 'dissatisfaction' (*descontentamento*) (Rosa in Lorenz 1983, p. 68) – and echoes of which he recognized in Kierkegaard (Corpas 2000, p. 169; Kutzenberger 2005, pp. 157–212), whose works he read in French and perhaps also consulted in the original Danish (Kutzenberger 2005, p. 157). If tragedy for Unamuno is to be considered a 'perpetual struggle, without victory or hope of it; it is a contradiction' (Unamuno 1997, p. 33), a metaphor for life not only in his eyes but also in Rosa's, who, however, reads life's texture as a kind of paradox: 'life, death, everything is, in the end, paradox' (Rosa in Lorenz 1983, p. 68). In other words, awareness of the tragic dimension of life does not trap Rosa within the confines of a pre-Nietzschean metaphysics. Every metaphysical temptation is mitigated by that of scepticism, which appears in the *Tutaméia* collection where three quotations from Sextus Empiricus are set in the text. One, in particular, is significant for our purposes: 'In order, however, to have a more accurate understanding of such antitheses, I will give the Ways of obtaining the suspension of judgment' (Rosa 2009, p. 313) – in other words, human existence is interwoven with contradictions and ambivalences, which need not be resolved to be understood.

This form of scepticism does not lead to a strategy of detachment from the tragedy of existence, however. Riobaldo's disenchanted view of the *sertão* does not prevent him from detecting the weight of every slight variation of meaning and significance that alters our perception of things and events. These slight variations can produce effects of great magnitude, as if to say that every particle of being has its own value and its own function in the world economy and in relation to the existence of man, who in turn represents a small part of the world as a whole.

To express this, Rosa recovers a word now in disuse, 'nonada' – something without value, a 'nothing', a trifle (Feitosa 2006, p. 2) – which is emblematically a synonym of 'tutameia', or 'mea omnia' (Rosa 2009, pp. 340–341), a term that exists not only in Portuguese but also in Castilian, and which Unamuno himself uses in his *Tragic Sense of Life* to indicate a vague feeling of existential tension, a kind of anguish in the face of the paradox of life. It is a feeling that reveals our standing as little more than nothing and our efforts to be more than nothing, to avoid being reduced to nothing, to avoid being nullified by the dark forces that deprive us of an aim, of a transcendent tension: 'As you penetrate into yourself and delve into yourself, you are discovering your own inanity, that you are not all that you are not, that you are not what you want to be, that you are not, in short, more than *nonada*' (Unamuno 1997, p. 153). *Nonada*, for Rosa, is that 'almost nothing' in which radical evil insinuates itself, but it is also the almost nothing to which radical evil is reduced once the gaze of the active nihilist has rested on it, preventing it from being reduced to nothing while refusing to interpret the death of God as a sign of decadence and passive nihilism.

For Rosa, the death of God coincides with the atheistic verdict of positivism, which, although not unreasonable, proves to be reductive compared to the paradoxicality and richness of life – even if life, like the narrative contained in *Grande Sertão*, plays itself out between one *nonada* and another.

Bibliography

Amorim Cristiane (2011): "Rosa e Nietzsche: entusiasmo dionisíaco em *Corpo de Baile*". In: *Revista Contexto* 19. No. 1, pp. 351–368.
Barbero, Carola (2013): *Filosofia della letteratura*. Roma: Carocci.
Bizzarri, Edoardo (1972): *João Guimarães Rosa: Correspondência com seu tradutor italiano*. São Paulo: T.A. Queiroz/Instituto Cultural Italo-Brasileiro.
Bonomo, Daniel Reizinger (2010): "A biblioteca alemã de João Guimarães Rosa". In: *Pandaemonium germanicum* 16. No. 2, pp. 155–183.
Carroll, Noël and John Gibson (Eds.) (2015): *The Routledge Companion to Philosophy of Literature*. London: Routledge.
Corpas, Danielle dos Santos (2000): "A 'reprise' de Kierkegaard no *Grande Sertão: Veredas*". In: Lélia Parreira Duarte (Ed.): *Veredas de Rosa*. Belo Horizonte: PUC Minas, pp. 168–172.
Cordeiro, Robson Costa (2008): "O Sertão de Riobaldo: uma leitura a partir de Nietzsche". In: *Revista Trágica: Estudos sobre Nietzsche* 1. No. 1, pp. 98–106.
Coutinho, Eduardo de Faria (Ed.) (1983): *Guimarães Rosa*. Rio de Janeiro: Civilização Brasileira.
Descombes, Vincent (1987): *Proust: Philosophie du roman*. Paris: Minuit.
Feitosa, Charles (2006): "No-nada. Formas brasileiras do niilismo" In: *Flusser Studies* 3, 11 pp. http://www.flusserstudies.net/sites/www.flusserstudies.net/files/media/attachments/no-nada.pdf
Frank, Manfred (1999): "Style in Philosophy: Part I". In: *Metaphilosophy* 30. No. 3, pp. 145–167.
Ginzburg, Jaime (1992): "A violência em *Grande Sertão: Veredas*". In: *Revista do Instituto de Estudos Brasileiros* 27, No. 34, pp. 87–100.
Gregório, Paulo Henrique da Silva (2010): "O trágico em *A hora e a vez de Augusto Matraga*: uma leitura nietzschiana". In: *Pandemonium germanicum* 16. No. 7, pp. 184–203.
Kutzenberger, Stefan (2005): *Europa in* Grande Sertão: Veredas. Grande Sertão: Veredas *in Europa*. Amsterdam, New York: Rodopi.
Lamarque, Peter (2009): *The Philosophy of Literature*. Malden, Oxford: Wiley-Blackwell.
Lorenz, Günter (1983): "Diálogo com Guimarães Rosa". In: Eduardo Coutinho de Faria (Ed.): *Guimarães Rosa*. Rio de Janeiro: Civilização Brasileira, pp. 62–97.

Martínez Pereiro, Paulo Carlos (2017): "Una transacción de ojos y retratos (La soberbissimice y esta estória de 'Os chapéus transeuntes')". In: Ascensión Rivas Hernández (Ed.): *João Guimarães Rosa: un exiliado del lenguaje común*. Salamanca: Ediciones Universidad Salamanca, pp. 327–349.

Magalhães, Maria Cristina Soares (2017): *O Trágico na Travessia do Sertão: Miguel de Unamuno e João Guimarães Rosa*. Curitiba: Editora CRV.

Martins, Ana Luiza Costa (2006): "Veredas de *Viator*". In: *Cadernos de Literatura Brasileira* 20–21, pp. 10–58.

Mazzari, Marcus Vinicius (2008): "Figurações do "mal" e do "maligno" no *Grande sertão: veredas*". In: *Estudos Avançados* 22. No. 64, pp. 273–290.

Nietzsche, Friedrich (1997): *Human all too Human, I*. Translated with an Afterword by Gary Handwerk. In: *The Complete Works of Friedrich Nietzsche*, vol. 3. Stanford: Stanford University Press, pp. XXX–XXX.

Nietzsche, Friedrich (2001): *The Gay Science with a Prelude in German Rhymes and an Appendix of Songs*. Edited by Bernard Williams and translated by Josephine Nauckhoff; poems translated by Adrian Del Caro. Cambridge: Cambridge University Press.

Nietzsche, Friedrich (2003): *Writings from the Late Notebooks*. Edited by Rüdiger Bittner and translated by Kate Sturge. Cambridge: Cambridge University Press.

Nietzsche, Friedrich (2014): "Beyond Good and Evil". In: *Beyond Good and Evil / On the Genealogy of Morality*. Translated with an Afterword by Adrian Del Caro. In: *The Complete Works of Friedrich Nietzsche*, vol. 8. Stanford: Stanford University Press, pp. 1–204.

Nuesch, Enrique V. (2008): "De profundidade e superfície: Guimarães Rosa e Schopenhauer sobre a compaixão e o sofrimento". In: *Estação Literária* 2. No. 2, pp. 85–95.

Nunes, Benedito (2006): "Guimarães Rosa quase de cor: rememorações filosóficas e literárias". In: *Cadernos de Literatura Brasileira* 20–21, pp. 236–244.

Piazza, Marco, and Denise Vincenti (2019): "Philosophy in Literature. A Strategic Approach to the Debate on Philosophy and Literature". In: *Odradek* 5. No. 2, pp. 7–27.

Plato, *Philebus*.

Retz Lucci, Vivian (2008): "*Grande Sertão: Veredas* foi escrito em Paris; veja entrevista com Vilma Guimarães Rosa Reeves". In: *Folha de San Paulo*, 28 June 2008. https://www1.folha.uol.com.br/multimidia/tvfolha/2008/06/416634-grande-sertao-veredas-foi-escrito-em-paris-veja-entrevista-com-vilma-guimaraes-rosa-reeves.shtml

Rosa, João Guimarães (1963): *The Devil to Pay in the Backlands*. Translated by James L. Taylor and Harriet De Onís. New York: Alfred A. Knopf.

Rosa, João Guimarães (1984): "'Cara-de-bronze'". In: *No Urubuquaquá, No Pinhem*. 7th ed. Rio de Janeiro: Editora Nova Fronteira, pp. 77–136.

Rosa, João Guimarães (2001): "Do diário em Paris – III". In: *Ave, Palavra*. Notas de Paulo Rónai. Rio de Janeiro: Editora Nova Fronteira, pp. 331–337.

Rosa, João Guimarães (2009): *Tutameia* (*Terceiras estórias*). 9th ed. Rio de Janeiro: Nova Fronteira.

Santiago Sobrinho, João Batista (2011): *Mundanos fabulistas: Guimarães Rosa e Nietzsche*. Belo Horizonte: Crisálida/Cefet.

Stocker, Barry, and Michael Mack (Eds.) (2018): *The Palgrave Handbook of Philosophy and Literature*. London: Palgrave MacMillan.

Sumiya, Cleia da Rocha (2015): "*Grande Sertão: Veredas* na perspectiva do trágico". In: *Revista Versalete* 3. No. 5, pp. 296–313.
Unamuno, Miguel de (1997): *Del sentimiento trágico de la vida*. Madrid: Allianza Editorial.
Vercellone, Federico (1992): *Introduzione a Il nichilismo*. Roma-Bari: Laterza.

Joseph G. Kickasola
Signifying Nothing? Nihilism, Violence, and the Sound/Silence Dynamic in Cinema

> Life is but a walking shadow, a poor player
> That struts and frets his hour upon the stage
> And then is heard no more. It is a tale
> Told by an idiot, full of sound and fury
> Signifying nothing.
> — William Shakespeare, *Macbeth* (Act 5, Scene 5)

Abstract: What does sound have to do with violence and nihilism? Inspired by Nietzsche, some philosophers believe this particular nexus forms a critical dynamic of reality. It also provides a site for an investigation of the sound and silence as a meaningful dynamic in cinema. In approaching it, there are two common interpretations of the experience of sound/silence dynamic: silence as 'cessation' and silence as 'receptivity.' I attend to the sonic experience in cinema, seeking to discover if and how sound plays a role in our feeling and experience of nihilism and violence. This essay argues that, if we are to approach a full phenomenology of sound and silence, we should realize that the cessation approach holds explanatory power, but is ultimately insufficient without receptivity. It details how the power manifest in a variety of film examples at the nexus of sound and violence might be characterized as nihilistic, generally speaking. However, additional examples suggest the viability and necessity of the receptivity thesis, which needs more precise articulation, both in its own identity and posture as well as its relationship to cessation.

1 Introduction

Macbeth's famous soliloquy presents three key elements—nihilism, violence, and sound—in one masterful rhetorical package. Here, at his most nihilistic moment, after his wife's death and gathering evidence that his vicious, bloody campaign will come to a brutal end, he casts his bitter verdict on life in sonic terms: a good amount of noise ("sound and fury"), "signifying nothing" because, in the end, it is a tale that "is heard no more." "Sound" is a touchstone of life, and "fury" an emblem of violence, that liminal threshold of existence and non-existence.

What does sound have to do with violence and nihilism? Just as Shakespeare links these concepts, many of the thinkers to be explored here believe that this particular triad is a critical dynamic of reality. This nexus provides a site for an investigation of the sound and silence as a meaningful dynamic in cinema, as well as human life in general.

In approaching this nexus, there are two common interpretations of the experience of the sound/silence dynamic. The first, epitomized by Macbeth's nihilism, is that sound has always signaled the hope of significance, and silence the final disappointment. On a sensory level, sound and silence are not merely symbols, but samples of the dynamics that constitute reality. Silence (which, in this essay, ranges from absolute silence to relative quiet[1]) is associated with the loss of vital power, manifest most concretely in weakness, trauma, or death. Violence functions as a liminal concept, hovering between sound and silence, strength and weakness, life and death.

An alternative approach is similarly to view sound as life, animation, and becoming, but to treat silence as 'receptivity,' a general term that may encompass a number of positive approaches to silence: humility and hope for revival, watchfulness for different streams of life, reflection upon life, and/or attention to a different order of life beyond earlier preconceptions of it. Critically, the receptive tendency leans toward hope for significance in silence.

I attend to the sonic experience in cinema, seeking to discover if and how sound plays a role in our feeling and experience of nihilism and violence.[2] This essay argues that, if we are to approach a full phenomenology of sound and silence, we should realize that the 'cessation' approach holds explanatory power, but is ultimately insufficient without receptivity. It details how the power manifest in a variety of film examples at the nexus of sound and violence might be characterized as nihilistic, generally speaking. However, additional examples suggest the viability and necessity of the receptivity thesis, which needs

---

[1] 'Silence' is almost never absolute. Multisensory connections between our visual systems, tactile vibrations, and the human auditory system also complicate the experience of silence. That said, the difference between auditory plentitude and relative silence, as a dynamic of human experience, still merits analysis and attention. As Lucy Fischer describes, we do not evaluate absolute silence, but "silence *perceived*" (Fischer 1985, p. 241).

[2] As numerous thinkers suggest, the cinema can be a kind of simulation, a rehearsal of emotions, thoughts, and existential choice that causes us to reflect on our posture, ideals, and deepest responses. Consider these summary articles: Sorfa (2016) and Coëgnarts (2017). If we better understand how sound functions in the cinema, that will likely yield new insights on how sound, violence, and nihilism function together in everyday life.

more precise articulation, both in its own identity and posture as well as its relationship to cessation.

In the following section, I analyze the cessation tendency. Though this tendency is exactly that—a tendency, rather than an explicit claim articulated by Nietzsche[3]—we shall see that those who follow this tendency tend to minimize the value of silence itself, either negatively casting it as a weakness or cessation of life, or positively characterizing it as not truly cessation, but as a shift to other sonic streams that are, presumably, always abiding. One of the more recent and interesting ideas in this line is the "sonic flux" theory of philosopher Christoph Cox.[4] So, this first section will largely consist of an engagement with central tenets of Cox's theory, bringing them into conversation with some other prominent thinkers on sound.

Subsequently, I will describe some cinematic examples of violence and evaluate them "sonically," in light of the theory detailed to that point. Here, cinematic sound serves as a kind of laboratory for examining functions of sound and silence, but also our experience of that dynamic.[5] As mentioned, I frame violence as a liminal ground between life (survival) and death, with foundationally sonic dimensions.[6] This aesthetic evaluation yields strong examples of the cessationist tendency, but also reveals some complications that beg for a different articulation of the value of silence.

By contrast, I then consider some curious instances of receptive cinematic silence, wherein relative silence seems to embody and signify a contra-nihilistic force, presence, or effect, even in the face of violence. The apparent virtues of silence, here, hint at another possibility: a different order that does not neatly

---

[3] I do not wish to suggest that my framing of these issues is the definitive account of how Nietzsche himself would have argued about the nature of nihilism, violence, sound, or silence. These are merely cultural tendencies prompted by Nietzsche and others, but they are, nevertheless, common and significant.

[4] Cox's (2018) materialist approach is built on thinkers (Schopenhauer, Nietzsche, Deleuze, and Meillasoux) who have been associated with nihilism at some level. Nietzsche and Schopenhauer often anchor the term, historically. Gilles Deleuze embraces Nietzsche's "active nihilism" in such a way as to throw the charge of true nihilism at all those who would diminish life in favor of "higher" ideals (like Christianity, according to Deleuze [1986, pp. 34–35]). Quentin Meillasoux's nihilism is even more complex, affirming some dimensions of classic nihilism, and attempting to transform other dimensions more positively (see Cesarale 2014).

[5] The restrictions of the laboratory obtain here: cinema is not "real life," so any conclusions here must be qualified, but it can serve as a means by which we can isolate that dynamic and gain new perspective on it.

[6] In so doing, I see violence in a wider lens than, perhaps, some do, encompassing any and all threats to life and existence, including natural, spiritual, and existential ones.

conform to the profiles of will (Nietzsche), "becoming" (Deleuze), or Sonic Flux (Cox). Such a possibility is not necessarily a defeater for these theories, but it does problematize some of those conceptions of silence, and softens their nihilistic force. It is here that I example a posture of receptivity, largely in light of the philosopher Jean-Luc Marion and some of his fundamental concepts: "givenness," "saturated phenomena," and "excess," concepts he uses throughout both his phenomenological and theological works. Theology is not required for serious engagement with these matters, but it helps to provide a more thorough investigation into the significance of sonic experience. If we are to take Macbeth seriously, we should also consider theological voices who have made silence an anchor for life, such as the Carthusian monks of Grand Chartreuse Charterhouse, featured in Philip Gröning's *Into Great Silence* (2005).

This essay is not intended as a precise argument for or against any of these thinkers, per se. Rather, as a phenomenological and aesthetic examination of Cox's neo-Nietzchean, Deleuzean hybrid idea at a variety of cinematic sites,[7] it articulates how the cessation and receptivity tendencies both have value. The conclusion suggests how they might be held together.

Finally, as Shakespeare indicates, the significance (or ironic lack of significance) of the web of experience is found in *living*, in the existential, sensory domain of feeling, experience, and time. The experiential register is our best means for engaging the dynamism around which Nietzsche built many of his most famous claims. To anchor us there, each section will begin with a "prompting" scene from Godfrey Reggio's *Koyaanisqatsi* (1982). It is not our only film example, but it is, perhaps, the most comprehensive sample of the complex web under investigation.

2 Cessation Tendencies in the Sonic Flux: Nihilism and Film Sound

Koyaanisqatsi opens on an image of ancient desert rock paintings, soon overtaken by an exploding fireball, revealed to an overlayed image of a launching rocket. The only sound to be heard is the accompanying music, which includes human voice chanting "Koyaanisqatsi." The spacecraft's powerful, steady rise moves in very

---

[7] In the spirit of film-philosophy, I approach film aesthetics as philosophically productive on its own terms, beyond serving as mere "illustration" of concepts (Sorfa 2016, 3). The notion that the aesthetic could be a form of reasoning and a counter-weight to rationality is, itself, a very Nietzschean idea.

slow motion, an inaugural temporal manipulation (slow motion, fast motion, time lapse cinematography, etc.) that will characterize the film. The images shift to monumental natural scenes: towering desert rock formations, churning oceans, soaring mountain peaks, wisping sand dunes, majestically billowing clouds in the heavens.

Koyaanisqatsi is a Hopi Indian word, translating "Life Out of Balance." With its lack of dialogue or obvious narrative, characteristic visual abstraction, temporal manipulation, and ubiquitous musical soundtrack, the film may be considered experimental, standing in the city-symphony tradition (e.g. Walter Ruttmann's *Berlin: A Symphony of the Great City*, 1927). These works tend to utilize specific cities or regions as sites for exploiting the aesthetic possibilities of cinematic form. However, *Koyaanisqatsi* does not limit itself to one location, seeking to make a universal statement through striking images of both nature and culture and a close, organic alignment of images and music.

Sometimes the images appear to be driving the score (composed by Philip Glass), and other, significant times the impression is the reverse. The film reaches its greatest heights when they become nearly indistinguishable, a powerful rhythm arising from their conjoined force and dynamic relation. Indeed, in this first "chapter" of the film, the music affords the elements we see (wind, fire, earth, and water) a grand temporality. Life pulses throughout, and Reggio proposes an animate rhythm to both natural and human life in general. We most often discern this at the "macroscopic" level, a wide, God's-eye view of human life, beyond ordinary spatio-temporal perspective.

Given this overarching experiential theme of "reality as flow," it is important to recall the cinematic sound theorist Michel Chion's claim that audition temporalizes the image (Chion 2018, pp. 13–14). Indeed, the science of audition is clear: temporal perception is a complex sensory and cognitive operation, but hearing is the temporal sense par excellence.[8]

In addition, there are phenomenologically distinct features to sound that impact our experience of it. Regardless of the material physics of sound and neural energies of the human auditory system, sound is perceived as immaterial. That is, phenomenologically, it is invisible and ungraspable. There is the sense of sound not being *immediately* accessible to our other, more explicitly "materially-oriented" senses (e.g. sight and touch), and yet it has a remarkable ability

---

8 "The temporal precision of the auditory system is about two-and-a half orders of magnitude greater than that of the visual system" (Patterson et al. 1999, p. 245). Also, hearing impairment affects temporal perception; see Bolognini (2012).

to entail and trigger those other senses at varying levels. What is more, it is evanescent, as communication theorist Walter Ong articulates:

> Sound exists only when it is going out of existence. It is not simply perishable but essentially evanescent and is sensed as evanescent. When I pronounce the word 'permanence,' by the time I get to the '-nence,' the 'perma-' is gone, and has to be gone.... All sensation takes place in time, but no other sensory field totally resists a holding action, stabilization, in quite this way. (Ong 1982, p. 32)

For these reasons, there has been a historical association between the mysterious concept of life and the "immaterial" time-endowing experience of audition that both exists outside us and resonates within us.

However, the philosopher Christoph Cox builds his philosophy on sound from an explicitly materialist point of view. He emphasizes that sound is not immaterial at all (dismissing its phenomenology), insisting it is "patterned matter-energy." Such energies, combined with raw matter, are "all there is." More specifically, he argues that many of the paradigms for thinking in the West arise out of visio-centric modes of attention that lead to idealisms of various kinds, but if we attend to sound first, that changes the philosophical frame entirely: "How does sonic thinking challenge the ontologies and epistemologies that prevail in our ordinary and philosophical thinking?" (Cox 2018b, p. 6).

Centrally, while there are many "flows" that constitute reality, Cox argues that "the sonic flux ... deserves special status insofar as it elegantly and forcefully manifests and models the myriad fluxes that constitute the natural world" (Cox 2018b, p. 3). The sonic "eludes analysis in terms of representation and signification," and helps us understand how Nietzsche, so invested in power and the mysterious "will" at the heart of reality, associated music so readily with those elements. "In the tensions and agitations of music, Nietzsche and Schopenhauer discerned flux, which renders sonorous the ceaseless becomings that constitute the real" (Cox 2018a).

In Cox's conception, energies, pulses, and flows all precede and transcend human perception of them, but these fundamental becomings are most directly accessed through the senses that attend to sound (and its absence). Philosophers from Schopenhauer to Nietzsche to Deleuze can be read in support of this thesis.[9] Silence is framed as part of the sonic flow, or flux. In due time, we shall examine which part and what role/significance silence has in this system.

---

9 Cox (2018b, pp. 19–31) traces this lineage of thought, connecting Schopenhauer's ideas of "Will ... below representation" (via his *World as Will and Representation*), to Nietzsche's explicit and detailed efforts to liberate will from Kantian frames (among others), and how Nietzsche specifically tied will to art, largely by naturalizing art and, particularly, sound. Deleuze advances

In this line of thought, film sound serves not merely as analogue, but as sample of what is and what is not, ontologically. These samples may, then, be extended synecdochally to themes that given films may be trying to express: regarding the nature of the world, morality, the future, etc. That is, sound-silence is easily "analogized" and felt as life-death, because it really is a sample of a flux ceasing or diminishing.

What is important for these thinkers is this acceptance rejects any hierarchy of sensations, and minimizes (if not eliminates) the importance of the subject. In the end, silence does not hold significance, in itself, but is simply useful in its anti-humanistic instruction. "All art, then, is tragic…. [B]oth Nietzsche and Deleuze recommend that one hold on to the minimum of subjectivity, identity, and organism necessary to explore a multiplicity of nonhuman becomings while warding off complete annihilation" (Cox 2018b, p. 40). Within this paradigm, there are a variety of postures. Susan Sontag speaks of two styles in which contemporary artists advocate for silence: "loud and soft." The "loud" features a kind of existential, eternal dialectic of argument between "plenum" and "void," "frequently apocalyptic," "to prophecy the end, to see the day come, to outlive it, and then to set a new date of the incineration of consciousness" (Sontag 1969, p. 32). The "soft" approach is "more cautious" ("'reticence' to the nth degree"), epitomized by artists like the composer John Cage and the painter Jasper Johns. That is, one dismisses art's absolute aspirations and faces the void gently, "in a polite voice and as a sequence of playful affirmations," without expectations of meaning (Sontag 1969, pp. 32–3), as an occasion to perceive new things with a kind of groundless happiness that Nietzsche advocated.[10]

However, Sontag ends her essay with some skepticism about whether either approach is tenable, in the long run: "It seems unlikely that the possibilities of

---

this theme through unique and useful non-Kantian terminology (e. g. "virtual" replaces "possible," fueled by "the intensive," which "actualizes the virtual") throughout all his books, but Cox focuses most upon *Difference and Repetition* in this discussion, as well as comments on sound and music that prove thematic in his later works, (e.g., that music has the capacity "to render sonorous forces that are not themselves sonorous," [Deleuze 2003, p. 56]. For Cox, this lineage provides for an "immanent metaphysics" ("that accepts only entities generated by the material and energetic processes that constitute nature" [Cox 2018b, p. 6]), and a fundamental conception of flux as grounding all reality, with sound as a powerful access point to that flux. This is a unique way of pursuing sound and music, both of which are labeled "Dionysian" in both Deleuze and Nietzsche.

[10] "As long as life *is ascending*, happiness is the same as instinct," Nietzsche says, in TI Socrates 11. Bruce Ellis Benson summarizes this as happiness free from "justification" (Benson 2008, p. 80).

continually undermining one's assumptions can go on unfolding indefinitely into the future, without being eventually checked by despair or by a laugh that leaves one without any breath at all" (Sontag 1969, p. 34).

3 Sound and Fury: Film Violence as Liminal Experiential Ground

> [H]ow often the aesthetic of silence appears hand in hand with a barely controlled abhorrence of the void.
> –Susan Sontag (1969, p. 27).

After the inaugural Koyaanisqatsi *sequence, we witness 18 minutes of stately, wholly natural, spectacle: mountains, waters, and deserts. Suddenly, an explosion of earth and rock disrupts this, followed by foreboding images of gigantic mining machines. The stately power of the earth is upended in violence, wrought by humans. Icons of man-made power follow, expending and extracting the earth's resources. Humans emerge for the first time, at around 23 minutes. A mother and child sleep on the sand, under the shadow of a towering power plant. The imagery shifts to transportation (planes, cars, trucks) and machines of war, before changing to urban scenes. At this moment, the music is temporarily replaced by relative silence, filled only with "empty," natural (soft) urban noise and wind sounds. A wide, aerial, time-lapse image of the New York City skyline features graceful patterns of moving clouds slipping over the buildings, followed by about six somber minutes of musically-accompanied urban decay and destruction: run-down neighborhoods, broken lampposts, shattered windows, and building demolitions, one after another.*

In this passage of scenes, we see violence encroaching, accompanied by various and powerful musical aggressions and recessions. There is no doubt of the polemical, environmentalist bent to *Koyaanisqatsi*, but I imagine Nietzsche might appreciate the aesthetic and experiential power functioning here: flows and ruptures of all kinds, at multiple sensorial registers.

Here we explore how violence registers in the cinema, aesthetically and sonically, in hopes of better understanding the sound-violence-nihilism nexus. Instances of cinematic threat and/or violence are of particular interest, as violence is potently liminal: at once the height of death (threat) and the height of life/survival (movement-activity-sensation).

In Nietzschean terms, violence is part-and-parcel of existence itself, "something like the anthropogenic principle of human history," as Paweł Pieniążek summarizes (Pieniążek 2019, p. 14). Indeed, destruction and war are affirmed as natural touchstones to the constituting dynamic of existence, the pulse of the ever changing, primordial Dionysian unity of the world (Cox 2018b, p. 24). In Nietzsche's *Birth of Tragedy*, the nature of violence is not a struggle between being and non-being, but between two different principles of existence itself, the primordial unity of being (Dionysus) and rational individuation of persons (Apollo). This conflict (or violence, if you will), animates all of Greek thought and art, he claims, and serves as a foundation for western thought and culture (BT 1). However, this is no Hegelian dialectic, Cox explains, but a relation that ultimately bends toward the Dionysian as the primordial reality. Nietzsche constructs "an ontology in which forces, powers, movements, tensions, affects, and events precede the individual subjects and objects to which they are ordinarily attributed" (Cox 2018b, p. 26). As his thought progressed, and the notion of "the will to power" developed, violence became "the essence of life itself" (Pieniążek 2019, p. 19).

Of course, there is no lack of violence in cinema.[11] In keeping with our focus, I will lay out a few common scene types of film violence that are particularly interesting in regard to their sonic dimensions. By no means an exhaustive list, these types do portray some common approaches to the sonic aesthetics of violence.

3.1 Sonic Prompting – Aestheticized Dramatic Violence

A common approach to cinematic sound at dramatic moments is to mix natural "diegetic" sounds (that is, sounds from the "world" of the film) with non-diegetic music. This may be seen, aesthetically, as a compounding of forces. Together they represent the diegetic world unfolding, and function as emotional cues as to how the audience should be feeling. In terms of Sonic Flux theory, this is not the most interesting or revelatory case, but it could be conceived as a confluence of different streams of the flux, and testimony to its existence.

In a climactic violent scene like the church shootout in John Woo's *The Killer* (1989), the diegetic sound is often restricted to the most explosive elements (gunfire and sounds of destruction). Human sounds—even cries of pain or fright—are curiously muted, and other sounds, such as breathing, are minimized. The aesthetics are shaped, primarily, around force and character psychology. When the cop (played by Danny Lee) is first wounded, the soundtrack shifts to absolute silence for a moment, as a marker of dramatic peak and psychological trauma,

---

11 See Kendrick (2009, p.32).

but also as a kind of intensifier, the grand pause before the furious finale, in musical terms. This speaks to the affinity of music with flow and Sonic Flux, as Cox has described it. More explicitly, at a second dramatic lull in the fighting, after the wounding of Chow Yun-Fat's character (again, momentary silence) and the ensuing, furious gunfire that destroys the statue of the Virgin Mary, the natural sound completely yields to the musical soundtrack (the opening movement to Handel's *Messiah*, as it happens). In this moment, the sound shifts completely to the non-diegetic realm, which is something like a code for a switch from the material to the purely emotional realm, elevating this "happening" to a moment of significance. In addition, Woo is famous for his ballet-like fight choreography and use of slow motion, which—psychologist Sheena Rogers (2013) has shown—actually reduces the sense of immediate force in perception (softening our sense of impact), in favor of other kinds of granular details of movement and expression in the scene. Such a scene trades one sonic stream and its particularities for another, and may be seen as a strong, aggressive example of "loud" silence, as Sontag describes it (1969, p. 32).

3.2 Blunt Force, Blunt Reality

Films with more of an existential edge—that is, they endeavor to present violence as shocking and horrifying, yet, in a certain sense, inevitable—often withdraw non-diegetic music in favor of diegetic sounds of violence. Sam Peckinpah's *The Wild Bunch* (1969) features a final shootout that strategically silences non-diegetic music and, largely, restricts itself to the sound of incessant and furious gunfire. The cultural critic Jacques Attali conceives of "noise" as violent in its nature, and so the tsunami of gunfire we have heard is dramatically sufficient.[12] A great deal of human agony and pain is shown, but very little of it can be heard over the noise, which creates a kind of dramatic irony: that the significance of these individual (Apollonian) lives, at their liminal moments, are swallowed up and lost amid a torrent of violent (Dionysian) sound.

In contrast to Peckinpah's overwhelming wash of violent noise, Martin Scorsese's *Taxi Driver* (1976) demonstrates a more harsh, naked, and awkward reality. The gunshots in the climactic scene come at a sloppy, almost haphazard, chaotic pace. In-between these sounds, we hear extended raw cries of pain, anger, agony, etc. without any predictable rhythm or anticipation. This could have been "smoothed" out, experientially, with some non-diegetic music, but

---

[12] Attali (1985), p. 26.

Scorsese demurs. Instead, death comes capriciously. Not until the very end of the scene, after all the bullets have been spent and Travis has unsuccessfully attempted suicide, do police enter accompanied by Bernard Hermann's music, mixing with the natural sound of Travis simulating gunshots with his fingers and mouth. As a coda, everything stands still in the frame, save a slowly gliding overhead camera; the diegetic completely surrenders to the flow of a non-diegetic movement and soundtrack. In this case, the division between the material real and emotional reverberation stark.

3.3 Sonic Trauma

At the sound-violence-nihilism nexus, one of the more interesting categories involves a kind of multisensory evocation of the experience of trauma, prompted largely by notable silence or greatly diminished sound on the soundtrack.

In the D-Day scene of *Saving Private Ryan* (1998), the sounds of warfare (remarkably un-aestheticized), cut suddenly to heavily "occluded" sounds when the camera drops underwater. This natural "simulative" sound design replicates the experiences of the soldiers who have plunged below the surface, but also yields a kind of sensory excess that could be described as "resonant" or extensive of the general panic and trauma of the violent scene. Shortly after a few of these sonic "plunges" in and out of the water, we have a full demonstration of mental/emotional "occlusion," wherein the sensory world of Captain Miller (Tom Hanks) is utterly overwhelmed and short-circuited. Despite the explosions, screaming, ricocheting bullets, and crashing waves all around him, neither he nor we can hear any of that. The soundtrack only registers something like muffled wind—steady, neutral, and unidentifiable.

Among his observations on the "psychodynamics" of orality, Ong notes that hearing is experienced globally: 360 degrees around the subject. It places the hearer at the center of the auditory world (Ong 1982, p. 72). This, combined with temporality and other multisensorial functions of sound, has ramifications for a person's sense of control. Here that existentially-anchoring power of sound has disappeared, replaced by a "lost" and disoriented feeling.[13]

In terms of sonic flow, this sudden shift from chaotic, unregulated, and punctuated sound to utter steadiness and undifferentiated sound is sudden. However "peaceful" this might seem to be, the visual chaos has not changed.

---

[13] Indeed, in some horror movies, silence can suggest that control is being held by a nefarious "other" (creature, villain, etc.) leaving us powerless. See Elisabeth Weis (1985), p. 307.

Half of Miller's means of perceiving are hampered, stalling the entire cognitive operation.[14] Like Captain Miller, we are forced to live impossibly: to see in one flow, and regulate it, sonically, with a completely different, unrelated flow.

3.4 The Sound of the End

Finally, dramatic or unexpected alteration of sonic flow can more directly express true despair or nihilism. In the opening scene of *Women without Men* (2009), a woman jumps from a building (in slow motion) and the soundtrack shifts to silence. Her slightly smiling face is shown, as she slowly sinks through the air. After a few moments, her voice emerges on the soundtrack: "Now I'll have silence … silence … and nothing." Suicide is presented as a relief from the sound and fury of life, from the ever-surging sonic flow that the character deems emblematic of all that she cannot bear. The altered flow on the visual and sonic level clearly leans toward stasis. As scholars have noted, Nietzsche largely affirmed suicide as a rational choice, "emptied of morality" (Stellino 2013, p. 157). Though he dismissed any thought of individual life-after-death, he did argue—via proto-flux theory—for a sense of comfort in the impersonal idea "that beneath the flux of phenomena eternal life flows on indestructibly" (BT 18).[15]

In a different example, Ingmar Bergman's *Winter Light* (1963) plays ironically with cinematic tropes to achieve an exceptionally beguiling experience around one man's "enlightening" loss of faith as matched with another man's suicide. The chiasm expresses something of the burden of the eternal, existential questions that never easily resolve themselves. A troubled man comes to his pastor, at the behest of his wife, to seek encouragement and counsel. That pastor, however, cannot help but use the occasion to express, in naked terms, why he is a "rotten clergyman" due to his absolutely crippling doubt and disenchantment. He launches into a passionate, nihilistic sermon:

---

14 This effect can also express hearing impairment in the characters, as we see in the climactic street battle in *Copland* (James Mangold, 1997).
15 On the one hand, reflecting on *Birth of Tragedy*, Pieniążek (2019, p. 19) explains that this comfort is what Nietzsche calls "Dionysian wisdom" regarding our inevitable annihilation. On the other hand, Pieniążek also notes, Nietzsche remarks that the violence and "cruelty" of Dionysian nature and the danger of "the rupture of the *principium individuationis*" (BT 2) sets up an existential, "will-paralyzing mood" of "awe and horror," manifesting in "nauseating reflections on the awfulness or absurdity of existence" (BT 7).

If there is no God, would it really make any difference? Life would become understandable. What a relief. And thus death would be a snuffing out of life. The dissolution of body and soul. Cruelty, loneliness, and fear—all these things would be straightforward and transparent. Suffering is incomprehensible, so it needs no explanation. There is no creator. No sustainer of life. No design.

His parishioner leaves, obviously disturbed. The pastor stands, stunned and reflective, in absolute silence. As the camera noiselessly dollies in to an intense close up, the light through the window grows brighter, an ironic play on the timeless trope of sunlight as symbol of the Divine. "God, why have you forsaken me," he murmurs. It is, by all marks, a "de-conversion" moment, amid all the tropes of a conversion scene, with the exception of silence. There is no cue for emotional resolve, joy, or triumph, despite the visual radiance of the moment. He breaks down emotionally and declares himself "free" from the "fleeting hope that everything wouldn't turn out to be illusions, dreams, and lies."

Soon after, a townswoman arrives to inform him that his parishioner had just shot himself. The pastor rushes to the scene which, remarkably, plays at a large distance (primarily a panning wide shot), by a surging creek. The soundtrack is far from silent, and far from typical: the sound of the water is abnormally loud—a surging, roaring rhythm of wave and undulation, and when men (the pastor and investigator) speak, they can barely be heard over the natural, overwhelming sonic flow.

From Bergman's perspective, this might seem to be a marker of an utterly indifferent God, the "silence of God" so pointedly referenced at the end of the film ("My God, my God, why have You forsaken Me?"); a "loud" silence, as Sontag says (1969, p. 32). Or, perhaps, this is just indifferent nature, the larger eternal and amorphous flow that persists, unbothered by our existence or lack of it (à la Nietzsche and Cox). The silence in this scene is implied; it seems there ought to be a voice, a human commentary, on the significance of these souls, alive and departed, but no such sound can be heard.

There are, of course, other types of the cinematic violence-sound/silence dynamic that could be explored, but it is fair to say, at this point, Cox's theory seems to be operating in strength. Silences (particularly human silences) signal the end of noisy, violent flows of activity and movement, and an ultimate nothingness. Alternately, they may register a shift where the flow of human life is subsumed by larger, indifferent natural forces. The sound design of these scenes regulates and animates our experiences of violence, and powerfully exudes trauma, dislocation, and death as a void.

4 Silence as Receptivity, Reprieve, and Alternate Life

After the aforementioned scenes of urban decay, Koyaanisqatsi *charges into urban life in all its vitality. For just over 30 minutes, the rhythms of streets, factories, and numerous social hubs throb with life, a grand ballet of synchrony and regulation. The pace gradually becomes frenetic. Imagery of mediated reality–video games and television—start signaling violence amid all the daily activity. Destruction in the games link with explosions on various televisions. Finally, at the apotheosis of the scene, where the editing pace is outright frantic, we see a giant wall of televisions themselves exploding. This is intercut with streaking traffic imagery and mad camera dashes through crowded sidewalks until—suddenly—the music halts. Dead silence accompanies a dramatic, suspended view overtop a skyscraper, dreamily gliding and staring down at the streets below.*

I have shown this particular *Koyaanisqatsi* sequence to dozens of audiences, and the same reaction always follows: at the grand moment of silence, the audience holds its breath for a moment, followed by a gentle, collective exhale of relief.

As Cox has shown us, there is a natural alignment with the flows and energies of "life" and the sonic. Our temporal experience of silence so far has been framed as part of the agonistic dynamic of life and the threat of death, but ultimately bends toward the "nothingness" or "nihilism" of human existence; that is to say, ultimately, all our words, cries, songs, and utterances, ultimately do not hold any lasting significance. As mentioned, Cox has articulated relative silence as a shift from one flow to another, with no philosophical reason to prioritize the human over the natural that subsumes it.

So it may be. But can that explanation fully account for silence and our experience of it? Our final example from *Koyaanisqatsi* suggests something more may be operative. After all those throbbing experiences of societal life—compounding into a dizzying and uncontrollable technological ride to apparent oblivion—the film climaxes in silence, but does not, in fact, end. Rather, it mercifully retreats into a gentle, removed, yet observant cosmic silence from above— a God's eye view, beyond temporality and movement, beyond sound. Having fruitlessly tried to perceptually and cognitively control and manage our experience, we likely find the silence a relief, a release from the need to control. As Ong has shown us, this makes perfect "psychodynamic" sense.

But might this just be a suicidal leap into nothingness, as with the *Women without Men* example? Is it simply a tip of the hat toward the natural, independent flux that eternally moves on, indifferent to our societal trauma and terrors?

Perhaps not. The imagery gradually shifts into a series of contemplative wide shots, pairing similarly "designed" satellite imagery with Hopi Indian tapestries (parallel "creations"), followed by a seven minute, deeply empathic section, focused almost exclusively on human faces and gestures. For this last chapter of the film, we have returned from the cosmos to the intimately human, a welcome reprieve from our contemporary addiction to noise, and a call to relation.

At the very least, *Koyaanisqatsi* suggests that silence need not be prescriptively nihilistic. In that vein, Phoebe Pua articulates how Bergman's minimal soundscapes might reflect spiritual absence or emptiness, while Tarkovsky's films utilize relative silence (amid layered, "quiet" sounds) to make us attend more carefully to what we see and hear (Pua 2019, para. 32).[16] That attention yields previously undetected sounds amid the "silence," as an affirmation of deeper reality and, for Tarkovsky, belief in God (Pua 2019, para. 23–31).[17] This sort of "call to attention" is also present and affirmed in Cage and Cox, but it is not relational or existentially significant, as Tarkovsky's call seems to be.

Most of the thinkers we have considered so far have not left much room for religious faith. In discussing Nietzsche's view of nature, and its "extravagantly creative, endlessly generating … artistic powers," Cox states: "Nietzsche's assertion of nature as artist, then, will be read as metaphorical at best and theological at worst, since 'the creativity of nature' seems to imply a divine creator. Nietzsche, however, operates in the wake of the 'death of God' and commits himself to tracking down and eliminating all the vestiges of theological thought" (Cox 2018b, p. 25).[18] Cox sees Nietzsche anticipating Deleuze and others in critiquing a whole western mode of thought, in this regard: rejecting "hylomorphism" (the idea that "the genesis of entities requires the external imposition of form upon inert matter") in favor of a theory of self-organization. "For Nietzsche, matter itself is creative and transformative without external agency, a ceaseless becoming and overcoming that temporarily congeals into forms and beings, only to dissolve them back into the natural flux. Nietzsche's name for this flux is the 'will to power'" (Cox 2018b, p. 25).

---

16 Pua affirms what we have noted: "silence" is often relative silence, a diminishment of amplitude and cessation of the focal sounds, but not, necessarily, the complete elimination of all sounds altogether.

17 My thanks to Rebecca ver Straten-McSparran for pointing me to this reference.

18 However, there are alternate views on whether or not Nietzsche leaves room for some sort of "faith," albeit, not the institutional Christian faith he despised. See Benson (2008). Julian Young, more explicitly, argues the "anti-religious" portrait of Nietzsche is utter caricature, that he never truly was an atheist, and he never abandoned his vision for "religious communitarianism" (Young 2006, p. 2).

But what if, as we may have already intuited, the profound impact of cinematic silence is not univocal? What if our experience of silence sometimes yields new resources for living, even in the face of violence? The philosopher Jean Luc-Marion prefers to speak of realms and truths that exceed Being, a category that is inherently circumscribed by human thought, at some level. Through an intense "radical" or "new" or "counter" phenomenology (and, indeed, a very focused examination of phenomenality itself), he thinks about experiences as "gifts," that often reveal themselves as abundance, as "saturated phenomena."[19] So-called "empty" or "diminished" phenomena like silence might seem to be unlikely candidates for that designation, but Marion explicitly argues for different kinds of silence,[20] and delineates a difference between a vacuous, unmoored silence "inscribed in banality, in metaphysics, and even in Being/being" (what he calls "mute idols"), and a silence that remains "silent through and for *agape*," the highest form of love, which Marion argues is Divine and "exceeds Being" (2012, p. 107).[21] As every good minimalist artist will tell you, the minimal can reveal itself to be maximal with the right kind of attention. Silence is almost never an "absolute nothing." It is often a marker of the opposite, the inadequacy of sense, attention, and expression in the face of heretofore unperceived, ineffable abundance.

---

19 The notions of "the gift," "saturated phenomena," and "excess" are perennial themes in Marion's work, found in nearly all of his major works, including *Being Given: Toward a Phenomenology of Givenness* (2002a), and *In Excess: Studies of Saturated Phenomena* (2002b). As a "New Phenomenologist" (Simmons's and Benson's moniker [2013]), Marion is among those thinkers who have attended carefully "to that which would seem to remain excessive to classical phenomenological inquiry," namely, in establishing that "givenness" is "the *primary* aspect of phenomenology" (Simmons and Benson 2013, p. 63). More particularly, Marion attempts to move phenomenology's attention from the subject-limited dynamic (objects of consciousness, intentionality, etc., as in Husserl's transcendental phenomenology), to "genuine and immediate appearance" (even if the mode of appearing is not straightforward), an original appearing that precedes and is not beholden to an intuitional, intentional subject or any sort of limit or authority (Simmons and Benson 2013, p. 64). This "appearing" or "givenness" of phenomena is what makes the classical phenomenological situation possible, and, yet, exceeds the ability of any given subject to fully intend, perceive, or conceptualize it.

20 "The greatest difficulty doubtless consists more essentially in deciding what silence *says*: contempt, renunciation, the avowal of impotence, or else the highest honor rendered, the only one neither unworthy nor 'dangerous'" (Marion 2012, p. 54).

21 Marion goes on to grant that his characterization of agape as explicitly Christian and theistically grounded is a choice on his part, but insists that those who disagree must at least reserve a space for it: "Despite oneself, one must recognize that, if we do not love agape enough to praise it, we must at least preserve this impotence as the trace of a possibility" (2012, p.107).

Like John Cage, Cox agrees, at least partially: the silences enlarge our perception and cause us to attend to new levels of the sonic flux, even if the flux cares nothing for us. However, the nature of this shift is consequential to our conception of what the sonic flux is, and the gift-minded receive this experience as a call: to insist on meaning, to see the silence as a call to listen more deeply, more attentively, suspend the need for control, and to seek relation more intentionally. This perspective does not require an explicitly theological appraisal, but the relational dimension, in particular, prompts us to at least consider some theological voices, for a moment.

Into Great Silence is a documentary about such gift-minded listeners. Philip Gröning initially made a request to film in the Grand Chartreuse monastery, in the French Alps. The monks said they needed to think about it … for a decade or more. Sixteen years later, they granted him access, for approximately six months. The monks there, of the Carthusian order, are some of the most ascetic monks in all Christendom, having taken an austere vow of silence from which they are only released a few hours each week. The minimal daily speaking they perform is liturgically prescribed, and, so, human speech of any kind is sparse throughout the award-winning film. It captures the long, gentle rhythms of daily life at the monastery, much of which is governed by very little sound at all.

As critic Steven Greydanus remarks: "This back story to *Into Great Silence*… is more than a picturesque anecdote. It is a telling insight into a world in which time is experienced very differently than in the workaday world we live in" (Greydanus n.d., para. 7).

There is much at stake in this, as a young monk hears during his initiation: "Are you ready to adopt our monastic way of life, as the way through which God will lead your souls to the inner holiness, where He will reveal His existence to you and let you commune with Him?" The documentary features no commentary or music, except for diegetic chants and prayers the monks themselves sometimes provide. There are, of course, small diegetic sounds that characterize this film, and eventually those sounds come to appear abnormally prominent to the attentive viewer, but there are also whole stretches where nothing audible can be detected beyond the faintest room tone. For instance, a long shot of a mug of tea and bowl of fruit by a window is a still life; it could be a painting, but the dreamy wisp of steam from the mug and slight pulse of the grain of the video reminds us that this is a live event.

This is deeply significant for the monks, and many who choose to sit with them through this film. Greydanus testifies:

> [Gröning's] style of filmmaking makes demanding viewing, and takes some adjusting to. Yet as the film progresses, a mysterious thing happens. Like the rule of the monastery, which the monks experience as a path of joy and liberation and inner peace, the film's very austerity becomes the bearer of something more. Almost imperceptibly, rigor and discipline are swallowed up in beauty, harmony and transcendence. (Greydanus n.d., para. 29)

The anchoring concept of the flux—constant change, constant becoming, will as battle, tension, violence, à la Nietzsche and Deleuze—all this seems to be missing. This does not seem to be the description of a force that pulses, energizes and, in its own inherent, violent nature, constantly overturns. This appears to be a space where Dionysus has settled down, and Apollo has stopped insisting on individuation. With the normal markers of momentary time gone, we are left to much more general markers of time passing and cycling: night and day, winter and spring. "This is what a monastery is," Gröning said. "It's getting rid of all the superfluous stuff, and then things become much more transparent—time becomes transparent, objects too. There's this transparency, this inner freedom that comes, which is felt as joy, of course" (Greydanus n.d., para. 30). Perhaps the most relevant dimension of this film is the filmmaker's own journey in making it. Greydanus recounts:

> Toward the end of Gröning's stay at the Grande Chartreuse, the monks asked him (in notes, probably) what he had learned from them. The question came as a surprise to Gröning, who had "drifted away from speech by then" that he hadn't worked out his ideas in words. Eventually, he said, "I realized that what I had actually learned was that it is possible to live very much without fear, because this is what they do. They live without fear. I wanted the audience to be able to share this." (Greydanus n.d., para. 68)

All of our examples to this point have featured some dimension of violence. Gröning's remark shows us why this film, and these silences, should be brought into this conversation. In the monastery, one takes a different approach than that of Nietzsche, for whom life is found in the struggle.[22] Here, one submits to order that extracts much of the sonic from life. One withdraws from the struggle, min-

---

[22] It is worth noting that, unlike the vibrant character of his ontology, Nietzsche was famously drawn to silence and solitude for writing and thinking. The character of that silence was very different, perhaps, than that of religious ascetics, however. That is, he was not "receptive" or "de-individuated" as much as confessedly struggling in thought. Interestingly, amid this goal-oriented restlessness, he also confesses (in HH I 626) to an occasional envy of "one who is able to live thus happily and peaceably with himself even in the turmoil of life, saying to himself with Goethe: 'the best is the profound stillness towards the world in which I live and grow, and win for myself what they cannot take from me with fire and sword.'" My thanks to Paolo Stellino for directing me to this fascinating Nietzschean moment.

imizes conflict, and focuses only on prayer, worship, and serving the community. It is an exercise in releasing control, and strengthening trust in a higher power, anew; to stop fighting, and allow God to "reveal His existence to you and let you commune with Him."

Koyaanisqatsi was the first of our examples to suggest that silence could, possibly, be a positive *living* (i.e. non-suicidal) respite from violence; that is, an embodied suggestion that there are other ways of living, beyond the constant need for acquisition and mastery, beyond "progress," away from daily fear. The silences in *Into Great Silence* are a sign of a kind of life beyond the violence Nietzsche argues is necessary for existence. Despite the stereotypes, the film helps us see monasticism is not about retreat from "life," but an exchange of one kind of life/temporality for another.

Nietzsche, famously, criticizes the ascetic-monastic practices of Christianity, "seeing in them the expression of the individual's mastery over himself, over their corporeality and voluptuousness," according to Pieniążek (2019, p. 18). And why do they do this? According to Nietzsche, "This mastery is to compensate them for their weakness, impotence and inability to gain control over others" (Pieniążek 2019, p. 18)[23] In this view, we do witness "violence" in this film, and it is masochism.

We simply need to ask ourselves, after viewing this film, if Nietzsche's descriptions hit anywhere near the mark. If not, then we must re-assess the sonic flux in this new soundscape.

Of course, most of the world does not live in monasteries, and so the "different kind of life" envisioned here should not be overdetermined as normative. And yet, these new experiences also reveal an intuition that the initial "normal" frame is not entirely satisfying and does not preclude a wider reality. Marion, quite famously, has postulated a post-metaphysical God (a "God without Being") which is simply to give a contemporary reframing of what so many believers, from so many religions and quasi-religions, have always believed: that God is so very "other" that any conception or utterance of God risks being a kind of idolatry, a reduction of the deity that might be mistaken for all that God is. In this respect, we might say God is "silence" itself—beyond flow, beyond name, beyond utterance, beyond sound.[24] As Victor E. Taylor has noted:

---

23 This summary ties together several strands of thought about asceticism in Nietzsche, one of which is his critique of French Christianity (specifically "Quietists" and "Trappist Monks") [D 192]).

24 As a hedge against labeling Marion a garden-variety mystic, we should note that he does not suggest God is utterly incomprehensible, as Marion's concept of the "icon" (contra "idol") makes clear; he only claims that God cannot be reduced to "being" or any other philosophical concep-

While Marion is ready to accept the inadequacy of language and history to totally reveal God, even a trace of God, he is not willing to abandon God as the radical excess of cognition. In a theological maneuver, Marion's *In Excess: Studies in Saturated Phenomena* turns to early Church writings (Fourth Theological Oration and Fourth Lateran Council) to uphold his philosophical conclusion. (Taylor 2006, p. 6)

Robyn Horner expounds on this. In Marion's approach, "supplication" replaces "cognition" as a means of experiencing God (Horner 2005, p. 142):

> The Name [Above All Names] does not name God as an essence; it designates what passes beyond every name. The name designates what one does not name and says that one does not name it.... . "God as such cannot be spoken. The perfect knowledge of God is so to know him that we are sure we must not be ignorant of Him, yet cannot describe Him." The theologian's job is to silence the Name and, in this way, let it give us one—while the metaphysician is obsessed with reducing the Name to presence, and so defeating the Name. The dividing line has been established by an inescapable formulation: "between creator and creature no likeness can be recognized which would be greater than the unlikeness that is to be recognized between them." (Horner 2005, pp. 212–213)[25]

Given our analysis of *Into Great Silence*, we have framed Marion and the "receptivity" view as inherently theological, but it need not be necessarily so. Marion himself takes great pains to distinguish his phenomenology from his theology, and there is plenty of both on these matters.[26] Of course, the latter informs the former, but the distinction is important, here, in that the phenomenology merely suggests (does not prescribe) other options beyond (or, complementary to) those provided by Nietzsche, Deleuze, or Cox are possible.

On a purely phenomenological level, Nietzsche and Cox's insistence on dynamism renders their view of stability and silence as trending toward the negative, or, at least, the ancillary; a contracted, passing state that is not worthy of philosophical investment in itself. We have seen phenomenological strength in silence that belies that tendency. Similar criticisms could be leveled against Cox's materialism, which rises and falls on the strengths and weaknesses of that position, the chief being that it begins with "faith" claims (namely, that mat-

---

tion. For more on Marion, the apophatic tradition and "kataphatic correctives," see Simmons and Benson (2013, pp. 192–199).

25 The "Name Above All Names" title is from the New Testament (Philippians 2:9), and the quotes are from (respectively) Hilary of Poitiers, *De Trinitate*, II § 7, and the Fourth Lateran Council (1215), Canon II, in H. Denzinger, *Enchiridion Symbolorum* § 432.

26 It is also fair to say that Marion wishes to show deeper levels of overlap, historically, between these two categories, and so challenges our modern caricatures of what theology is about.

ter and energy are "all there is" and that sound gives us access to "the real") that cannot be proven any more than Marion's conception of a "God without Being."

From a phenomenological point of view, I find another latent concern in Cox's radically anti-humanist stance: that of potentially losing the subject altogether amid the "de-individuation" project. Stemming from Nietzsche, Cox has definitively claimed: the world is not *for us*. Rather, we should "as Nietzsche puts it ... 'translate humanity back into nature.'" (BGE 230)[27] We must ask, phenomenologically, where that leaves us as participants and agents in this grand flux. Cox declares his position beyond the "de-centering of the human subject" in poststructuralism, which he faults for "a re-centering on discourse and language that, at its core, remained deeply humanist" (Cox 2018b, p. 4). With little consideration of intervening positions, Cox appears to wipe away half the phenomenological equation, eliminating any significance of the human subject. It would seem that, as a result, there can be no self-world dynamic of any consequence, because to think about that dynamic is to reify the "self," as consciousness, with substance (Cox argues) it does not really possess. The goal is: "a philosophical naturalism and materialism that rejects the ontological and epistemological oppositions between subject and object, mind and matter, culture and nature" (Cox 2018b, p. 4).[28]

Is this conception of things nihilistic? This is a matter of interpretation and degree, it seems. With all efforts focused on eliminating "the subject" as a theological trace in western philosophy, radically de-centering and de-throning the human experience as anything more special, interesting, or significant than any other flow in the Grand Flux, we run up against the question of meaning itself, as Sontag noted (from a decisively non-theological point of view), some decades ago.

Cox missteps when he equates Enlightenment thinking with Christian thought in toto, overlooking whole swaths of theological history, including early church fathers and recent articulations from post-metaphysical thinkers like Marion (who, we should note, studied under both Jacques Derrida and Gilles Deleuze) (Horner 2005, p. 3). The heart of Marion's "giftedness" concept is an "Other" that extends

---

[27] Translation by Cox.
[28] Of course, Cox's final position is his own and we cannot assume his foundational thinkers would wholly assent to it, despite their obvious affinities. However, it does raise questions that all of them ought to answer. For instance, when Cox declares, that "listening" is "a way of contracting or capturing a portion of this flow through biological or mechanical means" (Cox 2018b, p. 4), we must ask who, or what, is doing the "contracting" or "capturing" and how. What is there to be "captured" without ontological or epistemological distinctions? More important, why does it matter?

itself to us through the world, evoking gratitude toward the giver. In this vein, the essence of creatureliness is dependence, not control. Lack of correlation between creatures and the rest of creation ought to be received by religious people as mystery, not presumption.

All this matters, because all cinema is, at root, an epistemological gesture, the world as it appears to us, and, in that sense, for us in the theater, in our living rooms, in our classrooms, before the screen. We wish to know it and receive it and, on some level, understand it.

But the best cinema, some of which is mentioned in this essay, challenges our power. It is a gift of wonder, for us, but not subject to us, at once enlightening us to new possibilities and unseen dimensions of reality, but never giving an easy sense that this world is now our possession. If anything, silence disarms us, and the power is in revealing, through awe, extremity and sensorial challenge, utterly new and mysterious dimensions of the real.

In this light, silence is also on occasion for clarity: for deciding whether or not one is to accept one's "self" as simply matter and energy that must change form, or whether there is such a thing as a subject, a "you," who can receive the gift and believe that sound and silence might mean something. In facing this decision, one is on liminal ground, for what is decided here, experientially, is a key to how all other questions of meaning will be decided.

5 Conclusion: Beyond Dichotomy

> And whoever must be a creator in good and evil – truly,
> he must first be an annihilator and break values.
> Thus the highest evil belongs to the highest goodness,
> but this is the creative one. –
> Let us speak of this, you wisest ones, even if it is bad to do so.
> Keeping silent is worse; all truths that are kept silent become poisonous.
> And may everything break that can possibly be broken by our truths!
> Many a house has yet to be built!
> Friedrich Nietzsche, *Thus Spoke Zarathustra* (Z II Self-Overcoming)

> For this is what the Lord God, the Holy One of Israel, has said:
> "In repentance and rest you will be saved,
> In quietness and trust is your strength."
> But you were not willing...
> Isaiah 30:15 (New American Standard Bible)

> There is an appointed time for everything.
> And there is a time for every matter under heaven—
> A time to be silent and a time to speak.
> Ecclesiastes 3:1 (New American Standard Bible)

I began this essay with a grand question, prompted by Macbeth: What do sound, violence, and nihilism have to do with each other? Though a full answer is not possible here, Nietzsche and Cox have affirmed that these three elements do seem to have a symbiotic relationship in much of our experience. Our survey of violent film examples has borne this out, with a variety of aesthetic modulations affecting how we experience this nexus as trending toward cessation and nihilism.

We have also registered that silence need not always be the realm of trauma, tragedy, or cessation. Within sound a kind of cyclical stability may also be operative, providing comfort, respite, and freedom from the pitfalls of the human desire to control. Perhaps a different approach to the flux may reveal an entirely different conception of it. Perhaps there is something else, outside the flux, complementing it. Perhaps 'flux' is not the most full or accurate descriptor. We cannot fully say, here, but our inquiry has fruitfully re-opened.

What of violence? It seems that Cox's approach rises and falls on the respective virtues and weaknesses of materialism in general. By placing his faith in eternal change, he relinquishes hope for ultimate stability. In denying meaning, he may also leave himself vulnerable to charges of embracing an ethics where violence is naturalized. Was Macbeth correct? If so, we may very well become Macbeth (or Zarathustra?), loudly "speaking" and "destroying" on his way to the abyss, dismissing any "strength" in "repentance ... rest ... quietness ... trust" that the prophet Isaiah recommends. All that violence, after all, may simply have been Macbeth's energetic part to play in the grand sonic concert, amid the flux of reality.

It is unfair to presume Cox's or Nietzsche's ethics, which lay beyond our basic analysis of sound. However, this inquiry has entailed violence, so certain questions are unavoidable. Nietzsche's ontology of will implies violence inherent in reality, and rejects a number of a historically useful tools for addressing it. While he never expressly condoned murder, he never formulated an explicit prohibition of it, and one might argue (given his aggressive anti-moral philosophy) he should have.[29] Our question here: does Nietzsche offer adequate resources for ethically addressing violence, and does he offer any comfort or hope for its vic-

---

[29] For a different reading, however, see the article by Stellino contained in this volume.

tims? Our experience of the sonic dimension, at what is arguably the experiential heart of Nietzsche's philosophy, suggests there may yet be other alternatives.

But to return to the basic phenomenological level, our analysis suggests a complementary position between cessation and receptivity might be possible. Both experiences of the sound/silence dynamic hold legitimacy and resound far beyond the moment of apprehension, prodding us to hold in tension all that our varied experiences might mean for us. Terror at the void of cessation, and receptivity of something greater within quiet, are fundamentally human experiences, a tension inherent within silence, and an expression of limits of our knowledge and experience.

Cox suggests that we see the rich opening soundscape as a kind of map, a cartography of the flux that founds the world. For him, it is the only real fundament of meaning, preceding all ontological or epistemological categories, as they have been classically understood. While the flux is not personal, and any "inherent giftedness" of it must be received as impersonal happenstance, the gift-minded may recognize the value of such a map and transform it into a catalogue. Such a detailed list of experiential meanings might ultimately contribute to a more unified understanding. That is to say, the opening up of meaning (stubbornly before any kind of obvious "sense-making" or categorical realm) may point to the promise of a helpful continuum rather than a hierarchy, where the sensory, emotional, and visceral forms of (historically-labeled) "low" meanings and "higher order" cognitive and conceptual meanings are leveled out, all encompassed in a grand assessment of human experience.

What is more, the nature of Marion's gift is an ongoing dynamic of giving, an eternal giftedness from a giver who never stops giving. This is markedly not a transactional affair, but the opposite: it is for us, but we never own it or control it, and there is so much beyond our ken. It is filled with excess that shows us our perceptual limits and vast regions beyond them.

What has been revealed is not a refutation of the cessation view, exactly, but rather a multi-dimensionality to silence that, if we are able to "hear" it, demands more attention, and even deeper listening. Again, silence is not fundamentally about absence, but about the possibility of excess. The final images of *Koyaanisqatsi* present powerful experiences that, I assume, both Cox and Marion could interpret differently, but would find agreement on this point: Art is as old as human consciousness, and any artwork can transcend the moment of its making.

We return to the rocket we witnessed launching in the film's first images. It ascends, the gently rhythmic, incessantly cyclical music of Philip Glass accompanying. Suddenly, without natural sound, flames silently engulf the rocket and the fig-

ure breaks apart. The camera follows a portion of one of the rocket boosters, over its long, Icarus-like fall back to earth. For several minutes, without only music heard and no distinct background seen except blue sky, one completely loses the sense the object is falling. As it spins and whirls, and flames occasionally spout in irregular intervals, it transforms into something utterly abstract, utterly different. This obvious image of destruction and—presumably—a warning against the relentless march of human progress cannot, in experience, be received so programmatically. Destruction? Yes. But also beauty and transformation, in a timeless, spaceless experience. This long cinematic fascination with the rocket finally crossfades to an image of ancient cave paintings, reprising the theme that started the film.

The opening shot to *Koyaanisqatsi* featured a painting of large dark figures, a prominent white one among them. This is actually the so-called "Holy Ghost" panel, a prominent group of life-size figures from the Great Gallery set of rock paintings in Horseshoe Canyon, Utah, in the American West. They are called this because of their floating, looming, mysterious presence rising above hikers in the Canyon. Photographer Larry Lindahl describes: "The sheer size of the shamanic figures draws me forward. Majestic, yes. Magical. Mysterious, too. A prominent seven-foot-tall supernatural figure tells us that observing the cosmos was significant and vital" (Lindahl 2014, para. 6). But the final image of the film reveals a different panel in that large gallery, depicting something more familiar: several adults and at least one small child; a family, portending a future, full of new knowledge, new things to see, and hear.

These paintings are estimated to be at least 1500 years old. If we make the long, dusty, arduous journey, beyond the throbbing noise into the relative stillness of the desert, we can still behold them.

Bibliography

Attali, Jacques (1985): *Noise: The Political Economy of Music*. Translated by Brian Massumi. Minneapolis: University of Minnesota Press.
Benson, Bruce Ellis (2008): *The Pious Nietzsche*. Bloomington: University of Indiana Press.
Bolognini, N., C. Cecchetto, C. Geraci, A. Maravita, A. Pascual-Leone, C. Papagno (2012): "Hearing shapes our perception of time: temporal discrimination of tactile stimuli in deaf people." In: *Journal of Cognitive Neuroscience* 24. No. 2, pp. 276–86.
Cesarale, Giorgio (2014): "The 'Not' of Speculative Realism." In: *Mute*, February 19, 2014. https://www.metamute.org/editorial/articles/%E2%80%98not%E2%80%99-speculative-realism, visited on March 5, 2021.
Chion, Michel (2018): *Audio-Vision: Sound on Screen*. New York: Columbia University Press.

Coëgnarts, Maarten (2017): "Cinema and the embodied mind: metaphor and simulation in understanding meaning in films." In: *Palgrave Communications* 3. Article no. 17067, pp. 1–15. (https://doi.org/10.1057/palcomms.2017.67)

Cox, Christoph (2018a): "Christoph Cox on Sonic Flux: Sound Art and Metaphysics at the Kitchen." In: *Artforum*, November 3, 2018. Video, 1:38:04. https://www.artforum.com/video/christoph-cox-on-sonic-flux-sound-art-and-metaphysics-at-the-kitchen-november-3-2018-77736, visited on March 5, 2021.

Cox, Christoph (2018b): *Sonic Flux: Sound, Art, and Metaphysics*. Chicago: University of Chicago Press.

Deleuze, Gilles (1986): *Nietzsche and Philosophy*. Translated by Hugh Tomlinson. London: Continuum.

Deleuze, Gilles (2003): *Francis Bacon: The Logic of Sensation*. London: Continuum.

Fischer, Lucy (1985): "*Applause:* The Visual and Acoustic Landscape." In: Elisabeth Weis and John Belton (Eds.): *Film Sound: Theory and Practice*. New York: Columbia University Press, pp. 232–245.

Greydanus, Steven (n.d.): "Voyage into Silence: Interview with Philip Gröning." http://www.decentfilms.com/articles/groning, visited on March 13, 2021.

Horner, Robyn (2005): *Jean-Luc Marion: A Theo-logical Introduction*. Burlington: Ashgate.

Kendrick, James (2009): *Film Violence: History, Ideology, Culture*. London: Wallflower.

Lindahl, Larry (2014): "Great Gallery of Canyonlands." In: *Larry Lindahl Photography*. https://www.larrylindahl.com/great-gallery-of-canyonlands/, visited on March 13, 2021.

Marion, Jean-Luc (2002a): *Being Given: Toward a Phenomenology of Givenness*. Stanford: Stanford University Press.

Marion, Jean-Luc. (2002b): *In Excess: Studies of Saturated Phenomena* New York: Fordham University Press.

Marion, Jean-Luc (2012): *God without Being*. 2nd Ed. Chicago: University of Chicago Press.

Nietzsche, Friedrich (1995): *The Birth of Tragedy*. Translated by Clifton P. Fadiman. New York: Dover Publications.

Nietzsche, Friedrich (1997): *Daybreak*. Translated by Reginald John Hollingdale. Cambridge: Cambridge University Press.

Nietzsche, Friedrich (2015): *Human, All Too Human*. Translated by Alexander Harvey. Hastings: Delphi Classics.

Nietzsche, Friedrich: *Thus Spoke Zarathustra* (2006). Translated by Adrian del Caro. Cambridge: Cambridge University Press.

Nietzsche, Friedrich (1997): *Twilight of the Idols, or How to Philosophize with a Hammer*. Translated by Richard Polt. Indianapolis: Hackett Publishing.

Ong, Walter (1982): *Orality and Literacy: The Technologization of the Word*. London: Routledge.

Patterson, R. D., C.M. Hackney, S.D. Iverson. (1999): "Interdisciplinary Auditory Neuroscience." In: *Trends in Cognitive Science* 3. No. 7, pp. 245–247.

Pieniążek, Paweł (2019): "The Concept of Violence in the Evolution of Nietzsche's Thought." In: *Eidos: A Journal for Philosophy of Culture* 3. No. 2, pp. 13–25.

Pua, Phoebe (2019), "The Silent God of Ingmar Bergman and Andrei Tarkovsky." In: *IIIIXIII. Fourbythreemagazine*. http://christine-jakobson.squarespace.com/issue/silent-god-of-bergman-and-tarkovsky, visited on February 3, 2022.

Rogers, Sheena (2013): "Truth, Lies, and Meaning in Slow Motion Images." In: Art Shimamura (Ed.): *Psychocinematics: Exploring Cognition at the Movies*. Oxford: Oxford University Press, pp. 149–164.
Simmons, J. Aaron, and Bruce Ellis Benson (2013): *The New Phenomenologists*. London: Bloomsbury.
Sontag, Susan (1969): *Styles of Radical Will*. New York: Picador.
Sorfa, David (2016): "What is Film-Philosophy." In: *Film-Philosophy* 20. No. 1, pp. 1–5. (https://doi.org/10.3366/film.2016.0001).
Stellino, Paolo (2013): "Nietzsche on Suicide." In: *Nietzsche-Studien* 42. No. 1, pp. 151–177.
Taylor, Victor E. (2006): "Conversation with Jean-Luc Marion." In: *Journal for Cultural and Religious Theory* 7. No. 2, pp. 1–6.
Weis, Elisabeth (1985): "Style and Sound in *The Birds*." In: Elisabeth Weis and John Belton (Eds.): *Film Sound: Theory and Practice*. New York: Columbia University Press.
Young, Julian (2006): *Nietzsche's Philosophy of Religion*. Cambridge: Cambridge University Press.

Filmography

Bergman, Ingmar, director. (1963): *Winter Light*.
Gröning, Philip, director. (2005): *Into Great Silence*.
Neshat, Sirin, director (2009): *Women without Men*.
Peckinpah, Sam, director. (1969): *The Wild Bunch*.
Reggio, Godfrey, director. (1982): *Koyaanisqatsi*.
Scorsese, Martin, director. (1976): *Taxi Driver*.
Spielberg, Steven, director. (1998): *Saving Private Ryan*.
Woo, John, director. (1989): *The Killer*.

Paolo Stellino
Aestheticizing Murder: Hitchcock's *Rope*, Nietzsche, and the Alleged Right to Crime of Superior Individuals

'Private morality is dead. We are an elite society
to whom everything is permitted. Those are Hitler's very words'.
(Aschenbach in Luchino Visconti's *The Damned*)

Abstract: This paper explores intersections between nihilism, the death of God, and the aestheticization of murder by considering the use of Nietzsche's theory of the overman in Hitchcock's *Rope*. This theory is invoked to justify the gratuitous murder around which the film's plot revolves. Although the interpretation of the overman in *Rope* does not substantially differ from other stereotypical readings of Nietzsche's philosophy put forward in the twentieth century, Hitchcock's film is nonetheless particularly interesting for it explores the fundamental issue of intellectual responsibility. The paper will thus focus on the most philosophical aspects of *Rope*, paying particular attention to its literary sources and contextualizing the reference to Nietzsche's overman. The final section will be dedicated to the analysis of both Nietzsche's and Hitchcock's role in the progressive tendency towards the aestheticization of murder in nineteenth- and twentieth-century European culture.

1 Introduction

One of the characteristics of the studies dedicated to the relationship between Dostoevsky and Nietzsche is a widespread tendency to interpret the former not only as foreshadowing but even as forestalling the dangerous nihilistic ideas of the latter's philosophy. More specifically, Raskolnikov's theory of the extraordinary men (to whom everything is permitted) and Ivan Karamazov's idea that all is permitted if there is no God and no immortality of the soul are often seen as anticipating Nietzsche's theory of the overman. Following the death of God announced by the madman in section 125 of *The Gay Science*, so the reading goes,[1] the new man, the overman, turns himself into a new god (Dostoevsky's

---

[1] On this, see Grillaert (2008) and Stellino (2015, pp. 145–152).

https://doi.org/10.1515/9783110699210-013

man-god),[2] acquiring one of the attributes of the former god: unlimited moral freedom. Thus, for the overman, all is permitted. As the devil, who appears to Ivan Karamazov in a dream, puts it: 'since God and immortality do not exist in any case ... the new man is allowed to become a man-god, though it be he alone in the whole world, and of course, in this new rank, to jump lightheartedly over any former moral obstacle of the former slave-man, if he need be. There is no law for God!' (Dostoevsky 1992, p. 649).

I have shown elsewhere that this reading of Nietzsche's overman poses several hermeneutic problems.[3] Beyond these problems, however, it is important to understand the logic underlying this reading: the negation of God (atheism) is directly linked to the temptation to transgress conventional moral boundaries. To borrow from French theologian Henri de Lubac, it is as if, without God, man could not but organize the world against man himself (de Lubac 1995, p. 14). In other words, once man kills God (the foundation of morality), the door stands open to any kind of violence, be it self-inflicted (as in the case of Kirillov's suicide in Dostoevsky's *Demons*) or directed towards others (from anthropophagy and parricide in *The Brothers Karamazov* to gratuitous murder in André Gide's *The Vatican Cellars* or Albert Camus's *The Stranger*). Indeed, this philosophical problem (that is, whether everything is permitted if God does not exist) was already debated in the Age of Enlightenment, when atheistic philosophers and theologians entered into a heated debate over the possibility of providing a solid foundation for a secular ethics.[4] An echo of this debate can also be found in Jacobi's well-known letter to Fichte (1799), where the former claims that he has no answer to the question 'what is the good?' if there is no God (Jacobi 2003, p. 133). It was with Dostoevsky and Nietzsche that the aforementioned philosophical problem became truly pressing, however, for in the second half of the nineteenth century nihilism emerged, bringing with it a normative and axiological void that would pave the way for the Karamazovian notion that everything is permitted.

It is against this background that we must understand the proliferation of the aforementioned mythopoem (according to which everything is permitted for the Nietzschean overman) in the twentieth century.[5] Given the several similarities between Raskolnikov's theory of the extraordinary men and Nietzsche's philosophy (the division of humanity into superior and lower men, the postula-

---

[2] The *chelovekobog* (man-god) is the man who, having denied God, becomes a god. He stands in opposition to the *Bogochelovek*, the God-man, i.e., Christ, the incarnated God.
[3] See the second part of Stellino (2015).
[4] On this, see Domenech (1989) and Lewy (2008).
[5] I borrow the term "mythopoem" from Nel Grillaert (2008, p. 41).

tion of two different moralities – master and slave moralities, to use Nietzsche's terminology – and his fascination with Napoleon, among other aspects), intellectuals and scholars began to interpret the overman as a superior individual who enjoyed a special right to crime – a right which would be sanctioned in virtue of the overman's superiority over the mass of ordinary people. It is exactly this mythopoetic reading that one finds in Hitchcock's *Rope*, where Nietzsche's theory of the overman is invoked to justify the gratuitous murder around which the film's plot revolves. Although the interpretation of the overman in *Rope* does not substantially differ from other stereotypical readings of Nietzsche's philosophy put forward in the twentieth century, Hitchcock's film is nonetheless particularly interesting for two main reasons: first, it shows the extreme dangerousness of denying the existence of equal rights for all human beings and, at the same time, of postulating special rights held by allegedly superior individuals; second, it explores the fundamental issue of intellectual responsibility by asking a very simple question: how far does the responsibility of intellectuals extend?

This paper is divided in four sections. In section 2, I focus on the aspects of *Rope* that are most relevant to the present analysis. Section 3 provides an answer to the question of why Hitchcock decided to associate Cadell's and Brandon's theory specifically with Nietzsche and his theory of the overman rather than other literary or philosophical sources. Section 4 deals with the question of how to assess Nietzsche's intellectual responsibility for the crimes committed, directly or indirectly, in his name. Finally, section 5 analyses both Nietzsche's and Hitchcock's role in the progressive tendency towards the aestheticization of murder in nineteenth- and twentieth-century European culture.

2 Hitchcock's *Rope*

Rope (1948), Hitchcock's first colour film, is generally known in the history of film for being edited so as to give the impression of comprising a single, long, continuous shot. Due to technical limitations (one reel lasted approximately ten minutes),[6] Hitchcock decided to shoot long takes, varying between four and ten minutes, devising ways to mask the cuts.[7] From a technical point of view, the film was highly innovative. As he confessed to François Truffaut, however, Hitchcock was not satisfied with the final result: 'I undertook *Rope* as a

---

[6] The digital technology that half a century later allowed Sokurov to shoot his masterpiece *Russian Ark* was obviously not available to Hitchcock.

[7] On his reasons for using this technique, see Truffaut (1985, pp. 179–180 and 184) and Wood (1989, p. 350).

stunt; that's the only way I can describe it. I really don't know how I came to indulge in it'. (Truffaut 1985, p. 179). Although Hitchcock's assessment may appear overly harsh, the film was not a critical success at the time of its release and has received less attention than other Hitchcock classics. Considered from a philosophical point of view, however, *Rope* deserves special attention among Hitchcock's rich filmography, not only for its explicit mention of Nietzsche's theory of the overman but also for exploring, among other topics, the aestheticization of crime, the risks linked to the relativization of morality, the obligations everyone owes to society and the extent and limits of intellectual responsibility.

Among these issues, Nietzsche's theory of the overman deserves special attention for an obvious reason: it provides a philosophical justification of the murder around which the film's plot develops. Following the opening titles and a very brief sequence filmed outdoors (a policeman ushers two children across the street and simultaneously stops a car – a detail which, as we will see, is particularly significant), the audience is presented with two young men, Brandon and Phillip, who strangle their former classmate David to death. It soon becomes apparent that the murder is essentially motiveless; Brandon and Phillip have simply killed for the sake of performing a perfect murder and with the intention of putting into practice the ideas preached by their former housemaster at prep school, Rupert Cadell (James Stewart), now a publisher with a penchant for philosophy books.[8] Cadell is described by Brandon as having no patience for social conventions, someone who thinks that murder is a crime for most ordinary men but the privilege of a few superior human beings.

After strangling David, Brandon and Phillip hide his body in a cassone (a wooden chest) and prepare for the party they have been organizing so that Mr Kentley, David's father and a book collector, can take the opportunity to examine rare volumes from Brandon's collection. Among the unaware guests are Cadell, Mr Kentley, Mrs Atwater (Mr Kentley's sister-in-law), Janet (David's fiancée), Kenneth (Janet's ex-boyfriend) and Mrs Wilson (the housekeeper). The dinner is macabrely served on the wooden chest – a kind of 'ceremonial altar', as Brandon ironically puts it – and most of the action takes place in a living room dominated by a fake panoramic view of the New York skyline. In the middle of the party, Cadell, Brandon and Mr Kentley have the following conversation, which gives a more detailed picture of Cadell's theory:

---

[8] The perfect murder was a recurrent theme in Hitchcock's films of the period. It is a central aspect of the plots of *Strangers on a Train* (1951) and *Dial M for Murder* (1954). See also the conversations between Charlie's father and the neighbour in *Shadow of a Doubt* (1943).

RC: Murder is, or should be, an art ... and as such, the privilege of committing it should be reserved for those few who are really superior individuals.
B: And the victims, inferior beings whose lives are unimportant anyway... .
Mr K: Then, may I ask who is to decide that a human being is inferior, and therefore a suitable victim for murder?
B: The few who are privileged to commit murder.
Mr K: And just who might they be? ...
B: The few are those men of such intellectual and cultural superiority that they are above the traditional moral concepts. Good and evil, right and wrong were invented for the ordinary average man, the inferior man, because he needs them.
Mr K: And obviously you agree with Nietzsche and his theory of the superman.
B: Yes, I do.
Mr K: So did Hitler.
B: Hitler was a paranoid savage. His supermen, all Fascist supermen, were brainless murderers. I'd hang any who were left. But then, you see, I'd hang them first for being stupid.

As time passes, Mr Kentley becomes concerned about his son's unusual absence. At the same time, Cadell, surprised by Phillip's nervous behaviour, notices that something strange is afoot and begins to suspect that Brandon and Phillip have something to do with David's absence. Cadell's suspicions are confirmed when, at the end of the party, Mrs Wilson gives him the wrong hat, which bears David's initials. He thus leaves the apartment but, pretending to have left his cigarette case behind, returns after a few minutes with the intention of discovering the truth. A further discussion – during which, as Phillip puts it, Brandon and Cadell play cat and mouse – leads to the denouement: Cadell's discovery of David's body in the chest and his final monologue, which deserves to be quoted almost in its entirety for its philosophical content:

> Brandon, till this very moment, this world and the people in it have always been dark and incomprehensible to me, and I've tried to clear my way with logic and superior intellect, and you've thrown my own words right back in my face, Brandon. You were right too; if nothing else, a man should stand by his word, but you've given my words a meaning that I never dreamed of, and you've tried to twist them into a cold, logical excuse for your ugly murder. Well, they never were that, Brandon, and you can't make them that. There must have been something deep inside you from the very start that let you do this thing, but there's always been something deep inside me that would never let me do it ... tonight you've made me ashamed of every concept I ever had of superior or inferior beings. But I thank you for that shame, because now I know that we're each of us a separate human being, Brandon, with the right to live and work and think as individuals but with an obligation to the society we live in. By what right do you dare say that there's a superior few to which you belong? By what right did you dare decide that that boy in there was inferior and therefore could be killed? Did you think you were God, Brandon? ... I don't know what you thought or what you are but I know what you've done – you've murdered! You've stran-

gled the life out of a fellow human being who could live and love as you never could ... and never will again.

To attract the attention of passers-by, Cadell fires three shots out the window. The film's ending is doubly symbolic. Inside the apartment, Brandon, Phillip and Rupert visually form a triangle, with Rupert at the apex so as to symbolize his share of the responsibility for the murder (Hemmeter 2011, p. 79). Outside, one can hear the voices of the passers-by and, subsequently, an approaching police siren. Both stand for the society to which Cadell makes explicit reference at the end of his monologue and to whose rules and laws every member is obliged – the same rules that are represented by the policeman who, at the beginning of the film, stops the car and ushers the children across the street (Gentili 2018, p. 266). *Rope* thus ends with the restoration of the social order that had been temporarily suspended by the illegitimate murder (note the circular structure of the film, which begins and ends with the police, a symbol of law, justice and order).

3 Why Nietzsche?

Hitchcock's movie, which is actually based on Patrick Hamilton's 1929 play *Rope*, abounds in literary references and allusions, some of them explicit, others less so.[9] To begin with, the idea that murder is or should be an art and that 'the power to kill can be just as satisfying as the power to create', as Brandon puts it, is a clear allusion to Thomas De Quincey's provocative invitation to consider murder one of the fine arts and to treat it '*aesthetically* ... that is, in relation to good taste' (De Quincey 2006, p. 11). The idea of committing a perfect, motiveless murder ('we've killed for the sake of danger and for the sake of killing', Brandon says to Phillip) recalls Lafcadio's *acte gratuit* in André Gide's *The Vatican Cellars*

---

[9] As Dave Kehr points out, 'though Brandon is a collector of paintings and Philip is an accomplished pianist, the art foregrounded in *Rope* is literature. Rupert is a publisher; Jan, the murdered man's fiancée (Joan Chandler), is a writer; Mr. Kentley, the victim's father (Sir Cedric Hardwicke), is a collector of fine editions. The party is being held, ostensibly, so that Mr. Kentley can examine some rare volumes from Brandon's collection, books that were packed in the chest that now contains his son's body. When Brandon makes a present of a few books to Mr. Kentley, he ties them up with the length of rope used in the strangulation. Books are the means by which the "superior people" define their superiority, define their lives. .... But through their insistent association with the crime, books become agents of death. The printed word is a murder weapon' (Kehr 2011, pp. 249–250).

(*Les caves du Vatican*, 1914), an arbitrary and unmotivated murder of a perfect stranger committed for fun ('par jeu'), merely for the thrill of it ('l'amour du risque')[10] (Gide 2009, p. 1142). Furthermore, Hitchcock's decision to rename Hamilton's character (Wyndham Brandon) Brandon Shaw is likely an ironic allusion to Bernard Shaw, the well-known Irish playwright, author of the play *Man and Superman* (first published in 1903).

Together with these literary sources, Dostoevsky's name inevitably comes to mind. Indeed, although neither the play nor the movie makes explicit mention of the Russian writer, Hitchcock's film particularly recalls two of Dostoevsky's novels: *Crime and Punishment* and *The Brothers Karamazov*. The title of the former is explicitly alluded to in the film when Phillip, pressed by Rupert's questions, loses his temper and says: 'Stop playing "crime and punishment", Rupert'.[11] Moreover, Cadell's and Brandon's division of humanity into two different anthropological categories inevitably recalls Raskolnikov's distinction between ordinary and extraordinary people,[12] while the privilege to commit murder, which Cadell and Brandon grant to superior individuals, evokes the right to crime that is reserved, according to Raskolnikov, for extraordinary people.[13] On the other hand, Cadell's intellectual responsibility for the murder perpetrated by Brandon and Phillip closely recalls Ivan Karamazov's moral responsibility for the parri-

---

10 In a similar way, Hamilton has Brandon say: 'I have committed passionless – motiveless – faultless – and clueless murder. Bloodless and noiseless murder. ... And immaculate murder. I have killed. I have killed for sake of danger and for the sake of killing' (Hamilton 2009, p. 3).
11 See the analogous scene in the novel, in which Police Inspector Porfiry Petrovich plays with Raskolnikov, who says, in his mind: 'Strike directly, then; don't play cat and mouse with me' (Dostoevsky 1993, p. 254). As shown above, cat and mouse is precisely the game that, according to Phillip, Brandon and Rupert are engaged in playing.
12 Mr Kentley's question about 'who is to decide that a human being is inferior, and therefore a suitable victim for murder?' recalls the ironic question that Porfiry Petrovich poses to Raskolnikov: 'But tell me this: how does one manage to distinguish these extraordinary ones from the ordinary? Are they somehow marked at birth, or what?' (Dostoevsky 1993, p. 262). The division of humanity into two different categories (a higher or strong one, and a lower or weak one) can also be found in Gide's *Les caves du Vatican* (see Lafcadio's [and Proto's] distinction between 'les subtils' and 'les crustacés' [Gide 2009, p. 1159]) and in Carlyle's *On Heroes, Hero-Worship, and the Heroic in History* (1841). Carlyle's hero worship is explicitly mentioned in Hamilton's play. Brandon says of Carlyle that 'he's got guts ... and a kind of angry righteousness, which you don't get nowadays' (Hamilton 2009, p. 32).
13 Raskolnikov's theory clearly differs from Brandon's in that, whereas the latter justifies murder for aesthetic reasons or 'for the sake of danger', the former suggests that an extraordinary man has the right to step over certain obstacles 'only in the event that the fulfillment of his idea – sometimes perhaps salutary for the whole of mankind – calls for it' (Dostoevsky 1993, p. 259).

cide committed by the lackey Smerdyakov (who puts into practice Ivan's aforementioned idea that if there is no God and no immortality, then everything is permitted). Even Cadell's confession – 'I've tried to clear my way with logic and superior intellect' – can be interpreted as a reference to Ivan's rationalism, whereas his final acceptance of responsibility mirrors Ivan's at the end of the novel.[14]

Given these points of convergence between Hitchcock's *Rope* and Dostoevsky's novels, one might wonder why Mr Kentley associates Cadell's and Brandon's theory (according to which the privilege to commit murder is reserved for superior individuals) with Nietzsche and his theory of the overman rather than with Dostoevsky and Raskolnikov's theory of the extraordinary man – all the more so if one considers that, whereas the latter theory explicitly sanctions a right to crime on the part of superior individuals, Nietzsche never seems to legitimate such a right in his writings. In reality, there are several considerations that explain, if not justify, the allusion to Nietzsche. First, as mentioned above, Hitchcock's *Rope* was based on Hamilton's play, which in turn bears a striking resemblance to a true story: the Leopold–Loeb case, known as "the crime of the century". On 21 May 1924, Nathan Leopold and Richard Loeb, two wealthy students at the University of Chicago, kidnapped and brutally murdered 14-year-old Bobby Franks. When they were apprehended, Leopold and Loeb confessed that they wanted to carry out a perfect murder, justifying their actions with reference to Nietzsche's theory of the overman. In particular, as Simon Baatz explains, Leopold's ambition was 'to become a perfect Nietzschean and to follow Nietzsche's philosophy all the way through' (Baatz 2009, p. 325). Leopold was specifically interested in Nietzsche's theory of the overman, which he interpreted in a rather peculiar, hedonistic way:

> Nathan also, in Richard's opinion, had a tedious obsession with the philosophy of Friedrich Nietzsche;[15] he would talk endlessly about the mythical superman who, because he was a superman, stood outside the law, beyond any moral code that might constrain the actions of ordinary men. Even murder, Nathan claimed, was an acceptable act for a superman to commit if the deed gave him pleasure. Morality did not apply in such a case, Nathan assert-

---

[14] Note, however, that whereas Ivan fully accepts and recognizes his guilt ('I'm not mad, I'm simply a murderer!', he says during the process [Dostoevsky 1992, p. 686]), Cadell, on the one hand, confesses that he is ashamed of every concept he ever had of superior or inferior beings, while, on the other hand, accusing Brandon of having given his words a meaning he had never dreamed of and of having twisted them into an excuse for the murder.

[15] It is noteworthy that a similar poisonous fixation on the works of Nietzsche (and Schopenhauer) was attributed to the 24-year-old Walter Fischer, who on 4 December 1901 was tried in Gotha for the murder of his lover, the 17-year-old Martha Amberg. On this, see Gilman (1983).

ed. The only consideration that mattered was whether it afforded the superman pleasure – everything else faded into insignificance. (Baatz 2009, p. 52)

Although Hamilton claimed he had not heard of the Leopold–Loeb case until after his play was produced (Biderman and Jacobowitz 2007, p. 34), there are several similarities between the case and the play – the reference to Nietzsche's philosophy and the misstep that incriminated Leopold and Loeb, among others – that cast doubt on the truthfulness of his claim.[16] Be that as it may, there is little doubt that Hitchcock knew about the close resemblance between the case and the play, although in order to reassure Warner Bros., he denied that his film had anything to do with the case (Barrios 2003, p. 210).

A second reason that explains the allusion to Nietzsche's theory of the overman in Hitchcock's *Rope* is the historical context. Indeed, it is important to recall that Hitchcock's film was made only three years after the end of the Second World War, at a time when Nietzsche's name was still strongly associated with Nazi ideology. Hitchcock was well aware of the atrocities that had occurred in the German concentration and extermination camps during the war given that in 1945, at Bernstein's request, he had acted as an advisor for the editing of *Memory of the Camps*, a film composed by documentary footage shot by the Allied forces when the camps were liberated (Adair 2002, p. 81). As Patrick McGilligan points out in his Hitchcock biography, 'in more than one postwar film, Hitchcock

---

16 The Nietzschean reference in Hamilton's play is particularly interesting, for it is paradigmatic of a certain widespread use (or better, abuse) of Nietzsche's philosophy. In the final part of the third and last act, Brandon takes Nietzsche's words out of context and uses them to justify the murder: 'You read Nietzsche, don't you, Rupert? ... And you know that he tells us to live dangerously. ... And you know that he's no more respect for individual life than you, and tells us – to – live dangerously' (Hamilton 2009, p. 63). The expression 'to live dangerously' (*gefährlich leben*) can be found in section 283 of *The Gay Science*. One need not read the text particularly closely or attentively to see that Nietzsche's call to 'live at war' and to 'be robbers and conquerors' (GS 283) has nothing to do with the idea of breaking every moral rule and killing for the sake of killing, as Brandon erroneously believes, but is rather directed to seekers of knowledge (*Erkennenden*) who must be determined and steadfast in their search. A similar distorted use of Nietzsche's expression 'to live dangerously' was made by Mussolini, a great admirer of Nietzsche's writings. On the occasion of the opening meeting of the National Council of the Fascist Party, held on 2 August 1924, Mussolini claimed that 'to live dangerously' should become 'the *motto* of the passionate, young Italian Fascism', meaning that the Fascist had to be ready for any kind of sacrifice, danger and action when it came to defending the fatherland and Fascism (Mussolini 1956, p. 37, my translation). In Meyer Levin's 1956 novel *Compulsion*, a fictionalized account of the Leopold–Loeb case, Mussolini is depicted as 'a real leader, bringing back the glory that was Rome – a kind of superman' (Levin 2014, p. 70). Levin's novel was adapted for the big screen in 1959 by Richard Fleisher. The homonymous film starred Orson Welles as the defence lawyer.

scattered such reminders of something he never forgave: the evil of Nazi Germany' (McGilligan 2003, p. 273). Such reminders are sometimes linked, as in *Rope*, to Nietzsche's philosophy: in *Lifeboat* (1944), for instance, the German U-boat captain is defined as an 'ersatz superman', whereas in *Notorious* (1946) Ingrid Bergman plays the role of Alicia Hubermann, the American daughter of a convicted Nazi spy, whose name clearly recalls Nietzsche's *Übermensch* (German for 'overman').

In *Rope*, Brandon rejects Mr Kentley's association of Nietzsche's theory of the overman with Hitler and his "supermen". Brandon's characterization of the Nazis as 'brainless murderers' and 'stupid' indicates that he considers them to be lacking the necessary depth to understand the complexities of Nietzsche's philosophy – complexities that he nonetheless deems himself able to understand. Note that whereas Brandon dismisses Mr Kentley's allusion to Hitler, he makes no objections to Mr Kentley's association of his (i.e., Brandon's) ideas with Nietzsche's theory of the overman. Brandon thus seems to imply that, whereas the Nazi appropriation of Nietzsche's thought was nothing more than a vulgar distortion of it, his philosophical defence of the right to crime enjoyed by superior individuals is coherent with and faithful to Nietzsche's theory of the overman. There is a certain irony, however, in the fact that Cadell later levels against Brandon precisely the same accusation that the latter levels against the Nazis, namely, that of having distorted his theory in order to justify murder.

The analogy between Brandon's distortion of Rupert's words, on the one hand, and the Nazis' manipulation of Nietzsche's philosophy, on the other, is revealing of Hitchcock's intention. To see this, we must consider the key character of the film: Rupert Cadell. Cadell is undoubtedly a fascinating man: he is charming, entertaining and clever. As Biderman and Jacobowitz point out, he 'is eminently comfortable in the world of ideas... . Rupert is fond of using concepts and theories to provoke and shock conventional people and bolster his reputation for "dangerous thinking", all the while treating such concepts merely as abstractions on the intellectual plane' (Biderman and Jacobowitz 2007, p. 35). Although in his final monologue Cadell seems to reject his share of responsibility for the murder – he accuses Brandon of having twisted his words and given them a different meaning – there is a detail in the film that is very illuminating on this issue. When Cadell tries to disarm Phillip, the latter fires a shot that causes a minor wound on the former's left hand. Cadell wraps his hand in a kerchief and then heads towards the chest, opening it and finding David's body within. At this point, Hitchcock inserts the final cut of the film (against the back of the lid of the chest). After the cut, we see Cadell's left hand in the foreground: the kerchief is now stained with blood, clearly symbolizing the fact that, like Brandon and Phillip, Cadell is partially responsible for the murder and therefore quite literally has blood on his hands.[17]

The message of the film is thus that the world of ideas and the world of actions are not separate, and that abstract theories and ideas can have concrete practical consequences.[18] Following Carlo Gentili, it is thus possible to interpret *Rope* as Hitchcock's 'indictment of the European intellectuals (of whom Rupert Cadell is manifestly a double; he is, perhaps, Nietzsche's double) for having handled dangerous ideas without realizing their pragmatic and political implications. They therefore bear direct responsibility for the horrible crimes committed, directly or indirectly in their name, by a fanatical ideology' (Gentili 2018, p. 262, my translation). In this context, the allusion to Nietzsche's name in *Rope* becomes fully meaningful. After all, like Cadell, Nietzsche himself called into question traditional morality and tended to bolster his reputation for "dangerous thinking".

4 The Responsibility of Intellectuals

How should we consider Hitchcock's indictment of Nietzsche (regarded here as a representative of the European intellectuals that, as Gentili puts it, handled dangerous ideas without realizing their pragmatic and political implications)? Is it true that, as Karl Löwith claimed, 'Nietzsche's ideas spiritually [*geistig*] opened up the path for the Third Reich, though pathfinders always opened paths *for others* that *they themselves* did not traverse' (Löwith 1995, p. 208)?[19] Or is the fact that Nietzsche's thought was distorted and manipulated by Fascist and Nazi ideologues, as has been abundantly shown, a sufficient condition for releasing Nietzsche from all responsibility for the crimes that were partly justified through

---

[17] The symbolism becomes even more explicit when we consider that in a previous scene, Phillip cuts his right hand when he breaks a glass due to anxiety. When Cadell is wounded later in the film, the blood is thus symbolically transferred from Phillip, the actual murderer, to Cadell, the theoretician who provided the theory that justified the murder. It is noteworthy that one can find an analogous symbolism in Dostoevsky's *Crime and Punishment*. Having assisted Marmeladov, the drunkard who is run over by a carriage, Raskolnikov is soaked in blood. When Nikodim Fomich draws Raskolnikov's attention to the blood on his waistcoat, the latter says: 'Soaked, yes... I've got blood all over me!', clearly alluding to his murder of the old moneylender and her sister (Dostoevsky 1993, p. 186).
[18] As Biderman and Jacobowitz point out, 'when Rupert finally flings open the chest to discover David's body, the books resting on it are thrown off, symbolizing the clash of the world of ideas and the world of actions' (Biderman and Jacobowitz 2007, p. 43).
[19] I owe this quote to Gentili (2018, p. 262).

an appeal to his philosophy? Commenting on this, Biderman and Jacobowitz rightly point out that 'not everything done in the name of Nietzsche is Nietzschean' (Biderman and Jacobowitz 2007, p. 42); at the end of their paper, however, considering Cadell's attempt to distance himself from Brandon, they also ask the following important question: 'Can Rupert, Brandon and Philip's mentor and teacher, so easily disavow responsibility here?' (Biderman and Jacobowitz 2007, p. 44). The same question can thus be asked in relation to Nietzsche: can the German philosopher so easily disavow responsibility here? On the one hand, Löwith acknowledges that Nietzsche was a declared opponent of the Second German Reich and explicitly stated that the *Will to Power* was not written for the aspirations of the German Reich.[20] On the other hand, however, he also claims that Nietzsche shaped German political thinking like no other philosopher of the nineteenth century and that it is a 'historical fact that Nietzsche, precisely as an opponent of everything that the "Reich" meant, was situated within the scope of Bismarck's and Wagner's will to power, and that, as an untimely one, he was also timely and remained so' (Löwith 1995, p. 208).

The question of how to assess Nietzsche's intellectual responsibility for the crimes committed by the Third Reich either directly or indirectly in his name is undoubtedly a complex one.[21] Indeed, notwithstanding the fact that Nietzsche's thought was intentionally distorted and manipulated by Nazi ideologues with the help and co-responsibility of his sister, Elisabeth, and granted that no one can be held responsible for another's ideas, it is still legitimate to ask with Löwith whether and to what extent Nietzsche's ideas paved the way for the Third Reich – or, to put it differently and less controversially, whether and to what extent his philosophy lent support to the later Nazi ideology.[22] It is indeed no secret that Nietzsche praised the masculine, healthy and strong instincts that, in his view, were ideally embodied in the conqueror, rapacious and master races. It is also well known that Nietzsche was a harsh critic of democracy. The first sections of the ninth part of *Beyond Good and Evil* are dedicated to showing that every enhancement thus far of the type 'man' has been the work of an aristocratic society (BGE 257); that a healthy aristocracy 'accepts in good conscience the sacrifice of countless people who have to be pushed down and shrunk into incomplete human beings, into slaves, into tools, all *for the sake of the aristocracy*'; that society exists 'only as the substructure and framework for raising an exceptional type of being' (BGE 258); and that 'mutually refraining from injury, vio-

---

[20] Löwith's reference is to NL 1887, 9[188].
[21] On this, see Stellino (2017).
[22] On this, see Golomb and Wistrich (2002).

lence, and exploitation' is a recipe for decline, whereas if a social body is healthy 'it will have to be the embodiment of will to power, it will want to grow, spread, grab, win dominance' – and this simply because life is will to power, that is, '*essentially* a process of appropriating, injuring, overpowering the alien and the weaker, oppressing, being harsh, imposing your own form, incorporating, and at least, the very least, exploiting' (BGE 259).

On the one hand, if these aspects, among others, do not prove per se that Nietzsche is to be held intellectually responsible for the crimes that were committed in his name, they nonetheless partly explain why Fascist and Nazi ideologues found fertile ground in Nietzsche's thought. On the other hand, however, those same ideologues could never have made use of Nietzsche's philosophy without distorting, manipulating or even concealing certain aspects of it. Indeed, it should be recalled that Nietzsche had a strong aversion towards anti-Semites and was an opponent of the nationalist movements of his time (accusing them of being dangerous and fomenting national hostilities), remaining a particularly staunch critic of German nationalism and its slogan: *Deutschland, Deutschland über alles*.[23]

Similarly (but reversing the perspective), it is possible to argue that Brandon's use of Nietzsche's theory of the overman in Hitchcock's *Rope* to justify an alleged right to crime on the part of superior individuals is simply illegitimate. Indeed, nowhere in his writings does Nietzsche theorize about the perfect murder, nor does he defend the idea that murder can be considered an art or that one is allowed to kill simply 'for the sake of danger and for the sake of killing', as Brandon puts it. Furthermore, Nietzsche never claims that superior individuals are permitted to arbitrarily commit murder in virtue of their intellectual and cultural superiority. To interpret Nietzsche's overman in this way is clearly to trivialize one of the most polysemic and complex concepts of Nietzsche's philosophy, ignoring its philosophical context (the death of God and the rejection of all met-

---

23 See section 475 of the first part of *Human, All Too Human*, in which Nietzsche argues that 'one should not be afraid to proclaim oneself simply a *good European* and actively to work for the amalgamation of nations' (HH, I, 475). On Nietzsche's attitude towards nationalism and his low opinion of modern Germans, see, in particular, the eighth part of *Beyond Good and Evil*, titled 'Peoples and Fatherlands'. See also Diethe (1992). On Nietzsche's scorn for the slogan *Deutschland, Deutschland über alles*, see NL 1884, 25[248]; GM III 26; EH Wagner 2; and TI Germans 1. For a detailed analysis of Nietzsche's political views, see Drochon (2016). On Nietzsche's critical stance towards anti-Semitism, see, among many others: NL 1886, 7[67]; the letter to T. Fritsch of 29 May 1887; the letter to Elisabeth, Nietzsche's sister, of 5 June 1887 and of the end of December, 1887; GM II 11; and EH Wagner 2. There is a rich secondary bibliography on this topic. See, in particular, Kofman (1994) and Yovel (2006).

aphysical aspirations,[24] on the one hand, and the critique of modernity, on the other)[25] and the fact that the overman is a regulative ideal that stands for the human possibility of self-overcoming.[26]

On the other hand, however, one might ask whether and to what extent Nietzsche himself paved the way for such interpretations (or better, misinterpretations) of his philosophy by claiming, for instance, that 'there is an *order of rank* [*Rangordnung*] between people' (BGE 228) and that 'there are superior and lower men: equal rights for everyone is the most exceptional injustice' (NL 1883, 17[8], KSA 10, p. 535, my translation).[27] Nietzsche also sympathized with the 'morality of dominating types [*Moral der Herrschende*]', which is 'foreign and painful to contemporary taste due to its stern axiom that people have duties only towards their own kind; that when it comes to creatures of a lower rank, to everything alien, people are allowed to act as they see fit or "from the heart", and in any event, "beyond good and evil"' (BGE 260). Furthermore, he defined Cesare Borgia as 'a "higher man", a kind of *overman*' (TI Raids 37), and Napoleon as a 'synthesis of *Unmensch* (brute) and *Übermensch* (overman)' (GM I 16).[28] It is indeed

---

[24] It is worth recalling that Nietzsche presents the overman for the first time in the first part of *Thus Spoke Zarathustra*, more precisely, in the third section of the prologue. The first part of *Zarathustra* was written in 1883 and chronologically follows the first edition of *The Gay Science* (1882), which contains the announcement of the death of God (§ 125). From the very beginning, the overman is thus presented as a symbol of immanence. As Zarathustra puts it: 'The overman is the meaning of the earth. Let your will say: the overman *shall be* the meaning of the earth! I beseech you, my brothers, *remain faithful to the earth* and do not believe those who speak to you of extraterrestrial hopes!' (Z Prologue 3).
[25] In *Zarathustra*'s Prologue, the overman is presented together with his antithesis, the last man, 'the most contemptible person' (Z Prologue 5), a standardized man who has no goals in life except for happiness understood as material comfort.
[26] See the following well-known passage, in which Zarathustra speaks for the first time of the overman to those gathered in the market place: '*I teach you the overman*. Human being is something that must be overcome. What have you done to overcome him?' (Z Prologue 3). See also Kaufmann (1974, p. 309): 'The *Übermensch* at any rate cannot be dissociated from the conception of *Überwindung*, of overcoming'.
[27] Although this is a posthumous note not intended for publication, it is nevertheless revealing of Nietzsche's opinion on the matter. There is abundant textual evidence, both in the published writings and in the *Nachlass*, that Nietzsche was a strong opponent of the idea that all human beings have equal rights. See, for instance, GS 377; NL 1887, 11[157]; NL 1888, 23[1]; A 43.
[28] According to Walter Kaufmann, in the end Nietzsche did not consider the Corsican an overman, 'evidently not charmed by Napoleon's inhuman qualities' (Kaufmann 1974, p. 315). Contrary to this reading, Paul Glenn has drawn attention to the fact that, 'Given his [Nietzsche's] praise of hardness and cruelty, and his attempt to subvert the "humanitarian" ethics of Christianity, it stands to reason that "inhuman" could be worn as a badge of honor by Nietzsche, as he wore the term "immoralist" with pride' (Glenn 2001, p. 139). A posthumous fragment from the autumn of

no coincidence that Nietzsche's philosophy has often been associated with Raskolnikov's theory – which, as mentioned above, explicitly sanctions a right to crime on the part of superior individuals. Although this association is fundamentally wrong – as we have seen, Nietzsche never claims that superior individuals are entitled 'to shed blood *in all conscience*', as Raskolnikov maintains (Dostoevsky 1993, p. 263) – it is undeniable that there are several similarities between Nietzsche's philosophy and Raskolnikov's theory.[29]

There is little doubt that Nietzsche was conscious of the possibility of his name's being used in the future for purposes that had nothing to do with his philosophy. At the beginning of May 1884, he wrote the following to his friend Malwida von Meysenbug: 'And I am horrified by the thought of all the unqualified and wholly unsuitable persons who will one day appeal to my authority' (Bf. to Malwida von Meysenbug, 05.1884, KGB III/1, Bf. 509, my translation). Yet was Nietzsche fully aware of the horrifying practical consequences that would be drawn from some of his philosophical ideas? His enthusiastic reaction to Joseph Viktor Widmann's review of *Beyond Good and Evil* suggests not only that he did not ignore the danger of these implications but that, in a certain way, and unlike Rupert Cadell, he sought them out,[30] for he firmly believed that the decadence of modern man was a direct consequence of the ideals promoted by the democratic movement ('the universal, green pasture happiness of the herd, with security,

---

1887 support's Glenn's reading: 'Man is beast [*Unthier*] and superbeast [*Überthier*]; the higher man is inhuman [*Unmensch*] and superhuman [*Übermensch*]: these belong together. With every increase of greatness and height in man, there is also an increase in depth and terribleness: one ought not to desire the one without the other – or rather: the more radically one desires the one, the more radically one achieves precisely the other' (NL 1887, 9[154], KSA 12, p. 426).

29 See Stellino (2015, pp. 190 – 203).

30 Widmann's review appeared in the Swiss daily newspaper *Der Bund* on 16/17 September 1886 with the significant title "Nietzsche's Dangerous Book [*Nietzsches gefährliches Buch*]". In the present context, the review is particularly interesting because it directly raises the issue of the practical implications of Nietzsche's philosophy. In pointing out the dangerous character of Nietzsche's new publication, however, Widmann did not mean to be critical of the author and his work. On the contrary, according to Widmann, 'intellectual dynamite, like all explosives, can be useful and its uses don't have to be criminal' (Widmann 2000, p. 195). On Nietzsche's enthusiastic reaction to the review, see in particular EH Books 1, and the letters sent to Ernst Wilhelm Fritzsch and to Widmann himself (24 and 28 June 1887, respectively). In the letter to Widmann, Nietzsche confessed that Widmann's review was 'by far the "most intelligent" review' that had been written on his 'unpleasant book' (Bf. to Josef Viktor Widmann, 28.06.1887, KGB III/5, Bf. 869). It is thus reasonable to assume that he essentially agreed with its content and, by implication, with Widmann's approach to the dangerous practical consequences of his philosophy.

safety, contentment, and an easier life for all' [BGE 44]) and that, on the contrary, every elevation and enhancement of the type "man" was to be obtained under dangerous and unstable conditions. As Nietzsche puts it: 'We think that harshness, violence, slavery, danger in the streets and in the heart, concealment, Stoicism, the art of experiment, and devilry of every sort; that everything evil, terrible, tyrannical, predatory, and snakelike in humanity serves just as well as its opposite to enhance the species "humanity"' (BGE 44). Thus, far from being ignorant of the fact that his philosophy was intellectual dynamite, Nietzsche purposely sought to bring about a crisis, hoping that humanity would benefit from it. As he prophetically puts it in *Ecce Homo:* 'I know my lot. One day my name will be connected with the memory of something tremendous, – a crisis such as the earth has never seen, the deepest collision of conscience, a decision made *against* everything that has been believed, demanded, held sacred so far. I am not a human being, I am dynamite' (EH Destiny 1).

5 Aestheticizing Murder

Unlike Rupert Cadell, Nietzsche did not have the occasion to see his theories 'put into practice', but one can speculate that he would have been appalled by the fraudulent use of his name made by Fascist and Nazi ideologues – just as he would likely have considered Brandon a bourgeois decadent, a typical nihilist only able to use his qualities for destructive, unproductive ends. An altogether different and more complex question is whether what happened in the twentieth century proves that Nietzsche was fundamentally wrong in desiring and even promoting an 'even more terrible flaring up of the old flame', that is, of the aristocratic ideal and its 'terrible and enchanting counter-slogan: *priority for the few!*' (GM I 16). Indeed, one could argue that as soon as we deny equal rights for everyone, as Nietzsche repeatedly did in his writings, the door stands open to injustice and, in the worst cases, to the most ignominious and repulsive acts.

This does not mean, however, that Nietzsche sanctioned criminal acts – either directly or indirectly. And if from the end of the nineteenth century the maxim 'nothing is true, everything is permitted' was mistakenly interpreted as summarizing the core of Nietzsche's philosophy – fostering an identification with Ivan Karamazov's aforementioned idea that, if there is no God and no immortality of the soul, then everything is permitted – this was only because the same maxim was taken out of its original context and its meaning distorted.[31]

---

[31] On this, see Stellino (2015, pp. 169–188). The maxim, which was the watchword of the Order

As early as 1936, Karl Jaspers warned Nietzsche scholars of the facility with which this maxim could be falsely interpreted. According to Jaspers, 'when removed from context, such a statement – often repeated by Nietzsche – is unintelligible.[32] Taken by itself it expresses complete lack of obligation; it is an invitation to individual caprice, sophistry, and criminality' (Jaspers 1966, p. 227).

Here lies the main difference between Nietzsche's overman and Dostoevsky's man-god. Both have as their precondition the death of God and the emergence of nihilism. However, whereas Dostoevsky understands the man-god as someone who is subject to no moral law and to whom everything is permitted, even crime – recall the devil's exclamation 'There is no law for God!' in the passage from *The Brothers Karamazov* quoted above (Dostoevsky 1992, p. 649)[33] – Nietzsche neither deifies his overman, as is often wrongly assumed,[34] nor grants him licence to lightheartedly ignore or break every moral law or social convention. On the contrary, far from understanding the new freedom deriving from the death of God as a complete lack and absence of moral and social norms, Nietzsche encourages his disciples not only to create new values and give new laws to themselves but also, and most importantly, to assume responsibility for this choice.[35] This is why Brandon's appropriation of Nietzsche's philosophy

---

of Assassins, an Islamic sect dating from the eleventh to the thirteenth century AD, appears twice in the published writings (Z IV The Shadow and GM III 24) and in a few posthumous fragments from the period from spring 1884 to winter 1884–85.

32 Even Jaspers, with the best of intentions, mistakenly claims that the maxim is often repeated by Nietzsche. On this, see n. 31.

33 It is precisely in this context that Cadell's questions to Brandon in the final monologue of Hitchcock's *Rope* must be understood: 'By what right did you dare decide that that boy in there was inferior and therefore could be killed? Did you think you were God, Brandon?' Cadell's reference to God is motivated not only by the fact that God has the right to dispose freely of human beings' lives, but also by the fact that He is the legislator of the moral law, thus having the privilege of defining what is morally good and bad.

34 See the following paradigmatic passage from *Zarathustra*'s speech *On the Blessed Isles*, in which Nietzsche makes clear (through the voice of Zarathustra) that he does not conceive of his superman as a Feuerbachian man-god: 'Once people said God when they gazed upon distant seas; but now I have taught you to say: overman. God is a conjecture, but I want that your conjecturing not reach further than your creating will. Could you *create* a god? – Then be silent about any gods! But you could well create the overman' (Z II Blessed Isles).

35 This is a key point, which Heidegger did not fail to notice, as the following passage clearly shows: 'It is easy but irresponsible to be outraged by the idea and the figure of the overman, which was designed to be misunderstood; it is easy but irresponsible to pretend that one's outrage is a refutation. It is difficult but for future thinking unavoidable to attain the *high responsibility* [*hohe Verantwortung*] out of which Nietzsche reflected on the essence of that humanity destined ... to undertake mastery over the earth. The essence of the overman is not a warrant

to justify gratuitous murder is fundamentally wrong, being nothing more than a grotesque and macabre distortion of his philosophy.

There is no denying that Nietzsche flirted with the idea of committing crimes. However, these crimes were not physical but *intellectual*, that is, linked to the smashing of the traditional idols of religion, metaphysics and morality. Similarly, if Nietzsche revaluated the criminal type in his writings, this was because he saw the delinquent as the bearer of active and healthy instincts, the prototype of the strong person, not because he thought that everything was permitted for him or that he enjoyed a right to crime.[36] In this sense, Joel Black's attempt to present Nietzsche as the essential link between De Quincey's provocative invitation to consider murder one of the fine arts, on the one hand, and the definitive aestheticization of murder in modernist literature and in twentieth-century cinema, on the other, must therefore be refuted or at least relativized. If Black is right to emphasize the importance, for the later aestheticization of murder, of Nietzsche's critique of morality and his liberation of art from the dominion of morality, he can nevertheless present Nietzsche as 'the figure in whose name the crime of murder has been rationalized and raised from merely passive aesthetic experience to outright epistemological pursuits, and ultimately, to pure, often outrageous, spontaneous action – a path that De Quincey, in turn, would have feared to tread' (Black 1991, p. 82) – only at the cost of overemphasizing the aesthetic component of his philosophy. Thus, for instance, Black claims that 'Nietzsche succeeded in aestheticizing philosophy itself once and for all' (Black 1991, p. 78) and that his 'synthesis of literature and philosophy' involves 'the ultimate subversion of ethics by aesthetics' (Black 1991, p. 122). Aestheticizing Nietzsche's philosophy is not per se novel (in fact, similar readings can be traced back to the Italian poet Gabriele D'Annunzio and to his very early reception of Nietzsche's thought in the 1890s), and it is beyond the scope of the present work to assess the plausibility of such readings. What should not be overlooked in this context, however, is that Black's reduction of ethics to aesthetics is central to his reading of Nietzsche as a key figure in the progressive tendency towards the aestheticization of murder in nineteenth- and twentieth-century European culture:

> by considering murder as an art form rather than as a moral transgression ... De Quincey unwittingly prefigured Nietzsche's radical subversion of Kant's – and everyone else's – ethical system by aesthetics. It remained for later writers like Dostoevsky and Gide to show

---

for a fit of capricious frenzy. It is the law, grounded in being itself, of a long chain of the highest selfovercomings' (Heidegger 2002, p. 189, emphasis added).

36 On Nietzsche's revaluation of the criminal, see, for instance, TI Raids 45.

that murder may not only be a moral transgression or an artistic performance, but can be considered a cognitive, and even a creative, act as well. (Black 1991, p. 123)

Setting aside the problematic character of the assumption that Nietzsche radically subverted Kant's and everyone else's ethical system by aesthetics, I should like to point out that there is undoubtedly a certain irony in the fact that, in Black's study, Nietzsche and Hitchcock are seen as different moments in a single progressive tendency towards the aestheticization of murder, that is, the conversion of a 'moral transgression into an amoral, aesthetic digression' (Black 1991, p. 111). The irony lies in the fact that the same critique that Hitchcock levelled against Nietzsche (that of handling dangerous ideas without realizing their pragmatic implications) can be levelled against Hitchcock – mutatis mutandis, of course, for both the dangerous ideas and the pragmatic implications are obviously very different in Nietzsche's and Hitchcock's case. Still, one may legitimately ask whether Hitchcock's aestheticized and often humorous approach to murder does not represent an irresponsible playing with dangerous moral ideas. Another legitimate question concerns the extent to which Hitchcock paved the way for and contributed to the later hyper-aestheticization of violence and murder in film and in television – a hyper-aestheticization which, as Black rightly points out, risks prompting mimetic behaviour on the part of the spectator.[37]

Whereas Nietzsche never treated murder as an aesthetic digression, this is what Hitchcock repeatedly did both in his interviews – in an article published in 1958, for example, he sarcastically expresses regret that 'murder as a fine art ... has declined in recent years' (Gottlieb 2015, p. 87) – and in his films – think, for instance, of Joe and Herb's conversations about the perfect murder in *Shadow of a Doubt* (1943). In a talk delivered in 1965, Hitchcock also described De Quincey's *On Murder Considered as One of the Fine Arts* as a 'delightful essay' (Gottlieb 1997, p. 58). As Black points out in the introduction to his study, 'Alfred Hitchcock's films provide the most obvious examples of the degree to which the cinematic medium exploits the specifically artistic dimension of murder' (Black 1991, p. 17). With regard to Hitchcock's aestheticization of murder, *Rope* clearly plays a prominent role in his filmography, for it is in this film that De Quincey's suggestion that murder is an art finds its most explicit and powerful expression. If we consider that this theory indirectly provides the rationale for the murder just as much as Nietzsche's theory of the overman does (in its distorted form), then there is again a certain irony in the fact that if it is possible to read Rupert

---

[37] See, in particular, the second part of his study on the aesthetics of murder (1991).

Cadell as Nietzsche's double, as Gentili (2018, p. 262) suggests, then it is also possible to see Brandon as Hitchcock's surrogate, as Thomas M. Bauso argues (Bauso 1991). In fact, Hitchcock manipulates his audience just as Brandon manipulates both his guests and Phillip. Furthermore, 'that Brandon is Hitchcock's surrogate is also demonstrated by their common delight in perverse wit and in the unremitting pursuit of technical challenges that will finally enhance their works of "art"' (Bauso 1991, p. 231). Even Cadell's rhetorical question to Brandon in the final monologue (whether he thought he was God in taking the life of a fellow human being) facilitates the reading of Brandon as Hitchcock's surrogate – for, as Hitchcock famously claimed, 'in the fiction film the director is god' (Truffaut 1985, p. 102).

Nietzsche and Hitchcock as partners in crime: is this the paradoxical conclusion we ought to draw from *Rope*? Even worse, in providing us, the audience, from the very beginning of the film with information that the other characters (except the murderers) do not have, Hitchcock implicates us in the performance of the crime. As Bauso puts it: 'our mere knowledge establishes our complicity in the crime, and more importantly, it sets us up as an appreciative audience for the continuous flow of double entendres and "malicious" witticisms that swirl around the fact of David's death' (Bauso 1991, p. 233). We get Brandon's morbid jokes, and we cannot help laughing at them, becoming all the more implicated in the murder. *Incipit tragoedia*, as Nietzsche wrote, but also *incipit parodia*.[38] Manipulated by Hitchcock the director-god (just as the unaware party guests are manipulated by Brandon), we find ourselves entrapped in *Rope*, partners in a crime we would never have thought of committing ourselves – let alone enjoying.[39]

Bibliography

Adair, Gene (2002): *Alfred Hitchcock: Filming Our Fears*. New York: Oxford University Press.
Baatz, Simon (2009): *For the Thrill of It: Leopold, Loeb, and the Murder That Shocked Jazz Age Chicago*. New York: Harper Perennial.
Barrios, Richard (2003): *Screened Out: Playing Gay in Hollywood from Edison to Stonewall*. New York, London: Routledge.
Bauso, Thomas M. (1991): "*Rope*: Hitchcock's Unkindest Cut". In: Walter Raubichek and Walter Skrebnick (Eds.): *Hitchcock's Re-Released Films*. Detroit: Wayne State University Press, pp. 226–239.

---

[38] See GS Preface 1.
[39] This work was funded by national funds through the FCT – Fundação para a Ciência e a Tecnologia, I.P. – under the Norma Transitória – DL 57/2016/CP1453/CT0010.

Biderman, Shai, and Eliana Jacobowitz (2007): "*Rope:* Nietzsche and the Art of Murder". In: David Baggett and William A. Drumin (Eds.): *Hitchcock and Philosophy: Dial M for Metaphysics.* Chicago, La Salle: Open Court.
Black, Joel (1991): *The Aesthetics of Murder: A Study in Romantic Literature and Contemporary Culture.* Baltimore, London: The Johns Hopkins University Press.
De Lubac, Henri (1995): *The Drama of Atheist Humanism.* San Francisco: Ignatius Press.
De Quincey, Thomas (2006): *On Murder.* Oxford: Oxford University Press.
Diethe, Carol (1992): "Nietzsche and Nationalism". In: *History of European Ideas* 14. No. 2, pp. 227–234.
Domenech, Jacques (1989): *L'éthique des lumières : Les fondements de la morale dans la philosophie française du XVIIIe siècle.* Paris: Vrin.
Dostoevsky, Fyodor (1992): *The Brothers Karamazov.* New York: Vintage Books.
Dostoevsky, Fyodor (1993): *Crime and Punishment.* New York: Vintage Books.
Drochon, Hugo (2016): *Nietzsche's Great Politics.* Princeton, Oxford: Princeton University Press.
Gentili, Carlo (2018): "Friedrich Nietzsche e Rupert Cadell. Sull'obbligatorietà delle regole". In: Luca Renzi (Ed.): *Arte e scienza: Kunst und Wissenschaft.* Stuttgart: Franz Steiner Verlag, pp. 261–267.
Gide, André (2009): *Romans et récits. Œuvres lyriques et dramatiques,* vol. 1. Paris: Gallimard.
Gilman, Sander L. (1983): "The Nietzsche Murder Case". In: *New Literary History* 14. No. 2, pp. 359–372.
Glenn, Paul F. (2001): "Nietzsche's Napoleon: The Higher Man as Political Actor". In: *The Review of Politics* 63. No. 1, pp. 129–158.
Golomb, Jacob, and Robert S. Wistrich (Eds.) (2002): *Nietzsche, Godfather of Fascism? On the Uses and Abuses of a Philosophy.* Princeton: Princeton University Press.
Gottlieb, Sidney (Ed.) (1997): *Hitchcock on Hitchcock: Selected Writings and Interviews,* vol. 1. Berkeley: University of California Press.
Gottlieb, Sidney (Ed.) (2015): *Hitchcock on Hitchcock: Selected Writings and Interviews,* vol. 2. Oakland: University of California Press.
Grillaert, Nel (2008): *What the God-Seekers Found in Nietzsche: The Reception of Nietzsche's Übermensch by the Philosophers of the Russian Religious Renaissance.* Amsterdam, New York: Rodopi.
Hamilton, Patrick (2009): *Rope: A Play.* London: Samuel French.
Heidegger, Martin (2002): "Nietzsche's Word: 'God Is Dead.'". In: Heidegger, *Off the Beaten Track.* Cambridge: Cambridge University Press, pp. 157–199.
Hemmeter, Thomas (2011): "Hitchcock's Narrative Modernism: Ironies of Fictional Time". In: Thomas Leitch and Leland Poague (Eds.): *A Companion to Alfred Hitchcock.* Malden: Wiley-Blackwell, pp. 67–85.
Jacobi, Friedrich H. (2003): "Open Letter to Fichte". In: Ernst Behler (Ed.): *Philosophy of Idealism.* New York: Continuum, pp. 119–141.
Jaspers, Karl (1966): *Nietzsche: An Introduction to the Understanding of His Philosophical Activity.* Tucson: University of Arizona Press.
Kaufmann, Walter (1974): *Nietzsche. Philosopher, Psychologist, Antichrist.* Princeton: Princeton University Press.

Kehr, Dave (2011): "Hitch's Riddle: On Five Rereleased Films". In: *When Movies Mattered: Reviews from a Transformative Decade*. Dave Kehr. Chicago, London: The University of Chicago Press, pp. 247–263.
Kofman, Sarah (1994) : *Le mépris des juifs: Nietzsche, les juifs, l'antisémitisme*. Paris: Galilée.
Levin, Meyer (2014): *Compulsion*. Bedford: Fig Tree Books.
Lewy, Guenter (2008). *If God Is Dead, Everything Is Permitted?* London, New York: Routledge.
Löwith, Karl (1995): "European Nihilism". In: Richard Wolin (Ed.): *Martin Heidegger and European Nihilism*. New York: Columbia University Press, pp. 192–209.
McGilligan, Patrick (2003): *Alfred Hitchcock: A Life in Darkness and Light*. New York: Regan Books.
Mussolini, Benito (1956): "Vivere pericolosamente". In: Edoardo Susmel and Duilio Susmel (Eds.): *Opera Omnia di Benito Mussolini*, vol. XXI. Florence: La Fenice, pp. 37–40.
Nietzsche, Friedrich (1968): *The Will to Power*. Edited and translated by Walter Kaufmann. New York: Vintage Books.
Nietzsche, Friedrich (1996): *Human, All Too Human*. Translated by Reginald J. Hollingdale. Cambridge: Cambridge University Press.
Nietzsche, Friedrich (1998): *Twilight of the Idols*. Translated by Duncan Large. Oxford: Oxford University Press.
Nietzsche, Friedrich (2001): *The Gay Science*. Translated by Josephine Nauckhoff. Cambridge: Cambridge University Press.
Nietzsche, Friedrich (2002): *Beyond Good and Evil*. Translated by Judith Norman. Cambridge: Cambridge University Press.
Nietzsche, Friedrich (2005): *The Anti-Christ, Ecce Homo, Twilight of the Idols, and Other Writings*. Translated by Judith Norman. Cambridge: Cambridge University Press.
Nietzsche, Friedrich (2006): *Thus Spoke Zarathustra*. Translated by Adrian del Caro. Cambridge: Cambridge University Press.
Nietzsche, Friedrich (2006): *On the Genealogy of Morality*. Translated by Carol Diethe. Cambridge: Cambridge University Press.
Stellino, Paolo (2015): *Nietzsche and Dostoevsky: On the Verge of Nihilism*. Bern: Peter Lang.
Stellino, Paolo (2017): "Nietzsche and the Responsibility of Intellectuals". In: Ekaterina Poljakova and Yulia V. Sineokaya (Eds.): *Friedrich Nietzsche: Legacy and Prospects*. Moscow: LRC, pp. 467–477.
Truffaut, François (1985): *Hitchcock*. Rev. ed. New York: Touchstone.
Widmann, Joseph V. (2000): "Nietzsche's Dangerous Book". In: *New Nietzsche Studies* 4. No. 1/2, pp. 195–200.
Wood, Robin (1989): *Hitchcock's Films Revisited*. New York: Columbia University Press.
Yovel, Yirmiyahu (2006): "Nietzsche and the Jews: The Structure of an Ambivalence". In: Christa D. Acampora (Ed.): *Nietzsche's* On the Genealogy of Morals. Lanham: Rowman & Littlefield, pp. 277–289.

Filmography

Bernstein, Sidney, director. (1945/1984): *Memory of the Camps*.
Hitchcock, Alfred, director. (1943): *Shadow of a Doubt*.
Hitchcock, Alfred, director. (1944): *Lifeboat*.
Hitchcock, Alfred, director. (1946): *Notorious*.
Hitchcock, Alfred, director. (1948): *Rope*.
Hitchcock, Alfred, director. (1951): *Strangers on a Train*.
Hitchcock, Alfred, director. (1954): *Dial M for Murder*.
Sokurov, Aleksandr, director. (2002): *Russian Ark*.

Kevin Stoehr
Nihilism, Violence, and the Films of Michael Haneke

Abstract: This essay adopts a Nietzschean perspective in exploring intersections between nihilism and violence in the films of Michael Haneke, one of our most respected and discussed living film directors. Haneke's own essay "Violence and the Media" points to the nihilistic danger of passive spectatorship due to the saturation of violence in film, television, and social media. In his own films, Haneke seeks to combat that tendency by using certain self-reflexive techniques and narrative elements that hopefully make the viewer aware of her own role as a spectator. He does so by making the mediation of violence thematic as well as by presenting ambiguities or dilemmas that summon the moral engagement of the audience. The films discussed in this essay include *The Seventh Continent*, *Benny's Video*, *Funny Games*, *Time of the Wolf*, *Code Unknown*, *Caché*, *The Piano Teacher*, *The White Ribbon*, *Amour*, and *Happy End*.

1 Introduction

Michael Haneke has created a series of powerful cinematic works that explore the capacities of human beings to indulge in apathy, violence, injustice, and absurdity. However, this does not make Haneke or his films inherently nihilistic. By virtue of his very desire to make such films on a consistent basis, Haneke reveals the problems of both violence and nihilism in modern society and, like the philosopher Friedrich Nietzsche, seeks to point beyond these problems. Nietzsche's distinction between positive and negative forms of nihilism helps to clarify the director's overall moral vision. Much has already been published on violence and nihilism in Haneke's films, though these themes are often discussed separately. And more than several Haneke scholars have written on the director's "self-reflexive" strategies for evoking the viewer's reflection on these themes. This essay seeks to clarify the connections between nihilism and violence in his works and, most of all, to show how a Nietzschean perspective can help us to understand Haneke's overall anti-nihilism. This is especially the case when, while viewing his films, we witness violence that either results from or leads to loss of faith in fundamental values. Such values—including the values of freedom, truth, and life itself—help to anchor, orient, and hopefully enhance our existence amidst a world of flux and contingency.

Haneke's films typically demonstrate violence as a symptom of nihilism, though on occasion violence is also shown to be a cause, especially by way of the sense of indignation or injustice that can arise from violent acts. This filmmaker compels us to acknowledge the ugly truth of human reality and the ever-present possibility of falling into moral passivity, detached indifference, and even self-destruction. As Haneke once said in an interview:

> I think it can hardly be denied that each fictional story, no matter how cryptic or horrible, is a trifle compared with the horror that strikes against us in reality. In order to see this, one must not be a pessimist—it suffices if one is simply more-or-less awake.... What is positive can only be the merciless demand for personal truthfulness. Only: The truth is no longer beautiful. As Nietzsche already said in the past century: "For a philosopher it is an indignity to say that the Good and the Beautiful are the same. And if he should add 'the True,' one should clobber him. The truth is ugly." (Grabner and Haneke, 2008, pp. 12–13, my translation)

Or as Haneke said in a more recent interview:

> I always say I'm a realist.... But of course that's not enough in itself. You have to have hope in your private life, or in society—if you're a pessimist, it's a useless thing to be. But just hoping is insufficient. You have to believe that you can move people, or change people, or making the works would be completely useless. All artists are bound to believe in that. (Hasted 2017, para. 7)

More than a few Haneke scholars have pointed to this underlying hope and optimism, despite what appears at first glance to be a body of work driven by an obsessive sense of despair. For example, in her book *Michael Haneke's Cinema: The Ethic of the Image*, Catherine Wheatley explores the ways in which the director compels the thoughtful viewer to reflect on the morality of her own film spectatorship—and especially when the contents of the viewing experience include negative aspects of our psychology, ones with which we should reckon. In this sense, Haneke provides an occasion for moral self-reflection, a counter to the type of despair experienced by many of his characters (and especially in the face of violence). As Wheatley summarizes her argument in a separate essay:

> In my own book on Haneke, and again in a number of articles, I have posited that both the content and form of the director's work are shaped by a concern with the ethics of dominant film-viewing practices.... In this way, I have argued, the films are able to make their spectators aware of certain desires and motivations that may be less than admirable. (Wheatley 2011, pp. 10–11)

When focusing on the two versions of *Funny Games*, for example, Wheatley writes that Haneke, in both the original and American re-make, creates a "tension between a pleasurable absorption in the film's narrative and unpleasurable awareness of the film's constructedness" (Wheatley 2011, p. 11). Such a tension provides Brechtian distance between the viewer's immersion in the story and her awareness of being a viewer, resulting in the opportunity for evolving moral reflection and judgment about the contents of the film. This can save us from the type of nihilistic leveling of narrative content, and especially content involving violence, that Haneke warns about in his essay "Violence and the Media."[1]

In a similar vein, the co-editors of the collection *The Cinema of Michael Haneke: Europe Utopia* (2011), Ben McCann and David Sorfa, suggest in their Introduction that Haneke's aim is to point beyond the darkness that he so meticulously depicts in his films:

> In the cinema of Michael Haneke, there is a dystopian view of his own practice as a filmmaker just as much as there is one of the general functioning of contemporary society. And yet there is something in this almost nihilistic analysis that allows us to consider the possibility of future in which this terrible and (almost) inescapable guilt might not necessarily be true. It is this contingent and unlikely future that we find in Haneke. We find in his films a vision of Europe Utopia. (McCann and Sorfa 2011, p. 5)

One essay in their collection that explicitly supports such an approach is Lisa Coulthard's "Ethical Violence: Suicide as Authentic Act in the Films of Michael Haneke." She views acts (or at least temptations) of self-destruction in his works as occasions for possible breakthroughs in moral reflection, ones that can lead to positive life-transformation. In this sense, her essay nicely complements Wheatley's above-mentioned argument about the ethics of spectatorship. As Coulthard states, "Haneke's ethical violence stresses effects, not causes, and asks how we respond to the territories and consequences opened up by extreme acts" (Coulthard 2011, p. 48). According to such approaches, Haneke plunges us into extreme dramatic situations that engender violence and even nihilism on

---

[1] Wheatley's essay "Domestic Invasion: Michael Haneke and Home Invasion" centers on the ways in which the contemporary trend toward viewing films at home can complicate her original argument (in her book *Michael Haneke's Cinema*). This is especially due to the fact that our emotional absorption in the film narrative can be further disrupted by our own technical ability to manipulate the viewing experience (via the functions of pausing, re-winding, fast-forwarding, etc.). However, Wheatley ultimately argues that Haneke's "critical aesthetic," while "attenuated" during the home viewing experience, is not essentially undermined (Wheatley 2011, p. 19).

the part of the characters but, for the viewer, he uses certain strategies to convert our passive film-watching into ethical and self-reflective spectatorship.[2]

2 Nietzsche, Nihilism, and Haneke's Strategies

Haneke combats nihilism in a Nietzschean manner, but it is important to recognize the type of nihilism that he combats. Nietzsche viewed nihilism in general as the chief problem of the modern age—but a necessary one, given the development of the Platonic-Christian tradition. While Nietzsche addresses the idea of nihilism in various works, and most especially in *Thus Spoke Zarathustra*, some of his most illuminating writings on the subject appear among his unpublished notes that were later published in the collection titled *The Will to Power*. In a fragment at the very beginning of Book One (European Nihilism) in that collection, Nietzsche defines nihilism as follows: "What does nihilism mean?—*That the highest values devaluate themselves*. The aim is missing; 'Why?' finds no answer" (NL 1887, 9[35], KSA 12, p. 350). He tells us in another fragment from that same collection:

> A nihilist is a man who judges of the world as it is that it ought *not* to be, and of the world as it ought to be that it does not exist. According to this view, our existence (action, suffering, willing, feeling) has no meaning: the pathos of 'in vain' is the nihilists' pathos—at the same time, as pathos, an inconsistency on the part of the nihilists.
> (NL 1887, 9[60], KSA 12, p. 366)

A consistent and genuine nihilist would presumably overcome the feelings of empathy, sorrow, and disappointment associated with the rejection or negation involved here.

Once we start to doubt the idea of some objective moral structure underlying our existence, we may also begin to undermine the very threads that seem to hold our lives together. As Nietzsche tells us in another unpublished fragment: "Skepticism regarding morality is what is decisive. The end of the moral inter-

---

[2] Other essays that point to the presence of an underlying optimism and concern with the cultivation of ethical self-awareness (or "moral spectatorship") in Haneke's work, even if such a positive lesson is presented ambiguously in many of his films, include David Sorfa's essay "Uneasy domesticity in the films of Michael Haneke" (Sorfa 2006), Alex Gerbaz's "The Ethical Screen: *Funny Games* and the Spectacle of Pain" (Gerbaz 2011), Nemonie Craven Roderick's "Subject to Memory? Thinking after *Hidden*" (Roderick 2011), Tarja Laine's "Hidden Shame Exposed: *Hidden* and the Spectator" (Laine 2011), and John Orr's "*The White Ribbon* in Michael Haneke's Cinema" (Orr 2011).

pretation of the world, which no longer has any sanction after it has tried to escape into some beyond, leads to nihilism. 'Everything lacks meaning'" (NL 1887, 2[127], KSA 12, p. 126). Skeptical doubt can easily turn into indignation, non-belief, and rejection if it is driven far enough, especially in the wake of crises and other extreme experiences. And our loss of conviction in certain basic orienting values can then result in acts of violence toward others and toward ourselves, acts that express a negation of the values that have traditionally defined us as individuals living within a society of persons. On the flip side of the coin, our experience of extreme violence may shatter our personal value system to such a degree that we fall into a sense of general life-negation, one that can easily produce further violence.

According to Nietzsche, nihilism in general may be evoked by a loss of faith in unconditional ideals (religious or secular) and this can result in indignation toward that which is non-ideal (i.e. the earthly or perceived world along with the transience and finitude of human existence). But the crux of Nietzsche's teaching is that nihilism can also be viewed in a *positive* manner—as the necessary occasion for the emergence of a type of self-enhancing individuality that nonetheless accepts its limitations and transience. So, while nihilism *in general* expresses a basic loss of conviction in conventional and traditional values, Nietzsche also draws a clear distinction between negative and positive responses to this loss of faith. On the one hand, he tells us that passive or negative ("incomplete," "pathological") nihilism is a rejection of seemingly fixed values and institutions without the self-affirming spiritedness that allows one to become a creative individual. On the other hand, *active* or *positive* ("complete," "healthy") nihilism is the initiation of becoming a creative individual while rising above mere life-negation. As Nietzsche tells us in a further fragment of his unpublished writings: "Nihilism. It is *ambiguous:* A. Nihilism as a sign of increased power of the spirit: as *active* nihilism ... B. Nihilism as decline and recession of the power of the spirit: as *passive* nihilism" (NL 1887, 9[35], KSA 12, pp. 350–351). And so, when we speak of nihilism, we should recognize whether we are speaking of nihilism in general (as a general collapse of faith in traditional ideals and conventional values) or of a particular form of nihilism (i.e. as an active *or* passive reaction to such a loss of conviction).

Many of Haneke's films tend to depict passive or pathological forms of nihilism as a danger. These movies often evoke the kind of emotional estrangement that is engendered by the impersonal conditions and forces of a modern consumer society. Furthermore, more than a few of his movies illustrate the ways in which our inauthentic or apathetic responses to the contemporary world can lead to violence against others and ultimately against ourselves. Violence is presented in his films at times through the filter of the media (e.g. video recordings and TV news clips) so that we might reflect on the ways in which human aggression becomes conventionalized and even trivialized. Haneke has been especially interested in the ways in which violence is represented, not merely in cinema but also on television and through social media. And in his essay "Violence and Media," the director ponders how the rivalry between film and television has produced such an increasing saturation of represented violence that *content no longer seems to matter* to spectacle-obsessed audiences. The recurring flood of media-represented violence, then, leads to a type of nihilism about the very value of what we are watching—and above all, an outright lack of moral concern about the reasons why we are watching it.

In his recent film *Happy End* (2017), there is a poignant scene in which a declining (both mentally and physically) grandfather (Jean-Louis Trintignant) converses quietly with his troubled granddaughter (Fantine Harduin). After they share a few secrets about violent events in their pasts, the old man tells her that he was looking out the window a few days before and witnessed a hostile bird of prey attacking a smaller bird and then pulverizing it into a cloud of feathers. The grandfather then observes, reflecting back, that such events seem "almost normal" when we see them on television but, when we experience them in real life, they become extraordinary. Here we clearly see a recent example of Haneke's recurring concern with the ways in which violence can be softened, distorted, and "normalized" through certain kinds of media representation. (Haneke 2017)

As Haneke theorizes in his essay on this theme, the ways in which the media manipulate the image of violence may lead some to the false hope that violence can be likewise controlled in real life. But the increasing desire for more advanced forms of represented violence, whether for escape or curiosity or catharsis or all three combined, can lead to a type of disoriented embeddedness in such an artificial realm. This may then result in a nihilistic disregard of the moral value of what is being represented. This is especially true when we learn to substitute the significance of violence in the real world with artificially, technologically mediated forms of the same. Haneke tells us in this essay, in reference to the increasing depiction of violence over the course of the history of film and television:

> Violence became domesticated in its image and the pleasant chill of horror administered in homeopathic dosages was quite welcome. The controlled invocation of evil permitted the hope for its controllability in reality... . [F]or the sake of constantly increasing the impact of form, content has become an interchangeable variable.... The *absolute equivalency of all the contents* stripped of their reality ensures the universal fictionality of anything shown .... The question—limited to the topic of VIOLENCE—is not: "How do I show vio-

lence?" but rather: "How do I show the viewer his own position vis-à-vis violence and its portrayal?" (Haneke 2010, pp. 578–579)

Haneke seeks to combat the tendency toward the hyper-mediation of violence in a way that summons the thoughtful viewer to active reflection on the mediation itself (along with its potential psychological, moral, and even spiritual effects) and especially on the content of what is being represented. He does so in two basic ways. First, as mentioned previously in terms of recent scholarship, his films present violence in a way that meta-reflexively calls attention to the form of representation along with the viewer's participation in the experience of that representation, thus giving the audience "space" for reflection on the question of how violence is being represented. This is clear in *Happy End*, for example, and it occurs in several places in the movie. At the outset, we witness a woman in a bathroom and then a guinea pig in a cage, both presented through the narrow screen of a cell phone camera. Directly thereafter we witness a fatal accident at a construction site through the perspective of a security camera that has a time counter in the upper righthand corner of the screen. Later we become privy several times to a secret and highly erotic email correspondence through a social medium called "x3chat," as we can see when Haneke presents the electronic chat just as his characters see it. And at the very end of the film, a young girl pulls out her cell phone to record the attempted suicide of her grandfather, a suicide in which she has assisted, and we see the event occur as the girl sees it: through her cell phone screen. (Haneke 2017) In all of these cases, Haneke calls clear attention to the form of the representation. This same technique of self-reflexive consciousness-raising is evident in many of his earlier films: for example, the emphasis on the use of video in *Benny's Video* (1992) and *Caché* (2005).

And so Haneke seeks to trigger the viewer's awareness of the filmic mediation of violence so that we can then consider our own participation in this representation—and, ultimately, the moral value of our very choice and desire to watch it. It is this intention of producing self-awareness and ethical self-reflection that signals an anti-nihilistic stance on the part of the director. But there is a related way in which Haneke provokes reflection on the intersections between nihilism and violence. Some of his movies present narratives (almost always scripted by himself) that summon the viewer to make a personal moral judgment because the content and context of the filmic violence raise questions due to ambiguity and ambivalence. The remainder of this essay focuses chiefly on this latter strategy and discusses examples from Haneke's films that can evoke reflection on three basic forms of passive nihilism, ones that are connected with violence: the loss of faith in the three fundamental values of freedom, truth, and life itself.³

3 Violence and the Value of Freedom

One of the basic causes of a descent into pathological nihilism is the refusal to recognize and exercise one's inherent freedom to transform one's life. If anything, Nietzsche's critique of a herd-like slave-morality, along with his rejection of passive nihilism, emphasizes the choice that humans can make in asserting their individuality. On the one hand, slave-type personalities suffer anxiety or despair at the burden of responsibility that is entailed by the idea of their own inherent autonomy; they would rather live more comfortably, without such a burden, by conforming to others' values and expectations. Passive nihilists, on the other hand, use their autonomy to deny the intrinsic value of everything, including themselves, and therefore they reject the use of their freedom for any life-enhancing purposes.

Slave-morality and pathological nihilism can also be viewed as two different negative responses to one's psychological inability to cope with life's transience along with the inevitability of the past. This inability entails a failure to appreciate the opportunity of the conditioned moment, despite its contingency, in transforming the legacy of the past as an act of one's inherent, life-affirming freedom. As Nietzsche's character Zarathustra tells us in Part Two of *Thus Spoke Zarathustra*:

> To redeem those who lived in the past and to recreate all 'it was' into a 'thus I willed it'— that alone should I call redemption ... But now learn this too: the will itself is still a prisoner. Willing liberates; but what is it that puts even the liberator himself in fetters? 'It was'— that is the name of the will's gnashing of teeth and most secret melancholy. Powerless against what has been done, he is an angry spectator of all that is past.
> (Z 2 Redemption).

---

3 In her essay "How to Do Things with Violences," Eugenie Brinkema explores Haneke's early film *Benny's Video* (1992). Brinkema suggests a way to interpret the movie's representations of violence that rejects the typical "metaphysical" opposition between truth/reality and appearance. Taking as her departure point Jean-Luc Nancy's work on images and violence, she interprets the movie as showing how the image can itself be viewed as an instance of violence (broadly construed) rather than as merely the imitation of real-world violence (Brinkema 2010).

Nietzsche suggests two possible negative responses that one can make in the face of the irreversibility of the past: either "revenge" against the past or "weariness" in the face of the determinism of time.

Several of Haneke's films depict characters who express these types of weakness in trying to come to terms with their own freedom, especially in reference to how their past lives have shaped them. These movies present situations in which characters suffer from a feeling of malaise that is bred by the refusal to live a self-determined life. A repression of one's own autonomy and self-responsibility engenders the specter of slavish conformism and moral passivity and may in fact drive certain individuals to a loss of conviction in *any* values, leading to the overall attitude that *nothing* has intrinsic value, including one's own being. The rejection of one's own autonomy is a negative use of freedom that rules out alternative possibilities that are individualizing and life-enhancing. Furthermore, such self-repression can lead at times to violence, including violence against oneself, once enough resentment or guilt or self-loathing has accumulated through habitual decisions to limit or negate one's true instincts and desires.

In Haneke's first feature film *The Seventh Continent* (*Der siebente Continent* [1989]), a family is led to a horrifying act of self-destruction after suffering the deadening effects of an overly routine, conventional existence. They are too weak or indifferent to forge a new way of life or set of values, and so the only "rebellion" that they dare to undertake is that of total life-negation. They are gradually led to a violent reaction to the wearisome repetition that has arisen from the monotonous passage of their everyday existence. Even the parents' process of preparing for their act of collective suicide becomes methodical and robotic. Their only life-transforming act of freedom is to end their freedom and existence altogether. *The Seventh Continent* is based on the real-life story of a German family whose members committed such a gruesome act of shared suicide. Haneke intentionally focuses on scenes of recurring bourgeois boredom to evoke in the viewer a similar sense of gloom. Everything remains overly calm, cool, and conventional on the surface—and maddeningly so—until the climactic decision and its aftermath. Above all, it is the director's use of a delaying, meditative tempo that builds a sense of brooding unease. And, due in large part to the couple's own existential choices, they do not seem to know how to *fill* their time with the kind of meaning and purpose that would affirm the value of their lives. They can only dream of a distant place to which they might escape (as shown by recurring shots of a surreal beachscape which may symbolize tranquility as well as death). They have become imprisoned in the de-humanizing routine of mainstream suburban existence and their existential response is an eventual act of "revenge" against their own weary, detached lives—and taking along their young child, sadly. (Haneke 1989)

The audience is certainly prompted to condemn Georg (Dieter Berner) and Anna (Birgit Doll) by the ending of the film, especially given the forced involvement of their daughter Evi (Leni Tanzer) in such a pathetic scheme. And yet the very bleakness of the movie prompts questions that potentially call upon the viewer to reflect upon her participation in this viewing experience. What are the moral implications in having chosen to watch this sordid tale in which the dreary, troubling lives of the characters become mirrored by the dreary, troubling ritual of the movie-watching itself? What compels the viewer to continue watching such a film and what does such compulsion entail? If we fault the parents for having refused to exercise their freedom in changing their lives for the better—at the very least for the sake of Evi—then what changes will we make in our own lives after viewing the film? It is not the type of movie that allows the thoughtful spectator to remain a merely passive spectator without some queasiness about what this passive spectatorship entails. Haneke leaves moral judgment to the audience by choosing to focus only on the actions of his characters and refusing to include any explanations of the causes or motives behind their actions. He states in an interview about the movie:

> I tried to tell this story without giving any answers.... And it's up to the viewer to find his own answers .... The interest of the viewer always comes from the precision of what's shown.... The goal is to be precise enough in the details that the viewer, on account of this precision in the details, takes an interest in the people who are doing it.... I always try to find ambiguous solutions. (Toubiana, 2005)

In *The Piano Teacher* (*La Pianiste* [2001]), based on the novel by Elfriede Jelinek, the title character Erika (Isabelle Huppert) commits acts of sadomasochism after having devoted herself obsessively to her musical career as well as to her dominating mother. One can assume that she has had every chance to realize her freedom. But she has been shaped by her past: her mother is clearly controlling and Erika at one point refers to her father as having died at the Viennese Steinhof asylum after going mad. Her self-repressive behavior has stunted her life in a way that deprives her of any healthy and mature relationships. Her only outlets from such a life of self-denial take the form of self-punishment and self-abasement. These outlets, especially in terms of the turbulent relationship that she forms with the student Walter (Benoît Magimel), involve acts of momentary physical pleasure that undermine the path of a more fulfilling and mature life, one in which healthier freedom might flourish. In the potent final scene, her sudden and disturbing act of self-mutilation is the physical expression of her own longstanding impulse toward psychological self-harm. (Haneke, 2001)

The Piano Teacher draws the viewer into a troublesome emotional alignment with Erika and, in being both mesmerized and repulsed by her personality, the viewer senses a fair degree of moral ambivalence that summons a judgment about her morality—and perhaps our own. The viewer might feel disturbed by her visits to pornography shops where she watches sex videos and pleasures herself in an almost pathetic manner, and yet we find ourselves choosing to continue watching her. And as her sadomasochistic relationship with Walter unfolds, we continue observing as interested voyeurs. The writer-director has designed things so that we are provoked to reflect on our own participation as fascinated viewers of a deeply unhappy life.

One of the most controversial scenes in *The Piano Teacher* involves a dramatic act of sexual aggression against Erika by her student-lover Walter. On the surface, it is most clearly a rape scene. But as Jean Ma points out in an essay, Haneke complicates the scene and in a way that involves the idea of repressed freedom. Erika's seemingly paradoxical choice to deny her own freedom is contextualized by the story's emphasis on music and the teaching of music (Erika's passion and profession, respectively). This is because, just as a student submits to a teacher's authority and just as a musician's performance is dictated to a large degree by the composer's creative decisions, so does Walter's assault result partly from Erika's own instructions (given to him in a letter the day before) that explain how he is to bind, blindfold, gag, punch, and humiliate her. In other words, Walter's "rape" of Erika seems to be in accord with her own detailed and communicated fantasy. (Haneke, 2001) The act of sexual assault is still a deplorable act of violence and domination, but as Ma emphasizes, the context of the act invites moral questions. Ma points in a nuanced way to this intended ambiguity by also reflecting on the ways in which Erika has, throughout her career as both teacher and musician, exerted authority as disciplinarian over her students while subjecting herself to an almost masochistic life of discipline and sacrifice, one that "requires a negation of the will of the performer" (Ma 2010, p. 518). She has also subordinated herself to a domineering mother (Annie Girardot). Referencing Deleuze's essay "Coldness and Cruelty," Ma explores the ways in which Erika's expressions of masochism (both lived and imagined) should not be understood as mere sexual aberration; rather, her acts of self-punishment and even self-mutilation should be put into context as possibly the extension of the ways in which subjection and sacrifice have become "normalized" in her life. As Ma states after citing Deleuze:

> Such an account of masochism is striking for the way that it undermines the confidence with which we can define perverse or deviant sexuality in opposition to a norm, calling attention to the reverberations of normalized forms of violence within the realms of fantasy and desire. In *La Pianiste* we can begin to see how the ordinary world it portrays takes on a menacing cast when glimpsed through the reflecting lens of Erika's masochism, as it draws

to the surface the subtle forms of coercion coursing through the interactions of men and women to reveal a ubiquitous undercurrent of everyday violence. (Ma 2010, pp. 522–523)

The violence here becomes problematized for any reflective viewer and its representation calls for moral questioning and engagement.

4 Violence and the Value of Truth

Violence can also be a possible consequence of the will to deny, omit, or conceal the truth. This can take the form of the destructive (or even self-destructive) reaction of one person to another who has been untruthful. It can also be a violent response that expresses the forsaking of truth in general, as an act of sheer irrationality. Such acts of violence result from a nihilistic rejection of the value of truth, a rejection that forces us to subvert the stability and intelligibility of our lives. Our experience of this kind of irrationality forces us to confront the "horror of the void" since we immediately lose faith in the idea of any permanent foundations or unconditional guarantees. Haneke often emphasizes this type of nihilistic horror: our fear, not of some specific object or threat, but rather of the very emptiness that pervades our existence when the bedrock faith in the value of truth has been surrendered. Nihilistic horror may be evoked when there is an attempt at rational dialogue but where that attempt is resisted in a way that indicates no desire for mutual understanding. The violence in Haneke's films is most terrifying, not merely when it is unexpected and almost casual, but when the very will to rationalize or negotiate is condemned. By rejecting the need for truthfulness or truth-acquisition as an end-in-itself in our everyday lives, communication becomes a mere game at best. The negation of the value of truth itself as the basis of rational discourse may lead to a pathological form of life-denial because all moral propositions and beliefs become meaningless.

In Haneke's *Funny Games* (1997) and his American re-make of this film (2007), violence becomes a horrifying game played for senseless kicks, representing an encounter between civilized rationality and savage irrationality. This occurs in *Funny Games*, for example, when the father (Ulrich Mühe) asks the young antagonists (Arno Frisch and Frank Giering), "Why are you doing this?" The reply is chilling: "Why not?" When he later asks the same question, the response is a series of obvious lies about the influence of one hoodlum's mother's incestuous wishes and about their desire to obtain money for drugs. They make it conspicuous that these are arbitrary lies offered for their own sadistic amusement. A traditional game has rules, however. These are *funny* "games" because their players reject rational principles or goals that would otherwise allow one to win or lose. These games are there for sheerly selfish and absurd entertainment, but with no clear scheme or standard for victory other than power over another for the sake of cruel pleasure. The funny games played here are even scarier when nihilistic indifference itself become parodied, as when one of the hoodlums jokes with the couple that his partner in crime suffers from "world-weariness and ennui." (Haneke, 1997, 2007)

One telling instance of the rejection of rationality as the basis of truth is in *The Time of the Wolf* (*Le Temps du Loup* [2003]), when a family of hostile and hungry strangers has broken into another family's country house after some unexplained apocalyptic event. The victimized father (Daniel Duval) manages to convince his rifle-wielding counterpart to allow his two children to return to the family's car. When he then quietly suggests that they unload the car and eat, he is instantly shot dead and his wife (Isabelle Huppert), in a state of shock, can only respond by wiping the splattered blood from her face. Even the wife of the killer breaks down in a shocking fit of disbelief that her husband has actually pulled the trigger and killed a man in front of their own young son. (Haneke, 2003) Since Haneke does not give us any further clue about the killer's motive, we might surmise that it was the very proposal made by the now dead father, an attempt at reasonable negotiation (even in the face of a gun barrel), that prompted this man to fire unexpectedly. Interpreted this way, his act of violence is an act of nihilistic terrorism, an assault on the very value of rational discourse. But ultimately, in his typical manner, Haneke leaves the motive for the action unexplained, thus calling upon the audience's active interpretation. He challenges the type of passive spectacle-gazing that may result in a habituated, generalized lack of concern with the moral value of any film content.

In *The White Ribbon: A German Children's Story* (*Das weisse Band: Eine deutsche Kindergeschichte* [2009]), the rejection of truth is most apparent in the scene where the young teacher (Christian Friedel) confides his suspicion about the cause of recent violent events to the pastor (Burghart Klaussner). The film depicts a rural northern German village around 1913, one that has become plagued by a series of sinister, enigmatic events that point ever more increasingly to the diabolical intentions of the local children. The evil deeds appear to be the retaliatory actions of those whose youthful lives have been poisoned by their elders' almost fascist discipline and oppression. The rigid constraints on the children's freedom seem to be a primary cause of the violence, but it is in the scene where the teacher shares his suspicion about the village youth, including the pastor's own children, where we see the type of truth-denial that may engender future violence. It is clear from the pastor's face that he realizes the truth of what the teacher suspects. After all, he knows of the violence and acts of vandalism and he recalls having found his pet bird dead on his desk with a pair of scissors stabbed through its poor lifeless body, the scissors forming a crucifix. Given the pastor's behavior toward his daughter directly thereafter when he is administering communion in the chapel, we know that he is aware that his daughter was responsible for the heinous killing of the bird. So, when presented with the truth, a truth that he clearly and painfully realizes (and has no doubt suspected before, but then repressed), the pastor immediately scolds the teacher for such a suspicion, sternly warns him against speaking of it to others, and kicks him out of his house. Of course, we can see a clear line being drawn between 1913 and 1939, given the ages of these German children. Haneke wants us to see what type of widespread collective violence can result, even decades later, from such an ingrained repression of freedom and the truth. The seeds have been sown. (Haneke, 2009)

In the scene of the pastor's truth-denial in *The White Ribbon*, we are summoned to make a judgment about the pastor and those like him who not only repress others' freedom but also who repress the truth. The pastor is one of the reasons for the children's violent retaliations: the severe repression of their lives by their elders (along with sexual abuse, as in the case of the village doctor). And yet the violent events that have unfolded are by no means justified, even given the rigid tyranny of the elders, and the pastor reveals moments of tenderness toward his youngest son. And there is of course the question as to how much freedom can be allotted to young children in the first place. The pastor provides for his family and clearly believes that he is raising his children in the best way possible, even though he is sadly mistaken, given the consequences. And yet at the same time, he commands that the hands of his adolescent son be bound every night for weeks on end so that the boy will cease his obsessive masturbation. (Haneke, 2009) What do we make of this man's moral ambivalence? How do we judge him? Even if the children's revenge against the village elders is not morally justified in the eyes of the viewer, we are far from agreeing with the practices of the elders. In the chapel scene at the very end of the film, the camera captures the pastor joining his congregation in sitting before an invisible speaker who, we assume, is about to deliver a sermon. If we take this unseen speaker to be the film audience, then what kind of verdict should we deliver to those assembled? Here at the film's conclusion, Haneke gives us a cinematic image of the very idea of leaving moral judgment to the viewer.

5 Violence and the Value of Life Itself

Haneke's *Amour* (2012) is a far less ambiguous film than any of the director's earlier works. As he told an interviewer from *Sight & Sound:* "I'm trying to be less theoretical.... A film like *The Seventh Continent* wasn't a realistic film; it was a model.... [*Amour*] is hopefully ... getting closer to life" (Hasted 2017, para. 7). And yet the power of the movie's narrative, visual detail, and tempo manages to summon the active reflection and moral participation of the viewer. We are immersed in the claustrophobic private lives of the two main characters, Georges (Jean-Louis Trintignant) and Anne (Emmanuelle Riva). When Anne slips into sporadic dementia and then a paralyzing stroke, Georges is forced to cope with the overwhelming challenges of caring for her. Their daughter Eva (Isabelle Huppert), except for a few all-too-brief visits, proves to be of no assistance whatsoever, and one of the temporary day nurses turns out to be unreliable and even cruel. Haneke shows us in graphic terms—and in a slow, haunting tempo of montage—the solitary challenges and horrors of their daily existence. Most of the movie is set in the couple's apartment and the world beyond is glimpsed only through windows and doorways. The movie is a graphic meditation on aging, on the hour-to-hour repetition of suffering, and on the ever-present, looming shadow of death. (Haneke, 2012)

Amour ultimately presents us with a decision that seems, on the surface, to be as nihilistic as any that has appeared in Haneke's earlier works: the choice of Georges to terminate the life of his beloved Anne. This is his act of freedom in responding to his wife's deep suffering from the withering effects of her illness as well as in reacting to his own psychological misery. And yet this choice may also be viewed as a humane and even life-affirming one, especially given all that we have experienced up until this point. The film steers us toward empathy with Georges and thus with an acceptance of euthanasia as the best possible solution, given the circumstances. Georges's deep love for Anne is demonstrated in each small act of physical assistance and in each moment of coping with this horrible challenge. The tempo of these scenes, one after another, is such that the audience gains a clear sense of this husband's sacrifice for the sake of his beloved. It is also clear by the end of *Amour* that Georges's deep love for his wife has made it impossible for him to continue seeing her as a mere semblance of her former self.

Some may, perhaps for religious reasons, disagree with Georges's decision in terms of the killing of his wife and they may even agree with his daughter that he should have tried harder to put his wife into a hospital or hospice where proper care could be given to her. Haneke complicates the matter even further by showing that, in caring for his wife at home, at times with the temporary help of a caregiver, Georges adheres to a promise that he gave to his wife when she first returned from the hospital and asked him to vow never to let her return there (her fear of doctors and hospitals is referenced earlier in the film). Furthermore, Georges's self-absorbed daughter only visits on rare occasions when she happens to be in the area and simply tells her father that her mother should be hospitalized. In the final image of the movie, Eva enters their empty apartment to consider the awful twilight of lives she barely knew. She sits before the viewer in a way that seems akin to the chapel congregation in the final shot of *The White Ribbon:* awaiting the viewer's judgment. And so at its conclusion, *Amour* demands the reflective participation of the viewer, summoning a moral verdict not only about Eva's character and Georges's act of euthanasia but also about his own act of self-destruction. We briefly see Georges sealing the doors and windows of their apartment, obviously for the purpose of turning on the gas and joining his wife in a common fate. He loves her enough not to want to keep living without her. He may also not want to be the same type of burden for his daughter that he has just experienced. And while we can perhaps render a moral defense of Georges's act of euthanasia for the sake of Anne, we may find it more difficult to accept his suicide. After all, he is frail but not as agony-ridden and incapacitated as his wife had been. Haneke gives us no easy answers here and he even gives us space to criticize Anne herself, perhaps, for having requested that Georges promise never to return her to the hospital. (Haneke, 2012) Obedience to that promise had put her husband in the worst of all possible situations. So how do we judge these characters?

The viewer's experience of moral ambivalence about Georges's suicide is echoed in Haneke's most recent film *Happy End* (2017), where we return to the issue of euthanasia—along with the director's recurring critique of the contemporary bourgeoisie by emphasizing its tendency to result in family dysfunction, repression, apathy, and ennui. The film concerns the Laurents of Calais, an upper middle-class family whose members include the emotionally detached 85-year-old patriarch, Georges (Trintignant again). He is the wealthy retired owner of a construction firm who appears to be in the beginning stages of dementia and whose one goal now is the termination of his own increasingly frail life. There is reference to a prior suicide attempt and in the course of the story we witness Georges trying to end his life several times—once on his own, by driving a car into a tree, twice through seeking the assistance of others (a gang of African strangers as well as his barber), and once again with the help of his own granddaughter. We may assume that the reason for his intended self-destruction has to do with the onset of his dementia, though the film does not rule out the possibility that he also simply no longer views life as worth living since his family members present him with more headaches than with any inspiration to continue on. There is also evidence that, while he shows a few occasional moments of obvious forgetfulness and while he is now confined to a wheelchair, Georges is by and large quite lucid, especially in the poignant scene where he converses with his granddaughter Eve and tries to find out why she had intentionally overdosed on her mother's anti-depressants. It is in this scene where we learn that Georges had endured three years of his wife's agonizing suffering from an illness and that he had suffocated her to end her (and his) misery. (Haneke, 2017) And so there is a clear link to the storyline of Haneke's prior film *Amour*.

Eve also confides her own secret to Georges and there is good reason to suspect that Eve had secretly given her mother an overdose of anti-depressants, resulting in her vegetative state and eventual death. The Laurents form what appears to be a loveless family, for the most part, and if we can judge by the old man's persona as well as by his assumed influence on the behavior of his two children, Georges's recurring desire for an early termination to his life may simply be due to cold expediency. This desire is also highly selfish in that he seems to have no qualms in trying to involve the young African men as well as his barber and even his own granddaughter—despite the fact that he is asking them to consider accommodating a highly disturbing request that may well get them into trouble with the law (as his barber points out). Georges is a detached, imperious old man and we can very well picture him in his earlier years as a callous, profit-driven businessperson who ruled his company with mechanical efficiency. Is his air of unemotional passivity a symptom of his encroaching dementia or is it an expression of his long-standing character? His daughter Anne (Isabelle Huppert) has taken over the leadership of the construction firm and she exhibits a similar type of emotionally aloof character, as does his adulterous son Thomas (Mathieu Kassovitz). (Haneke, 2017)

When thinking about *Amour* and *Happy End* together, we can compare the different Georges characters (both played by Tringinant). They both express enough moral complications that the viewer is not given any easy answers in rendering a judgment about their motives and actions. The characters of both films clearly have similar reasons for wanting to terminate their lives sooner than Nature has intended. The Georges of *Amour* has suffered through the agony of caring for his invalid wife; he loves his wife enough that he does not want to continue living without her; he may not want to face the legal consequences of what he has done; and he is growing physically more frail and most likely does not want to live on his own, knowing that he may also soon need the very assistance that he had to provide for his dying wife. His daughter Eva, far from being loving and reliable, is as cold and mechanical as Georges's daughter Anne (also Huppert) in *Happy End*. And yet neither Georges is in a state of terminal illness or incapacitation. They are still fairly alert even if frail; they are not destitute and the Georges of *Happy End* can certainly afford as much assistance as he needs; and they both have children to lend some assistance even if their children are selfish. Again, Haneke problematizes any judgment about their characters and actions.

Finally, Haneke also summons the viewer of *Happy End* to make a judgment about young Eve, given that she seems capable of diabolical acts and yet has suffered a great deal from the break-up of her parents' marriage. She falls into a crying jag in the car with her father; he is quite clearly concerned and yet seems incapable of offering her a hug once he has pulled his car to a stop. The most that he can do is to tell her that he is "clumsy" in trying to be a father again. Later, when Eve is the hospital after attempting suicide by swallowing her mother's left-over sleeping pills, her father visits her and she tells him that she knows of his affair and that he is incapable of loving anyone. Thomas simply responds in silence with a vacant wide-eyed expression, one that seems to indicate that his young daughter is correct. It is the child who delivers the most mature judgment in the film, but how far can we extend our sympathy for Eve when we have also learned of her immoral actions? And we can ask the same question in reference to the rebellious Pierre (Franz Rogowski), the son of Anne. His own mother is driven to call him a "hopeless case," which he readily admits. We can see one cause of his disturbing, irresponsible behavior: he grew up in a family of self-absorbed individuals whose affection seems superficial and ritualistic at best. Pierre has also had foisted upon him responsibilities far above his maturity level. But can we simply blame his family for the chaos of Pierre's personality? After all, we witness his crazed (and seemingly drug-induced) karaoke performance and we see him thoughtlessly using African strangers (including the Moroccan servants in the Laurent mansion) as mere pawns when trying to rebel dramatically against his family. (Haneke, 2017)

In cleverly utilizing ambiguity, controversy, ellipsis, and the power of the violent image, Haneke raises moral questions about his characters' words and actions in extreme situations, including those in which the very value of human biological life is put into doubt. Through moments of dread and horror, he coaxes the viewer to become an active arbiter of values rather than a mere consumer of spectacle. He wants us to judge while showing us the dangers of sitting back and refraining from judgment—let alone action. Haneke gives us portraits of individuals who face violence and the specter of passive nihilism and he does so in a way that propels us into the type of reflection that illuminates our own implications in these problems and that awakens a need to cultivate our ethical self-consciousness. Like Nietzsche, Haneke gives us the occasion for recognizing our tendency to lapse into conformism or, even worse, sheer moral passivity. Such conformism or passivity can easily lead to a pathological form of detachment that levels qualitative differences of content and that casts doubt on those fundamental values (freedom, truth, and life itself) which otherwise help to guide us through the darkness.

Bibliography

Brinkema, Eugenie (2010): "How to Do Things with Violences." In: Roy Grundmann (Ed.): *A Companion to Michael Haneke*. Malden, Oxford: Blackwell Publishing Ltd., pp. 354–370.
Coulthard, Lisa (2011): "Ethical Violence: Suicide as Authentic Act in the Films of Michael Haneke." In: Ben McCann and David Sorfa (Eds.): *The Cinema of Michael Haneke: Europe Utopia*. London, New York: Wallflower Press, Columbia University Press, pp. 38–48.
Deleuze, Gilles, and Leopold von Sacher-Masoch (1991): *Masochism*. Cambridge: Zone Books.
Gerbaz, Alex (2011). "The Ethical Screen: *Funny Games* and the Spectacle of Pain." In: Ben McCann and David Sorfa (Eds.): *The Cinema of Michael Haneke: Europe Utopia*. London, New York: Wallflower Press, Columbia University Press, pp. 163–171.
Grabner, Franz, and Michael Haneke (2008): "'Der Name der Erbsünde ist Verdrängung': A Conversation with Michael Haneke." In: Christian Wessely, Franz Grabner, and Gerhard Larcher (Eds.): *Michael Haneke und seine Filme: Eine Pathologie der Konsumgesellschaft*. Marburg: Schüren Verlag, pp. 11–24.
Grundmann, Roy (Ed.) (2010): *A Companion to Michael Haneke*. Malden, Oxford: Blackwell Publishing Ltd.
Haneke, Michael (2000): "Beyond Mainstream Film: An Interview with Michael Haneke." In: Willy Riemer (Ed.): *After Postmodernism: Austrian Literature and Film in Transition*. Riverside: Ariadne Press, 2000, pp. 159–170.
Haneke, Michael (2005). "Michael Haneke on *The Seventh Continent* (1989)." Interview with Serge Toubiana. *YouTube*. Posted Dec. 27, 2018. https://www.youtube.com/watch?v=VaAbH9Wnelg
Haneke, Michael (2010): "Violence and the Media." In: Roy Grundmann (Ed.): *A Companion to Michael Haneke*. Malden, Oxford: Blackwell Publishing Ltd., pp. 575–579.
Hasted, Nick (2017): "Happy End: The Secret Kindness of Michael Haneke." In: *The Independent*, December 5, 2017. https://www.independent.co.uk/arts-entertainment/films/features/michael-haneke-happy-end-funny-games-amour-isabelle-huppert-oscar-piano-teacher-a8092356.html, visited on July 1, 2021
Laine, Tarja (2011). "Hidden Shame Exposed: *Hidden* and the Spectator." In Ben McCann and David Sorfa (Eds.): *The Cinema of Michael Haneke: Europe Utopia*. London, New York: Wallflower Press, Columbia University Press, pp. 247–258.
Ma, Jean (2010): "Discordant Desires, Violent Refrains: *La Pianiste* (*The Piano Teacher*)." In: Roy Grundmann (Ed.): *A Companion to Michael Haneke*. Malden, Oxford: Blackwell Publishing Ltd., pp. 511–531.
McCann, Ben, and David Sorfa (Eds.) (2011): *The Cinema of Michael Haneke: Europe Utopia*. London, New York: Wallflower Press, Columbia University Press.
Nancy, Jean-Luc (2005a): "The Image – The Distinct." In: *The Ground of the Image*. Translated by Jeff Fort. New York: Fordham University Press, 1–14.
Nancy, Jean-Luc (2005b): "Image and Violence." In: *The Ground of the Image*. Translated by Jeff Fort. New York: Fordham University Press, 15–26.

Nietzsche, Friedrich (1968): *The Will to Power*. Edited and translated by Walter Kaufmann. New York: Vintage.
Nietzsche, Friedrich (1977): *Thus Spoke Zarathustra*. In: Nietzsche, *The Portable Nietzsche*. Edited and translated by Walter Kaufmann. New York: Penguin Books, Viking Portable Library, pp. 103–439.
Orr, John (2011). "*The White Ribbon* in Michael Haneke's Cinema." In Ben McCann and David Sorfa (Eds.): *The Cinema of Michael Haneke: Europe Utopia*. London, New York: Wallflower Press, Columbia University Press, pp. 259–264.
Riemer, Willy (Ed.) (2000): *After Postmodernism: Austrian Literature and Film in Transition*. Riverside: Ariadne Press.
Roderick, Nemonie Craven (2011). "Subject to Memory? Thinking after *Hidden*." In: Ben McCann and David Sorfa (Eds.): *The Cinema of Michael Haneke: Europe Utopia*. London, New York: Wallflower Press, Columbia University Press, pp. 225–236.
Sorfa, David (2006). "Uneasy domesticity in the films of Michael Haneke." In: *Studies in European Cinema* 3. No. 2, pp. 93–104.
Wheatley, Catherine (2011). "Domestic Invasion: Michael Haneke and Home Audiences." In: Ben McCann and David Sorfa (Eds.): *The Cinema of Michael Haneke: Europe Utopia*. London, New York: Wallflower Press, Columbia University Press, 10–23.

Filmography

Haneke, Michael, director. (1995): *71 Fragments of a Chronology of Chance (71 Fragmente Einer Chronologie des Zufalls)*.
Haneke, Michael, director. (2012): *Amour*.
Haneke, Michael, director. (1992): *Benny's Video*.
Haneke, Michael, director. (2006): *Caché (Hidden)*.
Haneke, Michael, director. (2001): *Code Unknown (Code Inconnu)*.
Haneke, Michael, director. (1997): *Funny Games*.
Haneke, Michael, director. (2007): *Funny Games*.
Haneke, Michael, director. (2017): *Happy End*.
Haneke, Michael, director. (2001): *The Piano Teacher (La Pianiste)*.
Haneke, Michael, director. (1989): *The Seventh Continent (Der Siebente Kontinent)*.
Haneke, Michael, director. (2009): *The White Ribbon (Das Weisse Band)*.
Haneke, Michael, director. (2003): *Time of the Wolf (Le Temps Du Loup)*.

John Marmysz
"Supposing Truth is a Woman?": Nihilism and Violence in Nietzsche's *The Antichrist* and Von Trier's *Antichrist*

Abstract: This paper examines the parallels between Friedrich Nietzsche's book *The Antichrist* (written in 1888, but first published in 1895) and Lars von Trier's 2009 film *Antichrist*. I argue that an understanding of Nietzsche's book sheds light on the form and structure of the nihilistic violence depicted in von Trier's film. In both Nietzsche's book and von Trier's film, nihilistic violence is instrumental insofar as it is utilized as a tool for the overcoming of Christianity's denigration of nature. In this paper I argue that the instrumental, nihilistic violence utilized by Nietzsche and von Trier to dismantle Christian values finally inaugurates a difficult confrontation with a form of non-instrumental, expressive violence found in nature itself. Distaste for this natural, non-instrumental violence represents a final impediment to the embrace of nature on its own terms, raising questions about the possibility (or even the desirability) of the overcoming of nihilism.

1 Introduction

Lars von Trier has claimed that *Antichrist* is his most personal and important film. Made as he was emerging from a period of severe depression, he says it approximates a pure "scream" that expresses his feelings of anxiety, despair, and rage (Badley 2010, p. 144). The images of sex, violence, and sexual violence appearing in the film are so graphic and shocking that some audience members reportedly have fainted during screenings (Badley 2010, p. 141). Because of its extremity, numerous critics have condemned *Antichrist* as indecent, pornographic, and misogynistic (Brooks 2009).

But there is something more than indecency or self-indulgence at work in von Trier's *Antichrist*. While the explicit violence and brutality in the film may be expressive of the director's own emotional struggles, the significance of this imagery transcends his personal psychology, casting light on wider issues concerning the nature of human suffering and spiritual transformation. The violence in *Antichrist* is nihilistic in character; but it is nihilistic in an active sense, evoking a "violent force of destruction," which Nietzsche claimed precedes and opens the way for the transvaluation of values (NL 1887, 9[35], KSA 12, p. 351). This violence is an orgiastic paroxysm, both painful to watch and yet important to think about precisely because it lingers with rare and uncomfortable intensity on a ferocious, active purgation that clears the way for profound psychic transformation, revaluation, and recovery.

Von Trier confesses that the title of his film, *Antichrist*, was inspired by Friedrich Nietzsche's book *The Antichrist*; a book that von Trier claims to have kept on his nightstand ever since he was twelve years old (Badley 2010, p. 147). This biographical detail is an insight into how intimately the director has been influenced and affected by Nietzsche's thought; something previously noted by scholars such as Bodil Marie Stavning Thomsen (2009) and Ivan Krisjansen and Catherine Papadopoullos (2015). To understand von Trier's *Antichrist*, then, it helps first to understand Nietzsche's *The Antichrist*. The consonance between these two works sheds a great deal of light not just on the meaning of the violence in von Trier's film, but on the world-shattering nature of nihilistic violence in general.

In what follows, I shall first detail the structure of Nietzsche's book and then, in the second section, use it as a template to analyze the structure and trajectory of von Trier's film. Highlighting the structural parallels between these two works draws attention to the pivotal role that instrumental violence (both conceptual and physical) plays in the project of overcoming Christian nihilism. As I will argue in the final section of the essay, this instrumental violence ultimately inaugurates a confrontation with a form of non-instrumental, expressive violence found in nature itself. Distaste for this non-instrumental, natural violence constitutes the final impediment to the full embrace of nature, the overcoming of Christian nihilism, and the transvaluation of all values.

2 Nietzsche's *The Antichrist*

Nietzsche's *The Antichrist* is a violently angry work that, as Hans Küng writes, was intended "to wound" (Küng 2006, p. 405). It was initially planned as only the first in a multivolume "revaluation of all values," which would overturn the otherworldly ideals of Christianity and replace them with a new, non-Christian perspective rooted in nature (A Preface).[1] Christian thought deserves replacement, according to Nietzsche, because it is a "sickness" that has eaten away at

---

[1] Gary Shapiro and Daniel Conway both note that Nietzsche told his friend Georg Brandes that *The Antichrist* should be considered the entirety of *The Revaluation of All Values*, with his other book, *Ecce Homo*, representing a prelude (Shapiro 1988, p. 192; and Conway 2020, pp. 1–6).

the health of humankind through its denial of reality (A 1). By teaching followers to aspire toward an illusory, heavenly realm, Christianity repudiates nature in favor of supernatural falsehood. In the process, it cultivates a morality of pity for those who are naturally unfit—the weak and the sick—thus debilitating the human race as a whole while promoting an unhealthy, decadent form of civilization. For these reasons, Christianity is nihilistic, encouraging the negation of life (A 7, 20, 58). It must, therefore, be overcome.

Christian nihilism is insidious, Nietzsche tells us, and "is more extensive than generally supposed" (A 8). It has even infiltrated academic philosophy, where German Idealism has continued to spread the same sort of life-denying nihilism that Christianity spreads among the masses. According to Nietzsche's (debatable) account, we see this dramatically illustrated in Kant's Transcendental Idealism, which posits the existence of an objective, noumenal world of pure Being that is unknowable because it hides behind a subjective, phenomenal veil of human perception. Pure Being, the "true" world, is for Kant impenetrable. All that can be known about it is gained through human interpretation, which is achieved by means of the distorting, mental lenses of the a priori intuitions and the categories of understanding. These lenses shape and organize our perceptions of the unknowable "thing-in-itself," generating a world of phenomena that constitutes our actual, lived reality. Like the Christian Heaven, Kant's noumenal realm —objective reality—stands above and apart from the realm of phenomena, unseen and mysterious. In this way, Kant, at least according to Nietzsche, fractures the world in two, corralling human consciousness within a domain forever alienated from Being itself (A 10).

As with Christianity, the problem with Kantian nihilism, according to Nietzsche, is not simply an epistemological issue. It also has an ethical dimension. Kantianism encourages humans toward moral abstraction by holding that "true" morality, like "true" Being, lies in the absolute and the unconditioned. Consequently, Kantian morality advises us to ignore our natural, concrete, "all too human" urges toward pleasure and power in favor of an immaterial conception of absolute Goodness (A 11). Duty to an abstraction, the categorical imperative, replaces our natural inclinations to pursue concrete urges in the here and now. This is one of the most damaging consequences of Kantian nihilism according to Nietzsche, and it shows that Kant's idealist philosophy is just another manifestation of the "priestly type" of thinking (A 12). This kind of thinking negates life by distracting and deceiving us with hopes and dreams of a counterfeit, hidden, other world lying beyond our grasp. Transcendental Idealism promotes the same anti-natural lies among scholars as Christianity does among the masses (A 12), and thus, as Nietzsche writes elsewhere, Kant proves "in a way that would dumbfound the common man, that the common man was right: that was the secret joke of his soul" (GS III 193).[2]

Nihilism is not just a problem in the West. Nietzsche also criticizes Eastern Buddhism for being a nihilistic religion. Although "a hundred times more realistic than Christianity" (A 20), like Christianity and like Kantianism, Buddhism still involves reality denial. The difference is that while Christianity is a religion for "early" humans who are still in the process of taming their inner will to power, Buddhism is a religion for "late" humans who have already exhausted their will to power. Buddhists are reconciled to the fact that the natural realm is a place of suffering (the First Noble Truth), and as a result of their weariness have developed methods of withdrawal, ultimately aimed at the extinction of life altogether (Nirvana). Christians still actively resist the suffering caused by nature, and by internalizing their resentment they master, control, and civilize themselves in accordance with the priestly ideal. While Christianity makes humankind sick so that we can continue enduring the beastliness of the world, Buddhism is for civilizations that have reached a point of exhaustion with the world's beastliness altogether.

This is why the imagery of Christianity is so violent and vicious while the imagery of Buddhism is so passive and serene. Compare the tormented, bloody and beaten image of Christ on the cross with the serenity of Siddhartha as he sits beneath the Bo Tree. The violence inflicted upon Jesus is a manifestation of the Christian desire to subdue the fleshly, beastly aspect of humankind in preparation for a better, more spiritual life. The passivity of Siddhartha, in contrast, is a prelude to his complete and utter resignation to absolute nothingness. Both reactions are nihilistic, but in separate ways according to Nietzsche. Buddhist nihilism is passive. Christian nihilism is active and violent.[3]

The active, violent nihilism of Christianity is continuous with, rather than a break from, the earlier Jewish tradition, according to Nietzsche. Both Judaism and Christianity are religions of *ressentiment* (A 24), characterized by their hatred of reality. Over the course of history this hatred evolved into an increasingly abstract interpretation of the world, progressively distracting followers from the re-

---

[2] As Paul S. Loeb notes, Nietzsche's critique "will certainly seem unfair and excessive to admirers of Kant" (Loeb 2020, p. 112). Nietzsche, however, was not the first to accuse Kant of nihilism. The charge was first leveled against Kantian philosophy by Friedrich Heinrich Jacobi in his letter to Fichte (Jacobi [1799] 1994).

[3] Antoine Panaïoti has pointed out that Nietzsche's own philosophical project may in fact be more consonant with the doctrines of Buddhism than Nietzsche himself realized. For instance, both are concerned with the rejection of the myths of self, Being, and Bliss, as well as with the promotion of "great health" as an ethical ideal (Panaïoti 2013, p. 54).

alities of nature. Yahweh, the Hebrew God, began as a nature god, a rain-bringer, who, only after the Assyrian conquest of Israel, was transformed into a moral God. This transformation, Nietzsche claims, was in response to the suffering and lack of self-confidence experienced by the Jewish people after their defeat. When their nature god failed them, this god was reinterpreted as "a god who demands" and who violently punishes His people when they fail to remain obedient to Him (A 25). The victory of the Assyrians, thus, was not merely a military victory. It was a moral punishment for not obeying God's holy demands. But this raises the question: who is it that knows what God demands? The answer eventually provided by the defeated Jews was: the priests to whom God's will is revealed! In this, it is the inner vision of the priestly caste, rather than the physical strength of the King and his armies, that becomes the highest, holiest earthly authority. The priest becomes indispensable to society as the one who is in charge of consecrating and bestowing value on all natural occurrences in life (A 26). Nature becomes "desecrated" by the need for priestly blessing since it no longer is valuable in-itself, but only gains value through Heavenly sanction.

Jesus originally appeared among the Jews, according to Nietzsche, as something like a new Epicurus or a Western Buddha whose sensitivity to life's suffering turned him away from the outer, natural world, back inward, where he found the kingdom of Heaven inside his own soul. This, according to Nietzsche, constituted a rebellion against the priestly hierarchy of Judaism since Jesus taught that there are no chosen people (A 27), and that all humans are capable of channeling God's will directly, without priestly assistance. The spirit of God is within us all, and so there is no need for external authority or consecration of the natural world, according to Jesus.

But, writes Nietzsche, "there was only one Christian, and he died on the cross" (A 39). Jesus's teaching was about a way of life in *this* world, not a system of belief about another world. After his execution, this point became obscured when his followers—primarily Paul—gripped by the desire for revenge against his killers, interpreted Jesus's death abstractly. Unable to believe that Jesus was merely a man, they came to insist that he was God made flesh, and that his crucifixion was part of a Heavenly plan, which would culminate in a final judgment and the victory of the vanquished over their vanquishers. In another world, in a life after this life, the weak would dominate the strong. It was that other world that became the Christian standard of justice, and this world, the world of nature, became the embodiment of evil.[4]

---

[4] Anthony K. Jensen notes that Nietzsche's account of the transformation of the historical Jesus into the Christ of Christianity is "entirely speculative" and involves an "exaggerated psycholo-

Christian nihilism elevates the supernatural realm above the natural, earthly realm, denigrating the world of nature by judging it inferior to Heaven. Since what actually exists in nature is evaluated as imperfect, deficient, and in fact evil, nothing that concretely exists deserves to exist. What deserves to exist is only that which lies beyond the natural world. Contempt for the body is the consequence (A 56), and this contempt offers a justification for violence and the negation of life. In this, we encounter one manifestation of nihilistic violence. This sort of nihilistic violence attacks what actually does concretely exist in order to clear a path toward that which the Christian believes to exist in the spiritual realm. Yet, according to Nietzsche, since the non-concrete, spiritual realm is actually an illusion, what this sort of violence really inaugurates is nothingness. It clears away the only world that really does matter in service of a fantasy.

But the same sort of violence that is directed against nature by Christian thought can also be harnessed and redirected against Christian thinking. This, in fact, is what Nietzsche seems to be enacting as he writes *The Antichrist*. By first exposing the nihilistic, anti-natural character of Christianity, Nietzsche seeks to purge it from his own consciousness. He aims to turn the mechanism of Christian nihilism back on itself and subvert its abstract hierarchy of values so that nature becomes established as a new, self-validating standard of reality. He uses the violence of active nihilism as a tool to overcome nihilism altogether.

The violence of Nietzsche's attack on Christianity develops to an increasingly frenzied and violent pitch as *The Antichrist* progresses. The crescendo of this violence appears in the final section where Nietzsche proclaims:

> With this I am at the end and I pronounce my judgment. I condemn Christianity. I raise against the Christian church the most terrible of all accusations that any accuser ever uttered. It is to me the highest of all conceivable corruptions. It has had the will to the last corruption that is even possible. The Christian church has left nothing untouched by its corruption: it has turned every value into an un-value, every truth into a lie, every integrity into a vileness of the soul...
>
> I call Christianity the one great curse, the one great innermost corruption, the one great instinct of revenge for which no means is poisonous, stealthy, subterranean, small enough—I call it the one immortal blemish of mankind (A 62).

---

gism" (Jensen 2020, p. 131). He declares that *The Antichrist*, as a whole, "wildly oversteps the boundaries of scholarship" (Jensen 2020, p. 118). Panaïoti concurs, writing, "*The Antichrist* is terrible scholarship" (Panaïoti 2020, p. 43). And yet, as Jensen, Panaïoti, and others like Weaver Santaniello (1994, pp. 131–132) have also argued, Nietzsche seems not to have intended the work as a piece of tradional scholarship at all, but as "an interpretation intent on convincing only selective perspectives" (Jensen 2020, p. 135), a "cultural intervention" (Panaïoti 2020, p. 43), or as a "politically bold" statement (Santaniello 1994, p. 132).

Nietzsche's fevered tone explodes in this conclusion, finally bursting forth with an intensity embodying his passionate hatred for Christianity. The violence of this passage is itself nihilistic, serving to eradicate the influence of "priestly" thinking on his own consciousness. He has been building up to this, marshaling confidence for a final attack in which he steels his conviction to nullify the enemy.

And after this frenzied tirade, Nietzsche ends with a simple proclamation, "Revaluation of all values!" (A 62). The entire book was aiming at this goal, and when it is achieved, it arrives in a single sentence with no further explanation or elaboration. The actively destructive part of Nietzsche's project, the one occupying the bulk of the work, thus takes the most effort and seems to have been the most difficult for him to carry out. But it is an important part, clearing the way for his escape from Christian influence. Gary Shapiro notes that Nietzsche's literary executors actually removed a final, later section that Nietzsche had added to his book. Titled "Decree Against Christianity," this section proclaims "War to the death against depravity: depravity is Christianity." It then lays out seven propositions that repeat his condemnation of Christianity's "anti-nature." Nietzsche signed it, Antichrist (Shapiro 1988, pp. 212–213).

Nietzsche's violent attack on Christian life-negation clears the way for the emergence of the "overman" (A 4), the carrier of an alternative set of values rejecting otherworldly claims and who is rooted in nature itself. Free from ressentiment against the natural world and liberated from feelings of pity for the weak, the overman invests all value in the here and now world of lived, physical reality. This revaluation of the natural over the supernatural world is characterized by the affirmation of everything that actually does exist, including all suffering and hardship. When judged from the unnatural, idealist perspective of religion, the world we inhabit appears to be imperfect, cruel, and awful. But when reevaluated from the perspective of nature itself, everything is just as it should be. There is no difference between "is" and "ought." "'The world is perfect'—thus says the most spiritual, the Yes-saying instinct" (A 57). The overman wishes nothing to be other than the way it actually is and thus affirms life in the real world. This represents the overcoming of nihilism as life negation.

Stylistically, some scholars suggest that the violent tone of *The Antichrist* may be evidence of Nietzsche's own mental instability; an indication of his deteriorating mental condition and a precursor to the collapse that incapacitated him for ten years until his death in 1900 (Shapiro 1988, p. 192). While this may be true, it in no way invalidates the substance of what Nietzsche has expressed; any more than von Trier's own experience of depression invalidates the importance of his films. In fact, Walter Kaufman has even suggested that *The Antichrist*, and other books that Nietzsche wrote toward the end of his productive life, are among his greatest works of art, unleashing the Dionysian passion that had hitherto been obscured by too much Apollonian restraint (Kaufmann 1968, pp. 66–67).

3 Lars von Trier's *Antichrist*

Lars von Trier's *Antichrist*, like Nietzsche's book, has frequently been criticized as the product of a disturbed mind. As with Nietzsche's infamous book, von Trier's infamous film endeavors to exorcize traditional assumptions about the relationship between humans and nature in a single, intensely fierce act of purgation, violently and nihilistically nullifying systems of belief that falsely promise an idealized and untroubled state of existence—whether it be Heaven above or mental health within—beyond all earthly struggle and suffering. Echoing what Nietzsche wrote in *The Antichrist*, von Trier's *Antichrist* seeks to tear back the veneer of civilization in order to place humans "back among the animals" (A 14); a goal that, apparently, many critics believe only an unstable mind could possibly desire.

The role of physical violence in von Trier's film is congruent to the conceptual violence carried out in Nietzsche's book. In both, violence serves as an active force that dismantles and destroys belief in falsely idealized versions of reality, clearing the way for the embrace of nature as it concretely exists. In this sense, the film's violence is productive at the same time that it is destructive, exposing truth by clearing away falsehood and thus opening a path toward the transvaluation of our values. Like Nietzsche's book, the film's plot follows a trajectory beginning with the diagnosis of an underlying human condition, which is then followed by a progressively frenzied tone of aggression. After an explosion of nihilistic violence, von Trier's *Antichrist* ends, like Nietzsche's *The Antichrist*, with an affirmation, brief and simple in comparison to the frenzy that preceded it, but nevertheless representing the film's ultimate point and purpose. Destroying anti-natural falsehood liberates us to acknowledge and affirm the sublimity of nature as a place where "chaos reigns" (Trier 2009, 0:37:50–0:37:58) and where suffering has no transcendent purpose. It turns out that we do not suffer as a result of God's punishment. Rather, we suffer as a necessary consequence of living life in the natural world, and if we are able to love life, then we might come to embrace our suffering as well.

Antichrist's Prologue—filmed in slow-motion, black and white, and set to the music of Handel's "Let Me Weep"—establishes the film's central theme (Trier 2009, 0:00:41–0:06:16). In this Prologue, the film's two nameless protagonists He (Willem Dafoe) and She (Charlotte Gainsbourg) are having sex. He is a psychotherapist. She is a graduate student writing a master's thesis on the Christian persecution of witches. These two characters appear intended as archetypes for the male and female principles within nature. He represents reason, order, stability, and control while She represents emotion, fluidity, passion, and chaos. This dichotomy mirrors Nietzsche's early (but later modified) distinction, from *The Birth of Tragedy*, between the Apollonian and the Dionysian forces of nature.[5] For Nietzsche, as for von Trier, these forces are complementary, augmenting one another and functioning together to bring about all concrete expressions of Being. The male/Apollonian force channels and shapes the energy and passion of the female/Dionysian force, which is a "hidden substratum of suffering and of knowledge" pulsing through the heart of nature (BT 4). The chaos of Dionysus is unbearable as a raw potency; too vigorous and awful for the human mind to confront unmediated. The function of Apollo is to provide the necessary distance and perspective that allows us to endure the encounter with Dionysus. In the opening scene of *Antichrist*, these two forces literally interpenetrate one another as He and She have sex, forming a unity—like yin and yang—that is self-sufficient and indifferent to any reality beyond their reciprocal movements.

He and She are oblivious to the existence of the world outside of their shared blissfulness. Consequently, they are unaware that their young child has escaped from his crib, observed their sexual union, and subsequently fallen out of an open window to his death onto the sidewalk below. This sequence is startling in its contrast of the child's tragic demise with explicit shots of sexual penetration. Ian Christie has commented on the seeming "contradiction" in this opening scene between the beauty of the couple's lovemaking and the horror of the child's death (Christie 2010). Yet, there is no real contradiction between these images. They are, in fact, perfectly consonant with one another: children are the product of sexual union between men and women—two naturally complementary energies—and those who are born as the product of sexual union are also destined to die. The awful truth is that sex (at least very often) leads to birth, and birth (always) leads to death. In this short, provocational opening, then, von

---

[5] Shapiro notes that in 1886 Nietzsche criticized his own early distinction between the Apollonian and the Dionysian and that the forces became integrated in his later writings (Shapiro 2010, p. 252). As Kaufman writes, "The 'Dionysus' in the Dionysus versus Apollo of Nietzsche's first book and the '*Dionysus versus the Crucified*' in the last line of Nietzsche's last book do not mean the same thing. The later Dionysus is the synthesis of the two forces represented by Dionysus and Apollo in *The Birth of Tragedy*" (Kaufman 1974, p. 129). Alan D. Schrift argues that this synthesis culminates in Nietzsche's doctrine of will to power: "Opting instead for a polyvalent monism ... Nietzsche's announcement stands as a challenge to all subsequent dualistic attempts to divide and hierarchize the world into dichotomous groups" (Schrift 1995, p. 65).

Trier has compressed the entire trajectory of human existence. We are born into this world as a result of animal desire only to suffer and die as a result of the body's frailty and weakness. Our wish to cleave the "beauty" of lovemaking from the "horror" of death is symptomatic of our denial of reality and of our alienation from nature; an estrangement that Nietzsche aggressively denounces and that von Trier seeks to obliterate with horrifying violence in the remainder of his film.

"Supposing truth is a woman—what then?," writes Nietzsche in the Preface to *Beyond Good and Evil* (BGE Preface), and in *Antichrist* Von Trier eagerly sets his talents to answering this question. Traditionally, Truth has been viewed (at least in the West) as something stable, fixed, and objective. Christians and philosophers have thus dismissed as false whatever is fleeting, ephemeral, and rooted in subjectivity. Heaven and the noumenal world are taken to be more real than the earthly or phenomenal realms precisely because the former are stable and lasting while the latter are subject to flux and change. This, however, is a delusion according to Nietzsche, and his diagnosis of this delusion is that it results from the domination of Dionysus by Apollo. Ever since biblical times there has existed a fear of the violent, dynamic power of nature. This fear has encouraged philosophers to suppress the Dionysian aspects of the world and to instead emphasize its Apollonian aspects. In so doing, nature has been reified into a static illusion. Instead of a living, ambiguous and ever-changing organism, reality came to be conceived as an unchanging abstraction. For Nietzsche, as for von Trier, while it is the image of man that represents the formal, structuring force of Apollo, it is the image of woman that represents the chaotic, Dionysian dynamism in nature.

In *The Antichrist*, Nietzsche highlights how the fear of nature, and thus of woman, is on display in the book of Genesis, where it is Eve who tempts Adam with the fruit of knowledge, thereby incurring God's wrath. In this parable, it is woman who offers man the truth of the natural world; but this truth is too dangerous, threatening to eliminate the distinction between humans and God. As a consequence, God expels both Adam and Eve from Eden, condemning them to suffer for the rest of their existence. According to Nietzsche, this biblical myth illustrates the Christian urge to keep humans ignorant of the truth of the natural world so that they will remain preoccupied with thoughts of the un-true, supernatural world, which is held out as a reward for dutiful suffering (A 48). We might note as well that in this story it is man who is condemned to till the soil while it is woman who is condemned to childbirth. Tilling the soil aligns with man's role as the one who imposes structure and order onto nature, while childbirth aligns with woman's role as the one who renews life and vitality. Man is governed by Apollo, woman by Dionysus. The nihilistic genius of Christianity is that it has succeeded in separating and pitting these forces against one another through a strategy of divide and conquer.

In von Trier's *Antichrist*, Eden is the name of the couple's cabin retreat in the woods. She fears this place more than anything else; perhaps because Eden is where man and woman were turned against one another and humans became alienated from nature. In the film's first Chapter, "Grief," He determines that both He and She must return to Eden to confront her dread over the loss of their child and to pursue a therapeutic cure for her grief and despair. He resolves to heal her trauma with exposure therapy. Whereas in the opening Prologue of the film the terrible sublimity of life—from conception to death—was revealed in its full beauty and horror, in the film's following chapters He attempts to exert Apollonian control over nature's dynamism, offering a remedy for its horrors through the power of psychotherapy. The return to Eden is conceived by He as a strategy to cure her and to re-impose order to her "disordered" mind. But to do this, nature's complete truth must once again be confronted, suppressed, and controlled; and the more vigorously that He attempts to control it, the more violently nature resists until, finally, She explodes in an unrestrained orgy of sex, violence, and sexual violence. Prelapsarian Eden, it seems, is the wrong place to go if you want to silence Dionysus.

Upon the couple's return to Eden in Chapter Two: Pain (Chaos Reigns), the violence and callousness of nature is instantly unveiled. Amid the beautiful, lush forest setting, a deer struggles to give birth, but the fawn remains stuck and strangled as it hangs partially undelivered from its mother's birth canal (Trier 2009, 0:36:38 – 0:37:47). Oak trees drop hundreds of acorns that will die so that a few may take root and live (Trier 2009, 0:42:28 – 0:43:06, 0:56:04 – 0:56:22). A baby chick falls from its nest, is attacked by ants and then is snatched up and eaten by a bird of prey (Trier 2009, 0:46:59 – 0:47:20). A wounded fox consumes its own entrails, and in a startling and surreal episode growls the words, "Chaos reigns!" (Trier 2009, 1:00:11 – 1:00:50). In all of these images, nature shows itself to be violent and cruel. Creation is inextricably entwined with destruction, life with death, growth with decay. As the fox warns, this is a place where chaos reigns; a place where Dionysian frenzy and blind force rule over Apollonian structure.

She fears Eden. Her feet burn as she walks through the forest, indicating there is something uncomfortable and painful about this place (Trier 2009, 0:34:35 – 0:34:56). She tells her husband that nature is "Satan's Church" (Trier 2009, 0:53:39 – 0:53:46), a place of evil and darkness. But the real danger lies in what nature awakens inside of her; namely, an awareness of her own vicious, Dionysian essence. This essence, previously suppressed and dominated by the Apollonian forces of civilization, first broke through into her consciousness with the death of her child. With this, she peeked into the abyss beyond civilized life. At first this insight is profoundly disturbing, driving her to grief and despair. But after the commencement of exposure therapy in Eden, She begins to experience liberating exhilaration and an understanding that humans are continuous with animals and the natural world. With the recession of the orderly and comforting structures of society, raw Dionysian force courses through her and She becomes a conduit for the violent cruelty of nature. The return to Eden inaugurates her exploration of this truth. She is, as Nietzsche wrote, "back among the animals."

Upon being "cured" in Chapter Three: Despair (Gynocide), She unleashes, with unrestrained ferocity, all of her repressed feelings, passions, and fears. In this part of the film, the imagery becomes graphic and stomach-churning. She masturbates frantically among the roots of a tree and then furiously copulates with her husband (Trier 2009, 1:09:26 – 1:11:00). She flies into an uncontrolled rage after developing the fear that He will leave her. In her rage, she crushes his testicles with a wooden beam, and as he lays unconscious, she rubs his penis until he ejaculates blood. She then drills a hole in his leg and attaches a millstone to keep him from fleeing (Trier 2009, 1:14:57 – 1:20:35). In the following Chapter (The Three Beggars), as if exhausted by her own fury, She cuts off her clitoris with scissors (Trier 2009, 1:32:53 – 1:33:14). All of this visceral imagery builds to a crescendo, beginning with desperate and frenzied sex, then culminating in sexual violence and mutilation. A connection is thus forged between the two primal forces identified by Sigmund Freud as the foundation of human nature: sex and death, or eros and thanatos. As in the film's Prologue, the two are shown to coexist with one another; and yet the tone in this part of the film is much different from the film's earlier tone. Here, on the one hand, the frenzied violence is associated with fear, anger, and pain. The Prologue, on the other hand, evokes a sense of serenity, which is assisted by a classical soundtrack and slow motion, black and white photography. In contrast, Chapter Three is in color and filmed at regular speed. In the Prologue, the explicit shots of sexual penetration are associated with pleasure, joy, and melancholy sadness. In Chapter Three, the sex act is depicted as simply abject, horrifying, and associated with pain, injury, and suffering. Both evoke the connection between sex and death, but they operate on different emotional registers. The Prologue is rich with the ambiguity of both the positive and the negative facets of life while Chapter Three is skewed toward the negative, horrific aspects of life. This is because, in Chapter Three, the frenzied violence of her attack erupts as a nihilistic, nullifying reaction against his attempt to impose Apollonian control over Dionysian passion. In the Prologue, the forces of Apollo and Dionysus are in balance, integrated as one and working in concert. Here they are battling against one another. Her fear that He will leave her is an indication that things have gone out of balance. Her absolute abandon is an indication of what happens when Dionysus has gone wild, totally unrestrained and out of control.

She needs him to offer restraint and distance, just as He needs her to offer passion and energy. But as She falls deeper into the grips of her own nature, the inertia of her fervor increasingly resists his control and restraint. Yearning for catharsis, She also fears the consequences of total release. This is why She restrains her husband with a millstone; an image that offers an interesting and direct allusion to Nietzsche's *The Antichrist* where, illustrating the not-so deeply buried cruelty of Christianity, Nietzsche quotes Mark 9:42: "And whoever shall offend one of these little ones that believe in me, it is better for him that a millstone were hanged about his neck, and he were cast into the sea" (A 45). Resentment ties one to the object of resentment. In Christianity, resentment assures that Christians will remain preoccupied with, and hostile toward, nature. In von Trier's *Antichrist*, the resentment that She feels toward He keeps her longing for his comforting guidance and control even as She struggles to break free. The millstone is a concrete symbol of her craving for this restraint, which is the last inhibition to her total liberation.

In von Trier's *Antichrist* He finally kills She, strangling her to death and apparently inaugurating the triumph of Apollo once again. Yet the triumph is only apparent. In a black and white Epilogue that recalls the aesthetics of the opening Prologue, He attempts to escape Eden but finds himself overrun by a ghostly army of faceless women (Trier 2009, 1:40:07–1:42:49). These symbols of nature and of Dionysus easily ascend the steep hill that He unsteadily struggles to climb, passing him by as they head out of Eden. What is the meaning of this closing imagery? If Nietzsche's *The Antichrist* offers a guide for the structure of the film, it may be that what we are seeing in this concluding scene parallels Nietzsche's closing proclamation from the end of his book: "The revaluation of all values!" The violent battle between He and She has obliterated his domination over her, unleashing pure, Dionysian fury into our world. What this entails is left ambiguous, but it is significant that the ghostly female figures do not seem at all concerned with or threatened by the weakened, crippled male figure. Perhaps this suggests that the controlling force of Apollo has been so depleted by his struggle with Dionysus that He no longer poses the oppressive threat he once did. Or perhaps, as in Nietzsche's own later philosophy, the forces of Apollo and Dionysus have merged into a new unity—the will to power—ushering in an era that embraces nature as a singular, ferocious, yet self-regulating potency.

4 Forms of Violence in *(The) Antichrist*

The violence enacted in both Nietzsche's book and von Trier's film is aimed at nullifying Western, Christian attitudes concerning the moral inferiority of nature. The title *Antichrist* highlights this target of attack; but, due to the linguistic structure of the word 'antichrist' and its apocalyptic connotations, it also might obscure the fact that the assaults carried out by Nietzsche and von Trier are not exclusively negative. There is also a positive, transformational aspect to their use of violence insofar as it clears the way for an alternative set of values to be established and affirmed in place of what has been canceled out. Their violence, in the words of Jean-Paul Sartre, is similar to "Achilles' lance," which "can heal the wounds that it has inflicted" (Sartre 1963, p. 30). Theirs is an active form of nihilism, a "violent force of destruction" that opens a path toward transvaluation (NL 1887, 9[35], KSA 12, p. 351). The use of violence by Nietzsche and by von Trier is in this sense instrumental, being used as a means to an end and not intended as an end in itself. Likewise, the violence perpetrated by Christianity is also a form of active nihilism intended as a way to conquer nature's own cruelty and offer a new interpretation of reality. What Nietzsche, von Trier, and Christianity share in common, then, is that they all utilize nihilistic violence instrumentally.

Hannah Arendt claims that all violence is instrumental. She distinguishes violence from power or mere force, suggesting that violence is characterized by the use of implements (weapons) that are employed for a purpose. "Violence, being instrumental by nature, is rational to the extent that it is effective in reaching that end that must justify it" (Arendt 1970, p. 79). Because of this, she claims that it is a mistake to think of violence as an aspect of nature or as a manifestation of the "life process" (Arendt 1970, p. 82). Since nature lacks rational intentionality, it cannot pursue ends. Instead, what is found in nature is mere force, exerted without weaponry, guiding intention, or aim. However, others—such as Thomas Hobbes, Nietzsche, Walter Benjamin, and Giorgio Agamben—do refer to the violence of nature, indicating, contrary to Arendt, that violence might indeed be said to exist apart from the use of weapons or rational, means/ends calculations. In what follows, I will suggest, against Arendt, that in both versions of *Antichrist* we find many sorts of violence at work, including both instrumental and non-instrumental forms. I shall use the term 'violence' to refer to all of these destructive forces, whether conceptual or physical, intentional or non-intentional. This will give us the vocabulary to discuss a kind of natural violence, implied by both versions of *Antichrist*, that is both irrational and blind; something for which Arendt's definition has no room.

Walter Benjamin writes, "all violence as a means is either law making or law preserving" (Benjamin 1996, p. 243). Here 'law' indicates a governing value, and what Benjamin highlights is the fact that violence, when used as a means, already presupposes some desired end toward which it is directed (as Arendt claims is the case for all violence). In desiring such an end, the one using violence expresses the conviction that this goal has positive value worth establishing or preserving. In "legitimate" uses of violence, the end pursued is either legal, and thus sanctioned by the state, or natural, and thus in no need of state sanction (Benjamin 1996, p. 240). This is why revolutionary violence is often justified by an appeal to natural rights. Nature trumps convention, and so when state rules are held to be against nature, violence becomes a legitimate option for the reassertion of just laws consonant with nature. In both versions of *Antichrist*, this is precisely what seems to be occurring when Nietzsche and von Trier object to the anti-natural character of Christianity and seek its violent overthrow. Christian thought proves its own illegitimacy by virtue of the fact that it does violence against nature. This is deemed unjust, which in turn justifies the use of violence against Christianity.

If nature were completely pacific, then there would be no occasion to demand a justification for its own violence. However, neither Nietzsche nor von Trier believe nature to be tranquil or peaceful. Instead, they depict it as a realm of regular struggle, suffering, and violence. Nietzsche does this conceptually by characterizing all reality as a manifestation of unending power struggles (will to power) while von Trier does it visually by depicting the suffering and death of plants, animals, and humans. Their views on nature, in this sense, are similar to those of Thomas Hobbes, who in *Leviathan* famously asserts that in the state of nature, "men were in a condition of warre one against another," (Hobbes 2004, p. 93), and thus life was "solitary, poore, nasty, brutish, and short" (Hobbes 2004, p. 92). Civilization grows out of the desire to overcome the violence of nature and to inaugurate a state of stability and peace. Like Hobbes, Nietzsche and von Trier characterize nature as a realm where force, rather than law, is the highest governing principle. Unlike Hobbes, however, neither Nietzsche nor von Trier endorse the oppressive power of human institutions as a solution to the violence of nature. Rather, they endorse the revaluation of nature itself.

Under the control of a supernatural intelligence, nature's violence might be justified by reference to the authority of that higher power. However, nature, for both Nietzsche and von Trier, is conceived not as a manifestation of God's plan, but as a reality existing independent of supernatural influence. "God is dead" (GS III 125). Nature is chaos (GS III 109). Nature's violence has no ultimate point. It is blind and absurd. Violence just *is* an expression of the natural world. In this sense nature's violence, according to Nietzsche and von Trier, ironically shares similarities with what Benjamin designates as "mythic" and "pure" or "divine" forms of violence. Like the anger of a human being, these forms of violence, according to Benjamin, are *expressive* rather than instrumental. Mythic violence is a form of violence, exercised by the gods, which is "not a means to their ends, scarcely a manifestation of their will, but primarily a manifestation of their existence" (Benjamin 1996, p. 248). Pure or divine violence, likewise, is a mere manifestation of a singular God's unlimited power. The difference between the two is that pure or divine violence stands outside of mythic influence and thus is capable of destroying the boundaries and laws established by the whims and arbitrary desires of lesser gods.[6] In the Godless worlds of Nietzsche and von Trier, nature's violence, like mythic and pure/divine violence, is a manifestation of existence, seeking nothing and serving no higher authority. It is an absurd kind of violence that just is an expression of reality.

The instrumental violence employed by Nietzsche and von Trier seeks to reintegrate Apollo with Dionysus, healing the human relationship to nature so that we no longer harbor resentment against the reality of a world that is violent, painful, ephemeral, and fleeting. This new perspective would provide a vantage point from which humans could welcome and embrace the overall natural cycles of generation and decay, creation and destruction, life and death, pleasure and pain. In the pursuit of this end, both Nietzsche's and von Trier's instrumental uses of violence terminate with the acceptance of nature's own non-instrumental, absurd form of violence. It is the overcoming of our distaste for nature's violence then that constitutes the final step (and the final impediment) to our embrace of nature on its own terms. What makes this final step possible?

The non-instrumental violence of nature is a force that occurs as a reaction to nothing external to itself. It is this quality of nature that is so aggravating to the Christian mind according to Nietzsche. Unable to accept the absurd inevitability of natural suffering, the Christian posits a world beyond violence and suffering, a place of eternal comfort and peace, and in so doing transforms natural violence into a means that conveys us to this better place. In this, the violence of

---

6 In *Homo Sacer*, Agamben comments that, for Benjamin, divine violence is what originally establishes the connection between violence and law (Agamben 1996, p. 65). In *State of Exception*, he claims that "mythico-juridical" violence is "always a means to an end," while divine violence is "never simply a means" (Agamben 2005, p. 61). What Agamben obscures, however, is Benjamin's point that mythic violence, like divine violence, is a *manifestation* or *expression* of the gods' mere existence, and so is likewise never simply instrumental in nature.

nature takes on a provocative character.⁷ It provokes a response but does not itself occur in response to any prior provocation. In a Hegelian sense, this sort of violence can be compared to the initiating stage in the unfolding of Geist; a point at which the world is both in- and for-itself (Hegel 1977, p. 104; § 166). As a self-contained and complete entity, nature has no "other" against which to push. Any exercise of force occurs internally, perpetrated by and against nature itself. Von Trier's film opens by introducing us to this self-contained state of existence. The violent death of the child is integrated with the orgiastic ecstasy of the couple's lovemaking into a scene that encapsulates the natural journey from conception to extinction. Critics have repeatedly commented on the aesthetic beauty of this opening scene and yet have also repeatedly expressed their discomfort with the juxtaposition of explicit sex and the child's violent death. This discomfort may itself be an indication that the critics have already left Eden. They are unable to embrace nature (or this scene), in all of its cruel beauty, on its own terms. They have been *provoked* by what they have witnessed and now demand a justification.⁸

As Nietzsche has explained, the violence of Christian nihilism is a reactive response to the provocative violence of nature. While Jesus desired to withdraw passively from the world of suffering, the Christian Church actively engaged with the world, doing violence to it by denying all that actually does exist in service of an other-worldly illusion. Resentment against the cruelties of nature led to the development of a way of existence that denigrated the actual and the earthly in favor of the abstract and the heavenly. In von Trier's *Antichrist*, this same response is illustrated in the operations of His psycho-therapeutic treatment of Her despair. The couple's journey back to Eden is an attempt to confront the harshness of nature and to master it by means of psychotherapy's Apollonian force. Here, psychotherapy is the ally of Christian thought insofar as it treats suffering as a problem to be solved and overcome once and for all. Her complicity in searching for this solution is reflected in her thesis project: an exploration of the persecution of witches by the Christian Church. Psychotherapy and Christianity constitute a partnership in viewing her disordered, Dionysian nature as an illness that must be subdued, treated, and healed, and insofar as She is complic-

---

7 I adapt the following distinctions between provocative, responsive, and terminal forms of violence from Phillip P. Hallie's book *Cruelty*, where he highlights them as three distinct but interrelated types of cruelty in Gothic horror tales (Hallie 1982, p. 80).

8 At a press conference the morning after the premiere of *Antichrist* at the Cannes Film Festival, von Trier was confronted by an outraged Baz Bamingboyt from the *Daily Mail*, who "demanded the director justify his work." Von Trier responded that he felt no need to do so (Badley 2010, p. 142).

it in this course of treatment, She has adopted and endorsed the anti-nature stance. In Hegelian terms, this constitutes a negative stage of unfolding in which reality reflects back on itself in hostility, objectifying itself as a "thing" to be mastered. In this stage, a "life and death struggle" (Hegel 1977, pp. 113–114; §187) ensues as nature (*Geist*) views itself as an enemy to be conquered.

Except in the case of nature, provocative violence rarely comes from out of the blue. Rather, it is usually triggered by a previous cause to which it is a reaction, and thus provocative violence normally has a responsive or reactive element mixed in with it. In the case of Christianity, its violence against reality was a response to the violent cruelties of nature. But with the growth of the Church's power, it in turn became a force of provocation to those it oppressed and dominated. In the West, the establishment of Christianity was so insidious (according to Nietzsche) that it seeped into areas of life that, on the surface, seemed separate from religion: philosophy, science, politics, and psychology. Western nihilism became entrenched. The violence done by the Church thus itself came to constitute a provocation against which anti-Christian forces rebelled. The hostility and aggression unleashed by Nietzsche in his book and by von Trier in his film are expressions of this violent force of resistance. Like Christian violence against nature, this anti-Christian violence is both responsive and instrumental. It is responsive insofar as it reacts against Christianity's denigration of nature, and it is instrumental insofar as it is not an end in itself, but a means toward the nullification of Christian values in preparation for something new.

The final revaluation of nature and the overcoming of nihilism would require that these anti-Christians achieve a state of being different from the one in which the process began. There can be no absolute return to nature without the residual memory of preceding departure. Because of this, the return to Eden has to be undertaken beneath the cloud of previous exile. Therefore, the final goal sought after must be a state of being richer than the initial state of departure. This fuller state of being constitutes the goal of our Antichrists, and the violence that they enact in its service must finally be more than reactive or responsive. It has also to be *terminal* in the sense of being a violence that finally ends altogether the cycles of violence first initiated by Christianity. This final consummation can only be accomplished through "a cruelty that will not escalate or be repaid" (Hallie 1981, p. 80); a form of non-resentful violence that recognizes the necessity of its own cessation. In order to achieve this goal, one has to transcend the bitterness that has characterized the human relationship to nature stretching all the way back (at least) to biblical times. The world must be accepted as "perfect," embraced as it is, and not as we ideally wish or hope it could be. This is the perspective of the "most spiritual, the Yes-saying instinct" (A 57): the overman.

Yet, Christianity itself is a manifestation of the world that we inhabit. While its vision of a reality beyond nature may be viewed by Nietzsche and von Trier as an unnatural illusion, the sheer existence, history, and teachings of the Christian Church are nevertheless facts about our world. Christianity grew out of a human response to nature (so Nietzsche tells us) and insofar as human responses to nature are themselves natural phenomena, so must the natural history of Christianity be acknowledged. If the goal of the transvaluation of all values is to overcome resentment against nature – including its expressive violence – then this would imply that Christianity (as a natural manifestation of the human response to nature) must itself be embraced. To wish that it never existed would be to deny reality yet again, and to continue fighting resentfully against the Church would be to remain entangled in a cycle of hostility that the revaluation of nature requires we overcome. To successfully execute a transvaluation of values then, the Antichrist's own resentment against Christianity must also be transcended. The reality of Christian nihilism must be met with something other than continued rounds of reactive, nihilistic violence. It must be met with a terminal violence that brings all resentment to an end.

5 Conclusion

The preceding investigation leaves us with two open questions: 1) How successful were Nietzsche and von Trier in achieving their goal of overcoming Christian nihilism and of transvaluing all values?; and 2) Is the final goal of overcoming nihilism even desirable?

In response to question 1, I think it is unclear how successfully Nietzsche and von Trier have extricated themselves from nihilistic resentment. After all, the title of Nietzsche's book, his closing signature, and the title of von Trier's film all indicate their stances by reference to that which they are against. They remain tied to Christianity through an obsessive need to nullify and negate it. Thus, the bond between Christ and Antichrist remains a reactive, nihilistic bond. Both nodes in the relationship continue to oppose one another, and the positive, terminal synthesis of this opposition is only hinted at. Christianity remains a millstone for both Nietzsche and von Trier.

But suppose resentment against "the other" is actually part of our own nature, acting as the engine that propels human thought ever forward toward unrealizable ideals. If we could truly embrace the eternal struggle between Apollo and Dionysus as self-justifying—in the manner that Hinduism accepts the world's occurrences as a form of cosmic play (Lila)—then perhaps we could also embrace the never-ending struggle against nature as part of nature itself.

This offers an answer to question 2. Maybe the goal of overcoming nihilism mistakes itself. Perhaps in the transvaluation of all values we are obligated to reevaluate even the desirability of nihilism's final overcoming.

Bibliography

Agamben, Giorgio (1998): *Homo Sacer: Sovereign Power and Bare Life*. Translated by Daniel Heller-Roazen. Stanford: Stanford University Press.

Agamben, Giorgio (2005): *State of Exception*. Translated by Kevin Attell. Chicago: The University of Chicago Press.

Arendt, Hannah (1970): *On Violence*. New York: Harcourt, Inc.

Badley, Linda (2010): *Lars von Trier*. Urbana: University of Illinois Press.

Benjamin, Walter (1996): "Critique of Violence." In: Benjamin, *Selected Writings, Volume 1, 1913–1926*. Edited by Marcus Bullock and Michael W. Jennings. Cambridge: Harvard University Press, pp. 236–252.

Brooks, Xan (2009): "*Antichrist*: a work of genius or the sickest film in the history of cinema?" In: *The Guardian*, July 15, 2009. https://www.theguardian.com/film/2009/jul/16/antichrist-lars-von-trier-feminism, visited on January 13, 2022.

Christie, Ian (2010): "All Those Things That Are to Die." In: Lars von Trier, director. (2009): *Antichrist*. The Criterion Collection, 2010. 108 minutes. DVD.

Conway, Daniel (2020): "Introduction." In: Daniel Conway (Ed.): *Nietzsche and* The Antichrist: *Religion, Politics, and Culture in Late Modernity*. London: Bloomsbury Academic, pp. 1–6.

Hallie, Philip P. (1982): *Cruelty*. Middletown: Wesleyan University Press.

Hegel, Georg W. F. (1977): *Phenomenology of Spirit*. Translated by A. V. Miller. Oxford: Oxford University Press.

Hobbes, Thomas (2004): *Leviathan*. New York: Barnes and Noble.

Jacobi, Friedrich Heinrich (1994): *Jacobi to Fichte*. In: Jacobi, *The Main Philosophical Writings and the Novel* Allwill. Edited and translated by George Di Giovanni. Buffalo: McGill-Queens University Press, pp. 497–527.

Jensen, Anthony K. (2020): "Nietzsche's Quest for the Historical Jesus." In: Daniel Conway (Ed.): *Nietzsche and* The Antichrist: *Religion, Politics, and Culture in Late Modernity*. London: Bloomsbury Academic, pp. 117–139.

Kaufmann, Walter (1974): *Nietzsche: Philosopher, Psychologist, Antichrist*. Princeton: Princeton University Press.

Krisjansen, Ivan, and Catherine Papadopoullos (2015): "Nietzsche's Ausgang: Dissolution and Identity in the Cinema of Lars von Trier." In: *Studies in European Cinema* 12. No. 1, pp. 46–59.

Küng, Hans (2006): *Does God Exist?* Eugene: Wipf and Stock Publishers.

Loeb, Paul S. (2020): "Nietzsche's Critique of Kant's Priestly Philosophy." In: Daniel Conway (Ed.): *Nietzsche and* The Antichrist: *Religion, Politics, and Culture in Late Modernity*. London: Bloomsbury Academic, pp. 89–116.

Nietzsche, Friedrich (1968a): *Beyond Good and Evil*. In: *Basic Writings of Nietzsche*. Edited and translated by Walter Kaufman. New York: The Modern Library, pp. 179–435.

Nietzsche, Friedrich (1968b): *The Birth of Tragedy*. In: *Basic Writings of Nietzsche*. Edited and translated by Walter Kaufman. New York: The Modern Library, pp. 1–144.

Nietzsche, Friedrich (1968c): *The Will to Power*. Edited and translated by Walter Kaufman. New York: Random House.

Nietzsche, Friedrich (1974): *The Gay Science*. Edited and translated by Walter Kaufman. New York: Vintage Books.

Nietzsche, Friedrich (1984): *The Antichrist*. In: *The Portable Nietzsche*. Edited and translated by Walter Kaufman. New York: Penguin Books, pp. 565–656.

Panaïoti, Antoine (2013): *Nietzsche and Buddhist Philosophy*. Cambridge: Cambridge University Press.

Panaïoti, Antoine (2020): "Comparative Religion in *The Antichrist*: Pastiche, Subversion, Cultural Intervention." In: Daniel Conway (Ed.): *Nietzsche and the Antichrist: Religion, Politics, and Culture in Late Modernity*. London: Bloomsbury Academic, pp. 43–66.

Santaniello, Weaver (1994): *Nietzsche, God, and the Jews*. Albany: State University of New York Press.

Sartre, Jean-Paul (1963): "Preface." In: Frantz Fannon: *The Wretched of the Earth*. Translated by Constance Farrington. New York: Grove Press, pp. 7–31.

Schrift, Alan D. (1995): *Nietzsche's French Legacy: A Genealogy of Poststructuralism*. New York: Routledge.

Shapiro, Gary (1988): "The Writing on the Wall: *The Antichrist* and the Semiotics of History." In: Robert C. Solomon and Kathleen M. Higgins (Eds.): *Reading Nietzsche*. New York: Oxford University Press, pp. 192–217.

Shapiro, Gary (2010): "Aesthetics and the Philosophy of Art, 1840–1900." In: Alan D. Schrift and Daniel Conway (Eds.): *The History of Continental Philosophy: Volume 2*. Chicago: The University of Chicago Press, pp. 239–259.

Thomsen, Bodil, and Marie Stavning (2009): "*Antichrist*—Chaos Reigns: The Event of Violence and the Haptic Image in Lars von Trier's Film." In: *Journal of Aesthetics & Culture* 1. No. 1. https://www.tandfonline.com/doi/full/10.3402/jac.v1i0.3668, visited on December 4, 2020.

Zolkos, Magdalena (2011): "Violent Affects: Nature and the Feminine in Lars von Trier's *Antichrist*." In: *Parrhesia* No. 13, pp. 177–189.

Filmography

Trier, Lars von, director (2009): *Antichrist*. The Criterion Collection, 2010. 108 minutes. DVD.

Bülent Diken and Carsten Bagge Laustsen
"Is Something Funny, Asshole?": *Joker*'s Nihilist Violence

"I just hope my death makes more sense than my life." (The Joker)

Abstract: *Joker* is a film that explores the forms of nihilism and their intertwinement in contemporary society. Thus, it can be viewed as a piece of theorizing and social diagnosis. We start with looking at the Joker's violence. Why is it nihilistic and what sort of nihilism is that? But we can also see the Joker's violence as an act of anti-nihilism, as a way of challenging society's inherent nihilism. We discuss this in the following section. Is the Joker a revolutionary that criticizes society and opens up for a space for a new politics? In the third section, the article focuses on the film not as a narrative but as form: is it a comedy of pain or an attempt at overcoming nihilism? And, finally, by way of a conclusion, we ask what we should do with the Joker's obscene laughter. The pivotal intuition in our discussion is that the concept of nihilism is a central and necessary tool for a diagnosis of our political predicament and a way to rethink the possibility of a radical emancipatory act within it today.

Joker (Todd Phillips 2019) opens with the news from Gotham city, the fictional setting of the film. It is, the voiceover informs, the eighteenth day of the garbage collectors' strike. The rubbish is piling up everywhere and "super rats" are roaming the city. This is only part of the trouble, however. With increasing rates of poverty and inequality, Gotham is a breeding ground for violence. The situation is already so serious, the voiceover emphasizes, that the mayor has just declared a state of exception.

As the news goes on, the camera closes in on a sad-faced hobo clown, Arthur, who is preparing for his next job. We then see him at work in Gotham Square. He is holding up a sign in front of a music shop to attract the attention of bypassing pedestrians. Most people ignore him, except for a group of five boys. "Suck my dick, clown!" One of the boys kicks Arthur, another knocks the sign out of his hands. Then, laughing, the boys run across the street with the sign. But Arthur needs the sign, which belongs to the shop. He runs after the boys, "catching" them in a dark corner, where he is attacked by them in a cruel and malicious way. He takes the beating in passivity.

At this point, the title of the film—*Joker*—appears as a second layer imposed on the image of Arthur lying on the ground. Then, just before we move to the next scene, we hear grotesque laughter. We realize that it is Arthur's. The laughing fit ends. We see the tears in Arthur's eyes from laughing hard. He is in conversation with a social worker. "Is it just me, or is it getting crazier out there?" The social worker agrees that these are "tense" times. "How's the job? Still enjoying it?" Arthur responds that he "really likes" working as a clown. The social worker writes it down, looks at the clock; she is obviously overworked and indifferent. Arthur asks the social worker whether she could ask the doctor to increase the dosage for his medication, saying "I just don't wanna feel so bad anymore." A member of the precariat, Arthur's life rests on a fragile balance.

But things get worse. A few months later, Arthur is abandoned by the welfare system. "How am I gonna get my medication?" Then one day another party clown, Randall, gives Arthur a gun. "You gotta protect yourself out there, buddy. Too many wackos." Arthur takes the gun. But during a performance at a ward for sick children, the gun slips out of Arthur's pants. The children and nurses stop clapping, staring at the gun on the floor. His boss is furious. He does not accept Arthur's explanations. "Randall told me you tried to buy a .38 off him last week." Arthur is incredulous. "Randall told you that?" Arthur is fired.

Arthur copes with his misery through escapism. In one fantasy, Arthur, while watching the popular comedy show *Live With Murray Franklin*, imagines himself as a member of the audience. Franklin is running his usual style. "So, everybody has heard about the super rats we have in Gotham, right? Well, today the mayor said he has a solution. Are you ready for this?—Super cats?" Suddenly, Arthur interrupts the show by shouting "I love you, Murray." Surprised, but trying to capitalize on the interruption, Murray Franklin turns to Arthur and chats with him. Seizing the moment, Arthur wins the audience by saying, among other things, that his purpose in life is "to bring joy and laughter into this cold, dark world," that his mother has always told him "to smile and put on a happy face," and so on. Murray Franklin is touched and asks his name. "There is something special in you, Arthur, I could tell." After the show, Franklin thanks Arthur, and adds: "Listen, all this stuff, the show, the audience, I would give it all up to have a kid like you." Arthur and Murray Franklin hug each other.

But the reality is different. In reality, Arthur does not have a father. He lives with his mother, Penny, who calls him "Happy." Penny frequently writes letters to Thomas Wayne, a man for whose family she worked for twelve years in the distant past. Wayne is a rich man and a mayoral candidate in the coming elections. Penny thinks Wayne is Arthur's father—hence the letters. But since the letters are unreciprocated, Arthur decides to find Wayne himself and talk to him. "Dad!" Arthur calls. "Excuse me?" responds Wayne, nonplussed. "My name is Arthur. I'm Penny's son. I know you didn't know about me, and I don't want anything from you. Well ... maybe a hug." Arthur is smiling and tender. Wayne thinks that he is crazy. He tells Arthur that he is not his father. Arthur bursts out laughing. "Are you laughing at me?" But Arthur is laughing too hard to be able to answer. "You think this is funny?" Thomas Wayne punches Arthur in the face.

Arthur is also a notoriously unsuccessful comedian. This is evidenced in the film by his show in a Gotham comedy club where he keeps cracking up, unable to stop himself from laughing, and telling jokes that nobody else finds funny. His failure is so spectacular that he becomes material for the real Murray Franklin, who gets a videotape of Arthur from the comedy club and plays it in his own show. "Here's a guy who thinks if you just keep laughing, it'll somehow make you funny. Check out this joker." And so Arthur becomes the Joker.

This article is about nihilism in *the Joker*. The film is an exploration of the different forms of nihilism and their intertwinement in contemporary society, and, as such, can be viewed as social diagnosis. Is the Joker's violence nihilistic—a blind act that wants nothing except the destruction of society? Or is it a response to a society that has itself turned nihilistic—a society of pure enjoyment, in which "happiness," as the film suggests, coincides with infinite boredom? We start by examining the Joker's violence. Why is it nihilistic and what sort of nihilism is it? Is it an act of despair or disorientation, or perhaps both in the form of a disjunctive synthesis? In section 2, we argue that we can also view the Joker's violence as an act of anti-nihilism, as a way of challenging society's inherent nihilism. Is the Joker a revolutionary who criticizes society and opens up a space for the new in it? Is he making an attempt to transgress the contemporary predicament of global society: a permanent state of exception in which the event is suspended? Does the Joker succeed? In section 3, we focus on the film not as a narrative but as a form: is it a comedy of pain or an attempt at overcoming nihilism? And, finally, by way of a conclusion, we ask what we should do with the Joker's obscene laughter. Should we understand it as an instigation of the individual or as a reflection of society? Or is it rather the indeterminacy of the two that opens up for a politics that is beyond good and evil; that is, something that escapes the dialectics of self and society? The pivotal intuition in our discussion is that the concept of nihilism is a central and necessary tool for a diagnosis of our political predicament and a way to rethink the possibility of a radical emancipatory act within it today.

1 Nihilism

Is the Joker a nihilist? Let us define nihilism first. In Nietzsche's perspective, nihilism originates in a fundamental inability to accept pain, conflict, and antagonism. Since these are parts of life, the search for a pain-free life amounts to the denial of the world as it is, the invention of an illusory world, a transcendent heaven, in which pain, conflict, and antagonism cease to exist. This is why Nietzsche calls the three monotheistic faiths—Judaism, Christendom, and Islam—"nihilistic religions" (NL 1888, 14[13], KSA 13, p. 223). However, despite its genealogical tie with monotheistic religions, nihilism cannot be reduced to them. Nihilism does not disappear with modernity or secularization.

With modernity, or with the death of God, the originary religious nihilism divides itself into two different, symmetrical forms of nihilism: radical and passive nihilism. The first insists on transcendence by taking the negation of *this* world to its logical extreme, the annihilation of the actual world; the second, in becoming resigned to the actual world, gives up its essential qualities such as passions and values. Hence Nietzsche's definition: "A nihilist is a man who judges of the world as it is that it ought *not* to be, and of the world as it ought to be that it does not exist" (NL 1887, 9[60], KSA 12, p. 366). If, despite realizing that one's supreme values are not realizable, one still desperately clings to them, we confront radical nihilism: values without a world. If, however, existing values are disregarded while, at the same time, *this* world is preserved, we encounter passive nihilism, or a "world without values" (Deleuze 1983, p. 148).

So, there are two consequences of the death of God: despair (radical nihilism) and disorientation (passive nihilism). Despair, on the one hand, emerges because the ideal world cannot be realized within this one (Heidegger 1977, p. 66). Disorientation, on the other hand, occurs as an insight that if the highest values disappear, "then nothing more remains to which man can cling and by which he can orient himself" (Heidegger 1977, p. 61). On the one hand, this leaves values that cannot find a world; on the other hand, a world without values. There is therefore a strange symmetry between the two nihilisms, between willing nothingness and the annihilation of will. Thought of in this way, the relationship between radical nihilism and passive nihilism constitutes a dissipative, disjunctive synthesis in which will is captured in an oscillation between willing nothingness and not willing at all, between destructive violence and passivity. The two forms of nihilism, in other words, are opposed to each other while being bound together in a radical ambivalence. Both seem to be signs and effects of an impossibility to relate to the social order, to feel at home within it.

In a similar way, what strikes one in *Joker* is the uneasy combination of a cynical world without values and values that are without a world; passivity, on the one hand, and violent acting out, on the other. We meet these two poles sometimes within the Joker himself, sometimes in the relationship between the Joker and his surrounding society, which is abjectly cynical, farcically passive. This duality is established on the basis of Arthur's originary nihilism, which consists in his weakness, in his inability to fight, and, concomitantly, his escapism (the dream of becoming a comedian, of having a father). Only when escape proves to be illusory does the Joker resort to violence, to a more radical nihilism.

In other words, we have Arthur's passive nihilist society, which elevates smiling and "putting on a happy face" to the level of an imperative, a decisive element in the Joker's biography. A society that recognizes mediocrity, the absence of any desire for the sublime, as the only form of happiness, was the dystopia imagined in the nineteenth century, anticipating a future that promotes passivity, a "dampening of the feeling of life, mechanical activity, modest pleasures" (Nietzsche, GM III 19). This is the dystopia realized in the Joker's society. But the injunction to smile is never alone: the decaffeinated reality of passive nihilism is paradoxically accompanied by a desire to feel life as vibrantly as possible, a radical nihilism. The "sedating tranquilizer" joins the "stimulant" (Zupančič 2003, pp. 66–67).

Located in such a disjunctive synthesis, Arthur/Joker is a radical nihilist with a passion for the real. He desires to break free from a society that he despises, but he does not know how to, except through violence and destruction. Yet he is sure of one thing: he wills nothing, rather than accepting the tranquilizing, passive existence that society offers. Touching the void, the "nothing," becomes a promise of reality. Destruction becomes a means to achieve a near-life experience. If meaning is not possible in this world, and if one cannot tolerate a one-dimensional world without the possibility of creating meaning, one can just as well sacrifice the world: "I just hope my death makes more sense than my life."

Against this background, let us focus on the Joker's destructive violence, which unfolds as a series of killings. The first killing takes place on the subway. Joker is sitting in a subway car, in despair, contemplating what went wrong with his life. Three drunk Wall Street employees enter the car, immediately starting to bully a young woman sitting and reading. She tries to ignore them. Arthur cannot do anything to save her. Instead, he bursts out laughing. This diverts the three men's attention to him and the woman gets a chance to escape the car. "So tell us, buddy. What's so fucking funny?" "Nothing. I have a condition—" Arthur tries to get one of his "Forgive my laughter" cards out of his bag. But the men begin punching and kicking him. Arthur falls down, unable to get up. "Stay down, you freak." At this point Arthur pulls the gun and kills the men.

Next, Arthur kills Randall, who triggered it all by providing him with a loaded gun. And then it is his mother's turn. "Ma, remember how you used to tell me that God gave me this laugh for a reason? That I had a purpose? To bring laughter and joy into this fucked up world ... ?" His mother is confused. Joker continues. "It wasn't God, it was you or, or one of your boyfriends ... how could you let that happen?" His mother looks away. "C'mon, Ma, I know I was adopted. What's my name? Who am I really?" She can barely speak. "H-h-happ—" she stammers. "Happy?! I'm not happy. I haven't been happy for one minute of my entire fucking life." Joker seizes a pillow. "But you know what's funny? You know what really makes me laugh? I used to think my life was nothing but a tragedy, but now, now I realize it's all just a fucking comedy." He suffocates his mother.

The final killing takes the form of a television spectacle. After the videotape from the comedy club makes him "famous," the Joker receives an invitation from Murray Franklin's show booker to come to the show as a guest. The Joker accepts the offer. In the meantime, Gotham City sinks even deeper into the crisis. Anger and resentment build up. Protesters crowd the streets with banners: "Clown for Mayor," "Kill the Rich," "Mr. Wayne, Am I a Clown?" The reason for the reference to Thomas Wayne is that he has recently commented on the violent subway incident by calling the killer a jealous "coward" who "hides behind a mask." "And until that jealousy ends, those of us who've made a good life for ourselves will always look at those who haven't as nothing but clowns."

Against this background, on the Joker's arrival to the show, Murray Franklin first chats with him a bit, asking "So what's with the face? Are you part of the protests?" "No, I don't believe in any of that. I don't believe in anything. I just thought it would be good for my act." The Joker, in turn, asks Murray Franklin for a favor. "Hey Murray—one small thing? When you bring me out, can you introduce me as 'The Joker?'" After all, the Joker does not know what his real name is—and what is more, that is what Murray Franklin had called him on the show. "A joker. Remember?" And so the show starts. Murray Franklin opens with a question on politics. Is the Joker political? The Joker says he is not; he is "just trying to make people laugh." Is he working on "any new material," then? At this point, the Joker confesses to killing the three Wall Street guys and his mother in the manner of joking. Everybody is confused. Is it a joke or the Joker's confession? Murray Franklin asks him whether he thinks killing those three men is funny. "Yes," replies the Joker. "Besides, the way I see it, what happened was a good thing. All of you, Gotham, the system that knows so much, you decide, you decide what's right and wrong. What's real or what's made up. The same way you decide what's funny or not." This is followed by a characterization of contemporary society as one in which "nobody is civic anymore":

Nobody thinks what it's like to be the other guy. You think men like Thomas Wayne, men at ease, ever think what it's like to be a guy like me? To be anybody but themselves? They don't. They think we'll all just sit there and take it like good little boys. That we won't werewolf and go wild. Well, this is for all of you out there.

Murray Franklin counters this tirade by pointing out that it is sheer resentment. "So much self-pity, Arthur. You sound like you're making excuses for killing three young men. Not everybody's awful." The Joker looks Murray in the eye. "You're awful, Murray." There is silence in the audience. "Me? How am I awful?" "Playing my video, inviting me on the show—you just wanted to make fun of me. Well, it's easy to laugh at Frankenstein on a crowded beach, isn't it?" At the end of this conversation, the Joker shoots Murray in the head. The audience is terrorized. Two security guards tackle the Joker.

Next, we see him looking out the window of a police car, handcuffed, watching the violence in the city: the mob, the sirens, the fires set by people with Joker masks, looters. Suddenly the Joker hits his head against the metal cage. There is blood on his head. The police officer driving turns back to look at him, loses control and hits a parked car. Smoke rises from the burning cars. There is only one survivor, the Joker, who continues contemplating the city on fire.

2 Anti-Nihilism?

How, then, is anti-nihilism possible, if the Joker's is a nihilist violence? Anti-nihilism can only emerge by deconstructing dominant values and creating new ones, but doing so without recourse to religious, passive, or radical nihilism. In other words, anti-nihilism itself must, in a certain sense, become nihilistic: violence is needed to destroy the violence of nihilism. All creativity necessitates destruction in one way or another. This is why anti-nihilism must emerge as a paradoxical nihilism that turns back against itself, destroys and overcomes itself, to create immanent values, a new way of life. Thus, the anti-nihilist is one who wills to overcome oneself, one "who wants to perish" (Z Prologue 4). "To perish" is an act of affirmation, a response to the reactionary forces that overcomes one.

As we have already seen, nihilism is a multifarious concept with more than one meaning. It is, in one guise, a promise of creative destruction. In another, it can turn to sheer destruction, annihilating the very context of creativity. The two-in-one nature of nihilism moves it, in a way, "beyond good and evil"; like the *pharmakon* in the classical Greek sense, nihilism is both poison and remedy at the same time, capable of the best and the worst. It is therefore possible to say that the Joker's desire for revolt releases itself in a nihilistic revenge, a sentiment that "everything deserves to pass away" (Z II Redemption). The Joker is prepared, for hatred's sake, to spit his last breath at Murray Franklin. Yet he does not create new values. Seen through this prism, we could say that *Joker* fails to move beyond the framework of the three forms of nihilism, transfiguring them toward a "perfect nihilism." And as such, it is not only a film about nihilism, but also a nihilist film.

However, one should not reduce a film to what it shows and what it says. Cinematic images have a power that goes beyond that. If *Joker* disturbs the spectator's perception of the actual world through a shock, this shock provokes thinking. To be sure, the film takes nihilism as given, without showing any exit, any line of flight, in the world it depicts. What it shows (the three nihilisms), however, invokes something not shown, which could, in principle, be Nietzsche's "perfect nihilism" or any other form of radical politics. Thus, it:

> "is wrong to think that what we see towards the end of the film—Joker celebrated by others—is the beginning of some new emancipatory movement. No, it is an ultimate deadlock of the existing system; a society bent on its self-destruction. The elegance of the film is that it leaves the next step of building a positive alternative to it to us. It is a dark nihilist image meant to awaken us." (Žižek 2019)

One has to go through despair to be able to imagine the new. Only the "courage of hopelessness" can open up a new political space (Žižek 2018 and Žižek 2019; see also Agamben 2014). Recall the Joker's statement in the comedy show: "I got nothing left to lose, Murray. Nothing can hurt me anymore. This is my fate, it was always my fate. My life is nothing but a comedy." Precisely as such, *Joker* is a reminder of an aporia in relation to violence: any experiment with violence involves a radical contingency, an aporetic moment, precisely because it cannot provide a positive, definitive measure of its violence. In the lack of a calculus, any leap, all flight is potentially open to becoming destructive. Hence it is impossible to draw an absolute line between productive and unproductive, creative and destructive violence. After all, from the perspective of actual reality, every event is necessarily an excess that introduces an irrational, "impossible" element into the given world (cf. Žižek 1999, p. 44). Only when a new framework is re-established does the transgressive event retroactively ground itself and assume a positive, determinate character. The "meaning" of the Joker's violence is a meaning to come. For this to happen, however, the initial violence is unavoidable, for "there is none the less something inherently 'terroristic' in every authentic act, in its gesture of thoroughly redefining the 'rules of the game,' inclusive of the very basic self-identity of its perpetrator" (Žižek 1999, pp. 377–378).

Thus, the question that emerges is whether there is an opening, an escape route from the deceptive dichotomy of passivity, on the one hand, and the Joker's destructive anger, on the other. Is it possible to derive an affirmative moment either from passive nihilism or from radical nihilism? How can passivity or anger turn into a political asset? *Joker* does not prescribe a teleological necessity in this respect, but it evokes, as mentioned, the possibility of an opening. There is, to be sure, no guarantee for such affirmative transformations, but the possibility is there. One can (with Agamben, for instance) try to distil a political subjectivity from passivity, or one can (with Žižek, for instance) attempt to construct a political subjectivity on the basis of the radical (nihilistic) act.

Let us discuss passivity first. If the political gesture consists of subtracting oneself from prevailing consensus, it is obvious that a certain form of passivity is necessary for such subtraction. Let us, in this context, also recall that the Joker's is a society ruled by a state of exception. Significantly, from Hobbes to Schmitt, the state of exception is an ever-existing potentiality that can resurface as a ruler's response to a state of emergency; for Hobbes, the threat of civil war. That the Joker presents himself as one of those who "werewolf and go wild" at one of the most crucial moments of the film is significant in this respect. This reoccurrence of nature (of the "werewolf") *within* society, of a radically unbound and unregulated violence, is the necessary background for the state of exception. What makes the Joker dangerous in this context is that he becomes an ersatz figure of sovereignty who can reiterate the friend-enemy distinction instead of the state. "Look what you caused, you freak, the whole city is on fire because of you."

What the theory of exception seeks to do is basically to capture such anomie, inscribing the violence that pertains to it in the domain of state power as constituent power. This move, however, is problematic, for the state of exception cannot be inscribed within a juridical context as a necessary measure the state takes when faced with emergencies, because it designates a space in which the distinctions between constituent power and constituted power, between law and unlaw, and between the public and the private, lose their consistency (Agamben 2005, pp. 50–51).

Hence, violence is reducible neither to law-making (constituent) nor to law-preserving (constituted) violence, for it exists outside both. The theory of exception tries, precisely, to capture and neutralize this violence by inscribing it in a juridical context, thereby snatching it from figures like the Joker. One could say that the Joker unmasks this attempt by putting what Benjamin has called "pure violence" in the place of the state of exception (Agamben 2005, p. 64; see also Benjamin 1979, p. 139). What transpires in pure violence is not the destruction of the law as such but its de-activation, or another use of the law, which is nothing other than life itself, "life as it is lived" beyond the grasp of the law (Agamben 2005, p. 64). Hence what matters is not merely domesticating the state of exception, trying to contain it within temporal and spatial limits, so that the primacy of the law can be maintained in appearance. What is necessary is to de-activate the logic of exception, to expose its central fiction by showing that there is no considerable link between life and norm, between violence and law. This, in turn, necessitates a politics that is not contaminated by the law and thus can sever the bond between the law and violence. As long as this bond is not undone, politics can, at best, be thought in terms of law-making violence. But the Joker goes further than that by intimating the possibility of thinking of politics as what Agamben has called a "destituent power" (Agamben 2013).

However, the Joker is not only a figure of passivity but also a figure of anger and explosion, in which case the problem is how to move from anger to politics. Obviously, anger and political intervention are related, and anger can be conceived of as an impetus for social critique and politics (Schmidt 2006, p. 9). The problem of anger emerges only when it cannot articulate itself in terms of conflict; that is, when it cannot be translated into politics and thus turns into destruction. But why are we fascinated by the Joker's destructive single-mindedness? And what is the political significance of this?

Any radical politics, asserts Benjamin, must "win the energies of intoxication" (Benjamin 1979a, p. 236). For reality to transcend itself, an experience of discharge is indispensable (Benjamin 1979a, p. 239). Only a politics that can accommodate intoxication, a "poetic politics," can go beyond the domain of pragmatic calculations (Benjamin 1979a, p. 237). In other words, any true political intervention must be able to interweave the two dimensions of *kairos*, strategy and intoxication.

What fascinates us in the Joker is his possessed-ness, his courage to cut off the social bond. He is frightening as an instantiation of the "destructive character" who has "no vision" but is obsessed with one activity: "clearing away" (Benjamin 1979b, pp. 157–158). By the same token, he restages the paradox of *kairos*: strategy without intoxication is as useless as intoxication without strategy. Both sides of *kairos* are vital in politics. What matters is to keep them in relation. And since this relation cannot be a dialectical relation, since a synthesis is impossible or will result in antinomy, the relationship must be thought of as a disjunctive synthesis. But it is also not enough to say that this aporia must be maintained, for it will result in the infinite deferral of actualization. The Joker knows that the aporia can only be overcome in praxis.

Hence *Joker*'s tendency to border on a "bitter carnival" (Bernstein 1992). As Bernstein shows, the "abject hero," the romanticized loser of modernity, is a character that originated as early as the carnival in Saturnalian dialogues, in which the roles of the master and the slave are reversed (Bernstein 1992, p. 67–68). Crucially, the structure of the dialogues has a deeply bitter and negative strand that has survived throughout modern times. In contemporary culture, the abject hero remains a central figure who refuses to conform to the society that he despises. In this sense, the Joker adopts the discourse of the abject hero, of the slave in the carnival. Thus, it is easy to recognize in *Joker* an echo of Horace's satires: "All right, I admit I'm easily led by my belly, my nostrils twitch at a savoury smell, I'm weak, spineless—if you like, a glutton into the bargain, but you are exactly the same, if not worse" (Horace 2005, pp. 67–68). I am bad, but you are worse. What is the Joker's violence compared to the structural violence of the society in which he lives? But what makes the Joker violent is ultimately his self-awareness regarding his inauthenticity. Thus he can only become a monster in an indirect way, through joking, reminiscent of the abject hero "parodying a role that is, in reality, already his own, and imitating a state that he already inhabits" (Bernstein 1992, p. 31). This is also why the Joker's laughter seems to lack, at first glance at least, a joyful quality. Is the Joker's laughter, then, an incidence of what Bakhtin would call "romantic grotesque," a laughter that is "sent to earth by the devil" but can only appear to humans "under the mask of joy," as "angry satire" without any generating power (Bakhtin 1984, p. 38)? Can the Joker, in other words, turn terror into something truly comic?

3 Joker as Comedy

True, the Joker is a madman. Rephrasing the Marx Brothers, one could say that the Joker may talk like an asocial madman, and look like an asocial madman, but do not let that fool you: he really is an asocial madman. Yet, paradoxically, exactly at the point at which it seems most absurd, thus most transgressive in relation to the surrounding society, the Joker's laughter always also points out an anomaly, something absurd, at the heart of the social. This is a standard comic procedure that enables the spectator to see society in a new light, forcing her or him, through dis-identification, to move from a habitual way of seeing to another way of seeing. And imperceptibly, the dis-identification from society (from Wayne, Murray, his mother, Randall, and on and on) pushes the spectators toward a fascination, if not identification, with the Joker, a point at which the spectators cannot recognize themselves.

However, neither total dis-identification (with society) nor total identification (with the Joker) is possible. Their truth is a disjunctive synthesis, an "impossible joint articulation," which, Zupančič claims, is "the real comic object" (Zupančič 2008, p. 59). As such, the emphasis of the film is not on how society affects an individual—that would make it a "tragic" film that invites a sociological interpretation of the causal network behind the Joker's actions—but on the fact that society does affect an individual. Hence the film's repeated demonstration of incongruities and disparities that pertain to this relationship. As such, the Joker is not a tragic subject opposed to the social structure but a problematical instance of the structure going amok, which is why the film makes frequent use of the techniques of exaggeration and intensification (see Zupančič 2008, p. 196). In this respect, the Joker's reference to tragedy and comedy—his realization that his life is not tragic but comic—is crucial. The moment of this realization is also the point at which the Joker "accepts himself in all his despair as a comical figure and gets rid of the last constraints of the old world" (Žižek 2019).

But in what sense is the Joker comic and what does it have to do with nihilism? Marx said, famously, that history always occurs twice; first as tragedy, then as farce. But Marx thinks of tragedy and farce (or comedy) in terms of genres here. In contrast to tragedy, which necessarily causes disharmony and disruption by changing everything, farce builds upon harmony and consensus; it produces non-events within the confines of a given hegemonic discourse, and the only subject position that comedy allows for is that of types whose actions are a direct outcome of their social positions rather than of individual (tragic) choices. As Aristotle puts it in the *Poetics*, "comedy is ... an imitation of inferior people" (Aristotle 1996, p. 9). Consider "bedroom farce": couples get their beds mixed up, rushing in and out of different rooms, constantly connecting to the wrong people, and so on, but in spite of the infinite computation of relations and variables, nothing really happens; the outcome does not change anything, and, in contrast to tragedy, no change of perspective takes place. In the end, everybody occupies exactly the same position as in the beginning.

There is, however, another possibility if we follow Deleuze's reading of Marx. Deleuze, like Marx, deals with tragedy and comedy in terms of repetition. Differently, however, Deleuze does not deal with tragedy and comedy as pre-given genres. Therefore, comedy does not follow tragedy; rather, tragedy follows comedy. Repetition starts with the comic situation, in which the actor, like in Marx, "falls short" of creating something new, in which the event is "too big" to become worthy (Deleuze 1994, p. 89). Arthur is comic in this sense, as a nothing, for he progressively lacks a socio-symbolic content. Like the number zero, he comes to designate an absence, and the film treats this absence of the subjective content itself—Arthur's being reduced to nothingness—as a radical (nihilistic) critique of a passive (nihilistic) society whose basic operation is the destruction of every social bond. Only by becoming the Joker can Arthur become part of an event.

Comedy, in this sense, is the condition of repetition in *Joker*. His take on happiness is crucial to reflect on in this context. The Joker's society can think of happiness only in terms of feeling good, and elevates this to a "bio-moral" principle: A good person is a person who feels good and puts on a happy face, a principle that implies that the unhappy are "somehow corrupt already on the level of their bare life" (Zupančič 2008, p. 5). For the Joker, in contrast, happiness is the coincidence of destruction and laughter.

If history, as Benjamin said, consists of a pile of pseudo-events, the indistinct flow of empty time as a catastrophe, then the real catastrophe for the Joker is not the catastrophe he sets in motion, but, on the contrary, its impossibility. Passive nihilism is a hell, the ideal of which is bare repetition, the eternal recurrence of the same non-events that produce no difference. In turn, the catastrophic event that the Joker initiates works as a kind of "emergency break," which makes it possible to arrest the indistinct flow, to break free from bare repetition (Benjamin 1999, pp. 252–254). Thus, if history repeats itself as farce, if in pseudo-history the tragic reappears as farce, this is not necessarily a reason for melancholic detachment but rather an occasion for a joyful separation—history has this course "so that humanity should part with its past *cheerfully*" (Marx 1957, p. 46; see also Agamben 1999, p. 154). Happiness is separation from pseudo-history, the affirmation of an originary, immanent form of life, which is never fully exhausted in the social, political or cultural structures (Agamben 2000, p. 115). This immanent origin, life, is the core of the Joker's politics, which is of course not political in the usual sense of the word.

And yet, there can be no tragedy without comedy, no comedy without tragedy. We end up in a vicious circle of two nihilisms, passive and radical, which itself can appear farcical. (And which is why, to come out of this vicious circle, Marx needs a third repetition, social revolution, which can end the dialectic of tragedy and farce, and Nietzsche the overman, the anti-nihilist as a figure who wants to perish, that is, overcome himself as a nihilist). A clean-cut difference between tragedy and farce is not enough, for there remains an anachronism: insofar as repetition is a matter of dramatization, of masks, the difference between "tragedy" and "farce" seems to reside in "the difference of a time between two masks" (Derrida 1994, p. 141). What is crucial, therefore, is the contrast between the Joker's initial farcical mask—his smile, his happy face in the beginning—and his clown mask, which counters the surrounding society and his own subjection to it with a sign of cheerful destruction accompanied by his grotesque laughter.

4 Free will and Free Use

In *The Book of Laughter and Forgetting*, Milan Kundera dramatizes the opposition between two different forms of laughter in this way: When, in a crowded feast, an angel heard the Devil's laughter for the first time, he was horrified. He knew that the Devil's laughter was aimed against God. Yet, feeling weak and defenseless, "unable to fabricate anything of his own," he could do nothing except try to turn his enemy's tactics against him. So he opened his mouth and let out a "wobbly, breathy sound ... and endowed it with the opposite meaning." Whereas the diabolic laughter points out the nihilism of illusions, the angelic laughter rejoices in their rationality, beauty and goodness:

> There they stood, Devil and angel, face to face, mouths open, both making more or less the same sound, but each expressing himself in a unique timbre—absolute opposites. And seeing the laughing angel, the Devil laughed all the harder, all the louder, all the more openly, because the laughing angel was infinitely laughable. Laughable laughter is cataclysmic. And even so, the angels gained something by it. They have tricked us all with their semantic hoax. Their imitation laughter and its original (the Devil's) have the same name. People nowadays do not even realize that one and the same external phenomenon embraces two completely contradictory internal attitudes. There are two kinds of laughter, and we lack the words to distinguish them. (Kundera 1982, p. 62)

And so Arthur has moved from the angelic smile, from "putting on a happy face," to the Joker's grotesquely diabolic laughter that comes with the joy of destroying idols, albeit without creating new values, or "illusions." Indeed, all values are illusions or fictions necessary to live, to interpret life. Yet illusions must not, as monotheistic religions do, be treated as truths. And what is an illusion that knows that it is an illusion, if not the artistic fiction? *Joker*, as an artwork, tells the truth of the social world in the guise of fiction. This is why, for Nietzsche, the artistic "will to illusion" is more profound, more divine, than the will to truth. It is art that is the main antidote to the problem of nihilism (NL 1887, 11[415], KSA 13, p. 194).

Yet something remarkable in the Joker is his lack of free will, symbolized by his uncontrollable laughter, which transforms him into an automaton-like figure. Nietzsche argues that the notion of "free will" is invented by monotheistic religions to make humanity responsible to a transcendent God (GM II 7). One cannot sin without free will. Thus the genealogy of free will could shed light on the Joker's nihilism. As early as the third century, free will became a technical-theological term that designates "responsibility for sin" (Agamben 2018, p. 47). Free will is a necessary means to hold the subject accountable for its action. Likewise, in the juridical discourse, free will indicates inclusion in the sphere of the law. The law finds in free will that which it must presuppose, guilt as something interior to the subject, rendering the subject responsible for the events it sanctions. This implies that the guilt of the subject occurs only through the punishment that sanctions it (Agamben 2018, p. 13). No sanctioned action, no guilt.

Interestingly, the origin of the sanctioned action is usually located in ancient tragedy, which typically stages a conflict between an objective guilt ascribed to a heroic subject and its subjective innocence. Even though in tragedy the individual appears to be a free agent, in the end the necessity imposed by gods determines the decision. The tragic hero does not "choose" between options but rather "recognizes" the necessity of the one choice possible for her or him (Agamben 2018, p. 32). Along these lines—that is, in a tragic framework—it is possible to say that the Joker's actions are simultaneously free and necessitated. Such a tension is inherent in the very form of action: every human action is simultaneously related to a subject and external sanctions which forbid, prescribe, or condemn actions (Agamben 2018, p. 34). Further, in this tragic framework, in which the source of happiness is one's actions, one is always culpable and innocent at once, never able to experience being innocent without feeling guilt at the same time.

Comedy juxtaposes to this another framework in which human happiness is not determined by action, opening up a space where "the subject is removed from the hold of sanctioned action" and guilt gives way to innocence (Agamben 2018, p. 40). In this way, the opposition between tragedy and comedy reveals its true meaning in the context of the subject, as an opposition between its two destinies, subjection and freedom. Tragedy is a movement from a happy and serene beginning to guilt. This line of interpretation is also what a spontaneous reading of *Joker* would offer. But comedy reverses this, designating an opposite movement from guilt to innocence. While tragedy presents "the guilt of the just," comedy necessarily appears as "the justification of the guilty" (Agamben 1996, p. 7).

This other, comic framework, where happiness is not determined by action, brings us to the paradigm of free use. Happiness can only be imagined insofar as instrumental use (the apparatuses of sovereignty-governmentality) is rendered inoperative, brought to a "happy end." This end is not a teleological end or the effective realization of a potential but a condition in which free use is no longer appropriated or captured.

Comedy, in other words, testifies to the persistence of another approach to free will and free use that deals with responsibility in terms of not will but potentiality: one is responsible because one carries out an action—realizes a potentiality; not because one has willed the action. The implication of this is expressed in the Socratic maxim that "every evil action is actually ignorance" (Agamben 2018, pp. 31–32); that is, not a consequence of a choice on the basis of free will:

> This is to say that in the tradition of Western ethical and political thought there are two paradigms, which intersect and incessantly keep separating from one another in the course of its history. The first situates the essence of the human and the proper place of politics

and ethics in action and praxis; the second situates it instead in knowledge and contemplation (in *theōria*).... And if we wish, according to a gesture by now traditional in the history of philosophy, to mark each of the two paradigms genealogically with a name, the first would be situated in the wake of Aristotle, the second in that of Plato. (Agamben 2018, p. 35)

When one takes into consideration that the ancients dealt with action in terms of knowledge, referring guilt not to evil will but to ignorance, Plato's ideal republic, ruled by the philosopher king who excludes the tragic poet, is comprehensible as a "comic" paradigm of contemplation (Agamben 2018, p. 35). In this prism, *Joker*, too, follows Plato and the paradigm of contemplation. The Joker is fully exposed to affections as passionate automata. There is no free will in him. We imagine will to be contingent only because we are ignorant of the network of affections behind it.

This is where the sociological background given in the beginning of the film is crucial, for it shows that power is an apparatus—that which captures, enlists and directs the multitude of subjective desires in line with its own, imposing on them its own object of desire, appropriating their power, their capacity to act, for its own purposes, thereby diminishing their capacity to be put to other uses. Enrolled in this network of power that we call society, subjected to the distribution of the passions that it imposes, particular forms of life turn into a habitus of servitude, only feeling passive joy (putting on a happy face) that goes along with a feeling of impotence, sadness.

This problematical coincidence, which is the trademark of passive nihilism, is what Arthur's sad-clown mask signifies. His grotesque laughter, in turn, is what opens up a space for free use, that which pre-exists, persists in and escapes power's economy of instrumental use. In free use, the Joker relates to himself, others and the world without subjection, property and ownership. Thus, he denies his role in starting the protests, refusing even the ownership of his mask, imitated and appropriated by thousands of protesters.

Bibliography

Agamben, Giorgio (1996): *The End of the Poem*. Stanford: Stanford University Press.
Agamben, Giorgio (1999): *Potentialities. Collected Essays in Philosophy*. Stanford: Stanford University Press.
Agamben, Giorgio (2005): *The State of Exception*. Chicago: The University of Chicago Press.
Agamben, Giorgio (2013): "For a theory of destituent power." Paper presented at the Nicos Poulantzas Institute, Athens, Greece. November 16, 2013. http://criticallegalthinking.com/2014/02/05/theory-destituent-power/

Agamben, Giorgio (2014): "Thought is the Courage of Hopelessness," interview by Stuart Elden, *Progressive Geographies*, June 18, 2014, https://progressivegeographies.com/2014/06/18/thought-is-the-courage-of-hopelessness-interview-with-giorgio-agamben/.

Agamben, Giorgio (2018): *Karman: A Brief Treatise on Action, Guilt, and Gesture*. Stanford: Stanford University Press.

Aristotle (1996): *Poetics*. London: Penguin.

Bakhtin, Mikhail M. (1984): *Rabelais and His World*. Bloomington: Indiana University Press.

Benjamin, Walter (1979a): "Surrealism." In: Benjamin, *One-Way Street*. London: Verso, pp. 225–239.

Benjamin, Walter (1979b): 'The Destructive Character.' In: *One-Way Street*. London: Verso, pp. 157–159.

Benjamin, Walter (1979c): 'Divine Violence.' In: *One-Way Street*. London: Verso, pp. 132–154.

Benjamin, Walter (1999): *Illuminations*. London: Pimlico.

Bernstein, Michael (1992): *Bitter Carnival. Ressentiment and the Abject Hero*. Princeton: Princeton University Press.

Deleuze, Gilles (1983): *Nietzsche & Philosophy*. New York: Columbia University Press.

Derrida, Jacques (1994): *Specters of Marx. The State of the Debt, the Work of Mourning, & the New International*. London: Routledge.

Heidegger, Martin (1977): *The Question Concerning Technology and Other Essays*. New York: Harper & Row Publishers.

Horace (2005): *Satires and Epistles*. London: Penguin Classics.

Kundera, Milan (1982): *The Book of Laughter and Forgetting*. London: Faber and Faber.

Marx, Karl (1957): "Contribution to the Critique of Hegel's Philosophy of Right. Introduction." In: Karl Marx and Friedrich Engels, Friedrich: *On Religion*. Moscow: Foreign Languages Publishing House, pp. 41–58.

Nietzsche, Friedrich (1961): *Thus Spoke Zarathustra*. London: Penguin.

Nietzsche, Friedrich (1967): *The Will to Power*. New York: Vintage.

Nietzsche, Friedrich (1972): *Beyond Good and Evil*. London: Penguin.

Nietzsche, Friedrich (1996): *On the Genealogy of Morals*. London: Oxford University Press.

Žižek, Slavoj (1992): *Enjoy Your Symptom!* London: Routledge.

Žižek, Slavoj (1999): *The Ticklish Subject. The Absent Center of Political Ontology*. London: Verso.

Žižek, Slavoj (2018): *The Courage of Hopelessness*. London: Melville House.

Žižek, Slavoj (2019): "'System deadlock': Joker artistically diagnoses modern world's ills." *RT Question More* (blog), *World News*, November 3, 2019, https://www.rt.com/news/472541-joker-movie-horror-violence-zizek/

Zupančič, Alenka (2003): *The Shortest Shadow. Nietzsche's Philosophy of the Two*. Cambridge, MA: The MIT Press.

Zupančič, Alenka (2008): *The Odd One In*. Cambridge, MA: The MIT Press.

Filmography

Todd, Phillips, director. (2019): *Joker*.

Notes on the Contributors

Nolen Gertz is Assistant Professor of Applied Philosophy at the University of Twente and Senior Researcher at the 4TU.Centre for Ethics and Technology. He is the author of *The Philosophy of War and Exile* (Palgrave-Macmillan, 2014), *Nihilism and Technology* (Rowman-Littlefield International, 2018), and *Nihilism* (MIT Press, 2019).

George Pattison has held academic positions at the universities of Cambridge, Aarhus, Oxford, Copenhagen, and Glasgow and currently holds honorary posts in the universities of Glasgow and St Andrew's. Among his books on existential philosophy are *Kierkegaard and the Quest for Unambiguous Life* (Oxford University Press, 2013) and *Heidegger on Death* (Routledge, 2013). *A Metaphysics of Love*, the final volume of his three-part philosophy of Christian life, was published by Oxford University Press in 2021.

Luca Lupo is Assistant Professor in Moral Philosophy at the University of Calabria, where he teaches Ethics and Ethics of the Forms of Life. His research interests focus on Friedrich Nietzsche's thought and on the relationship between ethics and psychoanalysis. He has published widely on Freud, Foucault, Jung, Schopenhauer, and Wittgenstein. He is the author of *Le colombe dello scettico. Riflessioni di Nietzsche sulla coscienza negli anni 1880–1888* (Ets, 2006), *Filosofia della Serendipity* (Guida, 2012) and *Forme ed etica del tempo in Nietzsche* (Mimesis, 2018; recently translated into Spanish as *Formas y Ética del tiempo en Nietzsche*, Brujas, 2021).

Luís Aguiar de Sousa is Research Fellow at the Nova Institute of Philosophy, Nova University of Lisbon. His main areas of research are the self, self-consciousness and the nature of agency. He is the author of several papers on Schopenhauer, Nietzsche, and Merleau-Ponty. He is also the main editor of the volume *Phenomenological Perspectives on Intersubjectivity and Values* (Cambridge Scholars, 2019).

Agata Mergler is a researcher, Ph.D. candidate in the Department of Humanities (York University, Toronto), academic teacher, media artist, and translator. She is writing a doctoral thesis titled *The Cultural Translation of Latin American Digital Art*. She holds a Ph.D. in philosophy (A. Mickiewicz University, Poznań, Poland). Her current interdisciplinary research field encompasses digital art, media theory, cultural translation, and comparative literature. She is the editor of a forthcoming (2022) special issue of the *Canadian Review of Comparative Literature* on post-magical realism.

Gianfranco Ferraro is currently a Ph.D. Candidate in Global Studies (Theology, Studies in Religion) at the Universidade Aberta, Portugal, and an integrate member at the Nova Institute of Philosophy (IFILNOVA), Portugal. His research focuses on philosophical forms of conversion, particularly concerning Foucault, Nietzsche, and the history of utopian thought. Recently, he co-edited the book *The Late Foucault. Ethical and Political questions* (Bloomsbury, 2020). He is a member of the Red Iberoamericana Foucault and director of the international journal *Thomas Project: A Border Journal for Utopian Thoughts*.

Francescomaria Tedesco is Associate Professor of Political Philosophy, Political Systems and Cultural Pluralism, and History of Political Doctrines at the University of Camerino. In addition to essays and articles, he has published the following monographs: *Introduzione a Hayek* (Laterza 2004), *Diritti umani e relativismo* (Laterza 2009), *Eccedenza sovrana* (Mimesis 2012; English translation: *Sovereign Excess, Legitimacy and Resistance*, Routledge 2018), *Modelli europei di accoglienza dei rifugiati e richiedenti asilo* (Aracne 2016), *Mediterraneismo. Il pensiero antimeridiano* (Meltemi 2017; Voltaire Prize 2018). He keeps a blog for the Italian newspaper *Il Fatto Quotidiano*.

Derek Offord is Emeritus Professor of Russian Intellectual History and Senior Research Fellow at the University of Bristol. He has published books on the Russian revolutionary movement, early Russian liberalism, Russian travel writing, and the broader history of Russian thought, as well as two books on contemporary Russian grammar and usage. His prize-winning monograph *The French Language in Russia: A Social, Political, Cultural, and Literary History*, co-authored with Vladislav Rjéoutski and Gesine Argent, was published by Amsterdam University Press in 2018. His latest book, on *Ayn Rand and the Russian Intelligentsia: The Origins of an Icon of the American Right*, is due to be published by Bloomsbury Academic in their Russian Shorts series in May 2022.

Marco Piazza is Associate Professor in History of Philosophy at the Department of Philosophy, Communication and Performing Arts, University of Roma Tre. His research interests mainly focus on the relationship between philosophy and literature (especially in Rousseau, Maine de Biran, Proust, Pessoa, and Guimarães Rosa). He has devoted his most recent work to philosophies of habit. Among his recent publications are *Redimere Proust. Walter Benjamin e il suo segnavia* (Le Càriti, 2009), *Il fantasma dell'interiorità. Breve storia di un concetto controverso* (Mimesis, 2012), *L'antagonista necessario. La filosofia francese dell'abitudine da Montaigne a Deleuze* (Mimesis, 2015), and *Creature dell'abitudine. Abito, costume, seconda natura da Aristotele alle scienze cognitive* (il Mulino, 2018).

Joseph G. Kickasola is Professor of Film and Digital Media, Baylor University (USA), and Director of the Baylor in New York program. Select publications include *The Films of Krzysztof Kieślowski: The Liminal Image* (Bloomsbury, 2004), essays in *Film Quarterly*, *The Routledge Companion to Philosophy and Film*, as well as numerous anthologies on the cinema as it intersects philosophy, religion, and aesthetics. He lives in New York City.

Paolo Stellino is Researcher at the NOVA Institute of Philosophy and Invited Professor at the Faculty of Human and Social Science, NOVA University of Lisbon, Portugal. His main fields of research interest are the history of nineteenth- and twentieth-century philosophy, ethics, and philosophy of film. He has published many articles in international peer-reviewed journals and has authored several book chapters. He is the author of the books *Nietzsche and Dostoevsky: On the Verge of Nihilism* (Peter Lang, 2015) and *Philosophical Perspectives on Suicide. Kant, Schopenhauer, Nietzsche, and Wittgenstein* (Palgrave, 2020). He is currently co-editing with Michael Cholbi *The Oxford Handbook of the Philosophy of Suicide* (Oxford University Press, expected 2024).

Kevin Stoehr is Chair of the Division of Humanities and Associate Professor of Humanities in the College of General Studies at Boston University. His teaching and research interests include theoretical and applied ethics, history of philosophy, existentialism, philosophical literature, aesthetics, and film studies. His published books include *Ride, Boldly Ride: The Evolution of the American Western* (co-authored with Mary Lea Bandy, University of California Press, 2012); *John Ford in Focus: Essays on the Filmmaker's Life and Work* (co-edited with Michael C. Connolly, McFarland, 2008); *Nihilism in Film and Television: From Citizen Kane to The Sopranos* (McFarland, 2006); *Jung's Psychology as a Spiritual Practice: A Dialogue* (co-authored with William D. Geoghegan, University Press of America, 2002); and *Film & Knowledge: Essays on the Integration of Images & Ideas* (McFarland, 2002).

John Marmysz teaches philosophy at the College of Marin in Kentfield, California. He is the author of *Laughing at Nothing: Humor as a Response to Nihilism* (SUNY Press, 2003), *The Path of Philosophy: Truth, Wonder and Distress* (Cengage, 2011), *The Nihilist: A Philosophical Novel* (No Frills Buffalo, 2015), and *Cinematic Nihilism: Encounters, Confrontations, Overcomings* (Edinburgh University Press, 2017). He is coeditor (with Scott Lukas) of *Fear, Cultural Anxiety and Transformation: Horror, Science Fiction and Fantasy Films Remade* (Lexington Books, 2009). Marmysz is the recipient of a State University of New York Chancellor's Award for Excellence in Scholarship and Creativity, has served as a National Endowment for the Humanities fellow, and currently serves as an Associate Editor for the *Philosophy of Humor Yearbook*.

Bülent Diken is a Professor in Social and Cultural Theory in the Department of Sociology at Lancaster University and in the Department of Radio-TV and Cinema at Kadir Has University. His research fields are social theory, political philosophy, urbanism, cinema, and terrorism. His books include *The Culture of Exception* (co-authored with Carsten B. Laustsen, Routledge, 2005), *Nihilism* (Routledge, 2009), *Revolt, Revolution, Critique* (Routledge, 2012), *God, Politics, Economy* (Routledge, 2015), and *The New Despotism* (Rowman and Littlefield, 2021).

Carsten Bagge Laustsen is Associate Professor in Sociology at The Department of Political Science, Aarhus. His research fields are terrorism, the sociology of climate change, politics and popular culture, and social and political theory. His books include *The Culture of Exception* (co-authored with Bülent Diken, Routledge, 2005), *Sociology through the Projector* (co-authored with Bülent Diken, Routledge, 2007), *Textual Analysis for the Social Sciences* (with Kristoffer Leiding Kølvraa and Morten Brænder, Hans Reitzels Forlag, 2014), and *Social Theory* (with Lars Thorup Larsen, Mathias Wullum, Tine Ravn, and Mads P Sørensen, Routledge, 2017).

Names index

Agamben, Giorgio   150–152, 288, 290, 305–306, 309–312
Anaxagoras   30
Antonovich, Maksim A.   173, 176, 178
Arendt, Hannah   8, 16–23, 47, 60, 288–289
Aristotle   308, 312
Askochensky, Viktor   167

Bachofen, Johann Jakob   154–155
Bacon, Francis   144
Badiou, Alain   45
Bakhtin, Mikhail   26, 307
Bakunin, Mikhail A.   163, 176, 180, 183
Beck, Ulrich   124, 133 f.
Belinsky, Vissarion G.   162–164
Benjamin, Walter   90–97, 99 f., 104–107, 289 f., 305 f., 309
Bentham, Jeremy   174
Bergman, Ingmar   214 f., 217
Berlin, Isaiah   171
Black, Joel   248 f.
Bobbio, Norberto   143
Borsellino, Paolo   112 f., 118, 123, 129, 134
Bosse, Abraham   148
Bourget, Paul   115, 130
Brunetière, Ferdinand   115
Brusca, Giovanni   132
Buscetta, Tommaso   112, 120, 122 f.

Campanini, Massimo   148
Cheney, Dick   9
Chernyshevsky, Nikolai G.   174–176, 178, 182
Chinnici, Rocco   112
Chion, Michel   207
Coetzee, J. M.   54 f., 60
Coppola, Francis Ford   132
Cox, Christoph   205 f., 208 f., 211, 212, 215–217, 219, 222 f., 225, 226.

de Beauvoir, Simone   8, 12–15, 19 f.
De Palma, Brian   132

de Roberto, Federico   130
Deleuze, Gilles   205, 206, 208, 209, 220, 222, 265, 308
Democritus   30
Denaro, Matteo Messina   133
Derrida, Jacques   128, 152–154, 309
di Lampedusa, Giuseppe Tomasi   129
Dostoevsky, Fedor M.   1, 7, 26, 37, 115, 130, 163, 178–182, 184, 231 f., 237 f., 241, 245, 247
Duk, Kim Ki   57

Einstein, Alfred   55
Engels, Friedrich   148
Enyedi, Ildikò   53
Erlenbusch-Anderson, Verena   147

Falcone, Giovanni   112, 118, 123, 129, 134
Fircks, Theodor   177
Foucault, Michel   112, 119, 123 f., 125–127, 131, 133 f.
Fourier, Charles   175, 178
Freud, Sigmund   46–48, 55, 59 f., 61, 76, 286
Fuchs, Eduard   104

Gide, André   232, 236 f., 248
Ginzburg, Carlo   143
Girard, René   51
Gröning, Philip   206, 219 f.

Habermas, Jürgen   147
Haddad, Gérard   150
Haneke, Michael   255–258, 259 f., 263–273
Hayek, Friedrich   151, 153
Hegel, Georg Wilhelm Friedrich   33, 35, 291, 292
Heiberg, Johan Ludvig   34
Heidegger, Martin   8, 10 f., 12, 15, 20, 26, 31, 33, 35, 46, 115, 247 f.
Herzen, Alexander   164, 176

Hitchcock, Alfred 233–241, 243, 247, 249 f.
Hobbes, Thomas 74, 143–145, 147, 288, 289, 305
Hollande, François 140 f.
Homer 37
Honneth, Axel 148
Horace 307

Jacobi, Friedrich Heinrich 232
Jaspers, Karl 246
Jesus 56, 278 f., 291
John the Baptist 52 f.
Jung, Carl 50, 55

Kant, Immanuel 47, 49, 82, 147, 277 f.
Katkov, Mikhail 173
Kierkegaard, Søren 26–42
Kojève, Alexandre 151
Kolderup-Rosenvinge, J. L. A. 41
Kuhn, Thomas 112
Kundera, Milan 309 f.

Lacan, Jacques 61
Lefort, Claude 154
Leibniz, Gottfried Wilhelm 145
Lenin, Vladimir I. 175
Leucippus 30
Levinas, Emmanuel 54
Löwith, Karl 91 f., 241

Marion, Jean-Luc 206, 218, 221–223, 226
Martone, Mario 132
Marx, Karl 148, 308, 309
Mbembe, Achille 124, 127 f., 133
Meillasoux, Quentin 205
Mérimée, Prosper 66
Mori, Cesare 121
Moro, Aldo 131
Mosca, Gaetano 145 f.
Mosca, Gaspare 119
Mozart, Wolfgang Amadeus 36 f., 39

Napoleon III 122
Nasser, Gamal Abdel 148
Natoli, Luigi 120
Nechaev, Sergei 176, 179

Nietzsche, Friedrich 1 f., 8 f., 11, 15, 17, 19 f., 21 f., 45, 46, 56, 65–86, 91–95, 100, 106, 112, 114–118, 124, 130, 134, 192, 193 f., 197, 205 f., 208–211, 214, 217, 220–226, 231–233, 234, 238–250, 255, 258, 259, 262 f., 276–285, 287–293, 300, 304, 309 f.
Norwich, John Julius 124

Øhlenslæger, Adam 38
Ong, Walter 208
Ozhegov, Sergei 162

Pasolini, Pier Paolo 113
Paul 279
Peckinpah, Sam 212
Phalaris 36, 38
Pirandello, Luigi 130
Piromalli, Eleonora 148
Pisarev, Dmitrii I. 163, 173 f., 175 f., 178 f.
Pitrè, Giuseppe 119
Plato 8, 9 f., 12, 15, 19 f., 92, 152 f., 190 f., 312
Plautus 36
Pomialovsky, Nikolai G. 167, 178
Provenzano, Bernardo 113, 133
Pushkin, Alexander 37, 169

Raphael 37, 169
Riina, Salvatore "Totò" 113, 132
Rilke, Reiner Maria 53
Rizzotto, Giuseppe 119
Rosa, João Guimarães 189–199
Roy, Oliver 139

Saint Augustine 26, 34
Sartre, Jean-Paul 31, 288
Schlegel, Friedrich 34
Schmitt, Carl 41, 128, 146, 150 f., 152 f., 305
Schopenhauer, Arthur 33, 46 f., 49, 52, 56 f., 79 f., 205, 208
Sciascia, Leonardo 119, 122 f., 130–132, 134
Scorsese, Martin 212 f.
Shakespeare, William 204, 206
Siddhartha 278

Singer, Peter   52
Sontag, Susan   209, 212, 215, 223
Strauss, Leo   143

Tacitus   144
Tarantino, Quentin   132
Tarkosvky, Andrei   217
Thorvaldsen, Berter   38
Trier, Lars von   275 f., 282–293
Turgenev, Ivan   1, 7, 163 f., 166–172, 173–175, 182, 183, 184

Unamuno, Miguel de   198

Verga, Giovanni   130
Vernant, Jean-Pierre   151

Weil, Simone   22
Woo, John   211

Young, Edward   27

Žižek, Slavoj   144 f., 304 f.
Zupančič, Alenka   307

www.ingramcontent.com/pod-product-compliance
Lightning Source LLC
Chambersburg PA
CBHW020221170426
43201CB00007B/277